Better Homes and Gardens®

AMERICA'S HERITAGE QUILTS

D1401574

WE CARE!

The Crafts Department at Better Homes and Gardens® Books assembled this collection of projects for your crafting pleasure. Our staff is committed to providing you with clear and concise instructions so that you can complete each project. We guarantee your satisfaction with this book for as long as you own it. We welcome your comments and suggestions. Please address your correspondence to Better Homes and Gardens® Books Crafts Department, 1716 Locust Street, Des Moines, IA 50309-3023.

BETTER HOMES AND GARDENS® BOOKS

Vice President, Editorial Director: Elizabeth P. Rice
Art Director: Ernest Shelton
Managing Editor: David A. Kirchner
Project Editor: Marsha Jahns
Project Managers: Liz Anderson, Jennifer Speer Ramundt

Crafts Editor: Sara Jane Treinen
Senior Crafts Editors: Beverly Rivers, Patricia Wilens
Associate Crafts Editor: Nancy Reames

Associate Art Directors: Neoma Thomas,
   Linda Ford Vermie, Randall Yontz
Assistant Art Directors: Lynda Haupert,
   Harijs Priekulis, Tom Wegner
Graphic Designers: Mary Schlueter Bendgen, Michael Burns
Art Production: Director, John Berg;
   Associate, Joe Heuer;
   Office Manager, Michaela Lester

President, Book Group: Joseph J. Ward
Vice President, Retail Marketing: Jamie L. Martin
Vice President, Book Clubs: Richard L. Rundall

BETTER HOMES AND GARDENS® MAGAZINE

President, Magazine Group: James A. Autry
Editorial Director: Doris Eby

MEREDITH CORPORATION OFFICERS

Chairman of the Executive Committee: E. T. Meredith III
Chairman of the Board: Robert A. Burnett
President and Chief Executive Officer: Jack D. Rehm

AMERICA'S HERITAGE QUILTS

Editor: Patricia Wilens
Graphic Designer: Lynda Haupert
Project Manager: Liz Anderson
Contributing Illustrator: Chris Neubauer
Publishing Systems Text Processor: Paula Forest
Contributing Indexer: Barbara Klein

Cover project: See pages 8 and 9.

Special thanks to Jane Hall and Dixie Haywood for text from *Perfect Pineapples* (C&T Publishing, 1989).

Quilts are among the few tangible objects that reflect the role women played in the building of America. Log cabins, covered wagons, and split-rail fences evoke images of the rugged men who challenged the frontiers of the new land, but much of women's work did not survive the passage of time. The accomplishments of cooking meals and washing clothes disappeared with each passing day. Many quilts also vanished, used up in the wear and tear of living. But some quilts remain, as wondrous and diverse as the women who made them.

America's Heritage Quilts pays tribute to this legacy. We've assembled a collection of 70 quilts that exemplify the styles and techniques of quiltmaking throughout America's history. This book is designed to be a tool to help you *make* quilts, whether they're your first ones or the latest of many. As you use this book, we hope you'll learn more about the traditions of quiltmaking and be inspired to make the quilts of tomorrow.

In quiltmaking, you'll find the joy of working with your hands as you make something both functional and beautiful. For those of us who love quilts, making one is a labor of love and a means of self-expression. Your quilt becomes a lasting gift of hand and heart and is your personal contribution to the on-going legacy of American quilts.

> *Piecin' a quilt's like livin' a life . . . The Lord sends us the pieces, but we can cut 'em out and put 'em together pretty much to suit ourselves, and there's a heap more in the cuttin' and the sewin' than there is in the caliker . . . I've had a heap of comfort all my life making quilts, and now in my old age I wouldn't take a fortune for them.*
>
> Eliza Calvert Hall
> *Aunt Jane of Kentucky,* 1898

Patricia Wilens
EDITOR

Contents

How to Use This Book

America's Heritage Quilts presents an overview of the history and evolution of quiltmaking in the United States. It is not intended to be a complete history, but we invite you to do more in-depth reading about the historical aspects of quiltmaking that you find most interesting.

The chapters are organized chronologically, from colonial times to the present day. Each chapter focuses on one time period, touching upon social, political, and economic conditions that influenced quiltmakers of that period. The time periods in some chapters overlap, due to parallel developments during those times. For example, scrap quilts were being made by plains settlers at the same time wealthy women in cities were making Victorian crazy quilts.

Instructions for making the featured quilts follow the historical information in each chapter. (Instructions are not available for museum quilts or the quilts belonging to the quiltmakers featured in Chapter 11.)

About the Quilts In this Book

Most of the quilts pictured in this book were made during the historical period that they represent. However, due to the rarity of quilts made before 1860, a quilt made more recently may be shown. An estimated date of origin is given for each quilt, as is additional information about who made it and where it was made, if those facts are known.

The 70 quilt projects in this book were selected as representative of the different historical periods. For quilts with more than one name, we used the name we believe is most widely recognized.

About the Instructions in This Book

Use *America's Heritage Quilts* as a learning tool if you are a beginner, or as a reference guide if you are an experienced quiltmaker. Everything you need to successfully complete a quilt is in this book—step-by-step instructions for each quilt, full-size patterns, and tips on required sewing techniques.

Quilter's Schoolhouse (Chapter 12)

The Schoolhouse information on pages 280–309 is designed to help you through the quiltmaking process from start to finish. Even if you are an experienced quiltmaker, you may want to review the material on notions, selection and preparation of fabrics, and basic techniques. If you are making your first quilt, carefully read this section before you begin. As you proceed with your quilt, frequently refer to this section for guidance.

A glossary of terms is on pages 313–315.

Special Techniques

Tips on special techniques, such as ruching and quick-pieced triangle-squares, are presented on tinted pages throughout the book. These tips accompany quilts that are made with the described procedure, but the techniques are helpful for projects throughout the book.

Skill Levels

This book includes quilts that beginners can successfully complete as well as some that will challenge the most experienced quiltmakers.

Instructions for quilts that are particularly suitable for beginners (or anyone wanting a relatively quick and easy project) are labeled "BASIC." These quilts utilize fundamental quilt-making techniques.

The quilts labeled "CHALLENGING" are just that—complex and demanding projects that require precise and skilled workmanship. These quilts are not recommended for beginners.

The remaining project instructions in this book (those not labeled "BASIC" or "CHALLENGING") require average knowledge and skills. Once you have mastered the basics, you should be able to successfully complete any of the unlabeled projects in this book. Refer to the index for a listing of "BASIC" and "CHALLENGING" projects.

Individual Project Instructions

After reviewing the Schoolhouse information, select the quilt project you would like to make. Before buying fabric, however, *read all instructions for the quilt carefully*. Be sure you clearly understand the construction process before you decide to make the quilt.

The materials list for each quilt gives the fabric, batting, and notions required to make the quilt as it is pictured. Select fabrics in the colors of your choice in the quantities stated. If you want to change the dimensions of the quilt, adjust the fabric yardage and batting size accordingly.

As you gather the materials to make your quilt, here are guidelines to help you make some decisions about your quilt:

♦ The yardage requirements in the materials lists are given for 44-inch-wide fabric unless otherwise stated.

♦ 100 percent cotton fabric is recommended for both the quilt top and the backing of most quilts.

♦ Prewash fabrics and test for colorfastness before cutting.

♦ Cut pieces from each fabric in the order in which they are listed, cutting the largest pieces first. Cut smaller pieces from the larger pieces as instructed. This ensures efficient use of the yardage.

♦ Patchwork patterns are drawn with both the cutting line (solid) and sewing line (broken); the points on diamond and triangle patterns have been trimmed so your pieces will fit perfectly whether you sew by hand or by machine.

♦ Appliqué patterns in the book are drawn with the sewing line only. Add a $3/16$-inch seam allowance when cutting appliqué pieces from fabric.

♦ Press seam allowances to one side (unless otherwise stated), usually toward the darker fabric.

Spirit
OF
Independence

The Beginnings of
Quiltmaking in America

1800 ～ 1840

◆ **Burgoyne Surrounded**
Michigan, c. 1880;
83x101 inches. Instructions begin on page 19.

*I have plied my needle these fifty years and by my
goodwill would never have it out of my
hands . . . I have quilted counterpanes and chest covers
in fine white linen, in various patterns of my own
invention; I have made patchwork beyond calculation.*

A woman's letter to the London *Spectator*, 1700

◆ **Wholecloth Counterpane** *(top), made by Esther Wheat of Conway, Mass., c. 1780. Courtesy of the Smithsonian Institution. Instructions are not available for this quilt.*

◆ **Broderie Perse Medallion** *(bottom), made by Catherine Custis, Virginia, c. 1820. Courtesy of the DAR Museum, Washington, D.C. Instructions are not available for this quilt.*

The story of quilts in America begins with the first pilgrims who dared to brave the wilderness of the New World.

The colonists of the 1600s brought with them the skills and styles of their European homelands. They were familiar with wholecloth coverlets and garments quilted with hearts, feathers, and other traditional motifs.

Most early settlers used woven blankets, which were easier and less expensive to make or buy than quilts. Studies of colonial records find that a common blanket was valued at 10 shillings, a bed rug at 15½ shillings, and a quilt at 52 shillings. Such pricing sets the quilt apart as a luxury item.

Before 1800, most quilts were elegant works of silk, wool, linen, or chintz. The predominant style was wholecloth, fancifully quilted with designs of flowers and feathers—a showcase of a lady's fine handwork.

As cities grew and became prosperous, a new class of well-to-do tradespeople emerged who could afford fabrics imported from England. In addition to wholecloth counterpanes, affluent women of the late 1700s made quilts by appliquéing chintz cutouts onto a plain background in the broderie perse style.

Printed with large and colorful designs, chintz was ideal for this appliqué. The elaborate motifs were cut out and stitched onto the background with buttonhole embroidery.

Chintz appliqué would dominate quiltmaking until the mid-1800s, when new fabrics and economic conditions raised patchwork to unparalleled heights.

◆ **Nine-Patch Variation** *(opposite), Pennsylvania, c. 1860; 82½x103½ inches. Instructions begin on page 21.*

*I*n the early 1800s, both pieced and appliquéd quilts frequently were made in a medallion style. These quilts had a centered design enclosed by a series of borders.

The first patchwork designs were simple geometric patterns based

on the most basic shapes—the square and the right triangle. A few complicated star designs and circular Mariner's Compass patterns were devised by the very accomplished sew-ers.

Large-scale cotton prints remained the fabrics of choice, and many quilts combined these cottons with woolens and/or silks. Quiltmakers continued to demand Indian chintz, despite published comments by *Robinson Crusoe* author Daniel Defoe, who condemned these imported goods and the "passion for their fashion."

Some quilt design elements established in these years remain

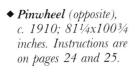

♦ *Pinwheel (opposite), c. 1910; 81¼x100¾ inches. Instructions are on pages 24 and 25.*

standards today. Early quilts abound with stars, pinwheels, flowers, and borders of appliquéd vines and swags, themes evident in earlier needlework forms, such as crewel embroidery and counted stitch samplers.

The roots of today's quilting motifs also are found in colonial quilts. Plain grids and parallel lines, as well as fancy flowers and undulating feathers, are seen on the earliest surviving whole-cloth quilts and petticoats.

But these quilted items remained the exclusive province of the wealthy

until after America became independent. When George Washington's mother bequeathed a blue and white quilt to him, its specific mention in her will showed that she considered it among her most valued possessions.

As the 19th century began, America had its own cloth industry. The first cotton textile plant opened in 1790 at Pawtucket, Rhode Island.

The resulting flood of inexpensive and washable cottons unleashed a new creativity in quiltmaking that came to flower in the American patchwork quilt.

♦ *Patchwork Medallion (above), made by Mrs. William Goosely of Virginia and her daughter; c. 1820. Courtesy of the DAR Museum, Washington, D.C. Instructions are not available for this quilt.*

Structured designs of patchwork emerged as the 1800s began. Nine-Patch, Irish Chain, Pinwheel, Sawtooth Star, and Flying Geese are some of the earliest patterns—the foundation for hundreds that followed.

The early American quiltmaker arranged basic geometric shapes in the patterns she saw in stenciling, architecture, weaving, and even the starry skies and furrowed fields of the countryside.

Written records show that a quilt top was usually pieced by one person. The quilting, though, was done either by the woman who sewed the top, by a professional quilter, or by a group of friends. By 1800, quilting bees were an important social activity; all the stages of a woman's life—girlhood, marriage, child raising, and death—were shared with the women of her community over the quilting frame.

After 1800, quiltmaking became more widespread.

Patchwork, quilting, and other forms of sewing and needlework formed the basis of a girl's education. All were fundamental skills she would need as a wife and mother.

Although American quiltmakers continued to make broderie perse and medallion quilts after the turn of the century, they also began to develop a new concept—the use of small, individual blocks.

The proliferation of patchwork block designs is thought by some historians to be among the most significant developments in quiltmaking and a purely American phenomenon. Blocks, made one at a time and later joined together, were practical, yet still met the maker's need for order and beauty.

Through quilting bees, prolific letter writing, and itinerant peddlers, block patterns traveled from Maine to Florida. In each region, a block acquired new names and variations.

◆ *Sawtooth Star* (left), *Pennsylvania, c. 1850; 85½x94½ inches. Instructions are on page 28.*

◆ *Irish Chain* (opposite), *c. 1880; 73¼x97¾ inches. Instructions are on pages 26 and 27.*

*Q*uiltmakers wanted to name their new blocks and frequently chose names to commemorate important people or events. This is how the classic Robbing Peter to Pay Paul block also came to be known as Dolley Madison's Workbox.

Often these quilt block names had no real tie to the historical figures they immortalized. But they did reflect women's desires to honor a famous person or to make strong political statements.

An example is the Burgoyne Surrounded block (on pages 8 and 9), which recalls the Revolutionary War battle of Saratoga. On October 17, 1777, a small force of Americans surrounded the army of British General John Burgoyne, forcing him to surrender. Ironically, the block's name immortalizes the defeated Burgoyne rather than the victor.

But is the pattern as old as its name implies? Was this block first made and named shortly after the battle at Saratoga?

The earliest known publication of this block pattern is 1890, and the

name was given as Beauregard's Surroundings. It was published later as Wheel of Fortune, Road to California, and Coverlet Quilt, but most often as Burgoyne Surrounded.

A pattern name that may be authentic is Lafayette Orange Peel. Its charming story tells of a Philadelphia belle seated at dinner next to the Marquis de Lafayette when he visited America in 1824. According to the tale, the marquis peeled an orange for the girl, who took the quartered rind home and copied the shapes in a quilt pattern, which she named for the general.

Fact or folklore? The pattern may not have anything to do with Lafayette. It too has been published under different names. But the earliest known surviving example of this pattern was made in approximately 1825, just after Lafayette's visit.

◆ *Robbing Peter to Pay Paul (left), made by Anna Gilderbloom and Retha Marsh of Pleasantville, Iowa; c. 1954; 68x98 inches. Instructions are on page 29.*

STRIP PIECING

In traditional patchwork, patches are marked, cut, and sewn together one piece at a time. But when squares and rectangles are combined in a repeated pattern, you can simplify assembly by using strip-piecing techniques.

This type of machine piecing eliminates tedious marking and cutting and significantly speeds up patchwork. In addition to saving time, strip piecing increases accuracy by eliminating the extra steps required by the traditional method of patchwork.

Strip piecing is ideal for several quilts in this book, including the Burgoyne Surrounded, Irish Chain, and Nine-Patch Variation quilts in Chapter 1, Checkers and Rails in Chapter 3, Amish Shadows in Chapter 7, and Carpenter's Square in Chapter 8.

Cutting strips

With strip piecing, you sew together a specified sequence of horizontal strips into a strip set. The strip set is then cut into vertical units, each of which represents a row or unit of a quilt block.

A rotary cutter is ideal for this kind of straight-line cutting. Used with an acrylic ruler that has ¼-inch markings, the rotary cutter cuts through several layers of fabric. You can use scissors if you prefer, but the rotary cutter/ruler is the fastest and most accurate way to cut strips.

Strips are cut ½ inch wider than the desired *finished* size of the patch to allow for ¼-inch seam allowances. For example, for a 2-inch finished square, cut a strip 2½ inches wide.

Cut strips on the crosswise grain. If the fabric is less than 42 inches wide, you may need more strips than the number given in these instructions.

Strip sets

By cutting units different widths or turning them upside down, a strip set is often used for more than one block row. In this book, the width, color, and number of strips are specified for each strip set and all strip sets are diagramed.

1 **Analyze the rows of the block** you wish to make to determine the repeated units. A simple block like the Nine-Patch, *above,* divides as shown. Most blocks require a separate strip set for each row; in this case, however, the first and third rows are the same, so only two strip sets are necessary.

2 **Cut strips of each fabric** for the strip set. Assume the strips in our example are 2½ inches wide. Sew the strips together, with right sides facing, using a standard ¼-inch seam. The strip sets for the Nine-Patch example are illustrated *above.* Press the seam allowances of each strip set toward the darker fabric.

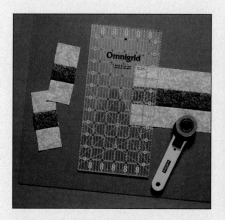

3 **Cut vertical units** from each strip set. Since the original strips of the set were each 2½ inches wide, these units also are cut 2½ inches wide.

4 **Join these units** in the appropriate sequence to complete the Nine-Patch block. The same strip sets can be used to cut units of different widths as shown *above;* these units can be combined with four Nine-Patch blocks to form a larger block.

Burgoyne Surrounded Quilt

Shown on pages 8 and 9.
The finished quilt measures approximately 83x101 inches. Each finished block is 15 inches square.

MATERIALS
7¼ yards of dark blue fabric
2¾ yards of muslin
¾ yard of binding fabric
6 yards of backing fabric
90x108-inch precut quilt batting
Rotary cutter, mat, and acrylic ruler

INSTRUCTIONS
This quilt is a 4x5-block straight set with sashing. The continuous look of the design is achieved with pieced, nine-patch sashing squares that connect the paths of squares in the surrounding blocks.

The pieces for this quilt can be cut and sewn individually, if you prefer, but these instructions feature quick strip-piecing techniques that greatly reduce the cutting and sewing time. These techniques also are likely to improve the accuracy in combining the 1-inch (finished size) squares.

For more information on strip piecing, refer to the *opposite* page.

Cutting the fabrics
For the best use of the fabric, first cut large pieces across the 42-inch width of the fabric as described. From each large piece, cut the strips and rectangles that are listed below it.

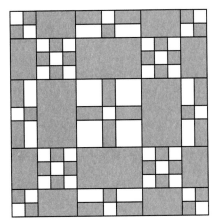

BURGOYNE SURROUNDED BLOCK

The 42-inch-long strips can be used for strip piecing or, if you prefer, individual pieces can be cut from these strips for traditional piecing.

The borders are cut longer than necessary, but they are trimmed after they are sewn to the quilt top.

From the dark blue fabric, cut:
◆ One 109x42-inch rectangle. Cut eleven 3½x109-inch strips. Set four of the 11 strips aside for borders. From each remaining strip, cut seven 3½x15½-inch sashing strips for a total of 49 sashings.
◆ One 40x42-inch rectangle. Cut seven 5½x42-inch strips. From each strip, cut twelve 3½x5½-inch pieces for patch A for a total of 80 A pieces.
◆ One 36x42-inch rectangle. Cut fourteen 2½x42-inch strips. From each strip, cut twelve 2½x3½-inch pieces for patch B. Cut a total of 160 B pieces.
◆ One 42-inch square. Cut 28 strips, 1½x42 inches each, for strip sets 1, 2, 3, and 5.
◆ One 21x42-inch rectangle. Cut eight 2½x42-inch strips for Strip Set 4.

From the muslin, cut:
◆ Forty 1½x42-inch strips. Set 10 strips aside for the inner border. Use the remaining 30 strips for strip sets 1, 2, 4, and 5.
◆ Twelve 2½x42-inch strips for Strip Set 3.

Preparing the strip sets
Note: For traditional piecing, the following four steps are not necessary.
1. The five strip sets are illustrated at *right*. To begin with the simplest one, Strip Set 5, sew one 1½-inch-wide muslin strip to a 1½-inch-wide blue strip, matching 42-inch lengths. Sew together six pairs of strips, making six of Strip Set 5 as shown.
2. Make strip sets 1 and 2 in the same manner, adding a third 1½-inch strip to each set as shown. Make four of Strip Set 1 and eight of Strip Set 2.

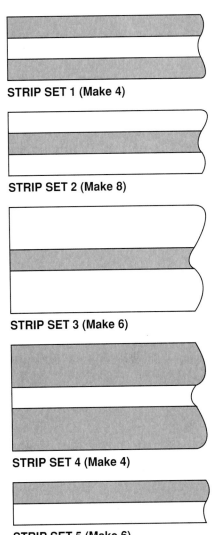

STRIP SET 1 (Make 4)

STRIP SET 2 (Make 8)

STRIP SET 3 (Make 6)

STRIP SET 4 (Make 4)

STRIP SET 5 (Make 6)

STRIP SETS FOR QUICK PIECING

3. Use one 1½-inch-wide blue strip and two 2½-inch-wide muslin strips to make one of Strip Set 3. Strip Set 4 is made in the same manner, with the colors reversed. Make six of Strip Set 3 and four of Strip Set 4.
4. Press all seam allowances toward the dark fabric.

Making the Nine-Patch units
TRADITIONAL PIECING: From the 1½-inch-wide blue and muslin strips, cut 1½-inch squares. Cut 440 blue squares and 550 muslin squares.

Assemble 110 Nine-Patch units as illustrated in Figure 1 on page 20. Press the seam allowances toward the dark fabric.

continued

STRIP PIECING: Cut twenty-eight 1½-inch-wide units from *each* of strip sets 1 and 2, cutting perpendicular to the strip edges as illustrated in Figure 2, *right*. Assemble 110 Nine-Patch units as shown in Figure 1, *right*.

Making the Four-Patch units

TRADITIONAL PIECING: Cut six 1½-inch-wide strips of *each* fabric into 1½-inch squares, cutting 160 squares of each color. Referring to Figure 3, *right*, assemble 80 Four-Patch units as shown.

STRIP PIECING: From each Strip Set 5, cut twenty-eight 1½-inch units. Assemble 80 Four-Patch units as illustrated in Figure 3, *right*.

Making the side units

TRADITIONAL PIECING: Cut 1½-inch-wide strips of *each* fabric into 1½-inch squares, cutting 80 squares of each color. From the 2½-inch-wide strips, cut 1½x2½-inch segments until you have 160 pieces of *each* fabric.

Assemble 80 side units as shown in Figure 4, *right*. Press all seam allowances toward the dark fabric.

STRIP PIECING: Cut eighty 1½-inch-wide units from *each* of strip sets 3 and 4. Assemble 80 side units as shown in Figure 4, *right*.

Making the center units

TRADITIONAL PIECING: Cut the remaining muslin strips into eighty 2½-inch squares and twenty 1½-inch squares. From the blue strips, cut eighty 1½x2½-inch pieces.

Assemble 20 center units as shown in Figure 5, *right*. Press all seam allowances toward the dark fabric.

STRIP PIECING: From the remaining Strip Set 3, cut forty 2½-inch-wide segments. From Strip Set 4, cut twenty 1½-inch-wide segments.

Assemble 20 center units as shown in Figure 5, *right*.

Assembling the block

The Burgoyne Surrounded block is assembled in five rows. Refer to Figure 6, *above right*, and to the block

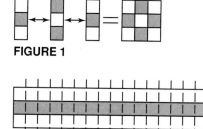

FIGURE 1

FIGURE 2

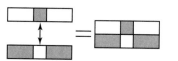

FIGURE 3

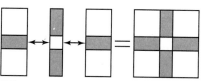

FIGURE 4

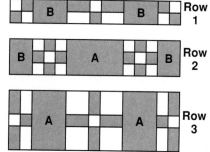

FIGURE 5

FIGURE 6

drawing on page 19 to assemble the rows. Position each unit carefully for correct color placement.

1. To begin Row 1, sew a B piece to each short side of one side unit. Complete the row with one Four-Patch unit on each end. Press all seam allowances toward the B pieces. Make two of Row 1 for each block.

2. For Row 2, stitch a Nine-Patch unit to each short side of one A piece. Complete the row with a B piece on each end. Press the seam allowances

toward the A and B pieces. Make two of Row 2 for each block.

3. To make Row 3, sew an A piece to opposite sides of one center unit. Complete the row with a side unit on each end. Press the seam allowances toward the A pieces. Make one of Row 3 for each block.

4. Join the five rows to make one block in a 1-2-3-2-1 sequence.

Make 20 blocks.

Assembling the block rows

1. Join four blocks in a horizontal row, sewing a sashing strip between each block.

2. Finish the row by stitching a sashing strip onto each end.

3. Make five block rows. Press seam allowances toward the sashing.

Making the sashing rows

There are 30 Nine-Patch units left for the pieced sashing.

1. Sew a Nine-Patch unit onto one end of 24 sashing strips; press seam allowances toward the sashing.

2. Starting with a Nine-Patch unit, join four sets of pieced sashing into a horizontal row so that Nine-Patch units and sashing strips alternate.

3. End the row by sewing one of the six remaining Nine-Patch units onto the end of the last sashing strip.

4. Make six rows of sashing. Press seam allowances toward the sashing.

Assembling the quilt top

Refer to the photograph *opposite* to assemble the quilt top. Join rows, alternating sashing rows and block rows. The first and last rows are sashing. Press seam allowances toward the sashing rows.

Note: In the photograph, it's easy to spot the mistake made by the quiltmaker. A side unit is turned around in the second block in the second block row from the top.

The assembled quilt top measures approximately 75½x93½ inches.

Adding the borders

1. Stitch three 1½x42-inch muslin strips together end to end for *each* side border strip. Sew border strips to sides of the quilt top; trim excess border fabric.

BURGOYNE SURROUNDED QUILT

Nine-Patch Variation Quilt

Shown on page 11.
The finished quilt measures approximately 82½x103½ inches. Each Nine-Patch block is 10½ inches square.

MATERIALS

6¼ yards of white or muslin fabric
2¾ yards of dark blue fabric
⅞ yard of binding fabric
6⅛ yards of backing fabric
90x108-inch precut quilt batting
Rotary cutter, mat, and acrylic ruler

INSTRUCTIONS

This quilt is a 7x9-block alternate straight set. Each block is composed of four basic Nine-Patch units, joined by a center crossbar.

The pieces for this quilt can be cut and sewn individually, if you prefer, but these instructions feature quick strip-piecing techniques that greatly reduce cutting and sewing time. Strip piecing also makes the assembly of the 1½-inch-square pieces (finished size) more accurate.

For more information on strip piecing, see page 18.

Cutting the fabrics
To minimize cutting and piecing, the fabric is cut into strips. These strips can be sewn together, then cut into small pieced segments for the block assembly, or individual pieces can be cut from the strips for traditional piecing.

For efficient use of fabric, cut large pieces across the width of the fabric as described below; then cut strips and rectangles from each large piece.

From the dark blue fabric, cut:
◆ Forty-three 2x42-inch strips. Set aside 10 strips for the middle border; use 33 strips for the Nine-Patch units.
◆ Two 2x33-inch strips for Strip Set 3.

continued

2. Sew two muslin strips together end to end to make one border for the top edge; repeat for the bottom border. Sew a border to each end of the quilt top; trim excess border fabric.
3. Assemble the outside blue borders in the same manner. Stitch them onto the quilt top as you did the muslin border, sewing side borders first, then the top and bottom borders.

Quilting and finishing

BACKING: Divide the backing fabric into two 3-yard lengths. Sew the two panels together; press the seam allowance open.

Layer backing, batting, and quilt top; baste the three layers together.

QUILTING: The quilt pictured *above* has straight lines of quilting that form a crosshatch pattern through each square of the patchwork and across the borders. Quilt as desired.

BINDING: See pages 306 and 307 for tips on making and applying binding. Use the ¾ yard of binding fabric to make approximately 324 inches of binding.

Adjusting the size of the quilt

The 83x101-inch quilt shown is suitable for most full- or queen-size beds.

To make a twin-size quilt, make 15 blocks into a 3x5-block set for a 68x101-inch quilt. For a king-size quilt, make 25 blocks into a 5x5-block set for a 101-inch-square quilt.

From the white fabric, cut:
- One 33x121-inch piece. Cut this piece into thirty-one 11-inch squares.
- Eight 2x42-inch strips. From these, cut sixty-four 2x5-inch pieces for the center cross pieces.
- Thirty-five 2x42-inch strips. Set aside eight strips for borders; use the remaining strips for the Nine-Patch units.
- Four 5x33-inch strips for Strip Set 3.
- Twelve 2x36-inch strips for borders.

Preparing the strip sets

Note: For traditional piecing, the following three steps are not necessary.

The three strip sets are illustrated at *right*.

1. For Strip Set 1, sew a 2-inch-wide blue strip to both sides of one 2-inch-wide white strip, matching the 42-inch lengths. Press seam allowances toward the blue fabric. Make 13 of Strip Set 1.

2. For Strip Set 2, sew a 2-inch-wide white strip to both sides of one 2-inch-wide blue strip. Press the seam allowances toward the blue fabric. Make seven of Strip Set 2.

3. Strip Set 3 is used for the center crossbar. It is made in the same manner as Strip Set 2, but it uses two 5x33-inch white strips with a 2x33-inch blue strip. For this set, press seam allowances toward the white fabric. Make two of Strip Set 3.

Making the Nine-Patch units

TRADITIONAL PIECING: Cut 31 of the 2-inch-wide blue strips and 25 2x42-inch white strips into 2-inch squares. Cut a total of 640 blue squares and 512 white squares to make all the Nine-Patch units.

Assemble 128 Nine-Patch units as shown in Figure 1, *right*. Press seam allowances toward the blue fabric.

STRIP PIECING: From *each* of strip sets 1 and 2, cut twenty 2-inch-wide pieces. Cut a total of 256 segments of Strip Set 1 and 128 segments of Strip Set 2.

Assemble 128 Nine-Patch units as shown in Figure 1, *right*.

STRIP SET 1 (Make 13)

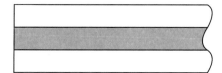

STRIP SET 2 (Make 7)

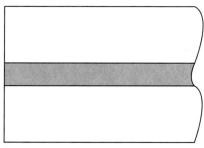

STRIP SET 3 (Make 2)

STRIP SETS FOR QUICK PIECING

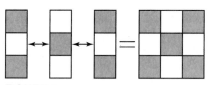

FIGURE 1

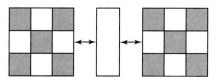

FIGURE 2

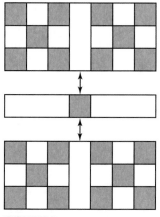

FIGURE 3

Assembling the block

1. Join pairs of Nine-Patch units with a 2x5-inch white piece between them as shown in Figure 2, *left*. Press these seam allowances toward the white center strip. Assemble 64 pairs of the Nine-Patch units.

2. Cut thirty-two 2-inch-wide pieces from Strip Set 3 for the center crossbar. If piecing traditionally, use the remaining strips to cut 2-inch squares of blue fabric and 2x5-inch pieces of white fabric to make 32 crossbars.

3. Stitch a Nine-Patch pair onto both sides of the 2-inch-wide crossbar to complete one block as shown in Figure 3, *left*. Press seam allowances toward the center strip.

Make 32 Nine-Patch blocks.

Assembling the block rows

There are seven blocks in each horizontal row. Alternating pieced blocks with plain blocks, make five rows that begin and end with a Nine-Patch block. Make four rows that begin and end with a plain block.

Assembling the quilt top

To assemble the quilt, join rows so pieced and plain blocks alternate. The first and last rows begin with a pieced block.

The assembled quilt top measures approximately 73½x94½ inches.

Adding the borders

1. Stitch three 2x36-inch white strips together end to end to make a border strip long enough for each side. Sew border strips to sides of the quilt top; trim excess border fabric.

2. Sew two 2x42-inch white strips together to make the top and bottom border strips. Stitch a border onto each end of the quilt top; trim excess border fabric. Press seam allowances toward the border.

3. Make the middle border in the same manner as the inside border, piecing three 42-inch-long blue strips for the side borders and two blue strips for the end borders. Sew side borders onto quilt top first, then attach the end borders. Press seam allowances toward the blue fabric.

4. Use the remaining white strips to piece the outside borders. Join three 36-inch-long strips for each side border and two 42-inch-long strips for each end border. Stitch these borders onto the quilt top as before, sewing the side borders first and then the borders at each end.

Quilting and finishing
BACKING: Cut the backing fabric into two 110-inch lengths. Sew the two panels together; press the seam allowance open.

Layer backing, batting, and quilt top; baste the three layers together.

QUILTING: The quilt pictured on page 11 has straight lines of quilting that cross through each square of the patchwork and across the borders. A maple leaf design is quilted in the plain squares; the pattern for the leaf design is *below*. Quilt as desired.

BINDING: See pages 306 and 307 for tips on making and applying binding. Use the ⅞ yard of binding fabric to make approximately 380 inches of binding.

**LEAF QUILTING DESIGN FOR
NINE-PATCH VARIATION QUILT**

Pinwheel Quilt

Shown on page 12.
The finished quilt measures approximately
81¼x100¾ inches. Each finished
Pinwheel block is 9¾ inches square.

MATERIALS
5¾ yards of muslin for setting
   squares and patchwork
2⅞ yards of solid yellow fabric for
   borders
2 yards of yellow print fabric for
   patchwork
⅞ yard of binding fabric
5¾ yards of backing fabric
90x108-inch precut quilt batting
Rotary cutter, mat, and acrylic ruler

INSTRUCTIONS
The Pinwheel block is assembled like
a nine-patch—five pieced Pinwheel
squares alternating with four plain
squares. The finished blocks are
joined in an alternate straight set and
framed with a wide yellow border.

   The instructions given for quick
piecing are adapted easily to traditional methods.

Cutting the fabrics
From the muslin, cut:
◆ One 42x83-inch piece.
  From this piece, cut thirty-one
  10¼-inch setting squares.
◆ One 42x45-inch piece.
  From this piece, cut 128 squares
  for the Pinwheel blocks, each 3¾
  inches square.
◆ One 42x72-inch piece.
  From this piece, cut eight 17-inch
  squares and three 8x17-inch
  rectangles for the triangle-
  squares.

From the yellow print fabric, cut:
◆ Eight 17-inch squares.
◆ Three 8x17-inch rectangles.

From the solid yellow border fabric, cut:
◆ Two 7x85-inch strips.
◆ Two 7x103-inch strips.

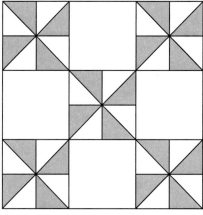

PINWHEEL BLOCK

Making the triangle-squares
Refer to page 114 for more detailed
instructions on quick-piecing triangle-squares.
1. On each 17-inch square of muslin,
mark a 6x6 grid of 2½-inch squares
as shown in Figure 1, *below.* Draw diagonal lines through the squares as
shown. Layer each muslin square,
marked side up, atop one matching
17-inch square of yellow print fabric.
2. For traditional piecing, cut the triangles apart on the marked lines. For
hand piecing, use a fabric pencil and
a gridded ruler to mark ¼-inch seam
allowances on each triangle.

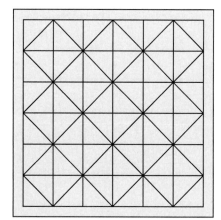

FIGURE 1

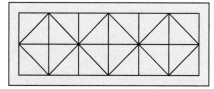

FIGURE 2

3. For quick piecing, stitch the grid as
described in Step 3 on page 114.
Each grid makes 72 triangle-squares.
4. Repeat the procedure with the
8x17-inch pieces, marking a 2x6 grid
of 2½-inch squares on each muslin
piece as shown in Figure 2, *below.*
Each of these grids will produce 24
triangle-squares.
5. Using either piecing method, make
640 triangle-squares. Press the seam
allowances toward the yellow fabric.
Discard any damaged or distorted triangle-squares.

Making the Pinwheel blocks
1. Join all the triangle-squares in
pairs, positioning the yellow print
fabric as shown in Figure 3, *below.*
Press all the joining seam allowances
in the same direction.

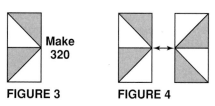

Make 320

FIGURE 3   **FIGURE 4**

2. Sew two pairs of triangle-squares
together to create one Pinwheel
square, turning one of the pairs upside down to position the fabrics as
shown in Figure 4, *above.* Make 160
Pinwheel squares.
3. Each Pinwheel block is made from
five Pinwheel squares and four 3¾-
inch muslin squares. Refer to the
block diagram, *above left,* and join the
squares in three rows.
4. Press the joining seam allowances
toward the muslin squares, then assemble the rows as shown to complete the block.
5. Make 32 Pinwheel blocks.

Assembling the quilt top
This quilt is assembled in nine horizontal rows of seven blocks each. See
page 295 for an illustration of an alternate straight set.

   Sew the blocks into rows, alternating Pinwheel blocks and plain muslin
blocks. Make five rows with pieced
blocks at both ends and four rows
with muslin blocks at both ends.
Press seam allowances toward the
plain blocks.

Join rows so the pieced and plain blocks alternate. The first and last rows start with pieced blocks so that all four corners of the quilt top have a Pinwheel block.

Adding the borders

See general instructions for mitering border corners on page 299. Following these instructions, sew the longer border strips to the quilt sides, then sew the remaining border strips to the top and bottom edges. Miter corners, then trim excess border fabric from the seam.

Quilting and finishing

BACKING: Cut the backing fabric into two 2⅞-yard pieces. Sew them together to make one wide panel.

Layer backing, batting, and quilt top; baste the three layers together.

QUILTING: The quilt shown on page 12 has an X quilted across each triangle-square. The same four-X design is repeated in the plain squares of each Pinwheel block. A feathered wreath fills the plain blocks; the pattern for this quilting design is at *right*. Quilt as desired.

BINDING: See pages 306 and 307 for tips on binding. Use the ⅞ yard of binding fabric to make approximately 370 inches of either bias or straight-grain binding.

Making a larger or smaller quilt

To keep the design properly balanced, this quilt should be made in odd-numbered rows. The quilt dimensions given are ideal for a full-size bed. This size also may work for a twin or a queen-size bed.

For a smaller quilt, try making a 5x9-block set. Because this will be narrow, you might consider adding another border to the sides only.

Adding another border is also an option for enlarging the 7x9 set to accommodate a queen-size bed.

For a king-size quilt, assemble nine more Pinwheel blocks and nine more plain blocks to make two additional vertical rows, or a 9x9 set. The finished size is 100¾ inches square.

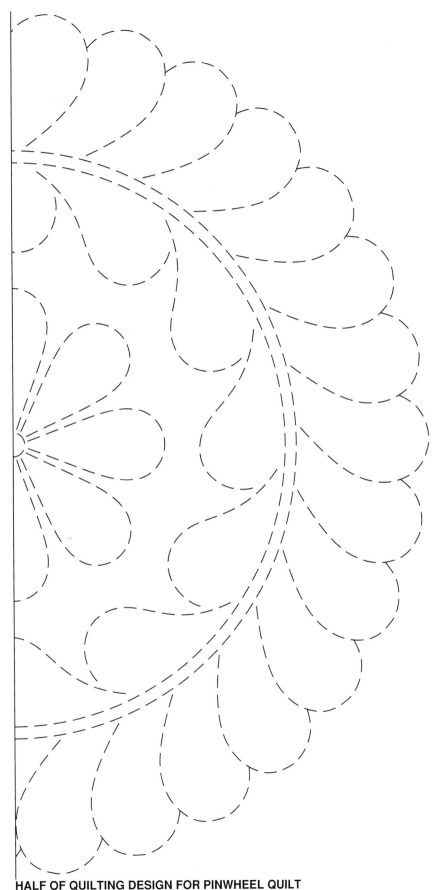

HALF OF QUILTING DESIGN FOR PINWHEEL QUILT

Irish Chain Quilt

Shown on page 15.
The finished quilt measures approximately 73¼x97¾ inches. Each finished block is 12¼ inches square.

MATERIALS
4 yards of muslin
3 yards of tan fabric, including binding
2½ yards of red fabric
6 yards of backing fabric
90x108-inch precut quilt batting
Rotary cutter, mat, and acrylic ruler

INSTRUCTIONS
This quilt is a 5x7-block alternate straight set. However, instead of being a plain square, the alternating block has piecing that connects to the main block to create the illusion of a continuous chain.

The pieces for this quilt can be cut and sewn individually, if you prefer, but these instructions feature quick strip-piecing techniques that reduce cutting and sewing time. These techniques also improve the accuracy of the 1¾-inch (finished size) squares.

See page 18 for more information on strip piecing.

Cutting the fabrics
Cut all fabrics in strips, as given below. For traditional patchwork, individual patches can be cut from these strips. For strip piecing, the strips are sewn together, then cut into small pieced segments.

From the tan fabric, cut:
◆ One 23x42-inch rectangle for binding.
◆ Ten 2½x42-inch strips for the outer border.
◆ Twenty 2¼x42-inch strips. Set aside 12 strips for Block A and eight strips for Block B.

From the red fabric, cut:
◆ Ten 2½x42-inch strips for the inner border.
◆ Twenty-four 2¼x42-inch strips. Set aside 20 strips for Block A and four strips for Block B.

IRISH CHAIN QUILT

From the muslin, cut:
◆ Ten 2½x42-inch strips for the middle border.
◆ Seventeen 2¼x42-inch strips for Block A.
◆ Four 5¾x42-inch strips for Block B.
◆ Eighteen 9¼-inch squares.

Preparing the strip sets
Note: For traditional piecing, the following three steps are not necessary.

The six strip sets are illustrated at *right.* The first four sets are for Block A; each is made by sewing together seven 2¼x42-inch strips.

Strip sets 5 and 6 are for the pieced edge of Block B.

1. Using the colors indicated in the illustration of each strip set, sew seven strips together to make strip sets 1, 2, 3, and 4, as shown.

2. Make strip sets 5 and 6 in the same manner, positioning a 5¾-inch-wide muslin strip in the center of each set as illustrated.

3. Make two of each strip set, except make only one of Strip Set 4. Press all seam allowances in one direction.

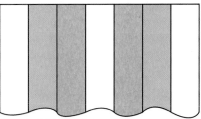

STRIP SET 1 (Make 2)

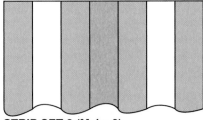

STRIP SET 2 (Make 2)

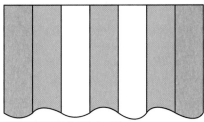

STRIP SET 3 (Make 2)

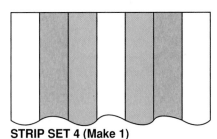

STRIP SET 4 (Make 1)

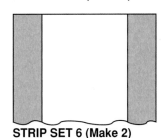

STRIP SET 5 (Make 2)

STRIP SET 6 (Make 2)

STRIP SETS FOR QUICK PIECING

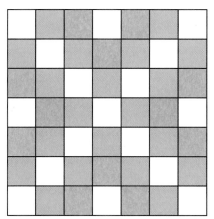

BLOCK A

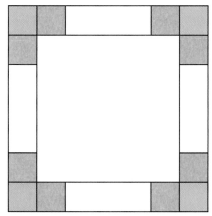

BLOCK B

Assembling Block A

Block A is assembled in seven rows. Refer to the block diagram, *above*, for placement of each square or strip segment. Position each unit carefully for correct color placement.

TRADITIONAL PIECING: Cut the 2¼-inch-wide strips designated for Block A into 2¼-inch squares. Cut 340 red squares, 204 tan squares, and 289 squares of muslin.

Assemble the squares in horizontal rows as shown in the block diagram, *above*. Press seam allowances toward the dark fabric. Join the rows as illustrated. Make 17 of Block A.

STRIP PIECING: Each strip segment represents one horizontal row of the block.
1. From *each* of strip sets 1, 2, and 3, cut thirty-four 2¼-inch-wide units. Cut 17 pieces 2¼ inches wide from Strip Set 4.
2. Each block requires two units from each of the first three strip sets and one piece from Strip Set 4.
3. Join the seven segments into a block in a 1-2-3-4-3-2-1 sequence. (See block diagram, *above*.)
Make 17 of Block A.

Assembling Block B

Block B is made by sewing pieced rows around a muslin square. Refer to the block diagram, *above*, for placement of each unit.

TRADITIONAL PIECING: Cut the 2¼-inch-wide strips designated for Block B into 2¼-inch squares. Cut 72 red squares and 144 tan squares.

From each 5¾-inch-wide muslin strip, cut eighteen 2¼x5¾-inch patches. Cut a total of 72 patches.

Assemble Block B as shown. For each block, make two units consisting of a muslin strip with a tan square sewn to each end. Make two more units in the same manner, adding red squares at each end.

Sew the shorter units to opposite sides of a 9¼-inch muslin square. Complete the block by sewing the longer units to the remaining sides. Press seam allowances toward the muslin square.
Make 18 of Block B.

STRIP PIECING: Block B is made by sewing units of strip sets 5 and 6 to a center muslin square.
1. Cut each of strip sets 5 and 6 into eighteen 2¼-inch-wide units. Each block requires two segments from each of these strip sets.
2. Sew units from Strip Set 6 onto opposite sides of one 9¼-inch muslin square. Complete the block by sewing units from Strip Set 5 onto the remaining sides of the square. Press seam allowances toward the muslin square.
Make 18 of Block B.

Assembling the quilt top

Note: See page 295 for an illustration of an alternate straight set.

Join five blocks into a horizontal row, alternating A and B blocks. Make four rows that begin and end with a B block and three rows that begin and end with an A block.

Alternating rows that begin with A and B blocks, join the rows to assemble the quilt top.

The assembled quilt top measures approximately 61¼x85¾ inches.

Adding the borders

1. Stitch three 2½x42-inch red strips together end to end to make a border strip long enough for each side. Sew border strips to sides of the quilt top; trim excess border fabric.
2. Sew two red strips together for the top and bottom border strips. Stitch a strip onto each end of the quilt top; trim excess border fabric.
3. Sew the middle and outer border strips together in the same manner; stitch borders onto the quilt top, sewing the side borders first and then the end borders.

Quilting and finishing

BACKING: Divide the backing fabric into two 3-yard lengths. Sew the two panels together; press the seam allowance open.

Layer backing, batting, and quilt top; baste the three layers together.

QUILTING: The quilt pictured on page 15 has straight lines of quilting that form a crosshatch pattern through each square of the patchwork and across the borders. Quilt as desired.

BINDING: See pages 306 and 307 for tips on making and applying binding. Use the remaining tan fabric to make approximately 350 inches of either bias or straight-grain binding.

Sawtooth Star Quilt

Shown on page 14.
The finished quilt measures approximately 85½x94½ inches. Each finished star block is 4½ inches square.

MATERIALS
4¼ yards of brown fabric
2¾ yards of muslin
Forty-one 5½-inch squares of assorted light fabrics for the star centers
Forty-one 9-inch squares of dark fabrics for the star points
¾ yard of green binding fabric
2⅞ yards of 90-inch-wide sheeting for backing fabric
90x108-inch precut quilt batting
Rotary cutter, mat, and acrylic ruler
Template material (optional)

INSTRUCTIONS
This quilt is a 17x19-block alternate straight set, with 161 star blocks and 162 plain brown squares. Each star has a light center and dark points against a muslin background.

Because the patches are so small, accurate machine piecing may be difficult. For hand piecing, mark seam lines on each cut piece using an acrylic ruler or templates for measuring.

Cutting the fabrics
In the quilt shown on page 14, many scraps are used in the pieced blocks. Some stars have more than one dark fabric for the points. A few blocks use light rather than dark fabrics for the points, but the light fabrics tend to disappear into the background.

Use a variety of colors and prints for a genuine scrap quilt. Plaids, shirtings, calicoes, pindots, solids, and stripes are used in the original quilt.

From the muslin, cut:
◆ Twenty-six 1⅝x42-inch strips. From each strip, cut twenty-five 1⅝-inch squares for patch A. Cut a total of 644 A squares.
◆ Fourteen 3½x42-inch strips. Cut twelve 3½-inch squares from each strip. Cut each square in quarters diagonally, creating four C triangles. Cut 644 C triangles.

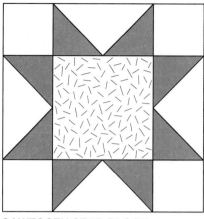

SAWTOOTH STAR BLOCK

From the brown fabric, cut:
◆ Four 5x90-inch strips for borders.
◆ 162 5-inch squares.

From each light scrap fabric, cut:
◆ Four 2¾-inch squares for star centers. Cut 161 center squares.

From each dark scrap fabric, cut:
◆ Sixteen 2-inch squares. Cut each square in half diagonally, creating 32 B triangles. Cut eight triangles for each star, or a total of 1,288 triangles.

Making the Sawtooth Star block
Refer to the block assembly diagram, *below,* as you make each block.

Each block requires one center square, four *each* of square A and triangle C, and eight B triangles.

Note: Although seam allowances are usually pressed toward darker fabrics, it is important to avoid building up bulk where seam allowances

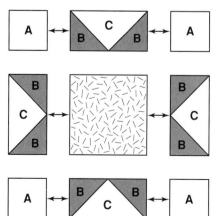

BLOCK ASSEMBLY DIAGRAM

meet. This requires pressing toward the lighter fabrics in this patchwork.
1. Stitch a B triangle to both short sides of each C triangle. Press seam allowances toward the C triangle. Make four BCB units for each block.
2. Sew a BCB unit to two opposite sides of the center square as shown in the assembly diagram. Press seam allowances toward the center.
3. Join an A square to each end of the remaining BCB units. Press seam allowances toward the A squares.
4. To finish the block, join the three rows. Press seam allowances toward the center square. Make 161 blocks.

Assembling the quilt top
Refer to the photo on page 14 and the diagram of the alternate straight set on page 295 for guidance.

Each horizontal row consists of 17 blocks, solid brown squares alternating with the pieced star blocks.
1. Make 10 rows, each with eight star blocks and nine solid squares. Make these rows with a solid square at both ends. Press seam allowances toward the plain squares.
2. Make nine more rows, using nine star blocks and eight solid squares and starting with a star block.
3. Alternating rows that start with a star block and a solid square, sew the 19 rows together.

Adding the borders
Stitch one border strip onto each long side of the quilt top. Press seam allowances toward the border strips; trim excess border fabric.

Join borders at top and bottom of the quilt top in the same manner.

Quilting and finishing
Layer backing, batting, and quilt top; baste the three layers together.

QUILTING: Quilt as desired. The quilt pictured has quilting that outlines the seams of the star points. Diagonal lines, ¼ inch apart, are quilted in the star centers, the brown squares, and the borders.

BINDING: See pages 306 and 307 for tips on making and applying binding. From the green fabric, make approximately 370 inches of binding.

Robbing Peter To Pay Paul Quilt

Shown on pages 16 and 17.
The finished quilt measures 68x96
inches. Each block is 7 inches square.

MATERIALS

6 yards *each* of white and red fabrics
5¾ yards of backing fabric
90x108-inch precut quilt batting
Template material

INSTRUCTIONS

This block appears to be pieced, but the curves are actually achieved by appliquéing four melon-shaped pieces (A) onto a solid fabric square.

Cutting the fabrics

Make a template for Pattern A, *below.*

From the white fabric, cut:
◆ One piece 20x108 inches. From this piece, cut four border strips 2½x108 inches and four border strips 2½x80 inches.
◆ Forty-eight 7½-inch squares.
◆ 192 of Pattern A.

From the red fabric, cut:
◆ One piece 10x108 inches. From this piece, cut two border strips 2½x80 inches and two border strips 2½x108 inches.
◆ One piece 8x98 inches for straight-grain binding.
◆ Forty-eight 7½-inch squares.
◆ 192 of Pattern A.

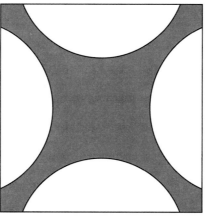

**ROBBING PETER
TO PAY PAUL BLOCK**

Making the blocks

1. On each A piece, turn under the seam allowance on the curved edges only. Clip the seam allowance if necessary to achieve a smooth curve; press or baste the seam allowance in place, if desired. Leave the straight edge flat, as this is sewn into the seam when adjacent blocks are joined.
2. Align the straight edge of one white A piece with one edge of a red square. There should be approximately ¾ inch of red fabric showing above and below the white melon shape on the straight edge. Appliqué the curved edge onto the red fabric.
3. Appliqué a white A piece onto each of the three remaining sides of the red square in the same manner.
4. Repeat, sewing four white A pieces onto each red square and four red A pieces onto each white square. Make 48 blocks of each color combination.

Assembling the quilt top

Join the blocks into 12 horizontal rows of eight blocks each, alternating red and white centers. Make six rows that begin with a red square and six rows that begin with a white square.

Join rows, alternating rows that begin with red and white squares and matching seam lines carefully. The assembled quilt top is approximately 56x84 inches.

Adding the borders

1. Match two white border strips with one red strip of the same length. Stitch the strips together lengthwise, with the red one in the center. Assemble four white-red-white borders.
2. Sew the longer border sections onto the sides of the quilt top; add the short sections at the top and bottom edges. See page 299 for instructions on mitering border corners.

Quilting and finishing

BACKING: Cut two 2⅞-yard pieces of backing fabric. Sew the two pieces together to make one wide panel.

Layer backing, batting, and quilt top; baste the three layers together.

QUILTING: The quilt shown on pages 16 and 17 has outline quilting around each A piece and the border seams. Quilt as desired.

BINDING: See pages 306 and 307 for tips on making and applying binding. Make approximately 332 inches of binding from the red fabric.

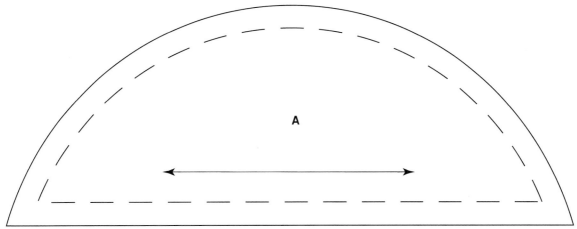

A

PATTERN FOR ROBBING PETER TO PAY PAUL QUILT

Antebellum Legacy

Appliqué Flowers
in Baltimore

1840 ∽ 1860

◆ *Rose Wreath, Virginia
or the Carolinas, c. 1860;
86x86 inches. Instructions
begin on page 38.*

We learned to sew patchwork at school while we were learning the alphabet; and almost every girl had a bed quilt of her own begun, with an eye to future house furnishing. I was not overfond of sewing, but I thought it best to begin mine early. So I collected squares of calico, and undertook to put them together in my usual independent way, without asking direction. I liked assorting those little figured bits of cotton cloth, for they were scraps of gowns I had seen worn, and they reminded me of the persons who wore them.

Lucy Larcom, *A New England Girlhood*

Quilts acquired new significance between 1840 and 1860 as women began to use them to raise funds and to make statements of friendship or social values.

An important trend was the creative, elaborate floral appliqué that started in Maryland and Pennsylvania, and then spread to other areas.

Paper albums inscribed with verses and autographs became popular in the 1820s, a fad encouraged by the new and influential magazine, *Godey's Lady's Book*. By 1840, the album craze extended to quilts.

These album quilts were presented to friends as gifts or kept by the maker to remember the friends and relatives who contributed blocks. Most appliqué album quilts were samplers of various block designs, whereas patchwork album quilts usually featured the same block made in different fabrics.

While quiltmakers all over the country stitched their friendship into quilts, the appliqué quilts made in and around Baltimore between 1846 and 1860 scaled the heights of this fashion.

The Baltimore Album quilts were mostly appliqué, and the women who made them apparently strove to outdo one another with elaborate creations of bouquets, wreaths, and cornucopias. Outstanding designers and stitchers, like Mary Evans of Baltimore, won lasting renown for the quality of their work.

Album sampler quilts, as well as other floral appliquéd quilts of the day, were made using nearly every technique available to the quilt-maker, including some we hardly recognize today. The ruched rose of the Rose Wreath Quilt, pictured on pages 30 and 31, is a fine example.

Wreaths were a favorite theme of the women who made these quilts. There were wreaths of grapes, cherries, laurel leaves, and tulips, but the wreath that was most beloved was one of roses and buds.

◆ *Bouquet Block* (above), Iowa, 1990; 16x16 inches. Patterns and instructions are on pages 44 and 45.

◆ *Album* (opposite), signed by C.A. Miles, Maryland, c. 1850; 74x74 inches. Instructions are not available for this quilt.

In the South, where slaves picked and cleaned the cotton that fueled the thriving U.S. textile industry, some female slaves were lent from one plantation to another to do sewing.

A slave who stitched fancy needlework, such as appliqué, was considered extremely valuable. Some of the finest appliqué

quilts of this period were made on Southern plantations, either by ladies of leisure or by the black women they owned.

The diversity of pieced patterns continued to grow, too. Stars sprouted feathered edges; triangles acquired curved corners and were joined to form blocks with colorful names, such as Hearts and Gizzards. Overall patterns of diamonds formed cubes or blocks, and hexagons made complex honeycombs.

These designs showed off the new roller-printed cotton fabrics, available in smaller prints than the old-fashioned plate and woodblock prints.

◆ ***Whig Rose*** *(above), Maryland, c. 1860; 82x82 inches. Instructions begin on page 46.*

*A*ppliquéd quilts reached unparalleled heights of beauty and workmanship during the 20 years preceding the Civil War.

Too time-consuming to be practical for a utilitarian quilt, appliqué became the hallmark of a lady of leisure whose greatest accomplishment was the creation of exquisitely elaborate needlework. To own an appliqué quilt was a statement of great affluence and prestige.

Some early album quilts had cutout chintz appliqués in the broderie perse style, but conventional appliqué replaced it during this period. Cutout chintz became a nearly forgotten style, along with stuffed work and wholecloth quilts. No longer did the quiltmaker cut out a preprinted chintz border of bows and swags; instead she created her own design. Birds, flowers, baskets, feathers, and other motifs were skillfully executed in dazzling abundance.

◆ ***Hearts and Gizzards*** *(opposite), c. 1900; 86¾x98 inches. Instructions are on page 50.*

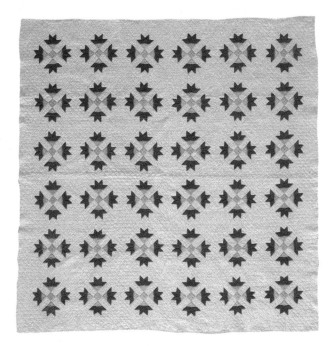

*A*n important ideal in quiltmaking set during the mid-1800s prevails today—the preference for a white or other light background for both patchwork and appliqué.

Green and turkey red on white is predominant among the quilts of this period. Appliquéd album blocks and many other quilt designs were executed in red and green calicoes, the small prints that became fashionable in the 1840s and 1850s.

Unfortunately, some green dyes in use then did not stand the test of time. Fabrics treated with natural dyes retained a green color, as in the Swirling Peony Quilt at *right*. The synthetic dyes adopted in the 1850s, however, eventually turned the fabric dull brown, as in the Goose Tracks Quilt, *above*.

The use of quilts in everyday life is reflected in memoirs of this prewar period. Girls growing up in these decades later recalled their first lessons in patchwork at home and at school. Quite a few women earned their living by quilting for others. Diarists frequently wrote of quilting frolics, parties, and bees as significant social occasions.

When the hardships of the Civil War and the isolation of distant prairies put an end to the widespread affluence of this well-mannered period, the scrap quilt emerged as yet another new form of the versatile patchwork quilt.

◆ *Goose Tracks* (*above*), *New York, c. 1860; 83½x83½ inches. Instructions are on page 51.*

◆ *Swirling Peony* (*right*), *Pennsylvania, c. 1850; 81x81 inches. Instructions begin on page 52.*

Rose Wreath Quilt

Shown on pages 30 and 31.
The finished quilt measures approximately
86x86 inches. Each appliquéd wreath
block is 20 inches square.

MATERIALS
8½ yards of muslin for the nine
    blocks, borders, and binding
4½ yards green solid fabric
3¼ yards red solid fabric
2¾ yards of 90-inch-wide sheeting
    for backing fabric
90x108-inch precut quilt batting
Template material
Rotary cutter, mat, and acrylic ruler
Acrylic triangle
Drawing compass and pencil
10 yards of ⅛-inch-wide cording
    for piping (optional)

INSTRUCTIONS
The ruched roses and buds on this
quilt are unusual. Although they are
rarely seen today, several ruching
techniques were used by Victorian ladies to tuck and gather fabric to create three-dimensional flowers and
other motifs for appliqué.

Step-by-step instructions for making ruched roses and buds are on
pages 42 and 43.

Another unusual feature of this
quilt is the red piping between the
border and binding. If you choose
not to make piping, you can insert a
⅜-inch-wide strip of folded red fabric or eliminate the trim altogether.

Cutting the fabrics
Refer to page 288 for tips on making
templates for appliqué. Make a template for each of patterns A through
C, *opposite,* and patterns D through F
on pages 40 and 41. When cutting
appliqués from fabric, add a ³⁄₁₆-inch
seam allowance around each piece.

Cut 5-inch circles of red fabric for
the wreath roses and 6-inch circles
for the border roses. Make templates
for each circle from the patterns giv-
en, *opposite,* or use a compass to draw
circles on the fabric.

If you wish to make traditional appliquéd roses, rather than ruched
roses, use patterns G and H.

ROSE WREATH BLOCK

From the green fabric, cut:
◆ One 10x20-inch piece for the
  border stems.
  From this piece, cut four 1x9½-
  inch stems for the corner border
  roses and twelve 1x7-inch stems
  for the side border roses.
◆ One 20-inch square for bias
  appliqué (wreath stems).
◆ 176 of Pattern A.
  Set aside 144 leaves for blocks
  and 32 leaves for border roses.
◆ 80 of Pattern B.
  Set aside 72 buds for blocks and
  eight for border corner roses.
◆ 16 of Pattern D and 16 of
  Pattern D reversed.
◆ 12 of Pattern F and 12 of
  Pattern F reversed.

From the muslin, cut:
◆ One 14x306-inch strip.
  From this piece, cut two
  13½x90-inch borders and two
  13½x62-inch borders.
◆ A 21x50-inch piece for binding.
◆ Nine 20½-inch squares.

From the red fabric, cut:
◆ One 24-inch square for piping.
◆ 80 of Pattern C.
  Set aside 72 bud inserts for the
  blocks and eight for border
  corner roses.
◆ 32 of Pattern E.
◆ Seventy-two 5-inch-diameter
  circles for ruched roses *or* Pattern
  G for traditional appliqué.
◆ Sixteen 6-inch-diameter circles
  for ruched border roses *or* Pattern H for traditional appliqué.

Preparing bias for appliqué
Using a triangle to mark a true 45-
degree angle, cut 1-inch-wide bias
strips from the 20-inch square of
green fabric. Cut at least 290 inches
of bias strips.

Lay each strip on an ironing board,
wrong side up. Fold both long edges
into the center, folding the strip into
thirds lengthwise. Press lightly. Each
pressed strip should be a scant ⅜
inch wide.

From the pressed bias, cut thirty-
six 6-inch-long stems and thirty-six
2-inch long stems. Do not turn under
the ends, as these will be covered by
the rose appliqués.

Preparing the ruched appliqué
Step-by-step instructions for making
ruched buds and roses are on pages
42 and 43.

Following these instructions, prepare seventy-two 5-inch circles for
the block roses, gathering the outer
edges into a 3-inch-diameter circle.
For the border roses, gather sixteen
6-inch circles to make 4-inch-diame-
ter circles.

Prepare 80 buds as directed on
page 43.

Appliquéing the blocks
1. For each block, turn under the
seam allowances of 16 A leaves. Also
use eight small roses, eight B buds,
four 6-inch pieces of prepared green
bias stems, and four 2-inch stems.
2. Fold each muslin square in half
vertically, horizontally, and diagonally; lightly press each crease to mark
positioning lines.
3. Using a compass or other tool with
a pencil, lightly draw a 14-inch circle
in the center of the muslin square.
4. Pin or baste a 2-inch length of bias
at the center top of the drawn circle,
placing the *inner* edge of the strip on
the pencil line. Position a rose at both
ends of the strip.
5. Tuck the end of a 6-inch bias strip
under the opposite side of each rose.
Curve the bias so the inside edge
aligns with the circle. Place a rose
over the other end of each strip.
6. Complete the circle in this manner,
alternating 2-inch and 6-inch lengths
of bias between roses.

continued

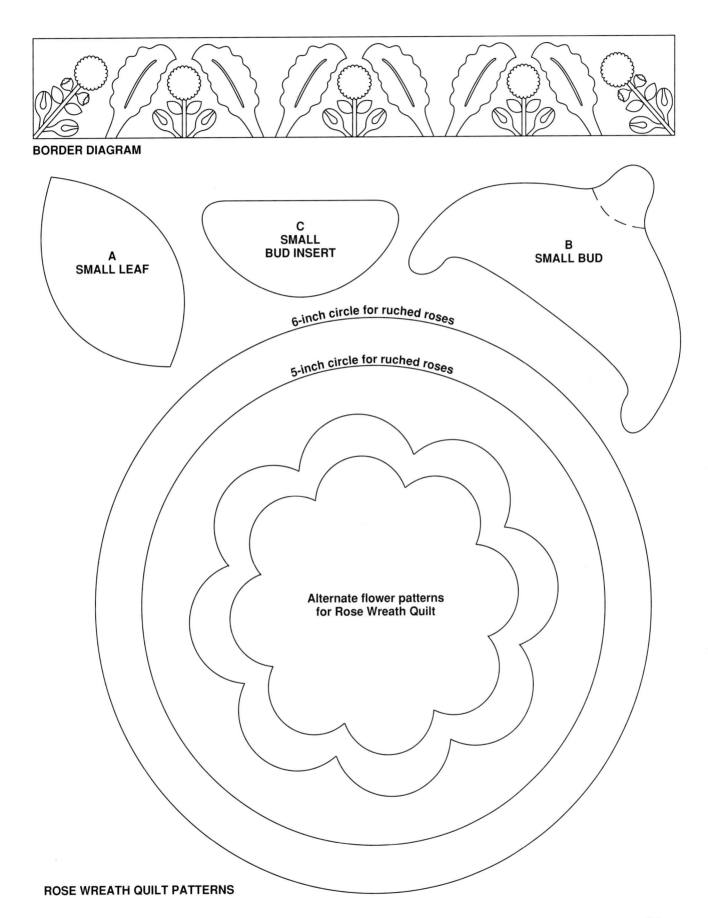

BORDER DIAGRAM

A
SMALL LEAF

C
SMALL
BUD INSERT

B
SMALL BUD

6-inch circle for ruched roses

5-inch circle for ruched roses

Alternate flower patterns
for Rose Wreath Quilt

ROSE WREATH QUILT PATTERNS

7. Pin leaves on both sides of each short stem piece. Alternate buds and leaves on the longer stems as shown in the block diagram on page 38.

8. Appliqué each piece in place on the background fabric. Make nine Rose Wreath blocks.

Assembling the quilt top
Join the nine appliquéd blocks in three rows of three blocks each to complete the center of the quilt.

Appliquéing the borders
Refer to the border diagram at the top of page 39 to position the design elements on the borders.

1. Trim the lengths of the 62-inch-long muslin border strips to match the lengths of opposite sides of the quilt top. Appliqué these borders as described below, before sewing them onto opposite sides of the quilt top.

2. Turn under the outside edges of each D bud. To prepare the insert area of each bud, carefully make a slit through the center; clip the seam allowance in the tight inner curve. Do not turn the inside edge under yet.

3. Turn under all seam allowances on the remaining appliqué pieces, except the bottom edges of the large leaves, stems, and buds. Those areas will be covered by other pieces or binding.

4. Pin or baste a stem in place at the center of each strip. Pin prepared leaves, buds, and bud inserts on both sides of the stem as illustrated. Turn under the small end of the E bud insert that is exposed. Top the stem with a prepared rose.

5. The center of the large leaf (F) requires *reverse appliqué* to reveal the fabric under it. Carefully slit the leaf fabric through the center of the area indicated by shading on the pattern. Do not turn under these edges yet.

6. Working outward from the center, position three rose units on each border as shown, surrounding each rose with an arch of large leaves.

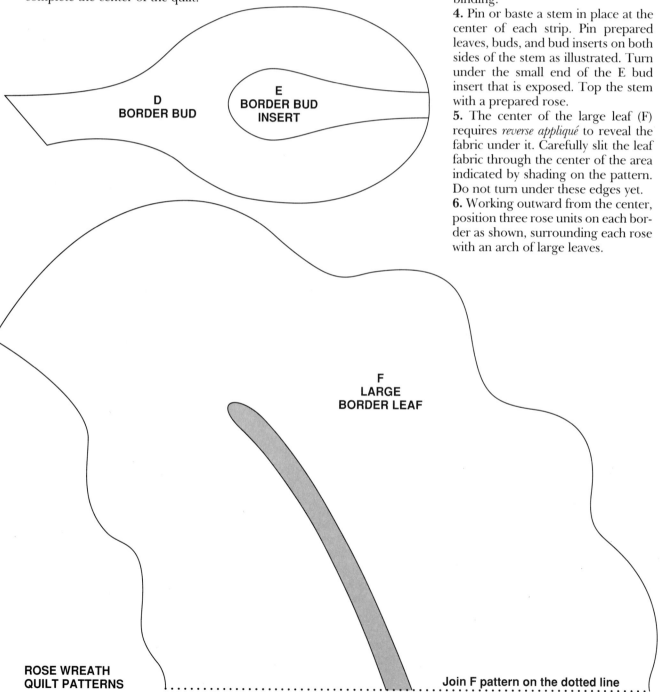

**D
BORDER BUD**

**E
BORDER BUD
INSERT**

**F
LARGE
BORDER LEAF**

**ROSE WREATH
QUILT PATTERNS**

Join F pattern on the dotted line

7. Appliqué all the border pieces in place. Use the needle to turn back the edges of the slit in the large leaves; appliqué them in place, revealing the muslin underneath. Sew the outer edge of each D bud in place, then use the needle to turn under the fabric covering the insert and appliqué the edge in place. Sew the exposed tip of the insert in place.

8. Sew the short borders onto opposite sides of the quilt top. Trim and appliqué the longer borders in the same manner, adding a corner rose unit at each end of these strips. Sew the longer appliquéd borders to the remaining sides of the quilt top.

Quilting and finishing

QUILTING: Layer the backing fabric, batting, and quilt top. Baste the layers securely together.

Quilt as desired. The quilt pictured on pages 30 and 31 has a different motif quilted inside each wreath, plus a ⅝-inch grid of squares overall.

PIPING: Refer to page 306 for tips on making continuous bias. Follow those instructions to cut 9¾ yards of 1-inch-wide continuous bias from the 24-inch square of red fabric.

Press the strip in half, wrong sides together. Insert cording in the fold.

Using a zipper foot or cording foot, machine-stitch right next to the cording as illustrated in Figure 1, *below*. Trim the seam allowance to a scant ⅜ inch.

Pin the raw edges of the piping around the edges of the quilt, positioning the stitching line on the piping at least ¼ inch from the edge. Machine-baste the piping in place, sewing on the same stitching line.

BINDING: Use the remaining muslin to make 350 inches of binding. See pages 306 and 307 for instructions on making and applying binding.

F
**LARGE
BORDER LEAF**

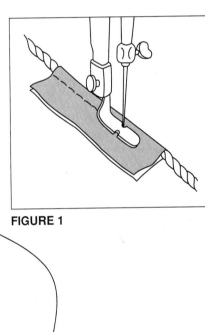

FIGURE 1

Join F pattern on the dotted line

MAKING RUCHED ROSES AND BUDS

One of the most elaborate techniques used in classic Baltimore Album quilts is ruching. Little used in this century, ruching was practiced by well-to-do ladies of the 1800s who devoted their time to creating extraordinary needlework.

Ruching (pronounced RU-shing) is a technique for gathering fabric that adds dimension and texture to otherwise ordinary appliqué.

Start with a circle

The renewal of interest in Baltimore Album quilts has reintroduced different types of ruching to quiltmakers.

Each rose of the antique quilt shown on pages 30 and 31 is made with a single large circle of fabric, tucked and gathered in the manner described here. We incorporated this ruching technique in our reproduction of the bouquet block from the Baltimore Album quilt; both projects are pictured on pages 32 and 33.

Circle patterns are given for the projects in this book, but you can draw circles directly on the fabric with a compass, if you prefer. The instructions for each project state the finished size of each ruched rose.

To apply this technique to other projects, the ratio of the finished rose to the cut circle is approximately 5:8. To determine the size of the cut circle, first select the desired finished size of the rose. For example, cut a 4-inch fabric circle for a 2½-inch rose.

Another way to figure this is by using percentages. The cut circle is approximately 160 percent of the finished size of the rose, so multiply 2.5 inches by 1.6 (2.5 x 1.6 = 4 inches).

Tools and materials

In addition to the materials generally used for appliqué, most ruching requires the use of a compass or a template to draw circles on the fabric.

It is important to use 100 percent cotton fabric for ruching, since cotton is more pliable than blends. Use thread that matches the color of the ruching fabric as closely as possible.

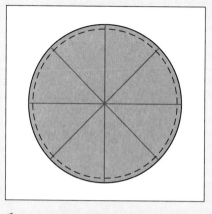

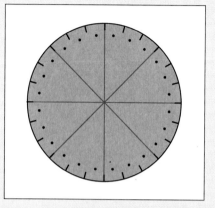

1a To make the roses, turn under and baste a ¼-inch seam allowance around the outside edge of the fabric circle. Fold and press the circle in half four times, folding *right sides together*, creasing eight equal wedges around the circle as shown *above*. Steam press; remove the basting thread.

1b Divide each wedge into thirds by making pencil marks on the folded edge of the circle, working on the right side. Make the marks on the pressed creases, too.

Make a second set of pencil marks about ⅜ inch to the inside of the folded edge, making a dot mark halfway between each edge mark as illustrated *above*.

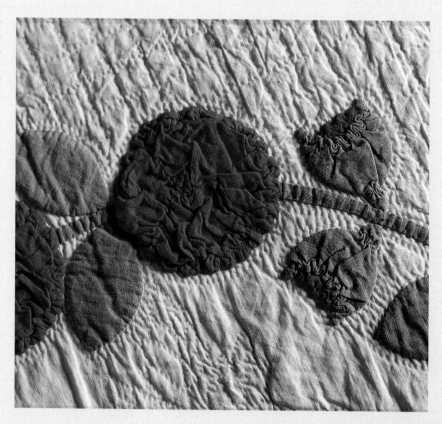

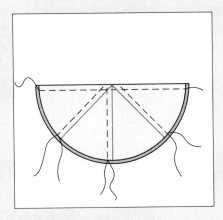

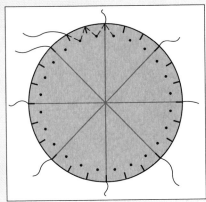

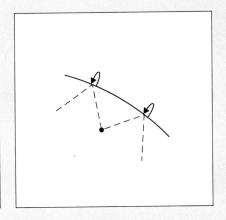

1c Fold the circle on one crease at a time, right sides together. Hand-sew a running stitch across the diameter of the circle right next to the fold through both layers, stitching a tiny tuck in the fabric. Begin and end each stitching line just over the raw edge of the seam allowance. Leave 4 to 5 inches of thread dangling at each end; this thread will be used later for gathering and appliqué.

1d Stitch a zigzag of tiny running stitches around the outer edge of the rose, connecting the pencil marks as shown *above*. With a new thread, start at any mark on the outer edge. Each time you complete a V, gently pull the thread to form a scallop.

1e Loop the thread around the edge to secure the gather in place, as shown *above*. Continue stitching the next V. Do not sew through the dangling pull-threads.

Pin the outer edge of the ruched rose in place on the block. Gently tug the pull-threads to gather the inner fabric of the rose. Use the pull-thread ends to appliqué the scalloped edges onto the background fabric.

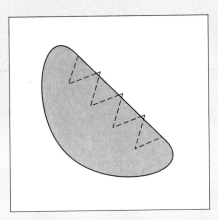

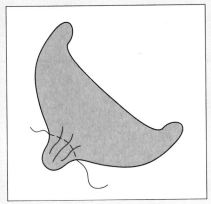

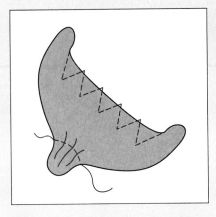

2 For each small bud, prepare the insert (Pattern C on page 39) by turning back a scant ¼ inch on the straight edge of the piece. Using thread that matches the color of the insert fabric, hand-sew a zigzag as shown *above*. Loop the thread around the edge each time in the same manner as for the ruched roses. Pull gently on the thread to scallop the outer edge. Pin the insert on the background fabric.

3a Prepare the outer bud (Pattern B on page 39) by turning back a scant ¼-inch seam allowance all around the piece. Using a matching thread color, hand-sew a gathering stitch through the lower base of the bud as indicated by the dashes on the pattern. Pull gently to gather the fabric; secure gathers with a loop knot.

3b Sew a zigzag of running stitches along the straight edge of the bud as illustrated *above*. Pull gently on the thread to gather the edge. Loop the thread around the fold at the top of each V as indicated.

Pin the bud in place on the background fabric, covering the unfinished edge of the insert. Position the ruched part of the insert as shown in the photograph, *opposite*. Appliqué bud and insert in place.

Framed Appliquéd Bouquet Block

Shown on page 33.
The finished size of the appliqué is 16 inches square.

MATERIALS

22-inch square of dark red fabric for background
18-inch square of green fabric for leaves and stems
14-inch square of dark rose print fabric for ruched roses, flowers, bow, and berries
Scraps of pink and beige print fabrics
20-inch square of low-loft batting
20-inch square of backing fabric
Nonpermanent fabric marker
Template material

INSTRUCTIONS

Refer to the general instructions for hand appliqué on page 292. Pin or baste all the appliqué pieces in place before you sew.

Cutting the fabrics

Refer to page 288 for tips on making templates for appliqué. Prepare templates for each pattern, *opposite.* Add a 3/16-inch seam allowance around each piece when cutting the fabrics.

From the green fabric, cut:
◆ Three 13-inch-long bias strips and two 6-inch-long bias strips, each 1¼ inches wide.
◆ 12 leaves.
◆ Two buds.

From the dark rose fabric, cut:
◆ Three 4-inch circles for ruched roses.
◆ Two flowers.
◆ Four berries.
◆ One of each of the five parts of the bow.

From the beige print fabric, cut:
◆ Two birds, reversing one.

From the pink print fabric, cut:
◆ Four flowers.
◆ Four berries.
◆ Two bud tips.

BOUQUET BLOCK DIAGRAM

Placing the center stems and leaves

1. Press the raw edges of each bias strip into the center to make ¼-inch-wide finished stems for the appliqué. Turn under the raw edges on one end of each 13-inch-long stem for the bottom of the bouquet.

Another method for making bias stems is to sew the long edges together using ¼-inch seams. Press the seam open, then turn the strip right side out. Press the seam to the center back of the strip. Handle the strips carefully; you'll get the best results if you use a bias pressing bar.

2. Fold the red square in half; make a crease to mark the centerline.

3. Pin one long stem over the center crease, positioning the bottom of the stem 3¼ inches from the bottom edge of the square.

4. Fold or press under the seam allowances on six leaves, the two buds, and the bud tips for the center stem. Do not turn under edges that will be covered by another piece, such as the bottoms of the bud tips.

5. Referring to the block diagram, *above,* pin a leaf on both sides of the stem, positioning the bottom of each leaf 6 inches from the bottom of the stem. Position two more pairs of leaves on the stem, spacing the bottoms of each pair 2 inches apart.

6. Pin the two buds approximately 1½ inches above the top leaves. Slip the ends of each bud piece under the stem fabric. Insert pink bud tips under the green bud fabric.

7. Pin a long stem in place on both sides of the center stem, curving each stem away from the center. Align the bottoms of the three stems, spacing them about 1 inch apart.

8. On each side stem, position a leaf about 5 inches from the bottom.

Positioning the flowers and bow

1. Pin one dark rose print flower at the top of each side stem, covering the unfinished end of the stem.

2. Position pink print flowers on the stem just below the rose flowers. Adjust the curve of the stem if necessary to allow enough space between the flowers and the center stem leaves.

3. Following ruching instructions on pages 42 and 43, prepare the 4-inch circles of rose fabric for appliqué. Pin one ruched rose at the top of the center stem and one between the leaf and the flowers on each side stem.

4. Position the bow knot approximately 3¼ inches from the bottom of the center stem. Pin the remaining bow pieces in place.

Positioning side stems and leaves

1. Referring to the block diagram, *above,* pin a short stem on both sides of the bow, inserting one end of each stem under the bow fabric. Curve each stem down, toward the bottom of the bouquet.

2. Pin two berries of each color onto the end of each side stem, as shown in the block diagram. Position a bird on both sides of the bouquet with each bird facing the center.

3. Pin a leaf on both sides of these stems, positioning them between the berries and the bow. Adjust the curve of the stems if necessary to allow space for all leaves.

Appliqué

Starting in the center of the bouquet, appliqué each piece in place. When all appliqué is complete, remove pins or basting.

Quilting and finishing

Sandwich the batting square between the backing fabric and the appliquéd block. Quilt as desired. The piece shown has outline quilting around each piece, as well as three lines of quilting in the body of each bird.

Stretch the finished piece taut over cardboard or some other stable material. Frame as desired.

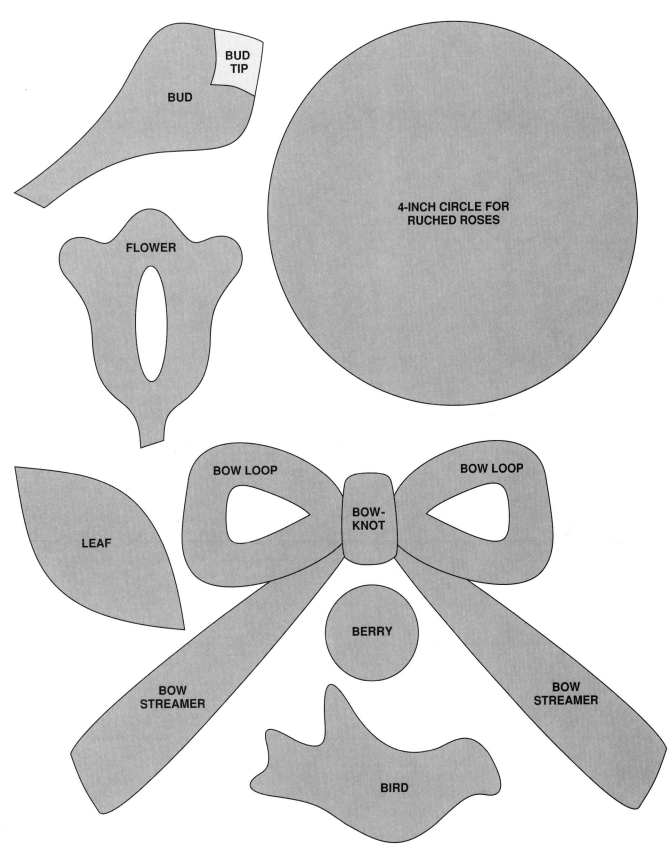

BOUQUET BLOCK PATTERNS

─────── CHALLENGING ───────

Whig Rose Quilt

Shown on page 34.
The finished quilt measures approximately
82 inches square. Each appliquéd block
is 29 inches square.

MATERIALS

5 yards of blue-green print fabric
   for background and outer border
3 yards of olive green print fabric
   for leaves, stems, tassels, and
   inner border
2 yards of pink print fabric for
   flowers, buds, and swags
¾ yard of yellow fabric for buds
   and flower centers
1 yard of red fabric for binding
2½ yards of 90-inch-wide sheeting
   for backing
90x108-inch precut quilt batting
Template material
Nonpermanent fabric marker

INSTRUCTIONS

The Whig Rose has four leaflike
shapes behind a central layered flower. Branches sprout between these
leaves, bearing leaves, buds, and secondary flowers. A single layered rose
is repeated in the center of the quilt
where the four blocks meet.

   This appliqué design also features
daisylike flowers on the branches,
which bear both pink and yellow
buds—impossible in real life, but
charming in this 19th-century quilt.

Cutting the fabrics

All the fabrics in this quilt are tiny
prints—so tiny that substituting a solid is a reasonable alternative.

   Refer to page 288 for tips on making templates for appliqué and to
page 292 for general instructions on
appliqué. Prepare templates for patterns A through N, *opposite* and on
pages 48 and 49. Add a ³⁄₁₆-inch seam
allowance around each piece when
cutting the fabrics.

From the blue-green print fabric, cut:
◆ Four 30-inch squares.
◆ Four 11½x42-inch strips (cut
   crosswise) for the side borders.
◆ Two 11½x61-inch strips for the
   end borders.

WHIG ROSE BLOCK

From the green fabric, cut:
◆ Four 1½x61-inch border strips.
◆ One piece 28x36 inches.
   From this piece, cut 16 of
   Pattern D.
◆ One piece 26x36 inches.
   From this piece, cut 16 *each* of
   patterns E and F.
◆ One piece 25x36 inches.
   From this piece, cut 32 *each* of
   patterns I and J.
◆ 44 of Pattern N.

From the pink fabric, cut:
◆ One piece 22x42 inches.
   From this piece, cut 36 border
   swags (Pattern L), adding a full
   ¼-inch seam allowance on the
   straight sides.
◆ One piece 10x42 inches.
   From this piece, cut four corner
   swags (Pattern M), then cut four
   of M reversed; add a full ¼-inch
   seam allowance to the straight
   side of each swag.
◆ One piece 25x42 inches.
   From this piece, cut 16 *each* of
   patterns G and K.
◆ Five of Pattern A.

From the yellow fabric, cut:
◆ One piece 12x42 inches.
   From this piece, cut 16 *each* of
   patterns H and K.
◆ One piece 14x42 inches.
   From this piece, cut five *each* of
   patterns B and C.

Positioning the appliqué

1. Fold each 30-inch background
square in half vertically, horizontally,
and diagonally; lightly press the folds

to establish placement guidelines for
the appliqué. If desired, trace the
complete design on the background
fabric with an erasable fabric marker.
2. Prepare the appliqué pieces for
each block by basting back the seam
allowances. It is not necessary to turn
under edges that will be covered by
another piece, such as the bottom
edge of the large leaves. Clip seam
allowances as necessary to achieve
nice points and curves.
3. Referring to the block diagram,
left, pin or baste all pieces in place on
the background before appliquéing.
Start in the center and work outward.
Slip the bottoms of the large leaves
(D) and large stems (E) under the
center flower (A). Align the leaf centers with the background placement
lines. Tuck the bottom of the short
stem (F) under the long stem. Position two leaves and two buds (one of
each color) on each short stem.

Appliquéing the blocks

1. Stitch the large leaves (D) in place
first. These anchor the other pieces.
2. Appliqué the center rose base (A)
in place next, then stitch the yellow
flower parts (B and C) on top of A.
3. Stitch all the stems in place, then
appliqué the small flowers, leaves,
and buds. When this appliqué is complete, trim away the background fabric behind the appliqués to reduce
thickness for quilting later.
4. Complete four Whig Rose blocks.
Press each appliquéd block. Trim the
blocks to 29½ inches each.

Assembling the quilt top

1. Join the four blocks in two rows of
two blocks each; join the rows into a
58½-inch square. Press seam allowances to one side.
2. Appliqué a layered rose over the
center seams. Do not trim the background fabric from behind this rose.
3. Stitch green border strips onto opposite sides of the quilt top. Press
seam allowances toward the border;
trim excess border fabric. Sew border
strips to the remaining sides.

Appliquéing the swag border

1. For each border, seam nine border
swags (L) end to end. Add a corner
swag (M or M reversed) at each end.

Press these seam allowances open. Turn under the seam allowances on the curved edges; press.

2. Match the center of one swag strip with the center of one 61-inch-long border strip. Pin the swags in place on the border, aligning the straight tops of the swags with the edge of the border fabric. The corner swags will extend past the ends of the strip. Repeat for second 61-inch-long border.

3. Piece two 42-inch-long strips to make a border long enough for each side of the quilt. Pin nine swags on these borders in the same manner.

4. With the quilt top on the floor, lay the borders in position. Check the corner swags where the border strips meet. The seam allowances of the corner swags should overlap at the corner of the inner green border. If corner swags do not meet properly, adjust the seam allowances of the swags to move the corner as necessary to fit. *Note:* The maker of the antique quilt pictured on page 34 surely had to do this, as few of the swags are precisely the same width.

5. Insert a tassel (N) under the swags at each swag seam line. Sew tassels and swags in place on each border; leave the corner swags unstitched.

Adding the borders

1. Match the center of a short border with the center of the bottom edge of the quilt. Pin the corner swag away from the seam. Sew the border in place; trim excess fabric at the ends. Repeat for the opposite border.

2. Add the side borders in the same manner. Press these seam allowances toward the green inner border.

3. Hand-sew the edges of the corner swags together where they meet, then appliqué the swags in place.

Quilting and finishing

Layer backing, batting, and quilt top; baste the three layers together.

The quilt pictured on page 34 has outline quilting around each appliquéd shape and parallel background lines. The large leaves are quilted from the bottom of each V down to the center rose. Quilt as desired.

Make 330 inches of binding. Refer to pages 306 and 307 for tips on making and applying binding.

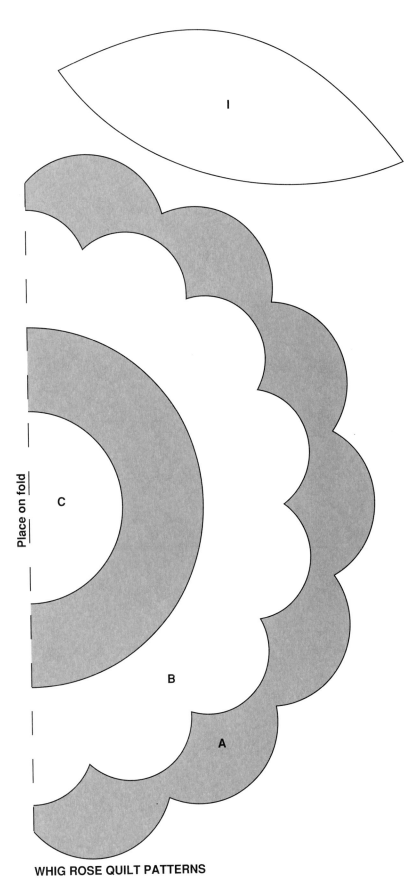

WHIG ROSE QUILT PATTERNS

Fold

D

K

J

G

H

N

WHIG ROSE QUILT PATTERNS

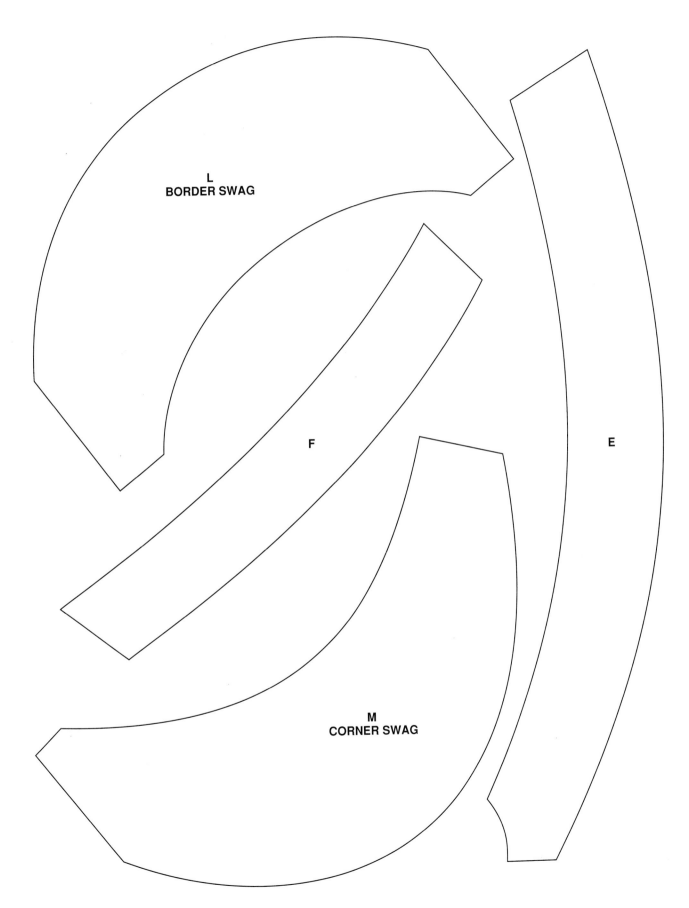

L
BORDER SWAG

F

E

M
CORNER SWAG

49

Hearts and Gizzards Quilt

Shown on page 35.
The finished quilt measures approximately 86¾x98 inches. Each finished block is 11¼ inches square.

MATERIALS

8¾ yards of white fabric, including borders and binding
7¼ yards of pink fabric
3 yards of 90-inch-wide sheeting for backing fabric
90x108-inch precut quilt batting
Template material

INSTRUCTIONS

This quilt is a straight set, consisting of 56 blocks sewn together in eight horizontal rows of seven blocks each. The quilt is bordered with 4-inch-wide strips of white fabric.

Cutting the fabrics

Refer to page 288 for tips on making templates for patchwork. Prepare a template for Pattern A, *below.*

From the white fabric, cut:
- Two 4½x100-inch border strips.
- Two 4½x81-inch border strips.
- One 33-inch square for binding.
- 112 6½-inch squares.
  Cut all these squares in half diagonally to obtain 224 triangles.
- 448 of Pattern A.

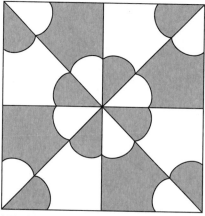

HEARTS AND GIZZARDS BLOCK

From the pink fabric, cut:
- 112 6½-inch squares.
  Cut all these squares in half diagonally to obtain 224 triangles.
- 448 of Pattern A.

Making the blocks

The Hearts and Gizzards block consists of four identical squares. Each square is made by joining triangles of different colors, but each triangle is first appliquéd with two half-hearts of the opposite color. At the center of the block, the joined squares form a wheel of hearts in an interchange of pink and white.

1. Baste under the curved edge of two pink A pieces.

2. Referring to the block diagram, *left,* for placement, pin or baste the prepared A pieces on opposite corners of a white triangle, matching all raw edges.
3. Appliqué the curved edges of both A pieces on the white triangle. When appliqué is complete, press lightly. Trim away the white fabric under the appliquéd A pieces, leaving a ¼-inch seam allowance of pink fabric under the curved edge.
4. In this manner, make 224 white triangles and 224 pink triangles.
5. Stitch one white triangle and one pink triangle together to form a square as shown in the block diagram, *left.* Make 224 squares.
6. Join four squares to complete a block, positioning squares as shown in the block diagram for correct color placement. Make 56 blocks.

Assembling the quilt top

Refer to page 294 for an illustration of a straight set assembly.
1. Stitch seven blocks together in a row. Make eight rows of seven blocks each. Press the seam allowances to one side.
2. Matching seam lines carefully, join the rows to complete the quilt top. The assembled quilt should measure approximately 78¾x90 inches.

Adding the borders

Stitch a short border strip to top and bottom edges of the quilt top. Press seam allowances toward the borders; trim excess border fabric. Add side borders in the same manner.

Quilting and finishing

QUILTING: Sandwich batting between backing fabric and quilt top; baste the three layers together.

The quilt pictured on page 35 has outline quilting inside each A piece and a shape resembling a fleur-de-lis quilted inside each triangle. A simple cable is quilted in the border strips. Quilt as desired.

BINDING: Make approximately 376 inches of binding. Refer to pages 306 and 307 for instructions on how to make and apply binding.

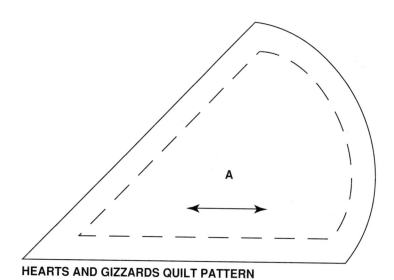

HEARTS AND GIZZARDS QUILT PATTERN

Goose Tracks Quilt

Shown on page 36.
The finished quilt measures approximately 83½ inches square. Each finished block is 9 inches square.

MATERIALS

6 yards of white or muslin fabric
1½ yards of dark red fabric
1 yard of gold-brown fabric
¾ yard of binding fabric
2½ yards of 90-inch-wide sheeting
   for backing fabric
90x108-inch precut quilt batting
Template material

INSTRUCTIONS

This quilt is an alternate diagonal set consisting of 36 pieced Goose Tracks blocks and 25 setting squares framed by a 3½-inch-wide white border.

Cutting the fabrics

For the best use of the fabric, first cut large pieces across the 42-inch width of the fabric as described. From each large piece, cut the required number of patches that are listed below it.

Refer to page 288 for tips on making templates. Prepare templates for patterns A, B, and C, *below.*

From the white fabric, cut:
◆ One 16x85-inch piece.
   Cut two 4x85-inch border strips and two 4x78-inch border strips.
◆ One 26x30-inch piece.
   Cut 288 of Pattern B.
◆ Twelve 2x24-inch strips.
   Cut each strip into 2-inch squares to yield 144 squares for patch D.
◆ Sixteen 2¼x42-inch strips.
   Cut nine 4¼-inch segments from each strip for 144 E rectangles.
◆ One 29x42-inch piece.
   Cut five 14-inch squares and two 7¼-inch squares. Cut each larger square in quarters diagonally, creating four setting triangles from each square. Cut the smaller squares in half diagonally to obtain four corner triangles.
◆ Twenty-five 9½-inch squares.

From the dark red fabric, cut:
◆ 576 A diamonds.

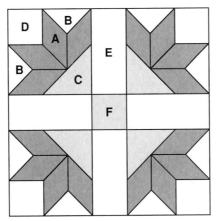

GOOSE TRACKS BLOCK

From the gold-brown fabric, cut:
◆ Six 3x42-inch strips.
   From these strips, cut 144 of Pattern C.
◆ Two 2¼x42-inch strips.
   Cut thirty-six 2¼-inch squares for patch F.

Making the Goose Tracks blocks

Refer to the block diagram, *above,* to piece this block. Because the block has set-in pieces, many quilters find it easier to piece this pattern by hand.

Make 36 Goose Tracks blocks.
1. Join four A diamonds as shown in the diagram. Leave ¼ inch at the end of each seam unstitched. Press seam allowances in one direction.

2. Set two B triangles and one D square into each four-diamond unit, as shown. Press the seam allowances toward the red diamonds.
3. Complete the square by stitching a C triangle to the bottom of the diamond unit. Press the seam allowance toward the triangle. Make four of these squares for each block.
4. Sew two squares to each long side of an E rectangle; press seam allowances toward the E patch. Repeat for the opposite side of the block.
5. Stitch an E rectangle to opposite sides of an F square; press seam allowances toward the center square.
6. Matching seam lines carefully, join the three rows to complete the block.

Assembling the quilt top

Refer to page 295 for a diagram of a diagonal set. Use this diagram as a guide to lay out the pieced blocks, setting squares, and setting triangles in diagonal rows.

Assemble the blocks and setting pieces in diagonal rows, then join the rows. The finished quilt top without the border should measure approximately 77 inches square.

continued

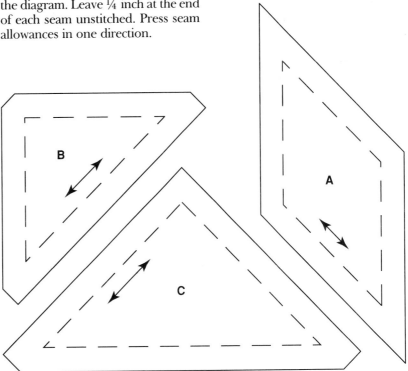

GOOSE TRACKS QUILT PATTERNS

Adding the borders

Sew the two shorter border strips to opposite sides of the quilt top; trim excess border fabric.

Sew the remaining border strips to the remaining sides of the quilt top; trim excess border fabric. Press seam allowances toward the borders.

Quilting and finishing

QUILTING: Mark quilting designs as desired on the quilt top. The quilt shown has outline quilting around the patchwork and a diagonal grid over the whole quilt.

Layer the backing, batting, and marked quilt top; baste the layers together. Quilt as desired.

BINDING: Prepare approximately 340 inches of binding and attach to quilt. Refer to pages 306 and 307 for tips on making and applying binding.

Swirling Peony Quilt

Shown on pages 36 and 37.
The finished quilt measures approximately 81 inches square. Each Peony block is 12 inches square.

MATERIALS

5¾ yards of white fabric
3¼ yards of green print fabric, including binding
1¾ yards of red print fabric
5 yards of backing fabric
90x108-inch precut quilt batting
Template material
Rotary cutter, mat, and acrylic ruler

INSTRUCTIONS

This quilt is an alternate straight set made of 13 pieced Peony blocks and 12 plain setting squares. The quilt is framed with a narrow border of red fabric, a wide white border featuring appliquéd trees, and a final narrow border of green fabric.

Cutting the fabrics

Refer to page 288 for tips on making templates for patchwork and appliqué. Make templates for patterns A, B, E, F, G, and H, *below* and *opposite.*

From the white fabric, cut:
◆ Two 9x81-inch border strips and two 9x64-inch border strips.
◆ One 38x50-inch piece. From this piece, cut twelve 12½-inch setting squares.
◆ Nine 2¼x42-inch strips. From these strips, cut fifty-two 2¼x6½-inch D rectangles.

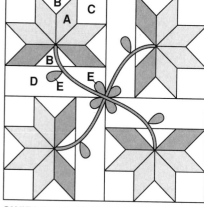

SWIRLING PEONY BLOCK

◆ Five 3¾x42-inch strips. From these strips, cut 208 B triangles.
◆ Six 2¼x42-inch strips. From these pieces, cut 104 C squares, each 2¼ inches square.

From the red fabric, cut:
◆ Four 1½x63-inch border strips.
◆ Six ¾x34-inch tree trunk strips.
◆ 208 of Pattern A.

From the green fabric, cut:
◆ One ½-yard piece for binding.
◆ Eight 1½x42-inch border strips.
◆ One 10x42-inch strip. From this piece, cut 26 *bias* strips for the peony stems, each approximately ¾x12 inches.
◆ One 15x42-inch piece. From this piece, cut 104 of Pattern A.
◆ One 10x42-inch piece. From this piece, cut 104 of Pattern E.
◆ One 21x42-inch piece. From this piece, cut 140 of Pattern F.
◆ 28 *each* of patterns G and H.
◆ 28 B triangles for tree bases.

Piecing the Peony block

Each Peony block consists of four quarter-block flower units. Refer to the assembly diagram, *opposite,* to make each unit.

1. Sew together two pairs of red A diamonds as shown. Leave ¼ inch at the end of each seam unstitched to accommodate the set-in pieces. Press the seam allowances of the pairs in opposite directions.

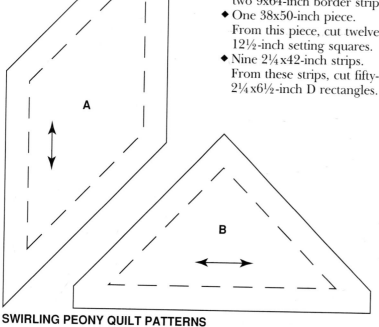

SWIRLING PEONY QUILT PATTERNS

2. Set in a C square in the corner of each diamond pair. Press seam allowances toward the diamonds.

3. Join the red diamonds by stitching the center seam. Press seam allowance to one side.

4. Sew a green A diamond onto both short legs of one white B triangle as shown. Press the seam allowances toward the triangle.

5. Stitch the four-diamond unit onto the ABA strip, carefully matching the seam lines at the center.

6. Set in three white B triangles at the top and sides of the unit. Press seam allowances toward the diamonds.

7. Sew a D rectangle to the bottom edge of the flower; press the seam allowance toward D.

8. Make 52 flower units for the blocks. Referring to the block diagram, *opposite,* for placement, join four flower units into a block.

Make 13 Swirling Peony blocks.

Appliquéing the stems and leaves
1. Fold and press the 12-inch strips of green bias into thirds lengthwise to make them ¼ inch wide.

2. Appliqué a flower stem strip into a gentle curve diagonally across the block, connecting flower centers as shown in the block diagram, *opposite.* Repeat, adding a flower stem between the remaining two flowers. Appliqué E leaves in the center and on stems as shown in the block diagram.

Assembling the quilt top
Refer to page 295 for a diagram of an alternate straight set. Join the blocks and setting squares in five rows of five blocks each. Make three rows that start and end with Peony blocks and two rows with setting squares at both ends. Join the rows to complete the inner quilt top.

Sew a red border strip onto opposite sides of the quilt top. Trim excess border fabric; press seam allowances toward the borders. Repeat to add borders to the remaining sides.

Appliquéing the tree border
1. Press each ¾x34-inch red strip into thirds to make them ¼ inch wide. Cut the pressed strips into twenty-eight 6½-inch lengths.

2. Turn under the edges of the remaining appliqué pieces, including the short legs of the green triangles.

3. Mark the center of each 64-inch border strip with a pin. Position another pin approximately 2½ inches from each end of the strip. At each pin, pin a green triangle on the bottom edge of the border, placing the long unturned edge of the triangle even with the raw edge of the border.

4. Place two more triangles between the center and each end triangle. The side points of the triangles will be approximately 10 inches apart.

5. Pin a red tree trunk at the top of each triangle, tucking the end of the strip under the triangle tip. Appliqué seven triangles on each border, leaving the trunks unstitched.

6. Pin a G treetop at the top of each trunk. Cover the bottom of the G piece and the top of the trunk with an H branch. Slip an F branch *under* the trunk just below the H branch. Space four more F branches under the trunk approximately ¼ inch apart, placing the bottom branch 2 inches above the base triangle. When all the tree pieces are correctly positioned, appliqué them in place.

7. Sew the two appliquéd borders to opposite sides of the quilt, matching the center of the border with the center of the side of the quilt top. Trim excess border fabric; press seam allowances toward the white border.

8. Appliqué seven trees to each 81-inch border, centering the middle tree and spacing the trees as on the shorter borders. Place first and last trees approximately 9½ inches from the ends of the border strips.

9. Matching centers, stitch the two appliquéd borders onto the remaining edges of the quilt top.

Adding the outer border
Join pairs of green border strips into four long borders; add to quilt top in the same manner as the red borders.

Quilting and finishing
BACKING: Divide the backing fabric into two 2½-yard lengths; split one piece in half lengthwise. Sew one narrow panel to each side of the larger one; press the seam allowances open.

Layer backing, batting, and quilt top; baste the three layers together.

QUILTING: The quilt pictured on pages 36 and 37 has crossed plumes of quilting in the setting squares, and close diagonal quilting on the pieced blocks and borders. Quilt as desired.

BINDING: Use the remaining green fabric to make approximately 330 inches of binding, either bias or straight-grain. Refer to pages 306 and 307 for instructions on making and applying binding.

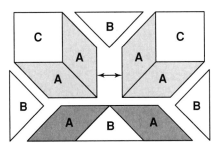

SWIRLING PEONY BLOCK ASSEMBLY DIAGRAM

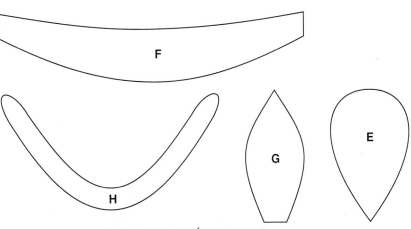

SWIRLING PEONY QUILT APPLIQUÉ PATTERNS

Westward Ho!

Pioneer Patchwork
Crosses the Prairies

1840 ~ 1860

◆ *Fruit Basket, c. 1870;*
81½x98½ inches. Instruc-
tions begin on page 62.

*I made quilts as fast as I could to
keep my family warm, and as pretty as I could
to keep my heart from breaking.*

A pioneer woman's diary

*N*ew opportunities for Americans to move westward came with the Louisiana Purchase—an event that doubled the size of the young United States and began the continental expansion.

Driving Indians from their ancestral lands to make way for pioneers, the U.S. Army established forts in the Ohio and Missouri territories. The Cumberland Gap provided a gateway through the mountains into Illinois, Indiana, and Missouri; and the Erie Canal opened the Great Lakes region.

Men going West sought adventure, fortune, and open spaces. The women who dutifully followed them into the wilderness left behind everything

they knew, picking out the few essential possessions they could carry.

The long trip by foot or wagon barred bringing niceties, such as furniture,

pictures, and family heirlooms. But quilts—even fancy "best quilts"—could be justified as bedding.

Pioneers used everyday quilts to cover cabin doors and windows, to shield crops from swarms of locusts and grasshoppers, and as shrouds to bury the dead. Yet some special quilts—mostly those made in the East and carried to new homes—survived the trip west and the years on the frontier because they were cherished souvenirs of another way of life.

Signature quilts were especially prized, since they symbolized ties to distant family and friends.

◆ *Wertman Family
Appliqué* (left),
*Pennsylvania, c. 1878;
93x108 inches; 31 family
names inscribed with inked
stamps. Instructions begin
on page 65.*

Westward Ho!

1840–1860

*T*he first pioneer women to cross the plains reached the Oregon Territory in 1836. It would be more than five years before the newly blazed Oregon Trail provided a reasonably safe passage across hostile lands and brought numerous settlers to the northwest region.

The first wagon train, carrying 47 people, left Independence, Missouri, on May 1, 1841. It took more than six months to reach California.

Many women found the pioneer experience a desperately lonely life. The social and aesthetic values of quiltmaking offered solace to them as they dealt with the isolation of their cold, colorless homes.

A quilt was functional, but it also was prized for beauty, sentimental value, and the quiltmaker's skill that it displayed. For such important work, only the most permanent materials would do. The continued popularity of indigo blue and turkey red was due in part to their ability to withstand fading.

Old quilt patterns came West with the pioneers, and new ones were made and named for the milestones of the journey. Kansas Troubles, Road to California, and Oregon Trail are pattern names that reflect a growing nation and the diversity of the patchwork tradition.

◆ *Sickle* (*above*), *c. 1870; 75x99 inches. Instructions are on page 67.*

◆ *Checkers and Rails* (*opposite*), *Indiana, c. 1870; 83x110¼ inches. Instructions are on pages 68 and 69.*

Westward Ho!

1840–1860

Girls learned to sew at a young age so they could help produce and mend the family's clothing and bedding. By the age of 10 or 11, most girls had a handful of quilts to their credit.

Pioneer brides made five or six quilts to set up housekeeping. Completion of a wedding quilt, her finest work, proved a girl's readiness for the responsibilities of marriage. Many outstanding quilts were made as bridal quilts and were preserved throughout women's lives as their best quilts, used only for honored guests.

Made by a bride alone or quilted with the help of friends gathered for a bee, the wedding quilt was a lasting barometer of a woman's sewing skills and social status. The elaborate elegance of some of these quilts belies the crude cabins in which they were made. Regardless of the homes where they were displayed, quilts brought comfort and pride to the women who cherished them.

◆ *Oregon Trail Quilt* (opposite), c. 1870; 72x96 inches. Instructions begin on page 69.

◆ *Optical Illusion* (below), Alabama or Georgia, c. 1865; 88x98 inches. Instructions are on pages 72 and 73.

Fruit Basket Quilt

Shown on pages 54 and 55.
The finished quilt measures approximately
81½x98½ inches. Each Fruit Basket
block is 8 inches square.

MATERIALS

5½ yards *each* of solid red and
  yellow print fabrics
3 yards of 90-inch-wide sheeting for
  backing fabric
90x108-inch precut quilt batting
Template material
Rotary cutter, mat, and acrylic ruler
Pencil and graph paper
Nonpermanent fabric marker

INSTRUCTIONS

This quilt consists of 32 basket blocks
set on the diagonal with wide sashing
strips and squares between them. Instead of plain setting triangles, half-
block "basket tops" fill in the sides.

Cutting the fabrics

Refer to page 288 for tips on making
templates for hand or machine patchwork. Prepare templates for patterns
A, B, C, E, and F, *opposite.*

   To make a template for triangle D,
draw a 4⅞-inch square, then divide it
in half diagonally—this is the *finished*
size of the triangle. Make a template
appropriate for your piecing method.

   Before cutting the fabrics, read the
following assembly instructions; decide whether you will use traditional
or quick-piecing techniques to piece
the triangle-squares. Even if you decide to make quick-pieced triangle-
squares, make templates for the A
and D triangles since single triangles
also are needed.

From the red fabric, cut:
◆ A 27x42-inch piece for binding.
◆ One 18x94-inch piece.
   Cut two 4½x94-inch borders and
   two 4½x86-inch borders.
◆ One 24x72-inch piece.
   Cut four 18x22-inch rectangles
   for quick piecing; for traditional
   piecing, cut 322 A triangles.
◆ One 12x24-inch piece.
   Cut 14 of Pattern D for the
   side triangles.

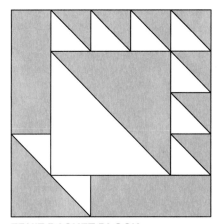

FRUIT BASKET BLOCK

◆ One 19x42-inch piece.
   Cut two 19-inch squares for quick
   piecing; for traditional piecing,
   cut 32 of Pattern D.
◆ Six 4½x42-inch strips.
   Cut 49 sashing squares, each
   4½ inches square.
◆ One 3x42-inch strip.
   Cut 28 of Pattern A for the
   setting triangles.
◆ One 4x42-inch strip.
   Cut four of Pattern F and
   28 of Pattern E for the corner
   setting triangles.
◆ 64 of Pattern B.
◆ 32 of Pattern C.

From the yellow fabric, cut:
◆ One 14x88-inch piece.
   Cut two 3½x88-inch borders and
   two 3½x77-inch borders.
◆ Sixteen 4½x42½-inch strips.
   Cut eighty 4½x8½-inch sashing
   strips.
◆ One 23x72-inch piece.
   Cut four 18x22-inch rectangles
   for quick piecing; for traditional
   piecing, cut 322 A triangles.
◆ One 19x42-inch piece.
   Cut two 19-inch squares for
   quick piecing; for traditional
   piecing, cut 32 of Pattern D for
   the blocks.
◆ 64 of Pattern A.
◆ 20 of Pattern E.

Making the basket triangle-squares

TRADITIONAL PIECING: Join yellow and red A triangles to assemble
322 small triangle-squares. Make 32
large triangle-squares with red and
yellow D triangles.

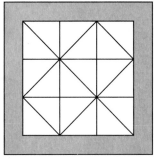

FIGURE 1

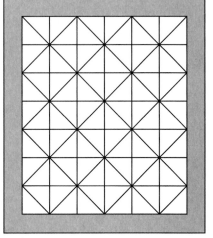

FIGURE 2

QUICK PIECING: Step-by-step instructions for quick-pieced triangle-
squares are given on page 114. Refer
to these instructions to stitch the
grids described here.
1. For the D triangle-squares, mark
the wrong side of each 19-inch yellow
square with a 3x3 grid of 5¾-inch
squares as shown in Figure 1, *above.*
Layer the yellow fabric, marked side
up, atop a matching red fabric piece.
2. Machine-stitch the grid as described in Step 3 on page 114. Each
grid makes 18 triangle-squares, so
you'll have 36 total. Thirty-two triangle-squares are needed; discard any
damaged or distorted ones.
3. To make the A triangle-squares,
repeat the procedure with the 18x22-
inch fabrics, marking each yellow
piece with a 6x7 grid of 2½-inch
squares as shown in Figure 2, *above.*
Each grid makes 84 triangle-squares.
The total of 336 is 14 more than the
322 needed.
4. Press all seam allowances toward
the yellow fabric.

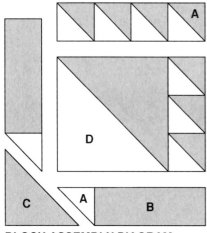

BLOCK ASSEMBLY DIAGRAM

Assembling the Fruit Basket block
1. Referring to the block diagram, *opposite,* and the block assembly diagram, *left,* join four of the small triangle-squares in a row. Make another row of three triangle-squares. Press the seam allowances toward the yellow triangles.
2. Stitch the shorter row to one large triangle-square, joining the small yellow triangles to the red D triangle and positioning the units as shown in the assembly diagram. Press the seam allowance toward the large triangle, then sew the four-square row to the top of this unit.

3. Sew a yellow A triangle to one end of a B rectangle as shown. Press the seam allowance toward the rectangle. Stitch this piece to the bottom edge of the center unit; press the seam allowance toward the outside of the block. Make another AB strip; add it to the left side of the unit.
4. Complete the block by sewing a C triangle across the base of the basket as shown. Make 32 basket blocks.

Making the setting triangles
Combine small triangle-squares and red D triangles to make the "basket tops" for the setting triangles at the sides of the quilt.
1. Follow Step 1 of the Fruit Basket block assembly to prepare two rows of triangle-squares.

continued

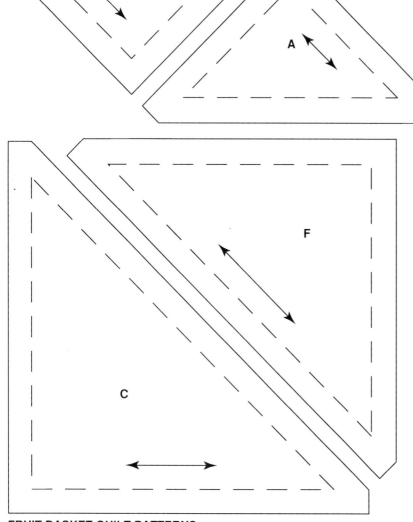

FRUIT BASKET QUILT PATTERNS

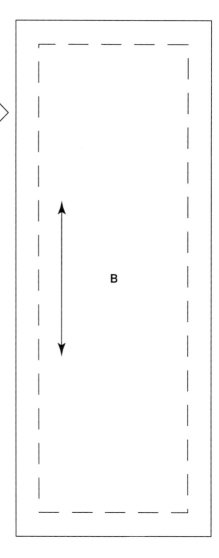

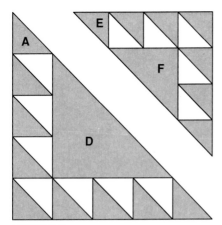

FIGURE 3

2. Stitch the triangle-squares onto a red D triangle in the same manner as in the block assembly. Add a red A triangle to each corner, creating a right triangle as shown in lower left of Figure 3, *above*. Make 14 "basket top" setting triangles.

3. Use E and F triangles to piece four corner triangles as illustrated in top right of Figure 3.

Assembling the quilt top

Refer to the quilt assembly diagram, *right*, to arrange the blocks, setting triangles, and sashing.

1. On the floor or a large table, arrange the basket blocks and sashing strips and squares as shown in the assembly diagram. Lay out the basket blocks in rows, placing sashing strips and squares between the blocks.

2. Fill in the sides and corners with the appropriate pieced setting triangles. Note that the sashing squares at the end of each diagonal row extend beyond the adjacent setting triangles.

3. Assemble all the blocks and setting triangles in the diagonal rows defined by red lines on the assembly diagram, stitching a plain sashing strip between blocks, and between blocks and setting triangles. Press the seam allowances toward the sashing.

4. Assemble diagonal rows of sashing strips and squares as shown. Press seam allowances toward the strips.

5. Alternating rows of basket blocks and sashing, assemble the quilt top as illustrated. Match seam lines of sashing strips and squares carefully.

FRUIT BASKET QUILT ASSEMBLY DIAGRAM

When the assembly is complete, trim excess fabric from the sashing squares at the edges of the quilt top so their edges are even with edges of adjacent setting triangles.

Adding the borders

Stitch the 88-inch yellow borders to the quilt sides. Trim excess border fabric; press seam allowances toward the border fabric. Sew the remaining yellow borders to the top and bottom edges in the same manner.

Join the red borders to the quilt top in the same manner, first stitching the longer border strips to the sides and then the shorter border strips to the top and bottom.

Quilting and finishing

Sandwich the batting between the backing fabric and the quilt top; baste the three layers securely together.

QUILTING: A grid of 1-inch squares is quilted over the surface of the quilt shown on pages 54 and 55. The grid is set straight over the basket blocks and sashing, but it is set on the diagonal in the borders. Quilt as desired.

BINDING: Use the remaining red fabric to make approximately 360 inches of bias or straight-grain binding. See pages 306 and 307 for tips on making and applying binding.

Wertman Family Appliqué Quilt

Shown on pages 56 and 57.
The finished quilt measures approximately 93x108 inches. Each appliquéd block is 13 inches square.

MATERIALS

7 yards of muslin
3½ yards of red fabric for appliqué; sashing, and binding
¾ yard *each* of green, dark green, pink, and brown appliqué fabrics
1⅜ yards *each* of navy blue, gold, and yellow appliqué fabrics
3⅜ yards of 108-inch-wide sheeting for backing fabric
120x120-inch precut quilt batting
Template material

INSTRUCTIONS

This quilt has 30 appliqué blocks in a straight set with sashing between the blocks. Each block is the same unusual pattern, a design reminiscent of the Pennsylvania Dutch.

Eight solid-color fabrics in 12 combinations of light and dark fabrics give the quilt a colorful appearance. Use additional fabrics if you want to achieve more of a "scrappy" look.

If desired, use a fine-point, permanent ink pen to inscribe signatures in the center of each block.

Cutting the fabrics

Refer to page 288 for tips on making templates for appliqué. Prepare templates for patterns A through H on page 66. When cutting the appliqués from fabric, add a ³⁄₁₆-inch seam allowance around each piece.

From the muslin, cut:
◆ Two 8½x110-inch border strips.
◆ Two 8½x80-inch border strips.
◆ Thirty 13½-inch squares.

From the red fabric, cut:
◆ Six 2½x95-inch sashing strips.
◆ Four 2¼x104-inch strips for straight-grain binding.
◆ One 26x33-inch piece for appliqué.
◆ Thirty-five 2½x13½-inch strips for horizontal sashing.

WERTMAN APPLIQUÉ BLOCK

From the red, green, dark green, brown, and navy blue appliqué fabrics, cut:
◆ 30 sets of dark fabric appliqués, each set consisting of one of Pattern A, two *each* of patterns B and G, four of Pattern F, and eight of Pattern E. The quilt shown has 10 blocks made with navy blue fabric, six blocks each with the dark green and red fabrics, and four blocks each with the green and brown fabrics.

From the pink, yellow, and gold appliqué fabrics, cut:
◆ 30 sets of light fabric appliqués, each consisting of two of patterns C and H, four of Pattern D, and four 1x3¼-inch stem pieces. Our quilt has six blocks with pink fabric and 12 blocks each with the yellow and gold fabrics.

Preparing the appliqués

Arrange the light and dark fabrics in pairs for 30 blocks.
1. On the quilt shown, the G and H pieces are seamed together at the straight edge rather than appliquéd. You may join these pieces with a ³⁄₁₆-inch seam or appliqué one piece atop the other.
2. Turn under the seam allowances on all appliqué pieces except the C circles. (These get slipped under the B posies.) On the other pieces, do not baste under edges that will be covered by another piece, such as the straight edges of the F pieces.
3. For the A, B, D, and H pieces, clip the seam allowances as needed to achieve nicely curved edges.

4. Cut out the center of the B posy, trimming the seam allowance to ⅛ inch. Do not turn this edge under yet.
5. Baste or press under ¼ inch on each long side of the stem strips.

Appliquéing the block

1. Fold each muslin square vertically, horizontally, and diagonally; press each fold to mark placement lines.
2. Referring to the block diagram, *left*, position and pin appliqués in place. Align the center curves of the A piece on the horizontal and vertical placement lines on the muslin block.

Tuck stems under the A piece on the diagonal placement lines; position a B or GH flower at the top of each stem as shown. Place a C circle under the opening in the B flower.

Tuck a D piece under the A fabric on the horizontal placement line as shown. Position two E leaves in the center of each D stem, and an F piece at the top.
3. When all the pieces are correctly positioned, appliqué them in place. For the center of the B posy, use your needle to turn back and appliqué the edge of the flower fabric, revealing the C circle underneath.

Make 30 appliquéd blocks.

Assembling the quilt top

Arrange the completed blocks in five vertical rows of six blocks each. In the quilt pictured on pages 56 and 57, all the blocks within a vertical row use the same light fabric—blocks in rows 1 and 5 have gold fabric, rows 2 and 4 have yellow fabric, and the middle row is made with pink fabric.
1. Join the vertical rows by sewing the blocks together with a short sashing strip between blocks. Finish each row with a sashing strip at the top and bottom edges. Press the seam allowances toward the sashing.
2. Assemble the rows, sewing a 95-inch-long sashing strip between the rows. Complete the quilt top by sewing a sashing strip to both sides of the assembled rows. Trim the excess sashing fabric even with the bottom of the quilt top.
3. Sew the 80-inch muslin border strips to the top and bottom edges of the quilt. Press seam allowances to-
continued

65

ward the borders; trim excess border fabric. Repeat to add side borders.

Quilting and finishing
Layer the backing, batting, and quilt top; baste the three layers together.

QUILTING: The quilt shown has outline quilting around the appliqués, diagonal lines in the sashing, and a cable quilted in the wide borders. Quilt as desired.

BINDING: Use the remaining red fabric strips to make 420 inches of straight-grain binding. Refer to pages 306 and 307 for instructions on making and applying binding.

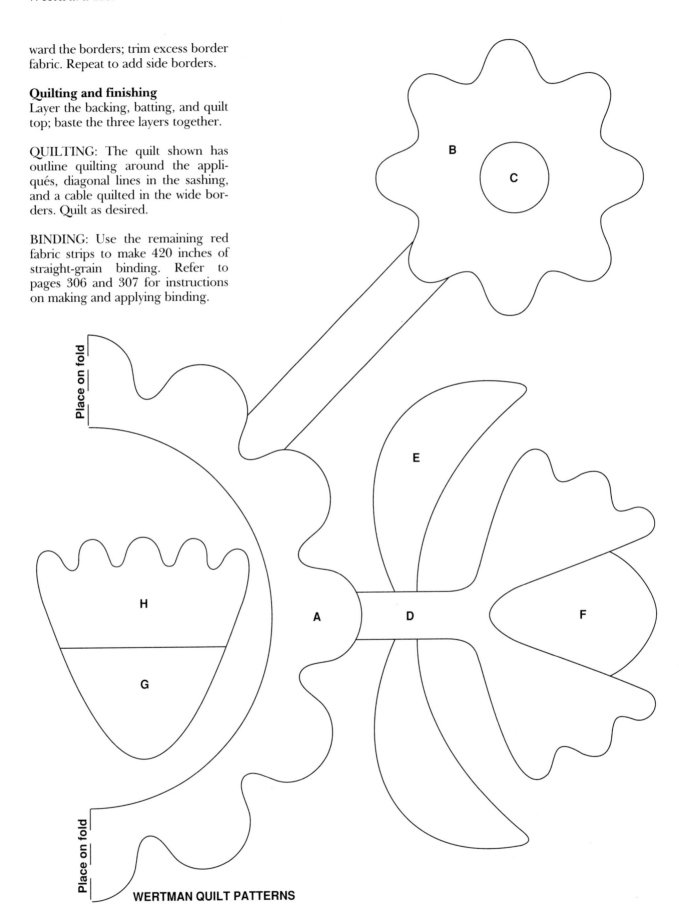

WERTMAN QUILT PATTERNS

Sickle Quilt

Shown on page 58.
The finished quilt measures approximately 75x99 inches. Each Sickle block is 16 inches square.

MATERIALS
3 yards of black print fabric
2⅝ yards of white print fabric
1⅛ yards of burgundy striped fabric
⅛ yard *each* of nine light and nine dark assorted print fabrics
¾ yard of dark red binding fabric
6 yards of backing fabric
90x108-inch precut quilt batting
Rotary cutter, mat, and acrylic ruler

INSTRUCTIONS
This block combines two four-patch squares with two squares consisting of large pieced triangles. The small four-patch units are scrap fabrics, but the consistent placement of light and dark fabrics preserves the illusion of a continuous diagonal chain.

Cutting the fabrics
For the best use of fabric, cut the large pieces as described below, then from those pieces cut the smaller patches listed below them. A rotary cutter is recommended.

From the black print fabric, cut:
◆ Five 6x70-inch strips for borders. Cut one of these strips in half resulting in two 6x35-inch strips.
◆ Eighteen 8⅞-inch squares. Cut each square in half diagonally to yield 35 triangles.

From the white print fabric, cut:
◆ Two 4½x90-inch border strips.
◆ Two 4½x58-inch border strips.
◆ Eighteen 8⅞-inch squares. Cut each square in half diagonally to yield 35 triangles.

From the burgundy striped fabric, cut:
◆ Eight 4½x42-inch strips. Cut seventy 4½-inch squares.

From each of the scrap fabrics, cut:
◆ Two 2½x21-inch strips.

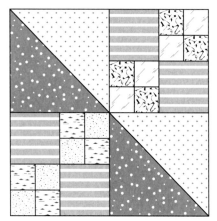

SICKLE BLOCK

Piecing the triangle-squares
Match the long edges of one white and one black triangle; stitch. Press the seam allowance toward the black fabric. Make 35 triangle-squares.

Piecing the four-patch squares
TRADITIONAL PIECING: Cut the scrap fabrics into 2½-inch squares. Cut 140 light squares and 140 dark squares. Arrange light and dark fabrics in pairs. Join 140 pairs.

Make 70 four-patch units as shown in Figure 1, *below*.

Continue as described in steps 4 and 5 below.

STRIP PIECING: Match light and dark scrap fabric strips in 18 pairs.
1. Stitch each pair together along one long edge. Press the seam allowance toward the dark fabric.
2. Cut eight 2½-inch-wide segments from each sewn strip as shown in Figure 2, *below*.

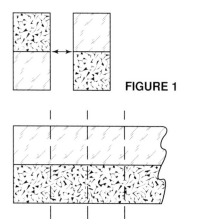

FIGURE 1

FIGURE 2

3. Join pairs of these segments to make 70 four-patch units as shown in Figure 1, *below*.
4. Sew a burgundy square onto each four-patch unit; press the seam allowance toward the burgundy square.
5. To complete the quarter-block, join two of these four-patch/square units, positioning the four-patches in opposite corners as shown in the block diagram, *left*. Make 35 of these quarter-block squares.

Assembling the Sickle block
Referring to the block diagram, join two triangle-squares and two quarter-block squares to make one Sickle block. Position light and dark fabrics as shown; press seam allowances toward the triangle-squares.

Make 15 Sickle blocks and five half-blocks with fabrics positioned as in the *left* side of the Sickle block.

Assembling the quilt top
Join five horizontal rows of three blocks each. Complete each row with a half-block at the *right* end. Join the rows to complete the quilt top.

Adding the borders
1. Stitch a 58-inch-long white border to the top and bottom edges of the quilt top. Press the seam allowances toward the border; trim excess border fabric even with the quilt sides.
2. Add the 90-inch-long white print borders to the sides.
3. Piece one 70-inch and one 35-inch black strip, creating a border long enough for each side. Sew the black border strips onto the quilt.

Quilting and finishing
BACKING: Cut two 3-yard lengths of backing fabric. Sew the two panels together; press the seam allowance open. Layer backing, batting, and top; baste the three layers together.

QUILTING: The quilt pictured on page 58 is quilted with an overall grid of 2-inch squares. Quilt as desired.

BINDING: Make approximately 360 inches of dark red binding. See pages 306 and 307 for instructions on making and applying binding.

Checkers and Rails Quilt

Shown on page 59.
The finished quilt measures approximately 83x110¼ inches.

MATERIALS

6½ yards *each* of muslin and blue print fabric, including binding
3⅜ yards of 90-inch-wide sheeting for backing fabric
120x120-inch precut quilt batting
Rotary cutter, mat, and acrylic ruler

INSTRUCTIONS

This quilt is unusual because the design is formed by pieced sashing rather than blocks. The quilt is assembled as a diagonal set.

Cutting the fabrics

For efficient use of fabric, cut large cross-grain pieces as stated below, then cut these into the strips and squares listed below the large pieces. Rotary cutting is recommended.

From the muslin, cut:

◆ Ten 2x42½-inch strips for the inner border.
◆ Ten 3x42½-inch strips for the outer border.
◆ Ten 6½x42-inch strips.
   Cut fifty-nine 6½-inch squares.
◆ Sixty 1¼x42-inch strips for checkers and rails patchwork.
◆ Two 9¾x42-inch strips.
   Cut five 9¾-inch squares; cut each square in quarters diagonally to obtain 20 setting triangles.
◆ Two 5⅛-inch squares.
   Cut each square in half diagonally to obtain four corner triangles.

From the blue print fabric, cut:

◆ One ¾-yard piece for binding.
◆ Twenty 2x42½-inch border strips.
◆ Seven 4¼x42-inch strips.
   Cut fifty-eight 4¼-inch sashing squares.
◆ Eighty-four 1¼x42-inch strips for the patchwork.
◆ Six 6½-inch squares.
   Cut each square in quarters diagonally for 24 setting triangles.

Piecing the sashing

Note: For this assembly, press all seam allowances toward the darker fabric.

TRADITIONAL PIECING: Use 24 muslin strips and 48 blue strips, 1¼ inches wide, for the rail units. Cut six 6½-inch-long pieces from each strip.

Sew one 1¼x6½-inch muslin strip between two matching blue pieces to make one rail unit as shown in Figure 1, *right*. Make 140 rails.

Cut the remaining 1¼-inch-wide blue and muslin strips into 1¼-inch squares for the checkers. Cut 1,120 squares of *each* fabric.

Use four squares of each color to assemble an eight-square row, alternating colors. Make 280 rows.

Join rows in pairs to complete the checker units, turning one row upside down so the fabric colors alternate. Complete 140 checker units.

STRIP PIECING: Refer to page 18 for tips on strip piecing.
1. Stitch one 1¼-inch-wide muslin strip between two matching strips of blue fabric. Complete 24 sets of pieced strips in this manner.
2. Cut six 6½-inch-long units from each pieced strip as shown in Figure 1, *right*. Cut 140 rail units.
3. For the checker units, stitch together four 1¼-inch-wide strips of *each* fabric, alternating the colors as shown in Figure 2, *right*. Make nine strip sets in this manner.
4. Cut thirty-three 1¼-inch-wide segments from each strip set as shown in Figure 2.
5. Join these checker segments in pairs, turning one upside down so that the fabric colors alternate. Make 140 checker units.

JOINING SASHING UNITS: Sew one rail unit to each checker unit, positioning the fabrics as shown in Figure 3, *right*. Press seam allowances toward the rails.

Assembling the quilt top

The quilt is assembled in the diagonal rows outlined in red in the assembly diagram, *opposite*.

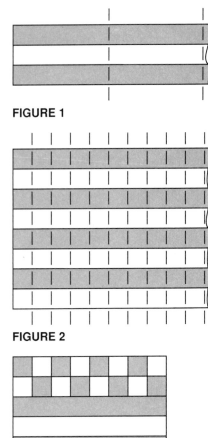

FIGURE 1

FIGURE 2

FIGURE 3

1. Referring to the assembly diagram, join diagonal rows of muslin squares and sashing units. Note the positions of the checkers and rails in each sashing strip. Each diagonal row ends with a muslin setting triangle. Press the seam allowances toward the muslin squares.
2. Assemble diagonal rows of sashing units and blue sashing squares. Refer to the assembly diagram to position the checkers and rails properly in each row. Each of these rows ends with a blue setting triangle. Press the seam allowances toward the blue sashing squares.
3. Starting at the bottom left corner of the diagram, stitch the rows together. Match seam lines carefully.

Adding the borders

1. Piece matching border strips end to end to make borders long enough for each side. With the blue strips, make four 2x126-inch borders and four 2x84-inch borders. In the same

CHECKERS AND RAILS QUILT ASSEMBLY DIAGRAM

manner, use the muslin strips to assemble two 2x84-inch borders, two 2x126-inch borders, two 3x84-inch borders, and two 3x126-inch borders.
2. For each side of the quilt, sew four border strips together lengthwise to make a single unit four strips wide with the widest (muslin) strip on the outside. Refer to the assembly diagram, *above,* for color placement.
3. Pin border units onto the quilt top. Refer to page 299 for instructions for borders with mitered corners. Sew borders to the quilt.

Quilting and finishing
The design area of the quilt pictured on page 59 is quilted diagonally with a grid of ¾-inch squares. Diagonal lines are quilted in the borders. Mark the quilt top with the quilting design of your choice.

Sandwich the batting between the quilt top and the backing. Baste the three layers securely together; quilt as desired.

BINDING: Use the remaining blue fabric to make approximately 400 inches of binding. Refer to pages 306 and 307 for instructions on making and applying binding.

Oregon Trail Quilt

Shown on page 61.
The finished quilt measures approximately 72x96 inches. Each finished block is 12 inches square.

MATERIALS
7¼ yards of white fabric
2½ yards of burgundy fabric
5¾ yards of backing fabric
90x108-inch precut quilt batting
Template material
Red embroidery floss (optional)

INSTRUCTIONS
This quilt has an unusual set of 14 Oregon Trail blocks and 12 setting squares arranged around a plain center. This center area makes an ideal showcase for fancy quilting.

The edges of the quilt are finished by hemming the top and backing, then securing the edges with decorative embroidery. Apply a traditional binding, if you prefer.

Cutting the fabrics
Refer to page 288 for tips on making and using templates for patchwork. A window template is recommended for this block. Prepare templates for patterns A and B on page 70.

Before cutting, review the information on marking and cutting curves on page 71.

From the white fabric, cut:
◆ Two 6½x86-inch borders.
◆ Two 6½x62-inch borders.
◆ Four 2¼x86-inch strips for straight-grain binding (optional).
◆ One 36½-inch square.
◆ Eleven 3½x42-inch strips. From these strips, cut 128 of Pattern A.
◆ Eleven 4x42-inch strips. From these strips, cut 112 of Pattern B.
◆ Twelve 12½-inch squares.

From the burgundy fabric, cut:
◆ Ten 3½x42-inch strips. From these, cut 112 of Pattern A.
◆ Twelve 4x42-inch strips. From these, cut 128 of Pattern B.

continued

Making the blocks

Refer to the teaching page, *opposite,* for tips on curved piecing.

1. Join white A pieces and burgundy B pieces along the curved edges to form squares. Make 128 square units in this coloration.

2. Make 112 square units in the opposite coloration, using burgundy A pieces and white B pieces.

3. Using two squares of each coloration, assemble four units into a quarter-block as shown in Figure 1, *right.* Make 56 quarter-blocks.

4. Referring to the block drawing, *top right,* join four quarter-blocks into a complete block. Make 14 blocks.

5. Assemble the remaining 16 square units into four border corners as shown in Figure 2, *right.*

Assembling the quilt top

1. Stitch pieced blocks onto opposite sides of one white setting square. Join this three-block row to one side of the 36½-inch center square. Repeat, adding another three-block row to the opposite side of the square.

2. Refer to page 295 for a diagram of an alternate straight set. Join the remaining blocks and setting squares in

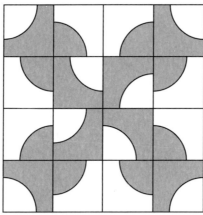

OREGON TRAIL BLOCK

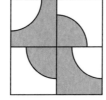 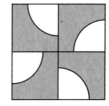

FIGURE 1   **FIGURE 2**

four rows of five blocks each. Two rows begin and end with pieced blocks and two rows have setting squares at both ends. Press seam allowances toward the setting squares.

3. Referring again to the diagram on page 295, join the rows and the assembled center section to complete the quilt top. Alternate the rows that begin with pieced blocks with those that begin with setting squares.

Adding the borders

1. Compare the 62-inch-long border strips with the top and bottom edges of the quilt. Trim the border strips so they are the same length as the edges, then stitch a border corner square to both ends of each strip.

2. Sew the 86-inch-long borders to the sides of the quilt top. Press the seam allowances toward the border; trim excess border fabric.

3. Matching the corner seam lines with the side border seams, sew the pieced borders to the top and bottom edges of the quilt.

Quilting and finishing

MARKING THE TOP: Select appropriate quilting designs for the center, setting squares, and the border. Refer to page 302 for tips on marking the quilting design on the quilt top.

If you plan to finish the quilt edges with embroidery as described below, mark and quilt the borders after the edges are finished. If you plan to bind the edges, quilt the borders before applying the binding.

BACKING: Divide the backing fabric into two 2⅞-yard lengths. Sew the two panels together; press the seam allowances open. Layer the backing, batting, and quilt top; baste.

QUILTING: Quilt as desired. The quilt shown has outline quilting around the seams of the patchwork.

EMBROIDERED HEM: Trim the backing even with the quilt top. Trim the batting so it is ¼ inch smaller all the way around than the quilt top and back. Fold in a ¼ inch hem on both the quilt top and backing. Secure the folded edges with a decorative embroidery stitch of your choice.

BINDING: If you prefer traditional binding, see pages 306 and 307 for instructions.

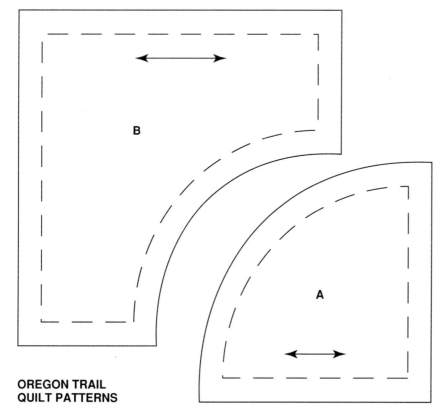

OREGON TRAIL QUILT PATTERNS

STITCHING CURVED SEAMS

Piecing a curved seam requires accuracy and precision. Curved seams can be stitched by machine, but most quilters prefer to hand-stitch curved seams for better control.

Refer to page 288 for tips on making templates. For precise cutting and piecing, window templates are recommended for curved patches.

Challenging patchwork

Achieving success with curves is like anything else—it takes practice. If you'd like to experiment with a curved-seam pattern, work with scrap fabrics. If your first attempt is a disaster, don't give up. By the time you've made four or five seams, you'll have much better results.

The Optical Illusion Quilt in this chapter is a good block to try, because the curves of its patches are not as severe as those for the Oregon Trail block. The Dogwood Quilt in Chapter 9 is a patchwork challenge that includes slightly curved seams.

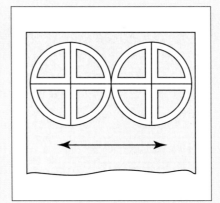

1 Mark curves on the bias by placing straight edges on the straight grain of the fabric. If possible, trace templates on the fabric in a manner that results in a mutual straight cutting edge as shown.

Mark both the cutting line and the sewing line for each piece on the *wrong side* of the fabric. Cut each piece carefully with sharp scissors.

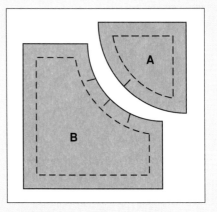

2 Clip the seam allowance in the center of each curve. To find the center, fold the piece in half; make a little cut in the seam allowance at this point, coming to within 1/16 inch of the sewing line. Make additional clips along the curved edge as necessary. Concave patches (B) usually require more clips than patches with convex curves (A).

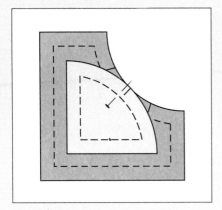

3 Matching center clips, pin the patches with right sides together. Bring the corners of the two pieces together, aligning the straight outer edges, and pin.

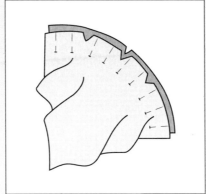

4 Add pins and clip as necessary to ease the concave patch (B) around the curve of the convex patch (A). More pronounced curves will require more clipping than gentle curves. Because the curved edges are on the bias, the patches should stretch to fit together smoothly.

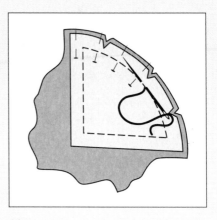

5 Stitch the seam by hand or by machine. Remove each pin just before sewing over it. Check the back of the work to be sure the stitches are exactly on the marked sewing line. Press the seam allowance toward the darker fabric; the seam allowance should lie flat in either direction.

Optical Illusion Quilt

Shown on page 60.
The finished quilt measures approxi-
mately 88x98 inches. Each block is
10 inches square.

MATERIALS

6¼ yards of dark green solid fabric
3¾ yards *each* of solid brown and
 gold fabrics
1½ yards of muslin, including
 binding
2¾ yards of 108-inch-wide sheeting
 for backing fabric
120x120-inch precut quilt batting
Template material

INSTRUCTIONS

The real name of this block is elusive. A similar quilt, handed down in an Alabama family, was called Snail's Trail. Pattern books published in the 1930s, however, referred to the block as Broken Stone, Lover's Quarrel, or New Wedding Ring.

Because of the wonderful interplay of color and shape, the current owner of this delightful antique quilt calls it Optical Illusion.

The quilt is made of 72 blocks in a straight set. The joined blocks form an allover pattern that obscures the visual definition of the blocks, creating a seemingly continuous swirl of circles and diamonds.

The slight curve of this block's seams can be sewn easily by hand or by machine.

Cutting the fabrics

Refer to page 288 for tips on making templates for patchwork. Because of the curves and set-in seams of this block, window templates are recommended to create accurate pivot points on each piece for either hand or machine piecing. Make templates for patterns A, B, C, and D, *opposite.*

From the dark green fabric, cut:
◆ Four 4½x94-inch border strips.
◆ 288 of Pattern A.

OPTICAL ILLUSION BLOCK

From the muslin, cut:
◆ One ¾-yard piece for binding.
◆ 288 of Pattern C.

From the brown fabric, cut:
◆ 72 of Pattern D.

From the gold fabric, cut:
◆ 288 of Pattern B.

Making the blocks

Before you begin, refer to page 71 for tips on piecing curved seams. Assemble each block as follows, referring to the block diagram, *above.*
1. For each block, use one D piece and four *each* of pieces A, B, and C.
2. Stitch a gold B piece to the curved edge of each A piece. Press the seam allowances toward the A pieces.
3. Join an AB unit to opposite sides of the D piece, as shown in the block assembly diagram, *below.* Press the seam allowances toward the B pieces.

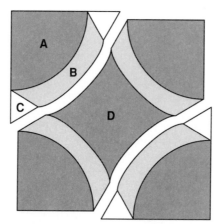

OPTICAL ILLUSION BLOCK
ASSEMBLY DIAGRAM

4. Add C triangles to both sides of the two remaining AB units as shown in the assembly diagram; press seam allowances toward the triangles.
5. Join the side ABC units to the center unit, setting in the angled seam.
 Make 72 Optical Illusion blocks.

Assembling the quilt top

Refer to page 294 for a diagram of a straight set. Join the blocks into nine horizontal rows of eight blocks each. When stitching blocks together, match the seam lines of the C triangles carefully to create the illusion of a single diamond.

Assemble the rows in the same manner. From edge to edge, the completed quilt top should measure approximately 80½x90½ inches.

Adding the borders

Stitch border strips to the 90½-inch sides of the quilt. Press the seam allowances toward the borders; trim the border fabric even with the top and bottom edges of the quilt top.

Sew a border strip to the top and bottom edges in the same manner.

Quilting and finishing

Sandwich the batting between the quilt top and the backing fabric. Baste the three layers together.

QUILTING: The quilt shown has outline quilting outside each seam and an X quilted through the center of the D pieces. Quilt as desired.

BINDING: Use the remaining muslin to make approximately 390 inches of binding, either bias or straight-grain. Refer to pages 306 and 307 for tips on making and applying binding.

Changing the quilt size

The 88x98-inch finished size of this quilt is suitable for either a full or a queen-size bed. To lengthen the quilt for a queen-size bed, make the top and bottom borders wider.

Make 54 blocks in a 6x9-block set for a 68x98-inch twin-size quilt.

For a king-size bed, make 100 blocks in a 10x10-block set for a 108x108-inch quilt.

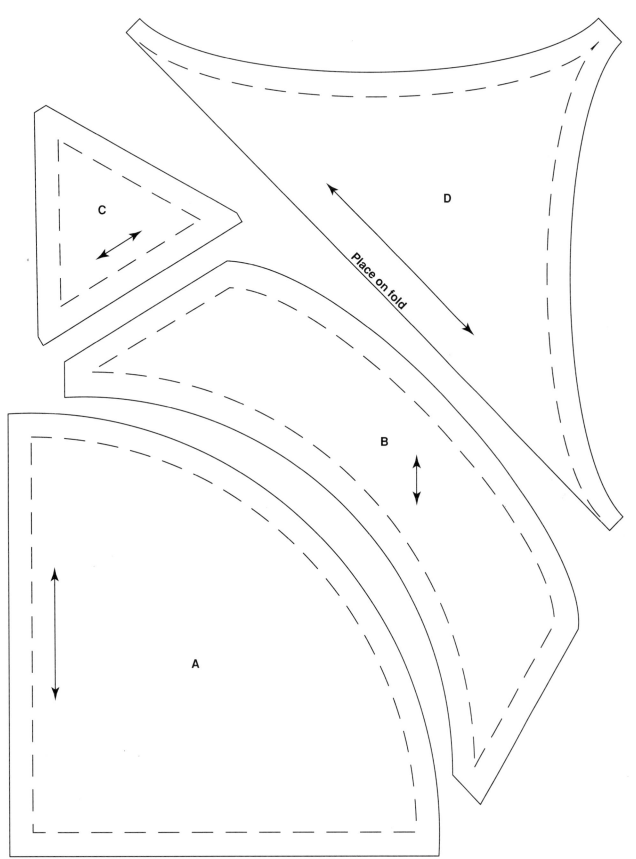

C

D

Place on fold

B

A

OPTICAL ILLUSION QUILT PATTERNS

Distant Trumpets

Log Cabins in
Lincoln's Union

1856 ∾ 1866

◆ **Whig's Defeat,**
Pennsylvania, c. 1940;
80x92 inches. Instructions
begin on page 84.

At the quilting bee, one might have learned . . . how to bring up babies; how to mend a cracked teapot; how to take out grease from a brocade; how to reconcile absolute decrees with free will; how to make five yards of cloth answer the purpose of six; and how to put down the Democratic Party.

Harriet Beecher Stowe

When 10 southern states seceded from the Union in 1861, one million men marched away to engage in an unprecedented slaughter. Left behind to wait and worry, women gathered over the comforting intimacy of the quilt frame to share their loneliness and fears.

At the sound of the call to arms, women on both sides of the Civil War mobilized to supplement inadequate supplies of bedding for soldiers and hospitals. They made so many quilts that one of every six soldiers slept under a quilt made behind the lines.

◆ *Straight Furrows (left), c. 1870; 80x100 inches. Instructions begin on page 88.*

Making quilts also was a means to raise funds for other supplies. Even before the Civil War, raffles and fairs, offering quilts for sale, supported the abolitionist cause.

Women's antislavery societies outnumbered the men's, and the movement—like the War— depended on women's fund-raising activities.

But the battle faded to a distant rumble for the settlers going West. The Homestead Act of 1862 guaranteed farmers free land in newly acquired territories. Lured by this promise of prosperity, men dotted the plains with log cabins, and the women who made these rough dwellings into homes created quilts to fit their new lives.

*T*he Log Cabin block dates from the 1860 presidential campaign of Abraham Lincoln, a "man of the people" whose origins were represented by the humble cabin of his birth.

The Log Cabin block is symbolic of the American frontier. The strips of fabric represent the inter-

locking logs of a cabin, built row upon row.

Most vintage Log Cabin blocks have a red center square that represents the hearth as the center of the cabin. Yellow centers symbolize candles in the cabin window. A few Log Cabin quilts of the Civil War era that have black centers were hung on the clothesline to subtly advertise a station of the Underground Railroad.

Log Cabin blocks in a Barn Raising set, *opposite*, depict the beams of a new barn; the Straight Furrows set on page 76 reflects

◆ *Barn Raising* (opposite), c. 1900; 82½x99 inches. Instructions begin on page 89.

patterns in a plowed field; Zigzag sets imitate the jagged split-rail fences that enclosed rural fields and gardens.

The Log Cabin has several block variations that deserve their own place in the patchwork encyclopedia. Courthouse Steps, *above*, and Pineapple on page 80 are two well-known variations. Like the Log Cabin, these blocks are made of strips sewn around a center square.

The decade before the Civil War was a time of national prosperity. Fabric became more affordable and available than ever, even reaching the farthest frontiers with some regu-

larity once the railroad crossed the Mississippi River in 1855. In 1856, Cranston Printworks produced nearly 1.5 million yards of calicoes per week with improved printing and colorfast dyes.

The sewing machine, patented by Elias Howe in 1846, was commonplace by 1870 and freed many women from the tediousness of sewing clothing and patchwork by hand. Some quilts of the 1850s and 1860s were machine-stitched, evidence of the quickness with which quiltmakers embraced a laborsaving innovation.

◆ *Courthouse Steps* (above), Kansas, c. 1870; 81½x98½ inches. Instructions begin on page 93.

◆ *Pineapple (above),
c. 1938; 80x98 inches.
Instructions begin on
page 94.*

*T*he social climate of
the years preceding the
Civil War boiled with
political turmoil. In the
antislavery fervor of the
Northeast, quiltmakers
began making political
statements in their work.

Many block names
preserve the issues and
events of the time. Clay's
Choice, Underground
Railroad, and Whig's
Defeat are a few.

The Whigs opposed
slavery in the 1850s, but
most voters still hoped for
compromise. When the
last Whig presidential
candidate lost to James
Buchanan in 1856, the
defeated party dissolved.

Henry Clay, a respected
Democrat, also lost his
chance to be president by
opposing slavery too
soon. Urged to moderate
his stand, he said, "I'd
rather be right than be
president." Clay's moral-
ity is honored in the quilt
block that bears his
name—Clay's Choice.

By 1861, the social and
economic issues of slavery
led the southern states to
secede from the Union
and the country was at
war. The bright calicoes
of Civil War era quilts
contrast with the harsh
realities of wartime.

The absence of hus-
bands gone to battle left
women alone to provide
for their families in hard

times. In areas where
battle ravaged the land,
survival was their only
care. An Alabama mother
wrote of riding 75 miles
by horseback to procure
salt, a commodity virtually
unobtainable in the South
as the War dragged on.

Many quilts were
destroyed during the
War. In the South, they
were lost to looting and
burning; in the North,
many quilts were donated
as hospital and field
blankets. In one month in
1863, more than 1,200
quilts were issued to
Union soldiers; some
were made specifically for
the troops, but others
were family quilts
sacrificed for the cause.

Thousands of men
from new midwest states
and the western territories
left home to join the
fight. Many pioneer wives
who hadn't wanted to go
West at all now faced life
alone in dark woods filled
with constant danger.

Women on the frontier
longed for the relative
refinement of their former
lives. They remembered
the pineapple, a symbol
of hospitality since
colonial times that was
traditionally worked in
wood or silver. Imitating
its jagged shape, the quilt
block that emerged shows
the simplification that
characterizes American
quilt design.

An interesting variation
of the Log Cabin block,
the Pineapple also
became known as Wind-
mill, Windmill Blades,
and Maltese Cross.

◆ *Log Cabin Medallion
(opposite), c. 1890;
94x102 inches. Instruc-
tions begin on page 97.*

Distant Trumpets

1856–1866

The cotton gin, invented in 1793, may have been one cause of the Civil War. It made slavery economically practical and thus led to a buildup of slavery in the South. And, it was that buildup that was at the root of the War.

Before the gin, cotton was barely a profitable crop for planters, even in warm southern climates. It took one slave nearly a whole year to pick the seed from a single bale, a labor-intensive and impractical process. But the new machine made cotton a cash bonanza, cleaning it quickly and efficiently. More cotton was planted and cheap slave labor was needed to pick it.

New England profited from the cotton crop, too. The establishment of cotton-spinning mills and weaving and fabric-printing plants began the industrial revolution that moved so much of the North away from an agricultural economy.

When the War began, the South saw the continuation of slavery as necessary for its economic survival. Although the immorality of slavery concerned some Northerners, most saw the preservation of the Union as the principal issue of the War.

The strong feelings on both sides inspired artistic works of patriotism and partisanship, including quilts. The surviving ones are mostly from the North, which suffered less physical devastation than the South. Symbols long associated with the United States were incorporated into northern quilt design.

Peterson's Magazine printed a color illustration of a red, white, and blue quilt in June 1861 and urged readers to quilt for the Union. The 34 stars in the design represented all 34 states, including those that seceded. Judging from the number of these quilts that survive, many readers applauded these Union sentiments.

The eagle, a favorite motif during the earlier Federalist period, enjoyed renewed popularity with quiltmakers and a four-square set of appliquéd eagles became known as a Union quilt.

Eagle quilts from the period are plentiful. They feature the bird in all sorts of styles, many with arrows or laurel leaves in their beaks and/or talons. Arrows, spears, and martial batons were emblems of war, while laurel was a symbol of peace.

Union quilts enjoyed renewed popularity during the patriotic fervor of the 1876 Centennial.

◆ **Eagles Union Quilt** (left), made by Sarah Winters, Pennsylvania, c. 1876; 74x74 inches. Instructions begin on page 101.

◆ **Underground Railroad** (opposite), c. 1870; 89x107 inches. Instructions begin on page 100.

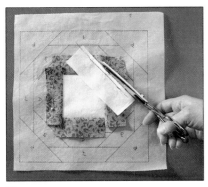

V

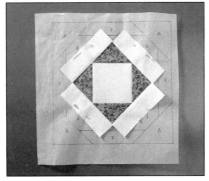

VI

pieces as shown in Photo IV, *opposite.* From the drawn side of the foundation, poke pins through all layers at both ends of the sewing line to aid in aligning the strip with the sewing line. Pin the strip in place; cut off the strip, leaving at least ½ inch for a seam allowance.

9. Turn the foundation over to the drawn side. Sew the muslin strip in place by stitching on the drawn line as you did in the first round. On the fabric side, check that the strip is sewn straight. Trim the seam allowance as necessary, cutting away the corners of the B pieces as shown in Photo V, *above.*

Note: Trim, press, and pin each strip as it is sewn. If you do not trim each seam allowance and the corners in turn, the excess fabric is trapped under the next round, causing bulk and distortion.

10. In the same manner, sew a strip on the opposite side of the block, then stitch the remaining two sides to complete the second round as shown in Photo VI, *above.*

11. Complete rounds 3, 4, and 5 in this manner, alternating colors. As the sewn pieces become longer, use more than one pin to hold them in place for sewing. Remove pins from any piece that is sewn on all sides.

12. When all the strip rounds are complete, the block is an octagon. Referring to the block diagram, *opposite,* sew the muslin G triangles onto the corners to make the block square. Make 80 Pineapple blocks. Do not remove the foundation material yet.

Assembling the quilt top
Make 10 horizontal rows of eight blocks each, then join the rows.

To align the seams of adjacent blocks, pin through the seam lines of both blocks so the tip of the pin holds the seams together. After stitching, check the matched points. If you are not satisfied with the join, open the seam on both sides of a mismatched point; with a little judicious adjustment, you can ease in a better match.

We recommend pressing the seam allowances open where the blocks are joined. Even if the seam lines are nicely matched, the bulk created by pressing so many seam allowances to one side makes the piecing appear inaccurate and hinders quilting.

REMOVING THE FOUNDATION: Make a small slit in the center of each foundation square. Slip your finger in the hole; gently tear the foundation along the seam lines and pull it away. Remove all foundation material.

Adding the borders
FIRST BORDER: Join three 2x33-inch green strips end to end to make one border strip for each long side. Matching the center of each strip with the center point of one side, stitch border strips onto the long sides of the quilt top. Press seam allowances toward the borders; trim excess border fabric at each end.

Join two 2x42-inch green strips to make one border strip for the top edge. Repeat for the bottom border. Add borders to quilt top as before.

MIDDLE BORDER: Combine three 1½x42-inch muslin strips for each side border and two strips for each end border. Add borders as before, sewing side borders first, then the end borders.

OUTER BORDER: Combine green strips as for the first border. Add border strips in the same manner.

Quilting and finishing
BACKING: Cut two 3-yard lengths of backing fabric. Stitch the two panels together lengthwise; press the seam allowance open. Sandwich the batting between the quilt top and the backing; baste the layers together.

QUILTING: Quilt as desired. The quilt pictured on page 80 has outline quilting in each log of the Pineapple block. Diagonal lines, 1 inch apart, are quilted in the borders.

BINDING: Make approximately 370 inches of binding. Refer to pages 306 and 307 for instructions on making and applying binding.

Log Cabin Medallion Quilt

Shown on page 81.
The finished quilt measures approximately 94x102 inches. Each Log Cabin block is 10 inches square; each Courthouse Steps block is 8 inches square.

MATERIALS
5¾ yards of black solid fabric for patchwork, borders, and binding
⅜ yard *each* of red and yellow solid fabrics for the Log Cabin blocks
Three 2½x42-inch strips of assorted light-colored fabrics for the Courthouse Steps blocks
Fifty-five 1½x42-inch strips or scraps of assorted light fabrics
Forty-five 1½x42-inch strips or scraps of assorted dark fabrics
2⅞ yards of 108-inch-wide sheeting for backing fabric
120x120-inch precut quilt batting
9½ yards of 1½-inch-wide red satin ribbon for bows
3 skeins of red No. 5 perle cotton
Rotary cutter, mat, and acrylic ruler
continued

INSTRUCTIONS

This quilt is an unusual mix of Courthouse Steps blocks and black squares set around a medallion of Log Cabin blocks.

The colors of the patchwork glow amid the black fabric, starting with fiery red and yellow in the center blocks of the medallion. Sparks of red appear in the centers of all the Log Cabin blocks, in the bows tacked onto each plain black square, and in the ties at all the block intersections.

Cutting the fabrics

Cut cross-grain strips for the blocks as described below. It is not necessary to make templates or to cut pieces to the specific length of each log or step.

Refer to the quilt assembly diagram, *opposite*, for guidance while cutting the fabrics.

From the black fabric, cut:
- Four 3½x98-inch border strips.
- One 30x42-inch piece for binding.
- One 10½x42-inch strip. From this strip, cut four 10½-inch squares for the medallion corners.
- Eighteen 1½x42-inch strips for the Log Cabin blocks.
- Fifty-three 8½-inch squares. Extra black fabric can be used to cut 2½-inch squares for the centers of the Courthouse Steps blocks.

From the red fabric, cut:
- Three 1½x42-inch strips.
- One 2½x42-inch strip. From this strip, cut sixteen 2½-inch A squares. Set aside 12 squares for the centers of the Log Cabin blocks; use the remaining squares for centers of Courthouse Steps blocks.

From the yellow fabric, cut:
- Three 1½x42-inch strips.

From the assorted light fabrics, cut:
- 2½-inch squares for the centers of the Courthouse Steps blocks. (Combined with the squares cut from the red and black fabrics, you need a total of 54 squares.)

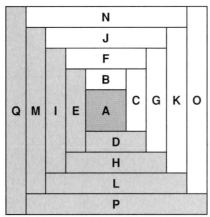

LOG CABIN BLOCK (Make 12)

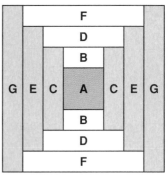

COURTHOUSE STEPS BLOCK (Make 54)

Making the Log Cabin blocks

Refer to the Log Cabin block diagram, *above*, and the general instructions for Log Cabin blocks on page 90 as you make each block.

Make 12 Log Cabin blocks. All the blocks use black fabric for the dark side of the block. Make two blocks using red strips for the light side and two more blocks using yellow strips. Use assorted light fabrics for the light side of the eight remaining Log Cabin blocks.

1. Begin each block with a red A square. Following the general instructions on page 90, add light-colored fabric strips for logs B and C and black strips for logs D and E.
2. Continue adding light and dark strips, referring to the block diagram, until each block is complete.

Making Courthouse Steps blocks

Refer to the Courthouse Steps block diagram, *above*, as you sew. Make 54 blocks, varying placement of light and dark fabrics if desired.

1. Begin each block with a 2½-inch square. With right sides together, stitch a light-colored strip onto one side of the square for Step B; trim the strip even with the sides of the square. Repeat on the opposite side of the square. Press the seam allowances toward the B pieces.
2. For Step C, stitch a dark-colored strip onto one long side of the BAB unit. Trim the strip even with the sides of the center unit; press the seam allowance toward the C piece. Repeat on the opposite side of the center unit for the other C step.

3. Continue adding strips of light and dark fabrics in alphabetical order until the block is complete.

Assembling the center medallion

Refer to the quilt assembly diagram, *opposite*, for the placement of *each* Log Cabin block.

1. Begin in the center with the four blocks made with red and yellow fabrics. Stitch the red edge of one block to the yellow edge of another. Press the seam allowance toward the red fabric. Join the second pair of blocks in the same manner. Join the two pairs of blocks together, sewing red edges to yellow ones.
2. Join two more Log Cabin blocks, stitching the black sides together. Add this pair to one side of the four-square center, positioning the fabrics as shown in the diagram. Repeat to add two blocks to the other side of the center, completing the two center horizontal rows of the medallion.
3. Join two more Log Cabin blocks, stitching the black edges together. Add a 10½-inch black square onto the light side of each block, creating a four-square horizontal row. Assemble the remaining blocks and squares in the same manner. Sew these rows onto the top and bottom edges of the center section as shown.

Assembling the quilt top

1. Referring to the quilt assembly diagram, *opposite*, join Courthouse Steps blocks and plain black squares in horizontal rows. Alternate blocks and squares in each row as shown, making seven 11-square rows. Make 10 three-square rows for the sides of the Log Cabin medallion.

LOG CABIN MEDALLION QUILT ASSEMBLY DIAGRAM

2. Join five three-square rows as shown, then stitch the assembled unit onto one side of the medallion. Repeat to add another five-row section to the opposite side of the medallion.
3. Referring to the assembly diagram, join four 11-square rows to the top of the center section and three more rows to the bottom edge.

Adding the borders
Stitch a border strip onto each long side of the quilt top. Press the seam allowances toward the borders; trim excess border fabric even with the quilt top.

Add the remaining border strips to the top and bottom edges in the same manner.

. continued

The quilt shown has red feather-stitching worked over the border seam lines with perle cotton. Use the embroidery stitch of your choice to embellish the borders. (See page 137 for stitch diagrams.)

Finishing
Sandwich the batting between the quilt top and the backing. Baste the three layers securely together.

TYING: The quilt pictured is tied with a cross-stitch of red perle cotton at the corners of each block.

To tie the quilt in this manner, bring the threaded needle from the back of the quilt to the front, leaving a 2-inch tail of thread on the back. Make a diagonal stitch, approximately 1 inch long, at the corners. Bring the needle back up in position to make another diagonal stitch that crosses the first one.

Tie off the thread with a knot on the back of the quilt.

If you prefer, the quilt can be tied traditionally with the knots on the top of the quilt. Refer to page 305 for tips on tying.

BOWS: Cut a 6-inch length of ribbon for each bow. With right sides together, stitch together the ends of each piece to make a loop. Turn the ribbon right side out; finger-press the seam allowance open.

Lay the ribbon piece flat with the seam at the back. Use sewing thread to hand-sew a loose gathering stitch through the vertical center of the ribbon, stitching through both layers.

Pull on the thread to gather the bow in the middle; wrap the thread tightly around the ribbon to secure the gathers.

Using perle cotton, tack a bow in place in the center of each plain black square. Stitch through the quilt top and the batting to secure the bow.

BINDING: Make approximately 400 inches of binding, either bias or straight-grain. Refer to pages 306 and 307 for instructions on making and applying binding.

BASIC

Underground Railroad Quilt

Shown on page 83.
The finished quilt measures approximately 89x107 inches.

MATERIALS
4¾ yards of black and white print fabric for the setting squares and the border
⅛ yard *each* of 25 light and 25 medium to dark fabrics for the patchwork, totaling 3⅛ yards *each* of light and dark fabrics
1 yard of binding fabric
3½ yards of 108-inch-wide sheeting for backing fabric
120x120-inch precut quilt batting
Rotary cutter, mat, and acrylic ruler

INSTRUCTIONS
This quilt is a 9x11-block alternate straight set. Some of the 50 different blocks are made with only two fabrics, one light and one dark, while others are a jumble of colorful scraps.

In the quilt shown, the fabrics are a cheerful mix of solids, prints, stripes, and plaids. The quiltmaker was creative in the manner in which she positioned the blocks, turning them this way and that to suit her fancy.

Because there are only four triangle-squares in each block, quick piecing is not efficient for this scrap quilt. However, if you are making many triangle-squares with the same fabric combination, refer to the instructions for quick-pieced triangle-squares on page 114 before cutting the fabrics as described.

Cutting the fabrics
Cutting requirements for blocks are given for one block, with the number required for the entire quilt shown in parentheses.

From the black and white print fabric, cut:
◆ Two 4½x100-inch strips for the side borders.
◆ Six 4½x31-inch strips (cut cross grain) for the top and bottom borders.
◆ Forty-nine 9½-inch squares.

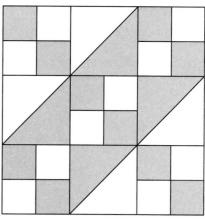

UNDERGROUND RAILROAD BLOCK

From each scrap fabric, cut:
◆ Four (200) 2⅜-inch squares. Cut each square in half diagonally to yield eight triangles of each fabric for the triangle-squares.
◆ Two (50) 2x21-inch strips for the four-patch units.

Choosing fabrics for each block
For each block, select one 2x21-inch strip of a light fabric and one of a dark color. These strips will be used to make the four-patch units.

For the triangle-squares, you may use the same combination of fabrics or you may change one or both fabrics to achieve a more scrappy look. Select four dark and four light triangles for each block.

Choose fabric combinations for 50 Underground Railroad blocks.

Making the triangle-squares
Match one light and one dark triangle. Stitch the two triangles together as shown in Figure 1, *below*. Press the seam allowance toward the darker fabric.

Complete four triangle-squares for each of 50 blocks.

Making the four-patch units
Make five four-patch units for each block, using one of the methods described here.

FIGURE 1   **FIGURE 2**

TRADITIONAL PIECING: Cut ten 2-inch squares from each 2x21-inch strip. Stitch one light square onto one side of each dark square; press the seam allowances toward the dark fabric.

Join two of these assembled units into a four-patch as illustrated in Figure 2, *opposite, bottom,* turning one unit upside down to position the fabrics as shown.

STRIP PIECING: Refer to page 18 for more detailed instructions on strip piecing.

For each block, sew the two 2x21-inch strips together, creating one 3½x21-inch strip. Press the seam allowance toward the dark fabric.

Cut 2-inch-wide vertical units from the sewn strip as illustrated on page 18. Turning one unit upside down, join two units into a four-patch as illustrated in Figure 2, *opposite.*

Assembling the block
1. Press each assembled unit. Identify the five four-patch units and four triangle-squares for each block. All the units should be 3½ inches square.
2. Assemble the nine units in three horizontal rows of three squares each, referring to the block assembly diagram, *above, right.* Press the seam allowances in the first and third rows in the same direction; for the middle row, press the seam allowances in the other direction.
3. Join the three rows to complete the block. Complete 50 Underground Railroad blocks.

Assembling the quilt top
Refer to page 295 for an illustration of an alternate straight set.
1. On a flat surface, arrange the blocks in 11 horizontal rows with nine squares in each row, alternating patchwork blocks with plain squares of the black print fabric.

Rows 1, 3, 5, 7, 9, and 11 will alternate five pieced blocks and four plain squares, with a patchwork block at both ends. Rows 2, 4, 6, 8, and 10 will alternate four pieced blocks and five plain squares, with a plain square at both ends.

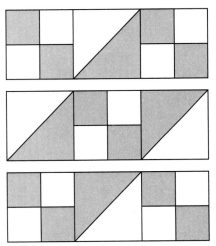

UNDERGROUND RAILROAD ASSEMBLY DIAGRAM

2. Join the blocks in each row, keeping all the squares in their correct positions. Press the resulting seam allowances toward the plain squares.
3. Assemble the rows, alternating rows with patchwork blocks at each end with rows that have plain squares at the ends. When all 11 horizontal rows are joined, the assembled quilt top should measure approximately 81½x99½ inches.

Adding the borders
1. Stitch a 100-inch-long border strip onto each long side of the quilt. Press the seam allowances toward the borders; trim excess border fabric.
2. Join three 31-inch-long strips of black print fabric end to end to make a border strip for the top edge of the quilt. Repeat for the bottom border.
3. Stitch the border strips onto the top and bottom edges of the quilt. Press the seam allowances toward the border fabric; trim excess border fabric even with the sides.

Quilting and finishing
Layer the backing, batting, and quilt top; baste the three layers together.

QUILTING: The quilt shown has diagonal lines of quilting over the entire quilt top. Quilt as desired.

BINDING: Make approximately 410 inches of binding. Refer to pages 306 and 307 for tips on making and applying binding.

Eagles Union Quilt
Shown on page 82.
The finished quilt measures 74 inches square. Each block is 30 inches square.

MATERIALS
3⅝ yards of light yellow fabric
2½ yards of red fabric for wings, leaves, border, and binding
½ yard of dark green fabric for heads, tails, and center wheel
⅓ yard of dark gold fabric for the shields, talons, and center ring
4½ yards of backing fabric
81-inch square of quilt batting
Red embroidery floss
Template material

INSTRUCTIONS
The size and the square shape of this quilt make it a great wall hanging. Each of the four bold-colored eagles is positioned diagonally and appliquéd on a square of light yellow fabric. The center motif is appliquéd over the seams after the squares are joined.

Cutting the fabrics
Refer to page 288 for tips on making templates for appliqué. Prepare templates for patterns A through H on pages 102–105. For the wing (A), make a complete template by joining the two halves of the pattern on pages 104 and 105.

For the tail (C), shield (E), wheel (F), ring (G), and leaf (H), you can either make a template of the complete shape or place a template of the half pattern on the fold of the fabric.

From the red fabric, cut:
◆ Four 2¼x76-inch strips for straight-grain binding.
◆ Four 3x68-inch border strips.
◆ Eight of Pattern A (wing). Cut four with the template right side up and four more with the template facedown.
◆ Four of Pattern H (leaf).

From the dark gold fabric, cut:
◆ Four *each* of patterns D (talon), E (shield), and G (center ring).

continued

101

From the light yellow fabric, cut:
- Four 30½-inch squares.
- Two 3x76-inch border strips and two 3x68-inch border strips.

From the dark green fabric, cut:
- Four *each* of patterns B (head) and C (tail).
- One of Pattern F (center wheel).

Appliquéing the block

1. Lightly press each background square in half *diagonally* in one direction to form a center guideline.

2. Refer to pages 292 and 293 for tips on hand appliqué. For each block, prepare two wings, one head, one tail, one shield, and one talon for ap- pliqué. Do not baste under edges that will be covered by another piece, such as the bottom of the head or the top of the tail. Do not baste under the tightly curved bottom edges of the wing and tail pieces.

3. Referring to the photo on page 82, position and pin the prepared appli- qués in place. Center the top of the eagle's head on the diagonal place- ment line approximately 13 inches from one corner of the block. Posi- tion other pieces; the shield overlaps the eagle's head, tail, and wings, as well as the talon.

4. Appliqué the pieces in place. Turn the tightly curving edges of the wing and tail pieces under with the needle as you appliqué.

5. Appliqué four eagle blocks. Use two strands of red embroidery floss to outline-stitch the eye, beak, and arrows on each eagle (see page 137 for stitch diagram).

Assembling the quilt top

Sew the four blocks together, posi- tioning the eagles' heads toward the center of the quilt. Press the seam allowances open.

Prepare the green center wheel, the four red leaves, and the four gold ring pieces for appliqué, turning back the seam allowances.

Align the spokes of the center wheel with the block seam lines. Pin a leaf at the end of each spoke, slipping the bottom of the leaf under the spoke. Position a gold ring piece be- tween adjacent leaves, with the red leaves overlapping the gold fabric.

When all the pieces are correctly positioned, appliqué them in place.

Adding the borders

Stitch a red border strip onto the top and bottom edges of the quilt top. Press the seam allowances toward the red fabric; trim excess border fabric even with the quilt top.

Sew the two remaining red border strips onto the side edges of the quilt in the same manner.

Stitch the 68-inch-long yellow bor- ders onto the top and bottom edges, then add the 76-inch borders to the sides. Press these seam allowances toward the red inner border.

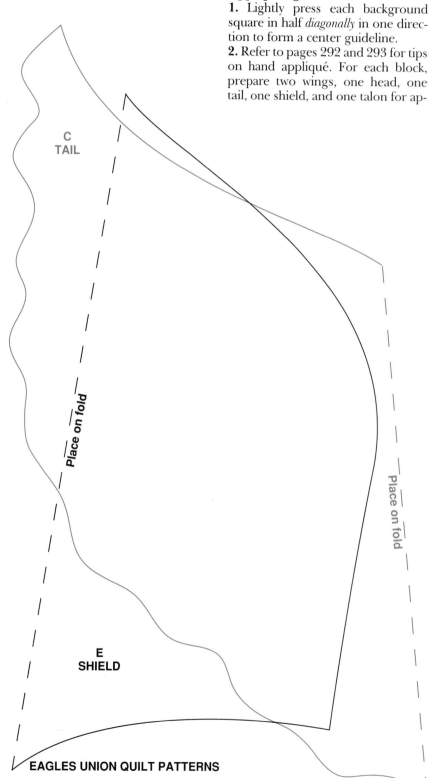

C
TAIL

Place on fold

Place on fold

E
SHIELD

EAGLES UNION QUILT PATTERNS

Quilting and finishing

BACKING: Cut the backing fabric into two 2¼-yard lengths. Sew the two panels together side by side to form the quilt backing.

Layer the backing, batting, and quilt top; baste the three layers securely together.

QUILTING: Quilt as desired. The quilt shown has a grid of diagonal squares over the center of the quilt, a cable pattern in the red border, and zigzag quilting in the outer border.

BINDING: Use the four 2¼x76-inch strips of red fabric for the binding. Refer to page 307 for instructions on applying straight-grain binding.

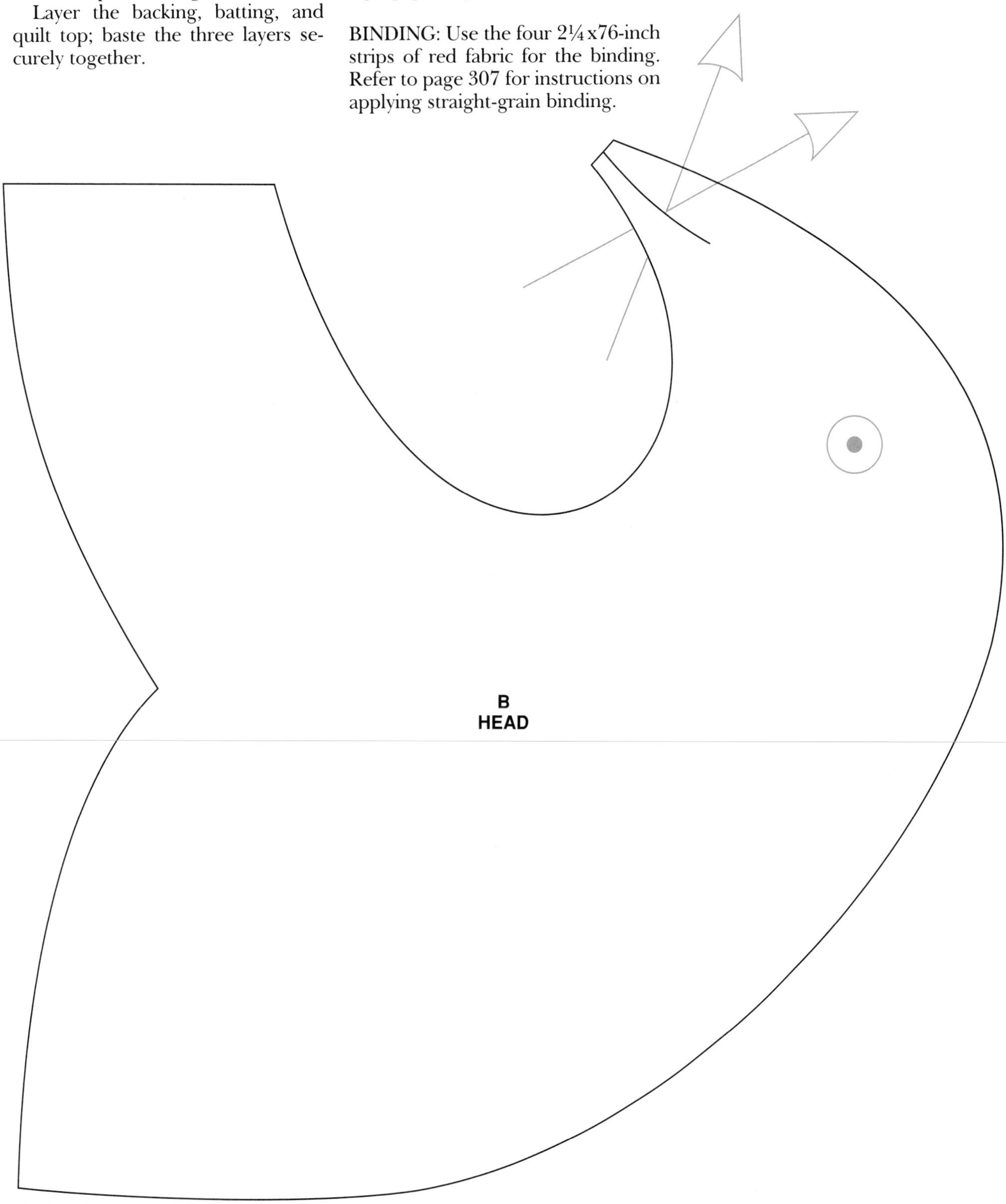

B
HEAD

EAGLES UNION QUILT PATTERN

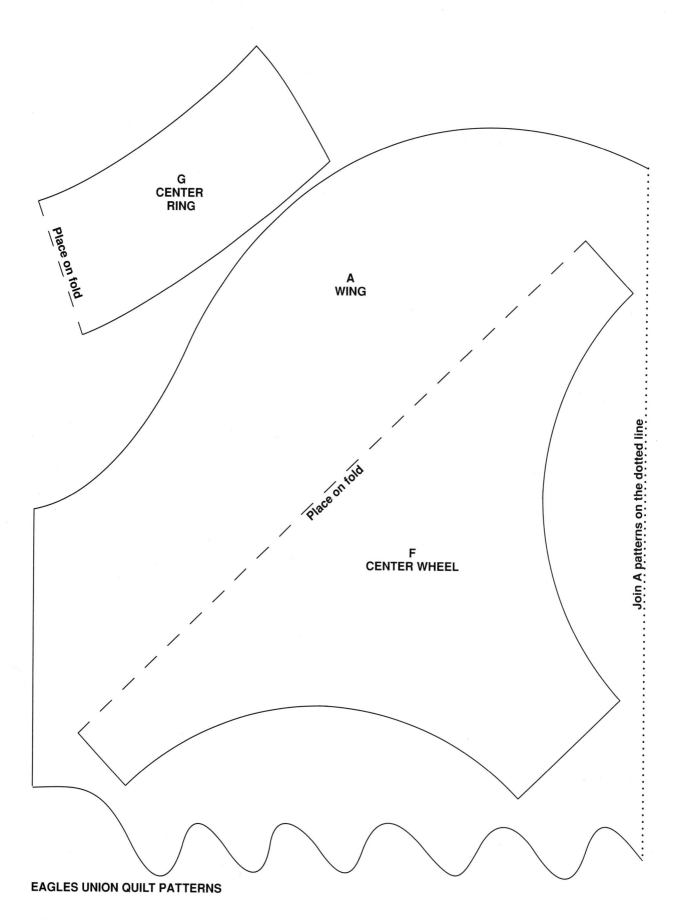

G
CENTER
RING

Place on fold

A
WING

Place on fold

F
CENTER WHEEL

Join A patterns on the dotted line

EAGLES UNION QUILT PATTERNS

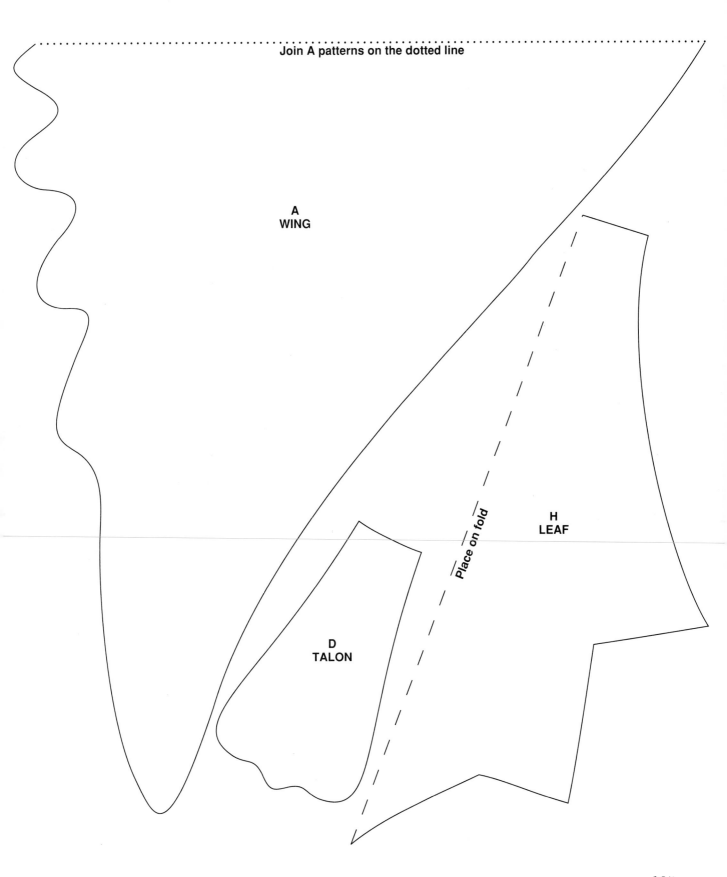

Join A patterns on the dotted line

A
WING

H
LEAF

Place on fold

D
TALON

◆ *Streak of Lightning,*
Indiana, c. 1880;
67½x82½ inches. Instruc-
tions begin on page 115.

The Virtue
OF
Necessity

Scrap Quilts Cover
The Plains with Pride

1862 ∽ 1890

The Virtue of Necessity

I have found nothing so desirable for summer covers as the old-fashioned scrap quilt of which our mothers were so proud. Every girl should piece one at least to carry away to her husband's home. And if her lot happens to be cast among strangers, the quilt when she unfolds it will seem like the face of a familiar friend, bringing up a host of memories . . . too sacred to intrude upon.

Annie Curd, *Good Housekeeping*, 1888

The patchwork scrap quilts created out of need in the late 1800s are still masterpieces of American folk art and ingenuity. They were made by a new generation of pioneers, who spread out over the prairies and made the land their own.

Times were hard nearly everywhere after the Civil War. The South was laid waste and the North struggled with the economic burdens of bank failures, labor disputes, and a growing class of urban poor. Opportunity lay to the west.

The open plains were up for grabs after the Homestead Act of 1862 guaranteed a free family farm to any man who staked a claim. From the East and the already populated states of Ohio, Illinois, and Missouri, men came to see this rich land of promise.

The railroad made traveling West easier for these settlers than it had been for earlier trail-blazers. Grace Snyder, later a renowned quilter, watched as furnishings, animals, and her mother's sewing machine were loaded onto a boxcar at the outset of her family's 1885 odyssey from Missouri to Cozad, Nebraska. There a lonely homestead sod house, or soddy, squatted over windswept fields and canyons.

The hard life of these settlers was brightened by nature's bounty, letters from home, and bits of cheerful calico. After the day's work, mothers and daughters gathered around their warm stoves to piece and quilt.

◆ *Flying Geese (right), c. 1880; 78x100 inches. Instructions begin on page 117.*

108

*I*n due time, towns grew up around the railroad depots that dotted the plains. In most towns, the general store included an array of calicoes among its wares.

Raising cattle and crops provided prairie farmers cash to buy this gay, inexpensive fabric. Calico curtains and other household items soon brightened the tidy frame houses that replaced the cold soddies.

Thrifty farm women created a new kind of quilt out of remnants from their scrap bags. They stitched together geometric pieces cut from cast-off clothing, worn linens, and sometimes new cloth from town.

Quiltmakers welcomed the laborsaving sewing machine into their busy lives. Americans bought more than 600,000 of the machines in 1879. Half of all quilts made after 1860 were machine-pieced.

Block names such as Hole in the Barn Door and Basket reflect farm life of the 1880s. New states were hailed with blocks, such as Texas Star and Idaho Beauty.

◆ *Texas Star Tablecloth* (above), Hector, Minnesota, 1989, made from scrap star blocks pieced in about 1930; 77 inches in diameter. Instructions begin on page 120.

◆ *Little Baskets* (opposite), c. 1885; 67x98 inches. Instructions begin on page 118.

*Q*uilting bees and county fairs remained social highlights of the late 1800s, when the distance between homesteads was great and travel was slow.

Sleeping in wagons or under the stars—sometimes for 10 days or more—families traveled to regional fairs and gatherings. One farm woman wrote in 1885 that she didn't get too lonely if there were "enough quiltings during the year."

Eager for a brief respite from the chores of country life, rural folks flocked to the agricultural fairs that became so popular at the end of the century. There they showed prize livestock and their best or newest quilt.

Toward the end of this period, quilting supplies and patterns arrived at even the remotest farms by way of the U.S. mail—even if the mail came only once a week.

In 1872, Montgomery Ward was the first to make these products available to the public via mail-order catalog. Sears, Roebuck & Co. followed in 1887, featuring dry goods such as fabrics, sheeting, batting, and some patterns.

◆ *Clamshell* (*opposite*), *c. 1936; 80½x94½ inches. Instructions begin on page 123.*

Ladies Art Company of St. Louis was the first to specialize in quilt patterns by mail. These came with templates and directions, as well as cardboard color cards individually hand-painted by the owner's children after school. From 1875 to 1940, the company's catalog offered more than 400 designs.

Catalogs popularized quilt patterns previously known to few and encouraged development of new ones. Clamshell and Postage Stamp, among others, were first known in the East but became favorites everywhere.

While fashionable city women fussed over their impractical crazy quilts, rural quiltmakers continued to piece scrap quilts well into the 20th century. Many women undoubtedly found pleasure in making quilts, but perhaps just as many thought it merely a fact of life, a task of womanhood as necessary to daily life as cooking or cleaning.

With no thought of recognition, but with tireless devotion, farm women diligently labored throughout their lives. They never imagined they would be honored years later for their quilts that would survive.

◆ *Postage Stamp* (*above*), *c. 1935; 78x78 inches. Instructions begin on page 124.*

QUICK-PIECED TRIANGLE-SQUARES

Pieced triangle-squares can be cut and sewn traditionally, but using this fast and easy machine-piecing technique is a definite time-saver.

By sewing triangles on a large piece of fabric before any cutting is done, you can eliminate the tedious task of marking triangles with a template, cutting out each one, and sewing the triangle-squares one by one. With this technique, a few minutes of sewing results in a pile of ready-to-go and *accurate* triangle-squares.

Fabric requirements
In this book, the size of the fabric piece needed for the quick-piecing grid is stated in the instructions for projects that can make use of this technique. The stated size of the fabric allows for a margin of at least 1 inch all around the outside lines of the grid and is large enough that individual triangles can be cut for traditional piecing, if desired.

It is best to work with fabric pieces that are no larger than 18x22 inches.

This technique is most useful when making many triangle-squares from one combination of the same two fabrics. If you want your quilt to have more of a "scrappy" look, then use this method with small grids of several different fabric combinations, or piece the triangle-squares traditionally using scrap-bag fabrics.

Marking the grid
The only tools needed are a ruler and a marker. Use a pencil, a washout marker, or a permanent ink marker. Do not use an ordinary ballpoint pen because the ink may run when the finished quilt is washed.

The project instructions state how many grid squares to mark on the fabric. *Each marked grid square produces two finished triangle-squares.* So, if each of 10 quilt blocks has four triangle-squares, then 40 triangle-squares are needed for the quilt; the instructions, however, will call for only 20 marked squares on the grid.

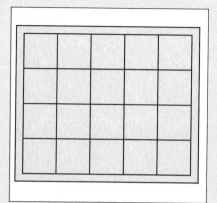

1 **Mark a grid of squares** on the *wrong side* of the lighter fabric. The size of each square, which is given in the project instructions, must be ⅞ inch *larger* than the desired *finished* size of the triangle-square. For example, if you want a 2-inch finished triangle-square, then each grid square should be 2⅞ inches square.

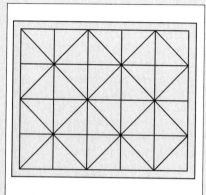

2 **Draw a diagonal line** through each square with the diagonal lines going in opposite directions in adjacent grid squares as illustrated, *above*. Place the marked fabric atop a piece of the dark fabric with right sides together and press. Pin the layers together along horizontal and vertical lines, away from intersections of diagonal lines, so the pins will not be in the way when you sew.

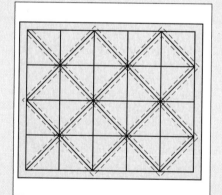

3 **Machine-stitch exactly** ¼ **inch** from *both* sides of all *diagonal* lines as illustrated, *above*. Pivot the fabric at corners without lifting the needle. When stitching is done, trim the excess fabric around the grid. Cut on all *horizontal* and *vertical* grid lines, cutting the fabric into squares. Next, cut on the diagonal lines between the stitching, cutting each square into two individual triangle-squares.

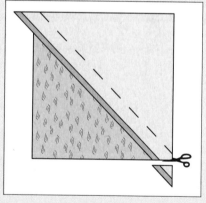

4 **Press seam allowances** toward the darker fabric. Cut off the "points" of the seam allowances, as shown, before you proceed. When handling the sewn triangle-squares, be careful not to pull on the seam line as this will stretch the bias, creating a distorted square.

Streak of Lightning Quilt

Shown on pages 106 and 107.
The finished quilt measures approximately 67½x82½ inches.

MATERIALS
3 yards of black print fabric
2¼ yards of muslin
Twelve 18x22-inch pieces of
  assorted print fabrics
⅝ yard of black checked fabric for
  binding
2⅛ yards of 90-inch-wide sheeting
  for backing fabric
72x90-inch precut quilt batting
Rotary cutter, mat, and acrylic ruler
Template material (optional)

INSTRUCTIONS
Most of the scrap fabrics in the pictured quilt are black, gray, and blue prints. Randomly placed triangles of pink, red, and gold add sparkle to the dark colors.

Instructions are given below for making triangle-squares traditionally or with quick-piecing techniques.

The assembly of this quilt is based on triangles. First six triangle-squares of print fabrics are joined with four individual small triangles to form a larger triangle. These larger triangles are then sewn to triangles of black print fabric in nine vertical rows. When the rows are assembled, the pieced triangles form a zigzag pattern across the quilt top.

Cutting the fabrics
Refer to page 289 for tips on cutting triangles from squares cut on the diagonal. To cut the small triangles traditionally, make a template of the triangle pattern, *right*.

From the black print fabric, cut:
◆ Twelve 16⅜-inch squares.
  Cut each square diagonally into quarters to obtain a total of 48 triangles. (This is three more than the 45 triangles needed.)
◆ Five 8⅜-inch squares.
  Cut each square diagonally in half to obtain 10 corner triangles; set aside the one extra triangle.

From the muslin, cut:
◆ Four 18x42-inch strips.
  Cut each strip into three 14x18-inch pieces for the triangle-squares.

From each scrap print fabric, cut:
◆ One 14x18-inch piece for the triangle-squares.
◆ Ten 3½-inch squares.
  Cut each square diagonally in half until you have a total of 216 triangles.

Making the triangle-squares
TRADITIONAL PIECING: Use the small triangle template to mark 24 triangles on each 14x18-inch piece of muslin and scrap print fabric. Cut 288 muslin triangles and 288 triangles of scrap print fabrics.

Join a muslin triangle to each print triangle. Make 288 triangle-squares. Press the seam allowances toward the darker fabric.

QUICK PIECING: Step-by-step instructions for quick-pieced triangle-squares are given *opposite*. Refer to these instructions to stitch the grids described here.
1. On the wrong side of each 14x18-inch muslin piece, mark a 3x4-square grid of 3½-inch squares as shown in Figure 1, *top right*. Layer each muslin piece, marked side up, atop a matching piece of print fabric.
2. Machine-stitch the grid as described in Step 3, *opposite*. Each grid makes 24 triangle-squares. Complete 12 grids to make a total of 288 triangle-squares.
3. Press all seam allowances toward the darker fabric.

Making the Lightning triangles
For each of the large triangles, select six random triangle-squares and four

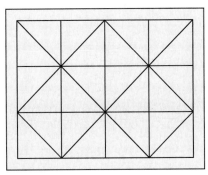

FIGURE 1

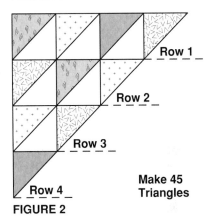

Row 1
Row 2
Row 3
Row 4

Make 45 Triangles

FIGURE 2

individual print triangles. Assemble each triangle in four rows as shown in Figure 2, *above*. Join the rows to finish the triangle.

Complete 45 large triangles.

continued

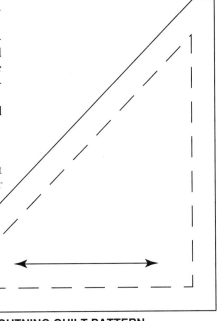

STREAK OF LIGHTNING QUILT PATTERN

CORNER TRIANGLES: For each corner triangle, select two different triangle-squares and four individual print triangles.

Sew a single triangle onto two adjacent sides of each triangle-square as illustrated in Figure 3, *below*, making a larger triangle. Matching seam lines carefully, join the two triangles to make one corner triangle.

Complete nine corner triangles.

Make 9 Corner Triangles
FIGURE 3

Assembling the quilt top

Join five pieced triangles and five triangles of black print fabric in a row as shown in Figure 4, *right*. End the row with a pieced corner triangle at the left end and a black print corner triangle at the right end, as shown in Figure 4. Press the seam allowances toward the black triangles.

Make nine vertical rows in this manner.

Lay all the assembled rows on the floor, each with the black print corner triangle at the top. Leave rows 1, 3, 5, 7, and 9 in place; turn rows 2, 4, 6, and 8 upside down so the pieced corner triangle is at the top. When the rows are correctly in place, you will see the zigzag pattern.

Stitch together the vertical rows to complete the quilt top.

Quilting and finishing

Sandwich the batting between the backing fabric and the quilt top; baste the three layers securely together.

QUILTING: A grid of 1-inch squares is quilted in the black print triangles of the quilt shown on pages 106 and

STREAK OF LIGHTNING QUILT

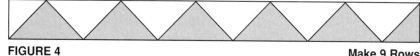

FIGURE 4   **Make 9 Rows**

107; the pieced triangles have outline quilting. Quilt as desired.

BINDING: Make at least 308 inches of binding, either bias or straight-grain. See pages 306 and 307 for tips on how to make and apply binding.

Making a larger quilt

Making more rows and/or adding more triangles in each row will enlarge the finished size of this quilt.

Add two more rows to make a full-size quilt, three rows for a queen-size, or five rows for a king-size quilt.

To make the quilt longer, add one or two of both pieced and plain large triangles to each vertical row.

For each additional row, you'll need at least ½ yard *each* of black print fabric and muslin, as well as two additional 18x22-inch pieces of scrap print fabrics.

Flying Geese Quilt

Shown on pages 108 and 109.
The finished quilt measures approximately 78x100 inches. Each Flying Geese block is 3x6 inches.

MATERIALS

3¼ yards of red print fabric for vertical stripping
1 yard of the same or a coordinating red print fabric for top and bottom borders
⅛ yard *each* of 10 medium or dark fabrics or scraps for the geese triangles
⅛ yard *each* of seven light fabrics or scraps for the sky triangles
1 yard of binding fabric
6 yards of backing fabric or 3 yards of 90-inch-wide sheeting
90x108-inch precut quilt batting
Template material
Rotary cutter, mat, and acrylic ruler

INSTRUCTIONS

This quilt gets its name from the triangular "geese" that "fly" up the quilt. The Flying Geese units are assembled in vertical rows that are then joined with alternating rows of unpieced fabric across the width of the quilt top.

Cutting the fabrics

Refer to page 288 for tips on making and using templates for patchwork. Prepare templates for patterns A and B, *right*. Cut notches in the templates as indicated on the patterns.

From the red print fabric, cut:
◆ Four 8½x85-inch strips for the inner vertical rows.
◆ Six 8½x29-inch strips for the outer vertical rows.
Add the remaining red print fabric to the dark print scraps.

From the red print border fabric, cut:
◆ Four 8½x42-inch strips.

From the light fabrics, cut:
◆ 140 of Pattern A.
Place the template grain line on the crosswise grain. Turn the template up and down to mark common cutting lines for adjacent triangles and to maximize use of the fabric.

From the medium and dark fabrics, cut:
◆ 280 of Pattern B.

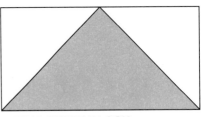

FLYING GEESE BLOCK

Making the Flying Geese blocks

For each block, match one A triangle with a pair of B triangles. Sort the cut triangles into sets for 140 blocks, varying the fabric combinations as much as possible.
1. With right sides together and matching both notches, sew a B triangle onto one side of the A triangle. Press the seam allowance toward the B triangle.
2. In the same manner, stitch the second B triangle onto the remaining notched side of the A triangle.
Make 140 Flying Geese blocks.

continued

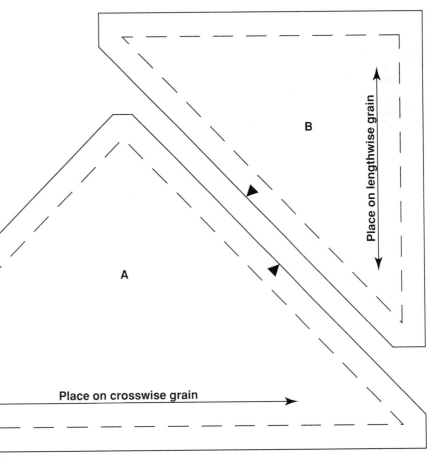

FLYING GEESE QUILT PATTERNS

Making rows of Flying Geese

Before sewing the blocks together, lay them out on the floor or another flat surface. Arrange the blocks in five vertical rows with 28 blocks in each row. Be sure the geese in each row are flying in the same direction.

Lay the print fabric strips between Flying Geese rows to help you see the effect. Move the geese blocks around to find a pleasing arrangement.

Join 28 blocks in a vertical row, sewing the top of one block to the bottom of the block above it. If your patchwork is precise, the seam line will cross the tip of each A triangle.

Press the joining seam allowances toward the A triangles. Stitch and press five rows of Flying Geese.

Assembling the quilt top

1. Fold *each* of the four 85-inch-long strips of red print fabric in fourths, or measure 21¼-inch sections down the length of the strip. Mark each quarter-section with a pin on both sides of the strip. This is important for matching the horizontal seam lines of the Flying Geese units.

2. Sew the four red print strips between the rows of Flying Geese, matching the marked points of each red strip with the horizontal seam line of every seventh geese unit.

3. Join three 8½x29-inch red print strips end to end to make one strip for each outside edge. Stitch these strips onto the long sides of the quilt; trim excess fabric even with the ends of the quilt top.

4. Join two 8½x42-inch strips of the red print border fabric to make one strip. On the top edge of the quilt, match the center seam of the border strip with the center of the middle row of Flying Geese. With right sides together, stitch the top border onto the quilt. Press the seam allowance toward the border fabric; trim the border fabric even with the sides of the quilt top.

5. In the same manner, make one more border strip; join it to the bottom edge of the quilt top.

Quilting and finishing

BACKING: To piece the backing fabric, cut two 3-yard lengths; split one piece lengthwise. Sew a narrow panel onto each side of the wide panel.

Layer backing, batting, and quilt top; baste the three layers together.

QUILTING: The quilt shown on pages 108 and 109 has a cable design quilted in the red fabric strips and outline quilting inside all the light triangles. Quilt as desired.

BINDING: Make 370 inches of bias or straight-grain binding. See pages 306 and 307 for tips on making and applying binding.

Making a larger quilt

The size of this quilt is suitable for most twin or full-size beds.

To make a wider quilt, simply add more vertical rows. To make the quilt longer, make additional Flying Geese units or add wider borders to the top and bottom of the quilt.

When making a larger quilt, remember to adjust the yardage for the red print fabric and the backing fabric. A larger batt also is necessary.

Little Basket Quilt

Shown on page 111.
The finished quilt measures approximately 67x98 inches. Each Basket block is 7 inches square.

MATERIALS

4 yards *each* of muslin and red plaid fabric
98 assorted 5x8-inch fabric scraps for baskets, totaling 2⅞ yards
1 yard of binding fabric
6 yards of backing fabric or 2¼ yards of 108-inch-wide sheeting
90x108-inch precut quilt batting
Template material

INSTRUCTIONS

Like the Streak of Lightning and Flying Geese quilts in this chapter, the Little Basket Quilt is set in vertical rows. Each of the seven rows has 14 Basket blocks. Three strips of sashing separate the vertical rows of blocks.

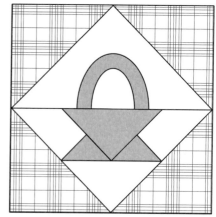

LITTLE BASKET BLOCK

Cutting the fabrics

Refer to page 288 for tips on making templates for patchwork and appliqué. Prepare templates for patterns A through E, *opposite.*

In the original quilt, the sashing strips are cut on the straight grain of the plaid and the block corners are cut on the bias. This makes the plaids contrast nicely, but it also requires more yardage and adds the difficulty of working with bias edges on the outside of the blocks. The yardage given below is for block corners cut on the straight of the grain.

From the muslin, cut:
◆ Twelve 1½x100-inch sashing strips.
◆ 98 *each* of patterns A, C, D, and D reversed.

From the red plaid fabric, cut:
◆ Six 1½x100-inch sashing strips.
◆ 196 4½-inch squares.
    Cut each square diagonally in half to get 392 corner triangles.

From each scrap fabric, cut:
◆ One *each* of patterns B and C. Add a ³⁄₁₆-inch seam allowance around the template when cutting the B basket handles.
◆ Two of Pattern E.

Making the Basket block

This block is a nice combination of patchwork and appliqué. The curved handle is appliquéd onto the muslin A triangle before the basket is pieced. Plaid corner triangles, sewn onto the basket square, complete the block.

1. Referring to the block assembly diagram, *below,* stitch an E triangle onto the bottom edges of the D and D reversed pieces. Press the seam allowances toward the E triangles.

2. Sew the DE units onto the short legs of the C triangle of scrap fabric, positioning the pieces as shown in the diagram. Press the seam allowances toward the C triangle.

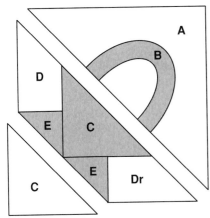

LITTLE BASKET BLOCK ASSEMBLY DIAGRAM

3. Complete the bottom of the Basket block with the muslin C triangle as shown in the assembly diagram; press the seam allowance toward the muslin triangle.

4. Turn under the seam allowance on the *curved* edges of the handle (B). Center the handle fabric on the muslin A triangle, matching raw edges. Appliqué the curved edges of the handle in place on the muslin.

5. Join the two halves of the basket block. Press the seam allowances toward the A triangle.

6. Complete the block by adding a plaid corner triangle to each side of the basket block. Press the seam allowances toward the plaid fabric.

Make 98 Basket blocks.

To assemble the quilt top
1. Join the blocks end to end in seven vertical rows of 14 blocks each.

2. Stitch a plaid sashing strip between two muslin sashing strips; press the seam allowances toward the plaid fabric. Make six muslin-plaid-muslin sashings.

continued

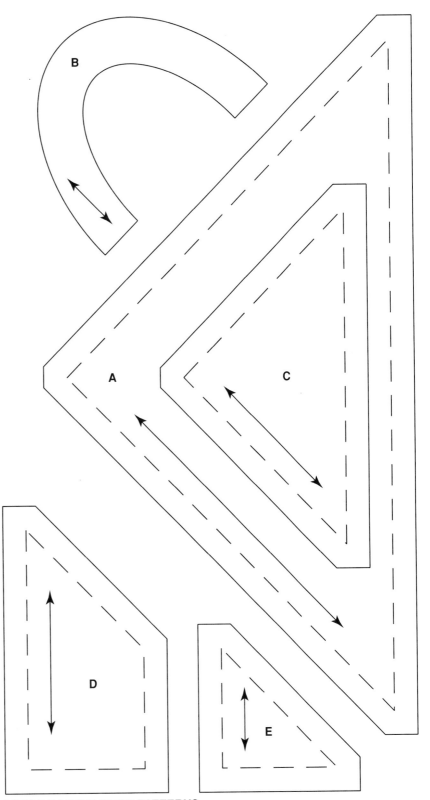

LITTLE BASKET QUILT PATTERNS

3. Starting 1 inch from the top of the sashing unit, measure 7-inch sections down the length of the strip. Mark each section with a pin on both sides of the strip. This is important for matching the horizontal seam lines of the Basket blocks.

4. Join the block rows with sashing strips between each row, matching the pins in each sashing unit with the block seam lines. Press the seam allowances toward the sashing. Trim the sashing even with the blocks at the top and bottom of the quilt top.

Quilting and finishing
BACKING: Divide the backing fabric into two 3-yard pieces. Sew the panels together; press the seam allowance open.

Layer the quilt top, batting, and backing fabric; baste the three layers securely together.

QUILTING: Quilt as desired. The quilt shown on page 111 has a diagonal grid of 1-inch squares stitched across the baskets and in the plaid corner triangles; a single line of quilting is stitched in the center of each sashing strip.

BINDING: Make 340 inches of bias or straight-grain binding. See pages 306 and 307 for tips on making and applying binding.

Texas Star Tablecloth
Shown on page 110.
The finished tablecloth is approximately 77 inches in diameter. Each finished Texas Star block is 12¾ inches wide.

MATERIALS
4¾ yards of muslin for patchwork and binding
Nineteen 10-inch squares of assorted print fabrics for the stars
Nineteen 4½-inch squares of assorted solid fabrics for the star centers
4¾ yards of backing fabric
81-inch square of quilt batting
Template material

INSTRUCTIONS
The tablecloth shown on page 110 has 19 hexagonal Texas Star blocks joined with hexagons of muslin. The vintage stars were bought at a yard sale and assembled into this tablecloth. Small projects of this type are ideal for using small numbers of blocks whether they are antique or leftovers from another quilt.

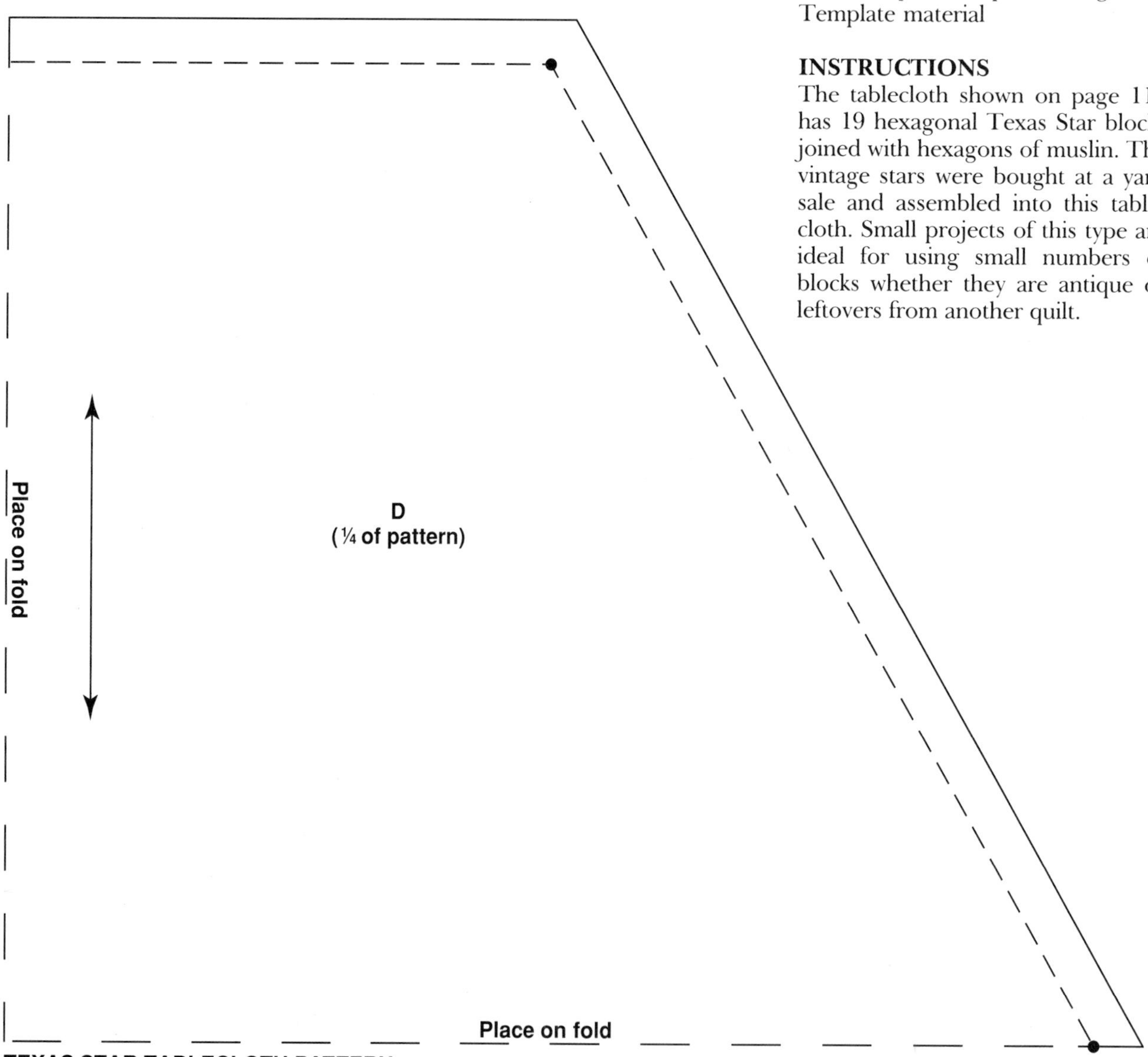

Place on fold

D
(¼ of pattern)

Place on fold

TEXAS STAR TABLECLOTH PATTERN

Hand piecing is recommended for this project because of the many set-ins. Refer to page 163 for tips on making set-in seams.

Cutting the fabrics
Refer to page 288 for tips on making window templates. Following these instructions, prepare templates for patterns A, B, C, and D, on this page and *opposite*.

To make a complete pattern for D, trace the pattern onto the template material four times, turning the tem-
continued

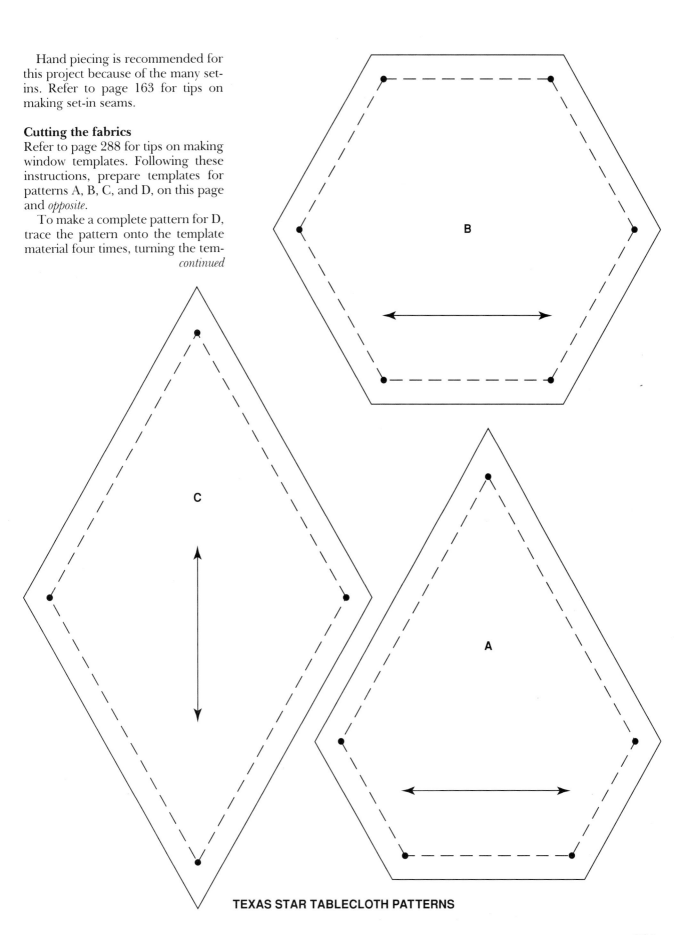

TEXAS STAR TABLECLOTH PATTERNS

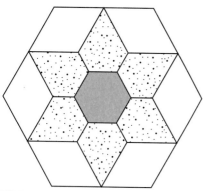

TEXAS STAR BLOCK

plate each time to draw another quarter of the hexagon. When tracing the templates on the fabrics, mark both cutting and sewing lines.

From each print fabric, cut:
◆ Six of Pattern A.

From each solid fabric, cut:
◆ One of Pattern B.

From the muslin, cut:
◆ One ¾-yard length for binding.
◆ 18 of Pattern D, cutting three across the width of the fabric.
◆ 114 of Pattern C.

Assembling the Star blocks
As you join the pieces, sew on the drawn seam lines only; do not stitch into the seam allowance. This is important, since the seam allowance must be available to receive the next set-in piece.

1. For each star, match one B center piece with a set of six A star points. Sew one A piece onto one side of the B hexagon. Press the seam allowance toward the A piece.
2. Referring to Figure 1, *below,* stitch another A piece onto the next side of

the B hexagon. Then bring the adjacent sides of the A pieces together with right sides together and stitch the seam. Press the A seam allowance toward the first A piece.
3. Continue adding A pieces around the star center in this manner until all six star points are connected.
4. Referring to the block drawing, *left,* set six C diamonds into the spaces between the star points. Press seam allowances toward the A pieces.
   Make 19 Texas Star blocks.

Assembling the tablecloth
Compare the completed Star blocks with the D hexagons—they should be the same size.
1. Refer to the tablecloth assembly diagram, *below,* as you join the Star blocks. Begin in the center of the tablecloth with a single block. Add blocks around the center in the order indicated in the diagram.

2. Add the muslin hexagons around the outside edge as shown.

Quilting and finishing
BACKING: Divide the backing fabric into two equal lengths. Sew the two panels together; press the seam allowance open. Sandwich the batting between the backing fabric and the quilt top; baste the three layers securely together.

QUILTING: The tablecloth shown on page 110 is quilted with a diagonal grid of 1-inch squares. Quilt as desired. Trim batting and backing even with the top.

BINDING: Use the remaining muslin to make approximately 300 inches of binding, either bias or straight-grain. See pages 306 and 307 for tips on making and applying binding.

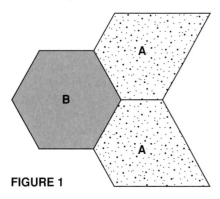

FIGURE 1

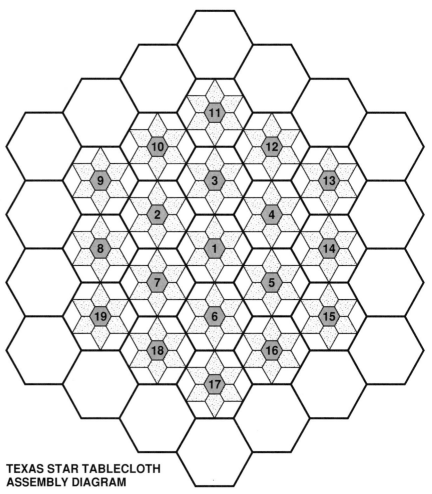

**TEXAS STAR TABLECLOTH
ASSEMBLY DIAGRAM**

Clamshell Quilt

Shown on page 112.
The finished quilt measures approximately 80½x94½ inches.

MATERIALS

5 yards of muslin or scraps of assorted light-colored fabrics for the clamshells
3½ yards or scraps of assorted medium- and dark-colored fabrics for the clamshells
2¾ yards of blue checked fabric for borders, binding, and shells
5¾ yards of backing fabric
81x96-inch precut quilt batting
Template material
Rotary cutter, mat, and acrylic ruler

INSTRUCTIONS

The Clamshell Quilt is made in alternating rows of light and dark fabrics. Our quilt has only muslin in the light-colored rows, but you may want to use a variety of light-colored prints and solids for a more scrappy look.

Cutting the fabrics

Refer to page 288 for tips on making window templates. Make a template for the clamshell pattern, *right*. Mark both the cutting and sewing lines on the right side of the shell fabrics.

From the blue checked fabric, cut:
◆ Two 4x83-inch strips and two 4x96-inch strips for the border.
◆ One 26x36-inch piece for binding.
Use the remaining border fabric to make shells.

From the muslin or light-colored fabrics, cut:
◆ 598 clamshells.

From the darker scrap fabrics, cut:
◆ 550 clamshells.

Assembling the quilt top

1. Baste back the seam allowance along the top curved edge of each clamshell, leaving the lower curves and the bottom unturned.
2. Working on a flat surface (an ironing board is ideal), lay out a horizon-

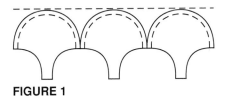

FIGURE 1

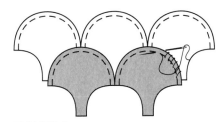

FIGURE 2

tal row of 23 light-colored clamshells. Referring to Figure 1, *above, top,* make sure the top edges are even and the sides touch, but do not overlap.
3. Position a row of 22 dark shells below the first row, lapping the second row over the bottom halves of the light shells as shown in Figure 2, *above.* Using a blind hemming stitch, appliqué the curved edges of the dark shells in place atop the light shells.
4. Continue to add rows of light and dark clamshells in this manner. Join

25 rows of dark shells and 26 rows of light shells. The light-colored rows are a half-shell longer on both sides than the dark rows.
5. The quilt top should be approximately 80½x91 inches. The light shells in the top and bottom rows and at the sides can be trimmed before or after the borders are added.

To trim the top, align a ruler ¼ inch above the top row of dark shells. With a rotary cutter, carefully cut away the top of the first row of light shells. At the bottom of the quilt top, cut ¼ inch below the tip of the last dark row, removing the bottom half of the last row of light shells.

On the right edge of the quilt top, place the ruler ¼ inch to the right of the dark shells to trim the excess fabric of the light shells. Repeat on the left edge of the quilt, cutting ¼ inch from the left side of the dark shells.

Adding the borders

Center the border strips on each edge of the quilt top. Refer to page 299 for instructions on sewing borders with mitered corners.

continued

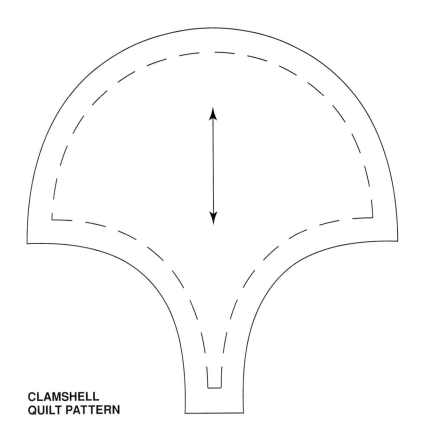

**CLAMSHELL
QUILT PATTERN**

Quilting and finishing

BACKING: Divide the backing fabric into two equal lengths. Sew the two panels together; press the seam allowance open.

Sandwich the batting between the backing and the quilt top; baste the three layers together.

QUILTING: The quilt shown on page 112 has outline quilting inside the curves of each clamshell. The border is quilted with straight lines perpendicular to the edges of the quilt. Quilt as desired.

BINDING: Use the remaining blue checked fabric to make approximately 360 inches of binding. See pages 306 and 307 for tips on making and applying binding.

Postage Stamp Quilt

Shown on page 113.
These instructions are for a finished quilt approximately 78x104 inches (see note below). Each block is 26 inches square.

MATERIALS

4¾ yards of yellow solid fabric for patchwork and binding
1¼ yards *each* of black and orange solid fabrics
1 yard of green solid fabric
Thirty-three ¼-yard pieces or scraps of assorted print fabrics
6⅜ yards of backing fabric or 3⅜ yards of 90-inch-wide sheeting
90x108-inch precut quilt batting
Rotary cutter, mat, and acrylic ruler

INSTRUCTIONS

This is the ultimate scrap lover's quilt. Even the tiniest scraps can be used in this timeless patchwork.

Note: The quilt shown on page 113 has three blocks across and 3¼ blocks down. (Because of all the piecing, it may be difficult to find the outline of each block in the photo.) To simplify the assembly and to achieve a more useful length, these instructions are for a 12-block quilt with three blocks across and four down.

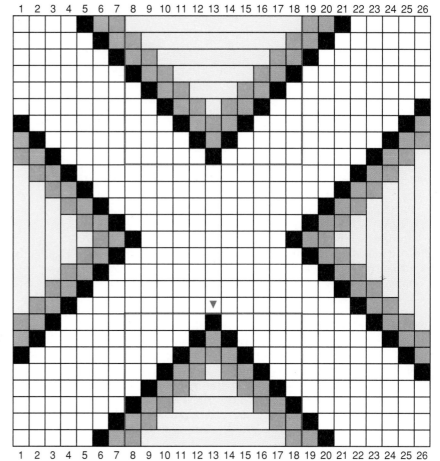

COLOR KEY ☐ Yellow ■ Black ▨ Green ▨ Orange
POSTAGE STAMP BLOCK ASSEMBLY DIAGRAM

Refer to the block assembly diagram, *above*, while cutting fabrics and making the Postage Stamp blocks.

Cutting the fabrics

From the yellow fabric, cut:
◆ Eighty-five 1½x42-inch strips. From these strips, cut 24 pieces 1½x11½ inches and 48 *each* of the following: 1½x9½ inches, 1½x7½ inches, 1½x5½ inches, 1½x3½ inches, and 1½-inch squares.

From the black fabric, cut:
◆ Twenty-nine 1½x42-inch strips.

From the orange fabric, cut:
◆ Twenty-five 1½x42-inch strips.

From the green fabric, cut:
◆ Twenty-one 1½x42-inch strips.

From each scrap fabric, cut:
◆ Five or six 1½x42-inch strips, cutting a total of 166 strips. From each strip, cut twenty-eight 1½-inch squares. Cut 386 squares of scrap fabric for each block, a total of 4,632 for the 12-block quilt.

Piecing the three-square and two-square units

In the quilt pictured, each yellow diamond is encircled by rows of green, orange, and black squares.

Using the following instructions, you can strip-piece these units before assembling the block to reduce the amount of piecing required later. If you prefer to assemble these units traditionally, one square at a time, you can sew them either by hand or by machine.

TRADITIONAL PIECING:

1. From the 1½x42-inch strips of green, orange, and black fabrics, cut forty-eight 1½-inch squares of *each* fabric for one block.

2. Sew one orange square between a black and a green square as shown at the left of Figure 1, *below*. Press the seam allowances toward the orange fabric. Make 48 three-square units for each block.

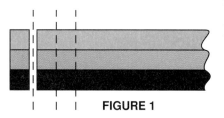

FIGURE 1

3. Make two-square units in the same manner, using squares of black and orange fabric. Press the seam allowances toward the orange fabric. Make eight two-square units for each block.

4. Cut the remaining four strips of black fabric into ninety-six 1½-inch squares for the block patchwork.

STRIP PIECING:

1. Machine-stitch one 1½x42-inch strip of orange fabric between strips of green and black fabrics as shown in Figure 1, *above*. Press the seam allowances toward the orange fabric.

2. Using a rotary cutter and a ruler, measure and cut 1½-inch-wide vertical units from the strip set as shown in Figure 1. Cut 28 three-square units from each strip set.

Each block has 48 three-square units, so start by making two strip sets for each block. Set aside the eight extra units from the second strip set until you have enough to use for a later block.

3. Make two-square units in the same manner, using strips of black and orange fabric. Press the seam allowance toward the orange fabric. Cut eight two-square units for each block.

4. Cut the remaining four strips of black fabric into ninety-six 1½-inch squares for the block patchwork.

Making the horizontal sections

The Postage Stamp block is assembled in 26 vertical rows as indicated in the assembly diagram, *opposite*.

However, because some of the yellow strips are horizontal, sections of the block are preassembled, as described below, to avoid awkward corners.

At the top and bottom of the block assembly diagram are sections outlined in red. Assemble these sections before joining the rest of the block. Begin with the section at the bottom of the block.

1. Start at the center of the section, indicated by the red arrow on the diagram. Stitch a 1½-inch square of yellow fabric onto the green square of one three-square unit. Press the seam allowance toward the yellow fabric.

2. Sew one scrap square onto the black end of two other three-square units; press the seam allowance toward the scrap fabric. Positioning the fabrics as shown in the diagram, sew the three units together with the yellow square in the center between the green squares as shown.

3. Sew a 1½x3½-inch yellow strip across the end of this assembled unit as illustrated. Press the seam allowance toward the yellow strip.

4. Join two scrap squares onto the black end of two other three-square units. Stitch one of these onto each side of the center section, aligning the green square of each unit with the yellow strip at the bottom of the center section.

5. Sew a 1½x5½-inch yellow strip across the end of the assembled unit. Press the seam allowance toward the yellow strip. Following the diagram, continue assembling the bottom section in this manner until the section is complete.

6. Follow steps 1 through 5 again to make the section at the top of the block. Complete *this* section by adding a 1½x11½-inch yellow strip at the top as shown in the diagram.

Assembling the block

1. Assemble the center scrap section of rows 8 through 18, positioning black squares in rows 8 and 18 as shown. Join the squares in vertical rows, pressing all seam allowances in the same direction. Then assemble the rows, turning alternate rows upside down to alternate the direction of the seam allowances.

2. Join the three sections of rows 8 through 18 to complete the center section of the block.

3. Referring to the assembly diagram, construct rows 1 through 7 by sewing scrap squares, three-square units, and yellow strips end to end in vertical rows.

4. Join rows 1 through 7, then stitch the assembled unit onto the left side of the center section.

5. Make rows 19 through 26 in the same manner; stitch this unit onto the right side of the center section.

Make 12 Postage Stamp blocks. As you finish each block, *mark the top of the block with a pin* to avoid confusion later.

Assembling the quilt top

Join the blocks in four horizontal rows of three blocks each. Make sure the pinned side of each block is at the top. Assemble the four rows to complete the quilt top.

Quilting and finishing

BACKING: Divide the backing fabric into two equal lengths. Sew the panels together; press the seam allowance open.

Layer the quilt top, batting, and backing fabric; baste the three layers securely together.

QUILTING: Quilt as desired. The quilt shown on page 113 has outline quilting on the yellow strips and a diagonal line quilted through each 1-inch square.

BINDING: Make 375 inches of bias or straight-grain binding. See pages 306 and 307 for tips on making and applying binding.

Making a larger quilt

The size of this quilt is suitable for most twin, full, and queen-size beds. Adding a fourth block to each horizontal row will make a wider quilt, suitable for a king-size bed.

When making a larger quilt, adjust the required yardage for all fabrics. A larger batt also is necessary.

Victorian Fancies

Fashion Demands Silks and Satins

1876 ∽ 1900

◆ *Crazy Quilt, c. 1884;*
74x74 inches. General
instructions for crazy quilts
begin on page 134.

You can spoil the prettiest quilt pieces that
ever was made just by putting them together with
the wrong color, just as the best sort of life
is miserable if you don't look at things right and
think about them right.

Eliza Calvert Hall, *Aunt Jane of Kentucky*

*I*n the 1880s, a man's measure of success was enhanced if his wife was considered a lady. A life of domestic chores was hardly a hallmark of prosperity, so a lady was expected to devote many leisurely hours to fancy needlework that she could use to decorate her ornate Victorian parlor.

The socially conscious Victorians wanted their homes to be places of elegance, culture, harmony, and spiritual enrichment. Believing that an attractive home contributed to the beauty of the soul, Victorians approached home decorating as a solemn duty.

European design trends were faithfully reported by the press. American women eagerly imitated Britain's Queen Victoria,

who gave her name to the era. Sentimental to a fault, Victoria collected keepsakes of her beloved Albert and their many offspring until she lived amid so many memorabilia that she had to hold court in the hallways of Windsor Castle because her rooms were too crowded to admit visitors.

Striving to emulate the Queen's clutter, Victorians covered their belongings with something extra. Lace, ribbon, ruffles, and fringe appeared in profusion on everything from garments to pillows.

Crazy quilting was an ideal and ladylike outlet for this decorative fervor. Crazy-quilted throws, piano scarves, and other impractical pieces were made with delicate and fragile fabrics, and embellished with sentimental messages and mementos of ribbons and cloth. Nearly useless as quilts, they served as elegant ornaments in the jumble of the Victorian home.

◆ *Victorian Fan (left),*
c. 1890; 80x96 inches.
Instructions begin on
page 138.

◆ *Crazy Quilt* (above),
c. 1880; 70x86 inches.
General instructions for
crazy quilts begin on
page 134.

Most Victorian crazy quilts are not quilts in the true sense because they were not layered with batting and then quilted; they were made to be decorative, not useful. Victorians loved ornamentation, and the more ornamentation, the better.

Unlike other patchwork, crazy quilting reflects the Victorian rejection of simplicity and right angles. *Godey's Lady's Book*, the first national women's magazine, published articles and instructions for making crazy quilts that warned against straight lines and "any angularities offending the eye."

With this type of guidance, Victorian women crafted knickknacks and bric-a-brac by embellishing everyday items with festoons of braid, tassels, or arrangements of beads, feathers, shells, lace, and even human hair.

This decorative labor, called fancywork, gave every woman—rich or poor—a way to enrich her home with found objects. *Godey's* urged women to be industrious in such work, since these items were "not trifles but *arts* that elevate human feeling above animal instincts."

Some quilt historians suggest that the Victorian fascination with crazy quilts started with a picture of a Japanese crazed pavement. The Japanese "cracked ice" china that was popular during the 1880s is another possible source of inspiration.

The Oriental influence is evident in many antique crazy quilts. The Centennial Exposition of

1876 was important to the evolution of American crazy quilting because the Japanese pavilion there was hugely successful.

Held in Philadelphia, the Exposition featured exhibits from many lands, but none was as popular as that from Japan. Visited by nearly 10 million people, the pavilion introduced Americans to new design concepts. Anything Japanese became all the rage; in the 1880s, even the word "Japanese"

became synonymous with asymmetrical design. Period fabrics, wallpapers, and embroidered pieces reflected the popularity of Japanese themes.

Embroidery designs for crazy quilts were available from mail-order firms and magazines. Some patterns were perforated so that ink or powder sprinkled over the holes marked the design on fabric. In 1883, *Peterson's Magazine* printed an array of Oriental fans and flowers for needle-work, saying the "superiority of the Japanese in designs of this kind . . . is universally conceded."

The crazy quilt shown *opposite* includes examples of such designs, including fans, swallows in flight, owls and other birds perched on gnarled branches, butterflies, and a kimono-clad couple.

◆ *Sunburst Block (above), a preserved segment of a tattered Victorian quilt, c. 1890; 12 inches in diameter. Instructions begin on page 139.*

♦ *Log Cabin Pillow*
(above), c. 1890;
20x20 inches. Instructions
begin on page 140.

Ornamental patchwork first became popular in the United States in the early 1850s, when American-made silk became widely available. At an 1852 fair, a blue ribbon was awarded for a quilt made entirely of silk and taffeta hexagons and trimmed with a silk fringe.

Godey's Lady's Book published instructions for similar quilts and recommended ornamental patchwork as "an agreeable and genteel occupation for ladies."

The fussy extravagance of Victorian high taste called for rich, dark fabrics in all forms of patchwork. Silk Log Cabin quilts, such as the one *opposite*, were described in the 1882 London edition of *The Dictionary of Needlework* as typical of American quiltmaking.

Even rural families did not escape fashion's demands. *The Good Old Days,* a reminiscence of country life at the turn of the century, described how a "silk quilt in intricate design set a woman high in the community." Such a quilt was valued as a status symbol for its expensive material rather than its intrinsic merit or workmanship.

Amid this extravagance, traditional quilts—so highly valued in Colonial times—acquired the label "poor man's comforters."

Most Victorians preferred to buy ready-made bedding from the new Montgomery Ward and Sears, Roebuck & Co. catalogs that enabled affordable goods to reach even the remotest farms. Both catalogs offered fabrics, batting, and a few patterns. In the 1890 Ward's catalog, materials for a full-size quilt cost only $1.60, but wool blankets cost $2.25 to $8.

Relegated to make-do status for the poor, traditional quilts were denounced by fashionable magazines as "ugly, common, and a menace to the public health." Even magazines aimed at rural readers, such as *Farmer's Wife* or *Farm and Fireside*, rarely offered quilt patterns until after 1900.

By the turn of the century, cheap manufactured products had nearly eliminated the need for home sewing. Except as ornaments, quilts began to lose their place in the American home.

♦ *Sunshine and Shadow*
Log Cabin (opposite),
c. 1890; 77x82½ inches.
Instructions begin on
page 141.

CRAZY-QUILTING TECHNIQUES

The charm of crazy quilting is that there is no set pattern, thus no two quilts are the same. A crazy quilt grows as it is worked—too much planning rarely produces the satisfactory results achieved by spontaneity.

In addition to the construction techniques described here, see pages 136 and 137 for tips on embroidery stitches and other embellishments.

Working on a foundation

Like string piecing, crazy quilting is stitched onto a base fabric that serves as a foundation. For a large quilt, it is practical to make small units that are then joined.

To make a crazy-quilted garment, begin with foundation pieces that are slightly larger than the corresponding pattern piece; once the foundation pieces are covered with crazy quilting, cut them to the size and shape of the patterns.

Victorian construction techniques

Victorian crazy quilters nearly always appliquéd the fabric pieces onto the foundation in a random fashion. In some cases, a large piece was basted onto the foundation and then smaller pieces were stitched on or around it.

In some quilts, construction units remain defined in the finished work, as in the quilt shown on page 130. In others, pieces at the edges of adjacent blocks were appliquéd over each other to obscure the joining line.

Modern construction techniques

Crazy quilting can be stitched by machine. The two techniques described here are similar to string piecing. Steps 1a–d, *right,* describe the Fan Method; steps 2a–c, *opposite,* explain the Center Method.

A combination of techniques is illustrated in steps 3, 4, and 5.

When the crazy-quilted piece is completely assembled, layer it atop backing fabric and bind the edges (few crazy quilts have batting between the layers). Tying the top and backing fabric together is optional.

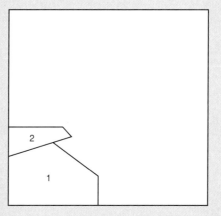

1a **With the Fan Method,** you start in a corner and build outward, fanning back and forth from one side of the foundation to the other. Begin by placing Piece 1 flush with one corner of the foundation. This piece should have four or five sides as shown *above.* Place Piece 2 on the top side of Piece 1 with right sides together; machine-stitch through the pieces and the foundation. Flip the second piece to the right side and press.

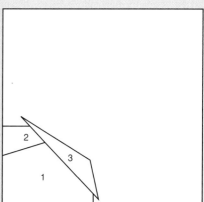

1b Align Piece 3 with the second side of the corner piece, making sure it extends over both of the previously sewn pieces. Stitch it down in the same manner as before. Trim any excess fabric from the seam allowance, then flip Piece 3 to the right side and press the piece flat.

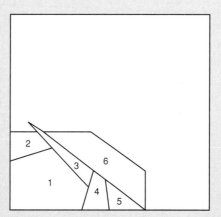

1c Cover the third side of the corner piece with Piece 4 in the same manner—sew it down, flip it over, and press. When all the sides of Piece 1 are stitched, start working back in the opposite direction to lay down the next level as indicated by pieces 5 and 6, *above.*

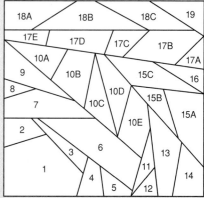

1d Fan back and forth from right to left, then left to right, adding pieces until the foundation is filled. If you encounter an awkward angle, it is easiest to appliqué the edges in place. To fill in a long edge, piece a separate unit that can be stitched in place as one piece (see pieces 10, 15, 17, and 18 *above*). Trim each seam allowance and press each piece flat before adding the next piece.

134

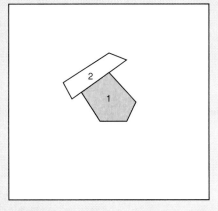

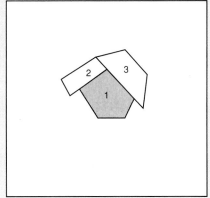

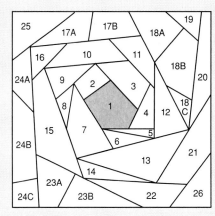

2a **Begin the Center Method** by placing Piece 1 at the approximate center of the foundation. If this is a dark fabric, it will appear to recede, bringing attention to the center; a light fabric will have the opposite effect. Piece 1 should have five or six sides. With right sides together, sew the next fabric piece onto any side of Piece 1 using a standard ¼-inch seam allowance. Flip Piece 2 over to the right side, then press it flat.

2b Stitch Piece 3 onto the next side of the center piece, making sure it completely covers the edges of pieces 1 and 2 as shown *above*. Trim excess fabric from the seam allowance, then press Piece 3 to the right side. The work can go clockwise or counter-clockwise, but maintain the same direction throughout construction of the block.

2c Continue adding fabric pieces in this manner, working outward from the center. To fill in a long edge, piece a separate unit that can be sewn in place as one piece (see pieces 17, 18, 23, and 24 in the example *above*). Once the foundation is filled, trim all pieces even with the edges of the foundation. If you are working with separate blocks, stitch embroidery designs on each block as desired before joining them.

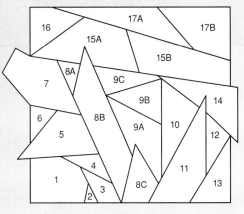

3 **Combine techniques** for added interest. As you sew, leave some points and angles unstitched so they can be appliquéd over an adjacent piece later (see pieces 8B, 8C, and 11 *above*). Overlapping pieces break up long seam lines. Leave some pieces at the block edges untrimmed (pieces 5, 7, and 14) so they can be appliquéd onto the adjacent block to obscure the joining seam.

4 **Appliqués cover seam lines** and trouble spots, and their varied shapes add charm to a crazy quilt. Hearts, crescent moons, bows, and flowers are some appliqué motifs that work nicely in crazy quilting. When the piecing is complete, hand-stitch appliqués over the seams to interrupt straight lines.

5 **Pieced fans** are frequently seen in antique crazy quilts. A fan can be appliquéd onto the crazy quilt piecing or stitched into a seam as shown *above*. The curved edge is left loose as you add more pieces, then it is appliquéd over the completed patchwork. This is an excellent way to introduce curves and other shapes that break up long, straight seam lines.

EMBELLISHMENTS FOR CRAZY QUILTING

It is the unrestrained profusion of varied fabrics and personalized decorative detail that makes antique crazy quilts interesting to examine and new crazy quilts so much fun to make.

Today's fabric stores stock a myriad of lush fabrics, delectable laces, buttons, and ribbons that offer great possibilities for crazy quilting.

SELECTING FABRICS

Because crazy quilts are rarely used and washed in the same manner as other quilts, any fabric can be used—even ones considered too fragile or impractical for traditional quilts.

For elegance, experiment with velvet, velveteen, moiré, satin, and silk. For a more informal look, use cotton, wool, and thin-waled corduroy. The remnant table at any fabric store is a wonderful hunting ground for small pieces of exotic fabrics suitable for crazy quilting.

Scraps of ribbon, clothing, handkerchiefs, neckties, upholstery, and leftover fabrics are fun to use, especially if they have sentimental value.

Mix textures, patterns, and solids

Use different fabric textures and patterns to achieve the integrated mix that makes a crazy quilt so delightful.

A solid fabric without nap shows embroidery to its best advantage, but a quilt made with just solids requires a lot of embellishment to be interesting—add random pieces of brocade or paisley print to balance the solids. In the same way, napped fabrics, such as velvet, will add interesting texture when mixed with other fabrics.

EMBROIDERY

Embroidery is to crazy quilting as frosting is to a cake. The stitches *opposite* and others can be used to cover seam lines or embellish a narrow fabric strip or ribbon. Victorian crazy quilts are rich tapestries of embroidered animals, flowers, and Oriental motifs. Outlines of a baby's hands or feet frequently appear.

EMBROIDERY DETAIL FROM CRAZY QUILT ON PAGES 126 AND 127

Stitch embroidery motifs and pictures onto large fabric pieces, which can be trimmed to fit into the patchwork, or onto a pieced block before the quilt is assembled.

Any drawing or photograph you can trace can become an embroidery motif. Victorians perforated magazine pictures with large needles so the printed image could be outlined on the fabric with a powder, such as talcum or cinnamon. Since powder rubs off as a piece is handled, lightly trace the outlined shape in pencil.

Spiders and webs

Victorian crazy quilts frequently feature an embroidered spider and a web. According to European folklore, spiders in needlework are a symbol of good fortune.

A web is easy to stitch. The spokes and concentric rings of the web are couched in place, as shown, *opposite*. Use metallic threads to make a web shimmer. A web is most effective when it is stitched in a light-color thread on a dark background.

Use beads for the spider's body; make lazy daisy or straight stitches for the legs.

OTHER EMBELLISHMENTS

Once the foundation is completely filled, add trims such as lace, ribbon, and appliqués. Small doilies and lacy handkerchiefs add interest.

Cover seam lines and appliqués with embroidery, then add beads and buttons as desired. Clusters of buttons create interesting shapes. Novelty buttons, such as flowers, stars, and animals, add a touch of whimsy.

BASIC EMBROIDERY STITCHES

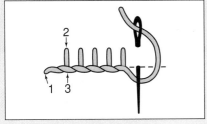

BUTTONHOLE STITCH

CHAIN STITCH

COUCHING STITCH

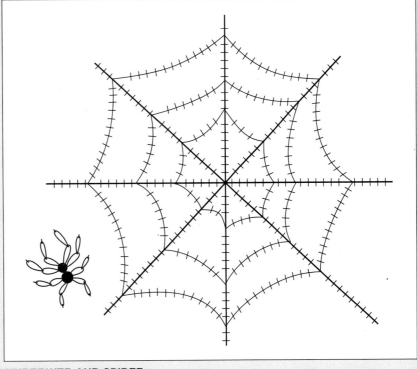

SPIDERWEB AND SPIDER

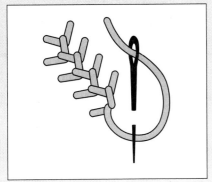

FEATHERSTITCH

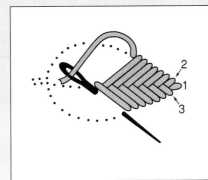

FISHBONE STITCH

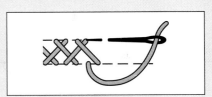

HERRINGBONE STITCH

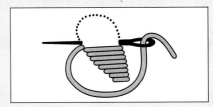

SATIN STITCH

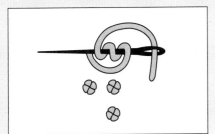

FRENCH KNOT

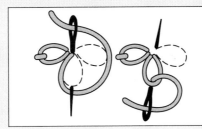

LAZY DAISY STITCH

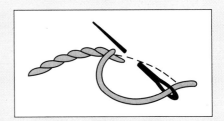

OUTLINE (or STEM) STITCH

Victorian Fan Quilt

Shown on pages 128 and 129.
The finished quilt measures approximately 80x96 inches. Each finished fan block is 8 inches square.

MATERIALS
6 yards of 44/45-inch-wide black solid fabric or 4½ yards of 60-inch-wide fabric
¼ yard *each* of 18 assorted light-color fabrics and 20 dark fabrics for the fans
1 yard of binding fabric
6 yards of backing fabric
81x96-inch precut quilt batting
Template material
Embroidery needles and assorted colors of embroidery floss or Size 5 perle cotton

INSTRUCTIONS
The antique quilt shown on pages 128 and 129 is made of lightweight wool. The black is a rich background for the jewel-tone fan fabrics of wool, silk, and cotton in an array of solids, prints, stripes, and plaids.

The quilt is a 10x12-block straight set of 120 fan blocks. After each fan

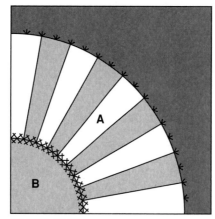

FAN BLOCK

block is completed, it is embellished with embroidery around the curved edge of the fan base piece (B) and the outside edge of the fan.

Cutting the fabrics
Refer to page 288 for tips on making and using templates. Prepare templates for patterns A and B, *below*.

Cutting requirements for the scrap fabrics are given for one block; the number required for the entire quilt is in parentheses.

From the black fabric, cut:
◆ 120 8½-inch squares.

From each light scrap fabric, cut:
◆ Five (600) of Pattern A.

From each dark scrap fabric, cut:
◆ Four (480) of Pattern A.
◆ One (120) of Pattern B.

Making the fan block
Use only two fabrics for each fan. Choose a B piece and four A pieces from the same dark fabric and five A pieces from one light fabric.
1. Stitch the nine A wedges together, alternating the two fabrics as shown in the block drawing, *left*. Pressing the seam allowances *open* will help you get a smooth curve when you turn under the seam allowance at the top edge of the fan.
2. Turn back the seam allowance on the curved edge of the B piece. Pin the prepared B piece to the bottom of the fan unit, placing B over the seam allowance of the A unit. Appliqué the B piece in place.
3. Turn under the seam allowance at the top edge of the fan.
4. Pin the fan onto a black square, aligning both sides of the fan with edges of the square. The B corner piece should be flush with the corner of the square. Appliqué the curved edge of the fan onto the black fabric.
5. Lightly press the completed block. Turn the block to the wrong side and trim away the black fabric under the fan, leaving a generous ¼-inch seam allowance at the fan seam line.
6. Referring to the stitch diagrams on page 137, embroider herringbone stitches along the curved seam line of the B piece. Position the stitches so they straddle the seam line as shown in the block diagram, *above*. Use the same floss to work three-stitch clusters of lazy daisy stitches along the outer curve of the fan.

Assembling the quilt top
Refer to page 294 for an assembly diagram of a straight set. Stitch the fan blocks together in 12 horizontal rows of 10 blocks each, then join the rows to complete the quilt top.

Quilting and finishing
BACKING: Cut the backing fabric into two 3-yard lengths. Join the two panels; press the seam allowance open. Sandwich the batting between the backing fabric and the quilt top; baste the three layers together.

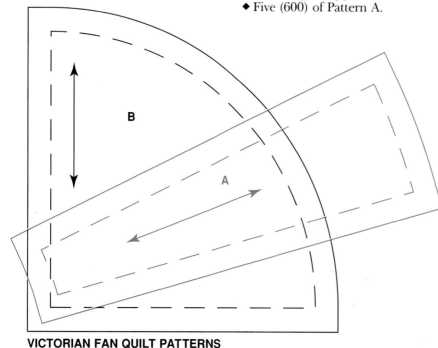

VICTORIAN FAN QUILT PATTERNS

QUILTING: Quilt as desired. The quilt shown on pages 128 and 129 has outline quilting at each seam line of the fans as well as a free-form wavy line stitched diagonally across the black corner of each block.

BINDING: Make approximately 370 inches bias or straight-grain binding. See pages 306 and 307 for tips on making and applying binding.

───────CHALLENGING───────

Sunburst Block

Shown on page 131.
The finished block measures 12 inches in diameter.

MATERIALS
For one block
⅛ yard *each* of muslin and pink print fabric
¼ yard *each* of green and red print fabrics
15-inch-square *each* of quilt batting and backing fabric
Template material

INSTRUCTIONS
Circular blocks, such as the Sunburst, usually have numbers of points divisible by eight; however, the antique block shown on page 131 defies the complications of geometry with an inner circle of 14 points. The quilt-maker made the points fit around the center circle even though they are not all the same size.

In order to provide accurate patterns that can be used consistently, these instructions are for a more traditional Sunburst block with a number of points divisible by eight.

This project, with its small pieces and set-in seams, is best suited to hand piecing. Instructions are given for one block.

Cutting the fabrics
Refer to page 288 for tips on making and using templates for patchwork. Prepare a template for each of patterns A through F, *right*.

continued

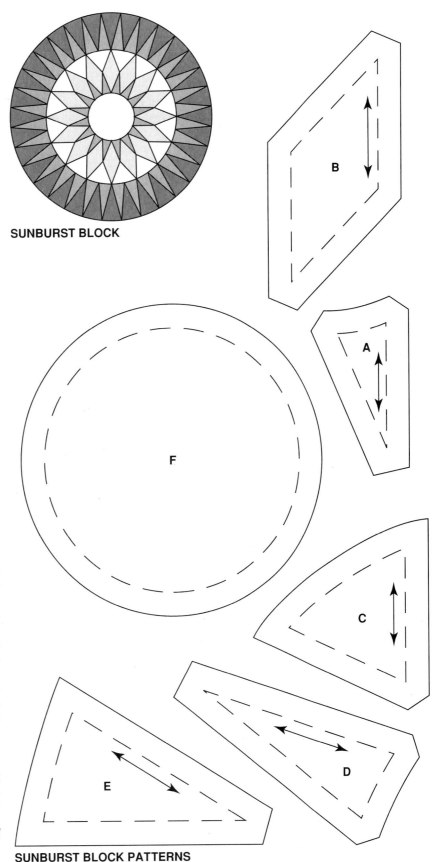

SUNBURST BLOCK

SUNBURST BLOCK PATTERNS

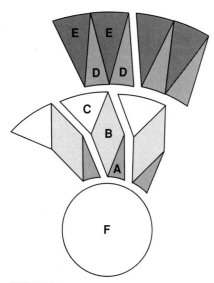

FIGURE 1

From the muslin, cut:
◆ One of Pattern F.
◆ 16 of Pattern C.

From the green print fabric, cut:
◆ 16 of Pattern A.
◆ 32 of Pattern D.

From the pink print fabric, cut:
◆ 16 of Pattern B.

From the red print fabric, cut:
◆ 32 of Pattern E.

Making the block
Refer to Figure 1, *above*, for guidance in assembling the block units.
1. Stitch an A triangle onto one side of each B diamond, as shown in the diagram. Press the seam allowance toward the B piece.
2. Add a C triangle to the opposite side of the B diamond, as shown. Press the seam allowance toward the C piece. Complete 16 ABC units.
3. Sew all the ABC units together to form a circle with an open center, carefully stitching the set-in seams.
4. Baste under the seam allowance of the F circle. Appliqué the circle over the center opening of the ABC circle.
5. Stitch D and E triangles together in pairs, as shown. Press all the seam allowances in the same direction. Join all the DE units into a circle.

6. Stitch the DE circle to the completed center section. If your pieces are perfectly aligned, the point of each B diamond will match up with the point of an E triangle.

Quilting and finishing
To finish the single block, center it over the squares of batting and backing fabric; baste the three layers together. Quilt and bind as desired.

The antique block shown on page 131 was once part of a larger quilt that became soiled and tattered beyond repair. The block is mounted on acid-free matboard and framed under glass, a nice way to preserve a remnant of a used-up quilt or display a single block.

Project suggestions
As a single block, the Sunburst can be framed, made into a round pillow, or inserted into a table or tray designed to display needlework.

One Sunburst block is an excellent addition to a sampler quilt. To make a Sunburst quilt, make 24 to 30 blocks in the same fabrics or an assortment of interesting scrap fabrics.

To use the Sunburst in a larger project, you may want a square block. Appliqué the completed Sunburst onto a 15½-inch square of fabric; trim away the background from under the circle, leaving a ¼-inch seam allowance all around. The finished block will be 15 inches square.

Log Cabin Pillow

Shown on page 132.
The finished pillow measures approximately 20 inches square. Each Log Cabin block is 5 inches square.

MATERIALS
⅛ yard of light blue solid fabric
½ yard *each* of ivory and dark blue solid fabrics
22-inch square *each* of quilt batting, lining fabric, and pillow backing fabric
Polyester filling for stuffing
Template material
Rotary cutter, mat, and acrylic ruler

INSTRUCTIONS
This pillow consists of 16 small Log Cabin blocks, joined in four rows of four blocks each. A border of prairie points adds interest to the outside edge of the pillow. The pillow shown on page 132 is made of satin in ivory and two shades of blue. Made with cotton fabric or prints, the pillow will have a more informal look.

Cutting the fabrics
Refer to page 288 for tips on using templates for patchwork. Make one template for the prairie point diamond pattern, *left*.

Cut cross-grained strips for the blocks as described below. These strips are cut the width of the logs plus ¼ inch on *both* sides for seam allowances. It is not necessary to make templates or to cut separate pieces for each log.

From the light blue fabric, cut:
◆ Three 1x42-inch strips.
◆ Four 1½-inch A squares.

From the dark blue fabric, cut:
◆ Nine 1x42-inch strips.
◆ Twelve 1½-inch A squares.
◆ 32 diamonds for prairie points.

From the ivory fabric, cut:
◆ Twelve 1x42-inch strips.
◆ 24 diamonds for prairie points.

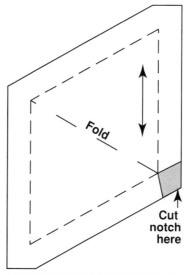

LOG CABIN PILLOW PATTERN

Fold

Cut notch here

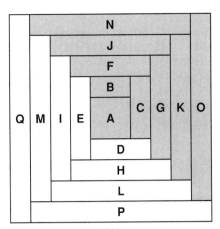

LOG CABIN BLOCK

Making the Log Cabin blocks

Refer to the block diagram, *above*, and the general instructions for Log Cabin blocks on page 90 as you make these blocks. Each block has ivory fabric on the light side of the block and the same blue fabric on the dark side of the block.

Make four blocks with the light blue fabric and 12 other blocks using the dark blue fabric.

1. Begin each block with a blue A square. Following the general instructions, use a strip of blue fabric to add logs B and C. Use ivory fabric for logs D and E.

2. Continue adding light and dark fabric strips in this manner until the block is complete.

Assembling the pillow top

Lay the blocks out on a flat surface in four vertical rows of four blocks each as shown in the pillow assembly diagram, *right*. Place the four light blue blocks in the corners of the pillow. Position the light and dark sides of the blocks as shown to achieve the Barn Raising set.

1. When the blocks are arranged as shown, join the four blocks in each row.

2. Center the batting square on the wrong side of the lining fabric. Securely baste the two layers together.

3. Baste or pin Row 1 at one edge of the batting. Lay Row 2 on top of Row 1 with right sides together. Match block seam lines as carefully as possible. Machine-stitch the two rows together, sewing through all four layers (Row 1, Row 2, batting, and lining).

Keep the lining fabric taut as you stitch to avoid sewing in puckers.

4. Turn Row 2 to the right side so it lies flat on the batting, covering the seam allowance. Check the back of the assembly to be sure the lining fabric is smooth.

5. Add rows 3 and 4 in the same manner. Trim excess batting, lining, and backing fabric even with the edge of the pillow top.

Making the prairie points

1. In each fabric diamond, clip a notch in one corner as indicated on the pattern, *opposite*.

2. Turn the clipped adjacent seam allowances back to the wrong side of the fabric and press.

3. Fold the diamond in half as indicated on the pattern, with the wrong sides of the fabric together; press. Prepare each of the 56 prairie points in this manner.

4. Match the raw edges of the prairie points with the raw edge on the right side of the pillow top. Pin 14 prairie points evenly spaced on each side of the pillow top, placing three ivory points at both ends and eight blue points in the center of each side. Machine-baste the prairie points in place with a ¼-inch seam allowance.

Finishing the pillow

Center the assembled pillow top on the backing fabric with right sides together. Machine-stitch a ¼-inch

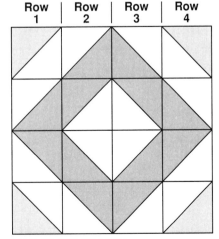

LOG CABIN PILLOW ASSEMBLY DIAGRAM

seam allowance through all layers around the edge of the pillow, leaving a 6-inch opening in one side for turning and stuffing.

Turn the pillow to the right side. Use a small tool or your fingernail to push the corners out from the inside. Insert stuffing through the opening and into the corners. When the pillow is stuffed as desired, close the opening with hand stitching.

———————*CHALLENGING*———————

Sunshine and Shadow Log Cabin Quilt

Shown on page 133.
The finished quilt measures approximately 77x82½ inches. Each Log Cabin block is 5½ inches square.

MATERIALS

⅛ yard *each* of medium red and dark red solid fabrics for the block centers
½ yard *each* of 13 light, 13 dark, and 26 medium-value fabrics in solids, prints, and plaids for the block patchwork
1 yard of binding fabric
5 yards of backing fabric
81x96-inch precut quilt batting
Rotary cutter, mat, and acrylic ruler
Assorted colors of embroidery floss or perle cotton, and embroidery needle for tying (optional)

INSTRUCTIONS

The quilt shown on page 133 is made of a medley of silk fabrics. Silk has a rich luster, but it is fragile and difficult to wash; today's quiltmakers may find it easier to work with cotton.

The dark sides of the blocks are made from a variety of prints, solids, and plaids in black, dark gray, brown, royal blue, hunter green, purple, and burgundy. The light fabrics are ivory, gold, light gray, peach, yellow, and aqua. Medium tones of all these colors also are widely used.

Each of the 210 Log Cabin blocks has a red center square. The light side of each block is made by alternating light and medium fabric strips;

continued

141

the dark side is made by alternating dark and medium strips.

Although no two blocks are made with the same four fabrics, the same two light or dark fabrics *must be present* in four adjacent blocks for the contrasting diamond pattern to appear when the blocks are joined. The instructions and diagrams that follow clarify the requirements of the fabric positioning. Study these carefully before you begin.

Cutting the fabrics

Cut cross-grained strips for the Log Cabin blocks as described. These strips are the width of the logs plus ¼ inch on *both* sides for seam allowances. It is not necessary to make templates or to cut pieces to the length of each log.

From each scrap fabric, cut:
◆ Seventeen 1x42-inch strips.

From each red fabric, cut:
◆ 105 squares, each 1 inch square, for the block centers.

Selecting fabric combinations for the Log Cabin blocks

This quilt is not difficult to make, but it requires careful planning of the fabric placement. As you read these instructions, refer to the photograph of the quilt, *below,* for guidance. We also suggest that you make a schematic drawing of the quilt to assist you in positioning the fabrics.

1. Divide your fabric strips into four tonal groups: light, medium-light, medium-dark, and dark.

2. Divide the dark and medium-dark fabrics in the same manner, selecting 42 dark/medium-dark combinations consisting of four strips of each fabric. Choose 21 dark/medium-dark combinations with just two strips of each fabric.

3. Select 49 light/medium-light fabric combinations, with four strips of each fabric in each group. Choose seven more light/medium-light combinations with two strips of each fabric in each combination.

4. As you make blocks, pull strips from these fabric combinations as described in the following steps. Each block will require a four-fabric set—a light/medium-light combination and one dark/medium-dark combination.

Making the Log Cabin blocks

Refer to Figure 1, *opposite,* and the general instructions for Log Cabin blocks on page 90 as you make the blocks. Note that this quilt's block is slightly different from other Log Cabin blocks—it is constructed *counterclockwise,* proof of the old adage that rules are made to be broken.

Make Block 1 as described in steps 1 through 3 below. Once you understand how to make a block, the only tricky part remaining is to arrange the fabrics correctly in each subsequent block.

1. Begin each block with a red A square. Follow the general instructions for Log Cabin blocks to add logs B and C, using a light fabric. Add logs D and E, using a medium-dark fabric.

2. Using a medium-light fabric, add logs F and G. Then use the darkest fabric in the set for logs H and I.

3. Continue adding light and dark logs in sequence as shown until the block is complete. Continue using the same fabric for each adjacent pair of logs, as shown in Figure 1.

4. Make Block 4 in the same manner, using the same light and medium-light fabrics in the same positions as in Block 1, but using a different combination of dark fabrics.

5. Make two more blocks (blocks 2 and 3) using the same two light fabrics, but reversing the positions of the light and medium-light fabrics as illustrated in Figure 1. Note that the dark fabrics are different in each of the four blocks.

SUNSHINE AND SHADOW LOG CABIN QUILT

Continue making blocks in groups of four in this manner. To assist you in positioning the fabrics correctly, we recommend laying the blocks on the floor in rows as illustrated in the quilt assembly diagram, *below, right.*

Select the fabrics for each block carefully as you work. The same dark fabrics should meet at the intersections of each four-block group just as the light fabrics do. This is an organizational challenge.

Use the eight-strip fabric sets to make the four blocks of the same combination. Use the four-strip sets where only two blocks of a color combination are needed around the outside edge of the quilt.

Make 210 Log Cabin blocks. You should have enough fabric strips left over to make additional blocks if you want to make a larger quilt.

Assembling the quilt top

Lay the blocks out on the floor or another flat surface in 15 horizontal rows of 14 blocks each. Referring to the photograph, *opposite,* and the quilt diagram, *right,* position the light and dark sides of the blocks as shown to achieve the alternating light and dark diamonds.

When the blocks are arranged as desired, join the blocks in each horizontal row. Sew the rows together to complete the quilt top.

Quilting and finishing

BACKING: Divide the backing fabric into two 2½-yard lengths. Stitch the two panels together; press the seam allowance open.

Sandwich the batting between the quilt top and the backing. Baste the three layers securely together.

QUILTING: Quilt as desired. The quilt pictured on page 133 is not quilted but is tacked at the corner of each block with embroidery floss. See page 305 for tips on tying.

BINDING: Make approximately 330 inches of binding. Refer to pages 306 and 307 for instructions on making and applying binding.

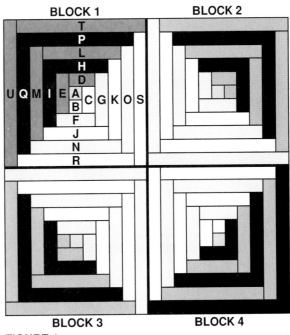

FIGURE 1

SUNSHINE AND SHADOW LOG CABIN QUILT
ASSEMBLY DIAGRAM

143

Plain Speaking

Amish Quilters Make A Colorful Statement

1880 ∽ 1920

◆ *Diamond-in-the-Square,*
Lancaster, Pennsylvania,
c. 1920; 82x82 inches.
Instructions begin on
page 154.

Plain Speaking

1880–1920

*Have nothing in your houses
that you do not know to be useful,
or believe to be beautiful.*

William Morris

*Q*uilts made by Amish women in the late 1800s and the early 1900s were made to be utilitarian, yet they are brilliant examples of rich, vibrant color. The austere Amish created quilts so visually dramatic that they are now hailed as great works of art.

The uncomplicated wholecloth and medallion quilts typical in the 1700s suited the principles of simplicity cherished by the Amish. These traditional styles were transformed into something unique by Amish sensibilities that were untarnished by fashionable tastes and values.

The Amish are part of a religious group called Anabaptists. Founded in Switzerland in the 1500s, the Anabaptists were conservative Protestants who rejected infant baptism, contending that a true commitment of faith can be made only with adult understanding. The group was subjected to severe persecution by church and state authorities.

The followers of Anabaptist Bishop Menno Simons (Mennonites) settled in Germany in the 1600s. The Germans' tolerance of their beliefs fostered ties of loyalty between the Mennonites and their neighbors.

This association offended some Mennonites who believed they should remain apart from all others. The group that became known as Amish followed Jacob Amman, who broke with the Mennonites in 1693 to pursue his fundamentalist beliefs. Believing in principles of simplicity and humility, the Amish adopted a strong discipline that insulated them from the world outside their own communities.

When the Amish came to America, their separateness and plain ways gave them a unique approach to quiltmaking.

◆ *Jacob's Ladder (right), Indiana, c. 1920; 68x95 inches. Instructions begin on page 160.*

146

*T*he first Amish families in America were among the thousands of German immigrants who settled in the vicinity of Lancaster County, Pennsylvania, in the 1700s.

These Germans—who inaccurately became known as Pennsylvania Dutch—had no heritage of quilting, but adapted their traditional folk-art

motifs to the crafts of their non-German-speaking neighbors. The Amish, avoiding contact with others, were slow to discover quilts and made very few before 1880.

The first Amish quilts were wholecloths, the simplest of styles. What had been discarded by others as out of fashion was acceptable to the Amish. Later, when the Amish made other quilts for everyday use, an elaborately stitched wholecloth quilt was often reserved for Sunday best.

Early Amish quilts were notable for their somber colors, as well as the plainness of their designs. This was due in part to the limited number of colorfast dyes available before 1880. In addition, the Amish rules that

♦ *Pillows* (opposite), 1990; Carolina Lily pillow (front) is 17x17 inches; Grape Basket and Cactus Flower pillows (back) are 12x12 inches. Instructions are on pages 162–167.

governed plainness of dress and life-style also applied to quilts.

These rules are set out in the *Ordnung*, the code of behavior for every aspect of daily life. First written in 1660, the updated *Ordnung* continues to guide the Amish and many Mennonites today.

The *Ordnung* of the 1880s forbade "striped or flowered clothing made according to the fashions of the world." An Amish home should not contain "proud kinds of furniture" and it was improper to have "unnecessary and

luxurious things," such as colored walls, curtains, and large mirrors.

But as groups of Amish migrated to Indiana, Ohio, Illinois, and Iowa, each community set its own guidelines for quilts. Rather than being written, these rules were more often decided by custom or by the group leaders.

On the prairie and the prosperous farms of Pennsylvania, change inevitably crept into Amish societies. By 1890, quilts had gained wide popularity among Amish women, who used the new fabrics available to them to make quilts unlike any ever made before.

♦ *Ocean Waves* (above), Holmes County, Ohio, c. 1925; 70x70 inches. Instructions begin on page 167.

◆ *Princess Feathers (above), probably Mennonite; Pennsylvania, c. 1900; 82x82 inches. Instructions begin on page 169.*

*D*espite the determination of the Amish to resist the encroachment of modern ways, change was inevitable. Around 1890, Amish quilters began to use a growing

palette of colors and fabrics in a wider range of quilt designs.

Homemade fabrics disappeared from Amish homes at this time, signaling the end of the self-sufficiency so precious

to earlier generations. Spinning wheels and looms were replaced by sewing machines and quilting frames. This new reliance on manufactured goods enabled Amish quilters to use the bright new fabrics introduced at the turn of the century.

The relaxation of rules in some church districts at the turn of the century allowed the Amish more choice of fabrics. Particularly in Ohio and Indiana, lighter colors found their way into Amish quilts.

Between 1880 and 1920, Amish quilters used cotton, cotton sateen, or

lightweight woolens of solid colors. The prohibition against print fabrics remained universal, but other rules varied widely.

Black was often used in the Midwest (see the Jacob's Ladder Quilt on pages 146 and 147), but rarely in Pennsylvania. Yellow was also avoided by the Pennsylvania Amish, but was acceptable to the more liberal Mennonites and Midwestern Amish. The Princess Feathers Quilt, *left*, was made in Pennsylvania, but the extensive use of gold and the appliqué motif indicates it is probably of Mennonite origin. White is rarely found in an Amish quilt.

While the Midwestern Amish made quilts using traditional blocks, such as baskets and Jacob's Ladder, the Pennsylvania Amish remained true to the medallion style. A Diamond-in-the-Square Quilt like the one shown on pages 144 and 145 almost always comes from Lancaster County.

Most groups in Ohio allowed quilts of simple blocks in two or three colors, but a conservative Nebraska district was restricted to Nine-Patch variations. Wholecloth quilts prevailed in some communities. Even today, the strictest of the Amish still shun patchwork, believing that cutting fabric and sewing it together again is "just for pride."

◆ *Amish Bars (opposite), Pennsylvania, c. 1900; 82x82 inches. This is the reverse side of the Princess Feathers Quilt pictured above. Instructions begin on page 173.*

*T*he wonderful profusion of color in their quilts seems to contradict the deliberate plainness of the Amish. Also, their classic feather quilting designs are much more elaborate than needed for a strictly utilitarian quilt.

The bright colors and fanciful stitching are evidence that quilting meant more to the Amish than just work—they enjoyed being creative. Mennonite women, too, helped preserve traditional forms of German folk art with quilts appliquéd in Pennsylvania Dutch motifs. A beautiful quilt was not frivolous because it was still functional.

Making quilts became a strong tradition among these plain people. In addition to providing bedcovers for her family, every mother worked to lay aside a supply of quilts and linens for each child's wedding day. Women found time for patchwork in summer between cooking, cleaning, gardening, and field work, so that plenty of quilt tops would be ready for quilting during the winter months.

Always vigilant against the evil of idle hands, the Amish used quilting and other needlework as proof of constant industry. As in all aspects of life, the Amish found guidance in the Bible: "Go to the ant, thou sluggard; consider her ways, and be wise." (Proverbs 6:6)

◆ *Amish Shadows* (above), 1990; 39½x46 inches. Instructions begin on page 174.

◆ *Pennsylvania Dutch Tulip* (right), c. 1910; 74½x90 inches. Instructions begin on page 175.

Diamond-in-the-Square Quilt

Shown on pages 144 and 145.
The finished quilt measures approximately 82x82 inches.

MATERIALS

3 yards of turquoise solid fabric
2 yards of dark red solid fabric
1⅝ yards of purple solid fabric
1¼ yards of dark green binding fabric
2½ yards of 90-inch-wide sheeting for backing fabric
90x108-inch precut quilt batting
Rotary cutter, mat, and acrylic ruler
Tracing paper
Nonpermanent fabric marker

INSTRUCTIONS

The quilt pictured on pages 144 and 145 is made of lightweight wool in classic Amish colors of purple, red, and turquoise. The graphic effect of the bold solid colors is enhanced by the elaborate quilting in black thread.

The pumpkin seed quilting design in the purple border is frequently found in Amish quilts, as is the diamond star and feather wreath in the center square. The floral quilting design in the red triangles is often found in Diamond-in-the-Square quilts made in Lancaster County, Pennsylvania, as are the glass fruit bowls quilted in the corners.

Patterns for the center motifs, the pumpkin seed border, and the fruit bowl quilting designs are given *opposite* and on pages 156–160.

Cutting the fabrics

Measurements given for cutting include ¼-inch seam allowances. Measurements stated for the turquoise border strips, however, allow a ½-inch seam allowance for the binding.

From the turquoise fabric, cut:
◆ Four 15¾x53-inch strips for the outer border.

From the purple fabric, cut:
◆ One 30½-inch square.
◆ Four 5½x42½-inch strips for the inner border.

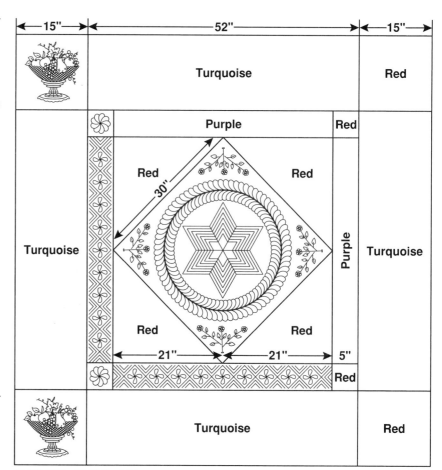

DIAMOND-IN-THE-SQUARE QUILT ASSEMBLY DIAGRAM

From the red fabric, cut:
◆ One 15¾x64-inch strip. Cut this into four 15¾-inch squares for the outside corners.
◆ Four 5½-inch squares for the inner border corners.
◆ Two 22-inch squares. Cut each square in half diagonally to obtain four triangles for the quilt center.

Assembling the quilt top

Refer to the quilt assembly diagram, *above,* as you work.
1. Stitch a red triangle onto opposite sides of the purple square; press the seam allowances toward the center. Join a red triangle to each remaining side of the square.
2. Stitch a purple border strip to the top and bottom edges of the center section; press the seam allowances toward the borders.
3. Sew a red corner square to each end of the remaining purple border

strips; press seam allowances toward the purple fabric. Add these borders to the sides of the center section, matching the seam line of each corner square with the seam line of the horizontal border. Press the seam allowances toward the border strips.
4. Join the turquoise outer borders to the quilt top in the same manner, stitching the top and bottom borders first and then adding the side borders with the red corner squares.

Marking the quilting designs

Extensive quilting of the kind featured on this quilt requires careful marking. See page 302 for tips about marking designs on quilt tops. Use a nonpermanent fabric marker to draw quilting designs on the top.
1. Make a tracing of the feather wreath pattern, *opposite,* marking the dots indicated on the pattern. Make one more tracing in the same manner. Tape the tracings together, over-

lapping them by matching the dots. The resulting curve is one-fourth of the feather wreath. Make a stencil of the design, if desired.

2. Make tracings or stencils for the quilting patterns on pages 156 and 157. The star and the floral bouquet quilting designs are used in the center purple square, and the pinwheel motif is used in the small border corners. Trace the pumpkin seed border pattern on page 160. To make a tracing of the fruit bowl design, join the two halves of the pattern as indicated on pages 158 and 159. Make or purchase additional quilting designs for the red setting triangles and the outer border.

3. Start marking in the center of the quilt. Using a yardstick for a straight-edge, draw a horizontal line from corner to corner of the center purple square. Draw another line to mark the vertical center. These lines will be erased later, but are important guidelines for placing the quilting motifs. The intersection of the two lines indicates the center of the square.

continued

FEATHER WREATH QUILTING DESIGN FOR DIAMOND-IN-THE-SQUARE QUILT

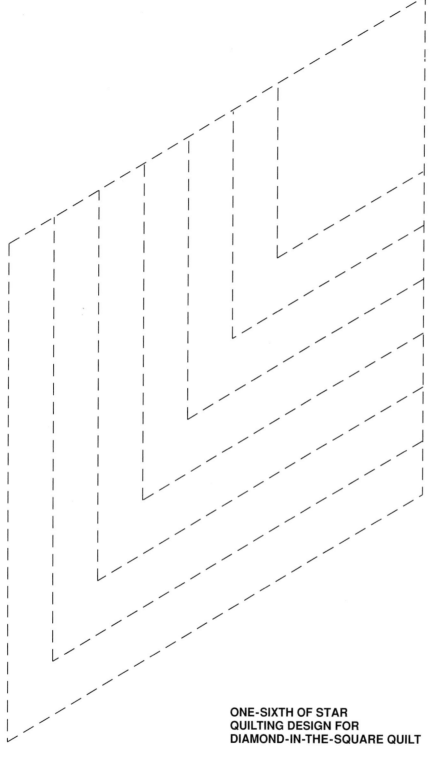

**ONE-SIXTH OF STAR
QUILTING DESIGN FOR
DIAMOND-IN-THE-SQUARE QUILT**

4. Measure 11¼ inches from the center of the center purple square along both vertical and horizontal placement lines. Mark these four points for placement of the spine of the feather wreath.

5. Align your stencil or tracing for the feather wreath with two placement points. If you have made a quarter section of the wreath, the dot at each end should align with a marked point. Mark this quarter section on the quilt top. Move the stencil to the next quadrant, again aligning the dots on the design with two placement points. Mark all four quadrants of the feather wreath in this manner.

6. Position one point of the star diamond on the intersection of the placement lines; place the opposite point on the *vertical* line. Mark quilting lines for that diamond. Move the stencil to the same position on the opposite side of the horizontal placement line; mark a second diamond.

7. Mark two more diamonds on each side of the first two, making a six-pointed star.

8. The floral design, *opposite,* fits in the corners of the purple center square. Mark one design in each corner, aligning the stem of the design on the placement lines.

9. If desired, remove the markings for the placement lines so you won't quilt them. Be careful not to erase markings for the quilting motifs.

10. Align the pumpkin seed motif with the center of each purple border strip. Mark pumpkin seed squares along the length of the border in both directions. Fill in the triangular spaces as shown on the pattern. At the end of each border, fill in the space between the last pumpkin seed square and the red corner with echo quilting as shown on the pattern.

11. Center and mark a pinwheel in each small red corner square.

12. Center the fruit bowl in each of the outer border corners; mark the design on each red square.

13. Mark the setting triangles and outer border strips as desired. The quilt shown has a floral bouquet quilted in each red triangle and elaborate undulating feathers quilted in the turquoise borders.

continued on page 160

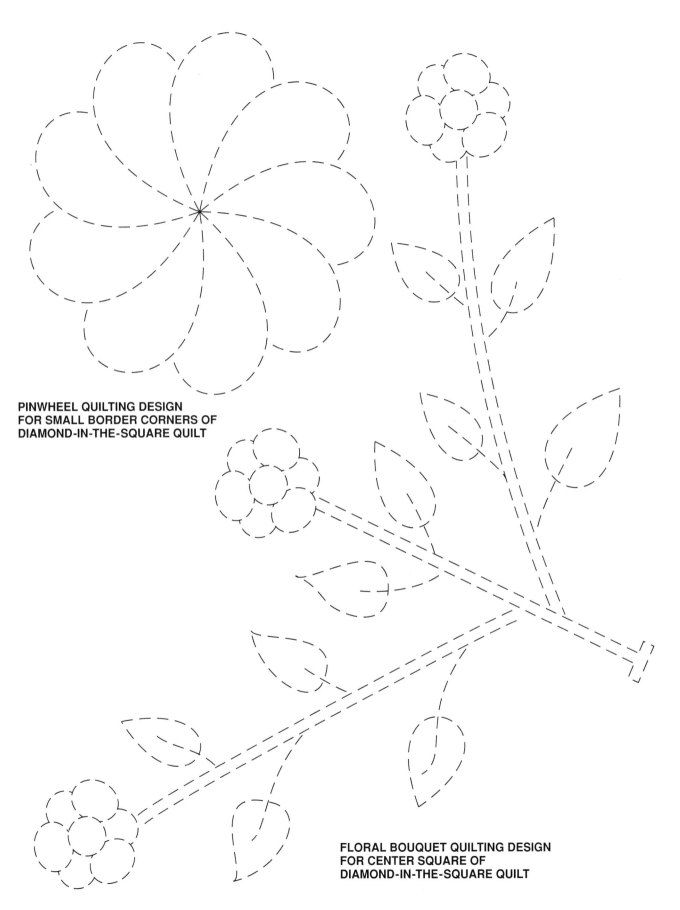

**PINWHEEL QUILTING DESIGN
FOR SMALL BORDER CORNERS OF
DIAMOND-IN-THE-SQUARE QUILT**

**FLORAL BOUQUET QUILTING DESIGN
FOR CENTER SQUARE OF
DIAMOND-IN-THE-SQUARE QUILT**

157

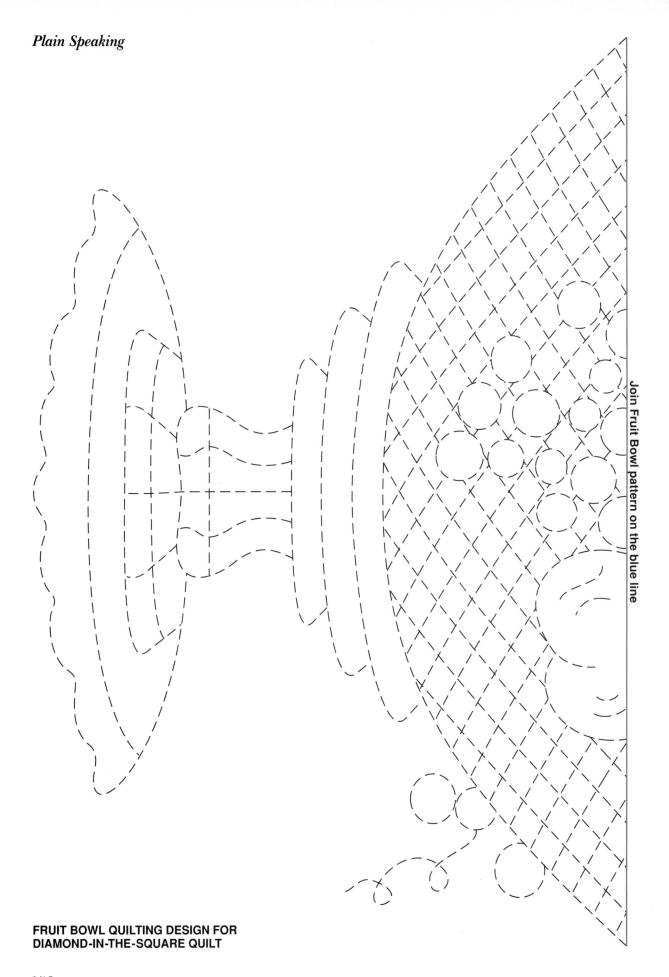

Join Fruit Bowl pattern on the blue line

**FRUIT BOWL QUILTING DESIGN FOR
DIAMOND-IN-THE-SQUARE QUILT**

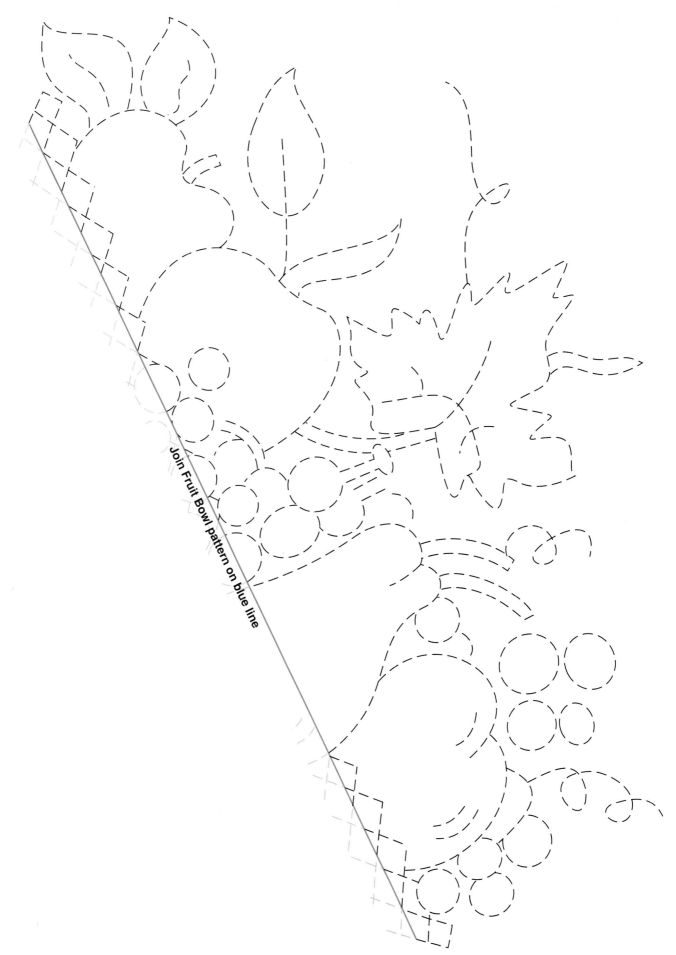

Join Fruit Bowl pattern on blue line

Seam line of border strip

**PUMPKIN SEED QUILTING DESIGN FOR
INNER BORDER OF DIAMOND-IN-THE-SQUARE QUILT**

Quilting and finishing

QUILTING: When the marking is complete, layer backing, batting, and quilt top; baste the three layers together. Quilt on all the marked lines. When the quilting is complete, remove the markings and basting.

BINDING: Cut the dark green fabric into eight 4½x42-inch strips. Refer to pages 306 and 307 for tips on making and applying straight-grain binding. Stitch the binding onto the quilt top with a ½-inch seam allowance. The finished binding on this quilt is ⅞ inch wide.

Jacob's Ladder Quilt

Shown on pages 146 and 147.
The finished quilt measures approximately 68x95 inches. The finished block is 9 inches square.

MATERIALS

4¾ yards of dark blue solid fabric for the blocks and outer border
4¼ yards of black solid fabric for the blocks, inner border, and binding
¾ yard of mauve solid fabric for the patchwork or ¼ yard *each* of three different shades of mauve or pink solid fabrics
6 yards of backing fabric
81x96-inch precut quilt batting
White or yellow fabric marker
Template material (for traditional piecing only)
Rotary cutter, mat, and acrylic ruler

INSTRUCTIONS

This quilt is made of 40 blocks in a 5x8-block straight set. All the blocks are the same, but they are turned different ways to achieve the overall design. Diagonal lines formed by the blocks' contrasting triangles create an illusion of connected "ladders" crisscrossing the surface of the quilt.

Instructions are given for making the blocks traditionally or with quick-piecing techniques.

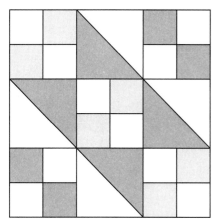

JACOB'S LADDER BLOCK

Cutting the fabrics

For the best use of fabric, cut the large pieces first; from these, cut the smaller patches listed below them. A rotary cutter is recommended.

Before cutting the fabrics, read the following assembly instructions; decide whether you will use traditional or quick-piecing techniques to make the triangle-squares. If you decide to sew the triangle-squares traditionally, make a template of the triangle pattern, *below, right*. A template is not necessary for quick piecing.

From the mauve or pink fabric(s), cut:
◆ Twelve 2x42-inch strips for the four-patch units.

From the dark blue fabric, cut:
◆ One 34x81-inch piece for the outer border.
  From this, cut two 8½x81-inch strips and two 8½x70-inch strips.
◆ One 42-inch square.
  From this, cut twenty 2x42-inch strips for the four-patch units.
◆ Four 20x24-inch pieces for the triangle-square units.

From the black fabric, cut:
◆ One 32x42-inch piece for binding.
◆ One 16x74-inch piece.
  From this piece, cut two 4x74-inch strips and two 4x54-inch strips for the inner border.
◆ Four 20x24-inch pieces for the triangle-square units.
◆ Eight 2x42-inch strips for the four-patch units.

Making the triangle-squares

TRADITIONAL PIECING: Use the triangle template to mark 40 triangles on each 20x24-inch piece of dark blue and black fabric. Cut 160 triangles of *each* fabric.

Join a dark blue triangle to each black triangle. Make 160 triangle-squares. Press the seam allowances toward the black fabric.

QUICK PIECING: Refer to page 114 for detailed instructions on quick-pieced triangle-squares.
1. On each 20x24-inch piece of blue fabric, mark a 4x5-square grid of 3⅞-inch squares as shown in Figure 1, *right, top*. Draw diagonal lines through the grid as shown.
2. Layer each blue piece, marked side up, atop a matching piece of black fabric. Stitch the grid as described in Step 3 on page 114. Each grid makes 40 triangle-squares. Complete 160 triangle-squares; press the seam allowances toward the black fabric.

Making the four-patch units

TRADITIONAL PIECING: Cut each 2x42-inch strip of dark blue, black, and mauve (pink) fabric into twenty 2-inch squares.

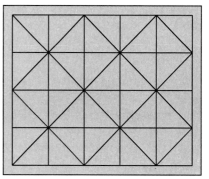

FIGURE 1

Stitch one dark blue square onto one side of each black and mauve square; press the seam allowances toward the dark blue fabric.

Join two blue/mauve units into a four-patch as illustrated in Figure 2, *below*, turning one unit upside down to position the fabrics as shown.

Stitch 120 blue/mauve four-patch units. Make 80 blue/black units in the same manner.

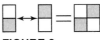

FIGURE 2

STRIP PIECING: See page 18 for tips on strip piecing.
1. Sew each 2x42-inch strip of mauve (pink) fabric to a matching strip of dark blue fabric, making one 3½x42-inch strip. Press the seam allowance toward the blue fabric.
2. Cut 2-inch-wide vertical units from each sewn strip as illustrated on page 18. Turning one unit upside down, join two units into a four-patch as illustrated in Figure 2, *above*.

Make 120 blue/mauve four-patch units and 80 blue/black four-patches.
continued

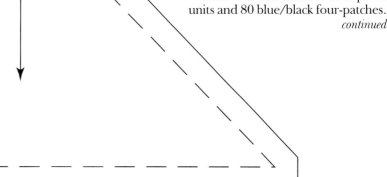

JACOB'S LADDER QUILT PATTERN

ROW 1

ROW 2

FIGURE 3

Assembling the block

1. Press each assembled unit. Each unit should be 3½ inches square. For each Jacob's Ladder block, use four triangle-squares, three blue/mauve four-patch units, and two blue/black four-patches.
2. Referring to the block diagram on page 161, assemble the units in three horizontal rows of three squares each. Press all joining seam allowances toward the triangles.
3. Join the three rows to complete the block. Make 40 blocks.

Assembling the quilt top

1. Lay out five blocks in a row, turning the blocks to position the squares and triangles as shown in Row 1 of Figure 3, *above*. Join the blocks, keeping each one in its correct position. Make four of Row 1.
2. Referring to Figure 3, make four of Row 2 in the same manner.
3. Stitch the assembled rows together in pairs, stitching one of Row 1 to one of Row 2. Match the block seam lines carefully. Join the four pairs to complete the quilt top.

Adding the borders

1. Stitch a 74-inch-long black border strip onto each long side of the quilt. Press the seam allowances toward the borders; trim excess border fabric even with the ends of the quilt top.
2. Stitch the 54-inch-long black border strips onto the top and bottom edges of the quilt. Press the seam allowances toward the black fabric; trim excess border fabric.
3. In the same manner, add the dark blue border strips to the four sides of the quilt top.

Quilting and finishing

BACKING: Cut two 3-yard lengths of backing fabric; sew the two panels together. Layer backing, batting, and quilt top; baste the layers together.

QUILTING: The quilt shown on pages 146 and 147 has diagonal lines of quilting over the entire quilt top. Quilt as desired.

BINDING: Make approximately 336 inches of binding. Refer to pages 306 and 307 for tips on making and applying binding.

———*CHALLENGING*———

Carolina Lily Pillow

Shown on page 148.
The finished pillow measures approximately 17x17 inches. The finished block is 12 inches square.

MATERIALS

⅛ yard *each* of light turquoise and dark turquoise solid fabrics
¼ yard *each* of green, dark purple, and slate blue solid fabrics
⅝ yard of black solid fabric
20-inch square *each* of muslin and quilt batting
2 yards of ¼-inch-diameter cotton cord for piping
Polyester filling
Template material
Rotary cutter, mat, and acrylic ruler

INSTRUCTIONS

This pillow is made of a single block set on the diagonal and finished with pieced corners. The rich colors of the solid fabrics are typical of vintage Pennsylvania Amish quilts.

Cutting the fabrics

Refer to page 288 for tips on making templates for patchwork and appliqué. Make templates for patterns A, B, and G on page 164.

From the black fabric, cut:
◆ One 18-inch square for the back.
◆ Two 6-inch squares.
  Cut each square in half diagonally to yield four corner triangles.
◆ One 12-inch square.
  From this square, make 70 inches of 2-inch-wide continuous bias for the piping. See page 306 for tips on making continuous bias.

From the slate blue fabric, cut:
◆ Two 3⅜-inch squares.
  Cut each of these squares in half diagonally to get four F triangles; discard the one extra triangle.
◆ Eight 2½x7½-inch pieces for the pillow border.

From each of the light turquoise and dark turquoise fabrics, cut:
◆ Six of Pattern A.

From the dark purple fabric, cut:
◆ Six of Pattern B.
◆ Three 2¼-inch squares (C).
◆ Two 4x4¼-inch pieces (E).
◆ One 8¼-inch square (H).
◆ Four 2½-inch squares for the border corners.

From the green fabric, cut:
◆ One 5¼-inch square.
  Cut this square in half diagonally. Use one triangle for D; discard the extra triangle.
◆ Two of Pattern G.
◆ Two 1¼x10-inch *bias* strips for the stems.

Making the Carolina Lily block

1. Fold one stem piece in half lengthwise with right sides of the fabric together. Stitch together the long edges of the strip. Press the seam

continued on page 164

SEWING SET-IN SEAMS

When two patchwork pieces come together and form an angled opening, a third piece must be set into the angle. This happens frequently in designs made with diamonds, such as an eight-pointed star. Where two diamonds come together, a square or triangle is sewn or set into the angled opening. Setting in also is required for joining patches, such as hexagons, that have more than four sides.

For a design that requires setting in, use a window template to mark each shape's sewing and cutting lines on the fabric. On each patch, mark the exact point of each corner by making a dot on the sewing line. By matching the dots of adjacent pieces, you will be able to sew them together easily and accurately.

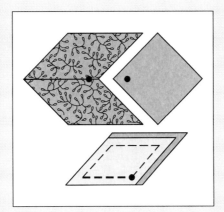

1 **Setting in** is required when you need to sew a piece into an angled opening formed by two adjacent pieces. The three patches should match at the points indicated by the dots. When you sew together the two pieces that form the angle, whether by hand or machine, be careful to *end the stitching at the dot*. This leaves the seam allowance open to receive the set-in piece.

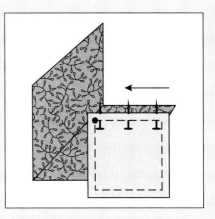

2a **To set in by hand,** pin the patch onto one of the sewn pieces with right sides together. Match the dots (corners) exactly, pushing a pin through both fabric layers to check the alignment of the dots. Hand-sew the seam from the open end of the angle into the corner as indicated by the arrow in the illustration, *above*. Remove pins as you sew. Backstitch at the corner to secure the stitches.

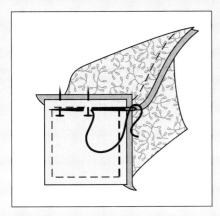

2b Bring the adjacent edge of the patch up and align it with the other edge of the angled unit. Insert a pin in the corner, matching the dots of both pieces, and pin the remainder of the seam. Hand-stitch the seam from the corner to the open end of the angle, removing the pins as you sew. See page 296 for tips on pressing.

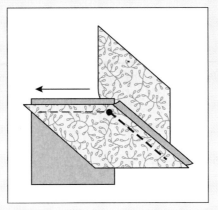

3a **To set in by machine,** pin one piece of the angled unit to one edge of the patch with right sides together. Match the corners, pushing a pin through both fabric layers to check the alignment of the dots. Machine-stitch the seam from the corner to the open end of the angle as indicated by the arrow in the illustration, *above*.

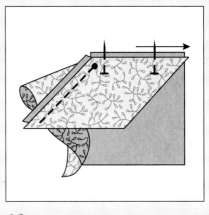

3b Bring the adjacent edge of the angled unit up to align it with the next edge of the patch. Insert a pin in the corner, matching the dots of both pieces, then pin the remainder of the seam. Machine-stitch from the corner to the open end of the angle.

allowance open, then turn the strip right side out. Press the seam line to the center back of the finished stem. Prepare the second stem piece in the same manner. Cut one strip in half, creating two short stems.

2. Fold the H square in half diagonally and finger-press a crease to mark the center placement line.

3. Designate one corner of the H square as the top corner. From that corner, measure 4 inches down one side of the square; mark that point with a pin. Pin a short stem to the square at this point, centering the end of the stem over the marking pin. Repeat on the other side of the block.

4. Pin the long stem piece over the center placement line, aligning one end of the strip with the top corner of the H square. Curve the short stems into the block as shown in the block assembly diagram, *right,* and tuck the ends under the center stem. Appliqué the stems in place.

5. Turn under the seam allowance on the long side of the green D triangle. Pin the triangle to the bottom of the H square, aligning its unturned edges with the sides of the square. Appliqué the turned edge in place over the bottom of the center stem.

6. Center the leaves in the spaces between the green triangle and the side stems. Appliqué the leaves in place.

7. Join two light turquoise A diamonds. Add a dark turquoise diamond onto each side of this pair, making a four-diamond unit. Make two more units in the same manner.

8. Stitch a slate blue F triangle to the bottom of each diamond unit.

9. Set a purple C square into the opening of each pair of light diamonds. Fill in the other openings with purple B triangles. (Refer to page 163 for tips on setting in.)

10. Referring to the assembly diagram, *above, right,* join the units to complete the Carolina Lily block.

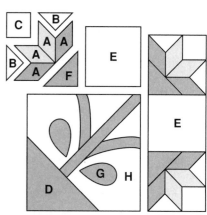

CAROLINA LILY BLOCK ASSEMBLY DIAGRAM

Adding the border corners

1. Stitch a 2½x7½-inch strip of slate blue fabric onto one short side of each black triangle. Press the seam allowance toward the black fabric. Do not trim the excess border fabric.

2. Sew a 2½-inch square of purple fabric onto one end of each remaining blue border strip. Press the seam allowance toward the purple fabric.

3. Stitch a pieced border strip onto the remaining short side of each black triangle.

4. Use the long edge of the black triangle as a guide to trim the excess border fabric. Align the edge of the acrylic ruler with the edge of the triangle so that the ruler extends over both borders. Use the rotary cutter to trim the border strips along the edge of the ruler.

5. Stitch a pieced corner unit onto one side of the Carolina Lily block, then stitch another corner unit onto the opposite side of the block. Press the seam allowances toward the corner units. Add corners to the remaining sides of the block to complete the pillow top.

Finishing the pillow

1. Sandwich the square of batting between the pillow top and the muslin square; baste the three layers together. Quilt as desired. Remove basting, then trim the batting and muslin even with the pillow top.

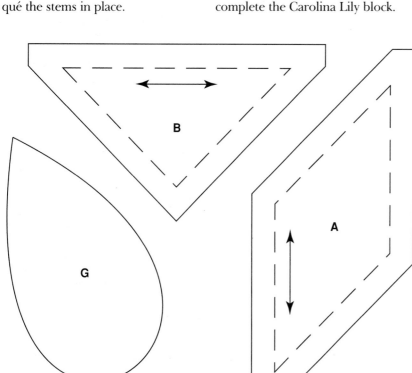

PATTERNS FOR CAROLINA LILY AND CACTUS FLOWER PILLOWS

2. Fold the continuous bias in half lengthwise, with wrong sides together. Put the cording in the fold, and, using a zipper foot, topstitch close to the cording.

3. Matching raw edges, baste the piping onto the pillow top aligning the topstitching of the cording with the ½-inch seam line at the edge of the block. Overlap the ends of the piping where they meet, leaving the excess in the seam allowance.

4. With right sides together, stitch the pillow back and top together with ½-inch seams. Leave a 3-inch opening in one side for turning. Turn the pillow right side out through the opening. Use a blunt pencil or crochet hook to push out the corners.

5. Stuff the pillow firmly, pushing the stuffing into the corners. Hand-stitch the opening closed.

———————*CHALLENGING*———————

Cactus Flower Pillow

Shown on page 148.
The finished pillow measures
approximately 12x12 inches. The
finished block is 6 inches square.

MATERIALS
½ yard of black solid fabric
¼ yard of dark purple solid fabric
One 8x10-inch scrap *each* of green, dark turquoise, light purple, and medium purple solid fabrics
14-inch square *each* of muslin and quilt batting
1½ yards of ¼-inch-diameter cotton cord for piping
Polyester filling
Template material
Rotary cutter, mat, and acrylic ruler

INSTRUCTIONS
The Cactus Flower block is similar to one quadrant of the Swirling Peony block in Chapter 1. The set-in triangles and squares make this block more difficult.

Cutting the fabrics
See page 288 for tips on making templates for patchwork. Make templates for patterns A and B, *opposite.*

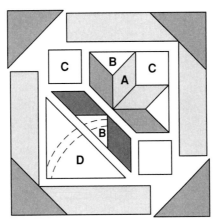

**CACTUS FLOWER PILLOW
ASSEMBLY DIAGRAM**

From the light purple fabric, cut:
◆ Four 2x7-inch strips for the inner border.
◆ Two of Pattern A.

From the medium purple fabric, cut:
◆ Two 4-inch squares.
  Cut these squares in half diagonally to get four border triangles.
◆ Two of Pattern A.

From the dark purple fabric, cut:
◆ Eight 2¾x8-inch border strips.
◆ Two of Pattern A.

From the green fabric, cut:
◆ One 1¼x6-inch bias strip.

From the dark turquoise fabric, cut:
◆ One 5¼-inch square.
  Cut this square in half diagonally to obtain one D triangle and one extra. Cut some of the smaller pieces from the extra triangle.
◆ Three 2¼-inch squares (C).
◆ Three of Pattern B.

From the black fabric, cut:
◆ One 14-inch square for the back.
◆ One 12-inch square.
  From this square, make 56 inches of 2-inch-wide continuous bias for the piping. See page 306 for tips on making continuous bias.
◆ Two 3-inch squares.
  Cut each square in half diagonally to yield four corner triangles.

Making the Cactus Flower block
1. Join the light purple diamonds into a pair. Sew one medium purple diamond onto each light diamond, making a four-diamond unit as shown in the block assembly diagram, *left.*
2. Set a turquoise C square into the opening of the light diamonds. Fill in the other openings with B triangles. (See page 163 for tips on setting in.)
3. Fold the green stem piece in half lengthwise with right sides together. Stitch together the long edges of the ⅝x6-inch strip. Press the seam allowance open, then turn the strip right side out. Press the seam line to the center back of the finished stem.
4. Pin the stem onto the remaining B triangle, matching the end of the stem with the raw edge of one short side of the triangle. The long edge of the stem should be parallel to the other short side of the triangle and approximately ⅜ inch from it. Sew dark purple diamonds onto the short sides of this triangle as shown in the block assembly diagram, catching the end of the stem in the seam.
5. Stitch the diamond/stem unit onto the four-diamond unit, aligning the corner of the B triangle with the center seam line of the diamonds.
6. Set C squares into the remaining openings.
7. Keeping the stem out of the way of the seam, stitch the large D triangle onto the bottom of the unit to complete the block.
8. Appliqué the stem in place, curving it to align with the bottom corner of the block. The end of the stem will be enclosed in the border seams.

Adding the inner border
1. Stitch a 2x7-inch strip of light purple fabric onto opposite sides of the block. Press the seam allowances toward the purple strips; trim the strips even with the sides of the block.
2. With right sides together, center one of the remaining light purple strips on an unstitched side of the block. Stitch the strip to the block, sewing across the seam lines of the first two strips. Add the last strip of light purple fabric to the remaining block side in the same manner. Do not trim these borders.

continued

3. Center a medium purple triangle diagonally at one corner of the block. With right sides together, sew the triangle over the border corners so the seam line crosses the corner of the Cactus Flower block. Sew a triangle across each corner in this manner.

4. On the wrong side of the block, use your rotary cutter with the acrylic ruler to trim the excess border fabric away from the seam allowance.

Adding the pillow corners

1. Stitch a 2¾x8-inch dark purple strip onto each short side of one black triangle, making a mitered corner. (See page 299 for tips on mitering corners.) Make four corner units.

2. Use the long edge of the black triangle as a guide to trim the excess border fabric. Align the edge of the acrylic ruler with the long edge of the triangle so that the ruler extends over both border strips. Use the rotary cutter to trim the border strips along the edge of the ruler.

3. Stitch a pieced corner unit onto one side of the center unit; stitch another corner unit onto the opposite side. Press the seam allowances toward the corners. Add the remaining corners to complete the pillow top.

Finishing the pillow

1. Sandwich the square of batting between the pillow top and the muslin square; baste the three layers together. Quilt as desired. Remove basting, then trim the batting and muslin even with the pillow top.

2. Fold the bias strip in half lengthwise, wrong sides together. Put the cording inside the fold. Using a zipper foot, stitch close to the cording.

3. Baste the piping onto the pillow top, aligning the topstitching of the cording with the ½-inch seam line at the edge of the block. Overlap the piping ends where they meet, leaving the excess in the seam allowance.

4. With right sides together, stitch the pillow back and top together with ½-inch seams. Leave an opening in one side for turning. Turn the pillow right side out. Use a blunt pencil or crochet hook to push out the corners.

5. Stuff the pillow firmly, pushing the stuffing into the corners. Hand-stitch the opening closed.

— BASIC —
Grape Basket Pillow

Shown on page 148.
The finished pillow measures approximately 12x12 inches. The finished block is 5⅝ inches square.

MATERIALS

½ yard of black solid fabric
One 14-inch square *each* of dark turquoise and dark purple solid fabrics
14-inch square *each* of muslin and quilt batting
1½ yards of ¼-inch-diameter cotton cord for piping
Polyester filling
Rotary cutter, mat, and acrylic ruler

INSTRUCTIONS

The basket has been beloved by quiltmakers for centuries and is a favorite of the Amish. In the first half of the 20th century, the Amish made classic quilts using blocks, such as the Grape Basket, that are comprised of simple geometric shapes.

Cutting the fabrics

All the pieces in this pillow can be cut using a gridded acrylic ruler and a rotary cutter; it is not necessary to make templates. Refer to the block assembly diagram, *right, top,* to identify each lettered piece of the block.

From the black fabric, cut:
◆ One 14-inch square for the back.
◆ One 12-inch square.
   From this square, make 56 inches of 2-inch-wide continuous bias for the piping. See page 306 for tips on making continuous bias.
◆ Four 3-inch corner squares.
◆ One 1⅝-inch square (A).
◆ One 2-inch square.
   Cut this square in half diagonally to yield two B triangles.
◆ One 3⅜-inch square.
   Cut this square in half diagonally. Designate one of the resulting triangles as D; cut the remaining triangle in half to yield two C triangles.
◆ Two 1⅝x3⅞-inch strips (E).

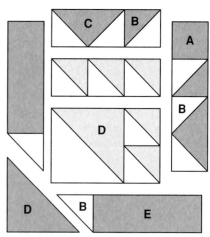

GRAPE BASKET BLOCK
ASSEMBLY DIAGRAM

From the dark turquoise fabric, cut:
◆ Two 5-inch squares.
   Cut each square in half diagonally to obtain four setting triangles.
◆ Seven 2-inch squares.
   Cut each square in half diagonally to yield 13 B triangles (discard the one extra triangle).
◆ One 3⅛-inch square.
   Cut this square in half diagonally; designate one of the resulting triangles as D and discard the extra triangle.

From the dark purple fabric, cut:
◆ Four 3x9-inch border strips.
◆ Three 2-inch squares.
   Cut these squares in half diagonally to get five B triangles (discard the one extra triangle).
◆ One 3⅛-inch square.
   Cut this square in half diagonally; use one of the resulting triangles for D and discard the extra one.

Making the Grape Basket block

Refer to the block assembly diagram, *above,* as you join the pieces for the basket block.

1. Join purple and turquoise B triangles in pairs, making five squares. Make two more squares with turquoise and black B triangles. Join the purple and turquoise D triangles in the same manner.

2. Stitch a turquoise B triangle onto both short legs of each black C triangle. Sew the remaining turquoise triangles onto one end of each E piece.

3. Press all the seam allowances toward the turquoise fabric.
4. Referring to the assembly diagram, join the pieced units in rows as shown, then join the rows. Add the black D triangle across the bottom corner to complete the block; trim the sides of the black triangle even with the sides of the block.

Adding the border
1. Stitch a turquoise setting triangle onto one side of the block; repeat on the opposite side. Press the seam allowances toward the triangles. Add the remaining triangles to the unstitched sides of the block in the same manner. The resulting unit should be approximately 8½ inches square.
2. Join a 3x9-inch border strip onto one side of the square, then add another border strip to the opposite edge. Press the seam allowances toward the border fabric; trim excess border fabric even with the sides of the square.
3. Sew a black corner square to the short ends of each remaining border strip. Stitch these strips to the remaining sides of the square. Adjust the seams of the corner squares if necessary to match the seam lines.

Finishing the pillow
Refer to the finishing instructions for the Carolina Lily Pillow on pages 164 and 165.

Ocean Waves Quilt
Shown on page 149.
The finished quilt measures approximately 70x70 inches.

MATERIALS
2¼ yards of black solid fabric
¾ yard *each* of light yellow and lavender solid fabrics
Scraps or approximately ⅝ yard *each* of six different solid fabrics
¾ yard of binding fabric
4½ yards of backing fabric
81-inch square of quilt batting
Template material
Rotary cutter, mat, and acrylic ruler

INSTRUCTIONS
The eight-pointed stars in the setting squares of the Ocean Waves Quilt set it apart from the ordinary. The center section is surrounded by a strip-pieced "piano key" border that repeats the scrap fabrics used in the center. The wide black outer border is typical of Amish quilts.

There are 864 small triangles in this quilt; most are joined to make 384 triangle-squares. Instructions are given below for making the triangle-squares traditionally or with quick-piecing techniques.

Cutting the fabrics
Refer to page 288 for tips on making templates for hand or machine piecing. Prepare a template for Pattern X on page 168. See page 289 for tips on cutting triangles from squares.

From the black fabric, cut:
◆ Two 8½x73-inch strips and two 8½x58-inch strips for the outer border.
◆ One 13¼-inch square.
Cut this square in quarters diagonally to get four setting triangles.
◆ Two 7-inch squares.
Cut each square in half diagonally to yield four corner triangles.
◆ Twenty 3-inch squares (Y).
◆ Five 4¾-inch squares.
Cut each square in quarters diagonally to obtain 20 Z triangles.

From each of the yellow and lavender fabrics, cut:
◆ Two 2x38-inch strips for the pieced border.
◆ Three 14-inch squares for the triangle patchwork.
◆ 20 X diamonds.

From each of the six scrap fabrics, cut:
◆ Three 14-inch squares for the triangle-squares.
◆ Two 2x38-inch strips for the pieced border.
◆ Eight 2⅞-inch squares.
Cut each square in half diagonally to create 16 triangles of each fabric.

Making the triangle-squares
TRADITIONAL PIECING: To make a template for the patchwork trian-

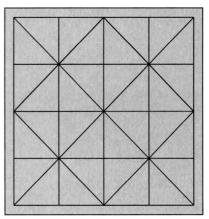

FIGURE 1

gles, draw a 2⅞-inch square on template material; draw a diagonal line through the square and cut out the triangles. Use these templates to mark 32 triangles on each 14-inch fabric square; cut 768 triangles.

Join two triangles to make one triangle-square; press the seam allowances toward the darker fabric. Make 384 triangle-squares.

QUICK PIECING: Step-by-step instructions for quick-pieced triangle-squares are given on page 114. Refer to these instructions to mark and stitch the grids described here.
1. On the wrong side of one light-colored 14-inch fabric square, mark a 4x4-square grid of 2⅞-inch squares as shown in Figure 1, *above.* Layer this square, marked side up, atop one matching square of another scrap fabric.
2. Machine-stitch the grid as described in Step 3 on page 114, then cut on all the drawn lines. Each grid makes 32 triangle-squares. Stitch 12 grids to make a total of 384 triangle-squares.
3. Press all seam allowances toward the darker fabric.

Assembling the blocks
Use the assembled triangle-squares to make blocks A, B, and C.
1. Select nine triangle-squares for one of Block A (see block diagram on page 168), avoiding similar fabric combinations. Assemble these triangle-squares in three rows of three squares each, then join the rows.
continued

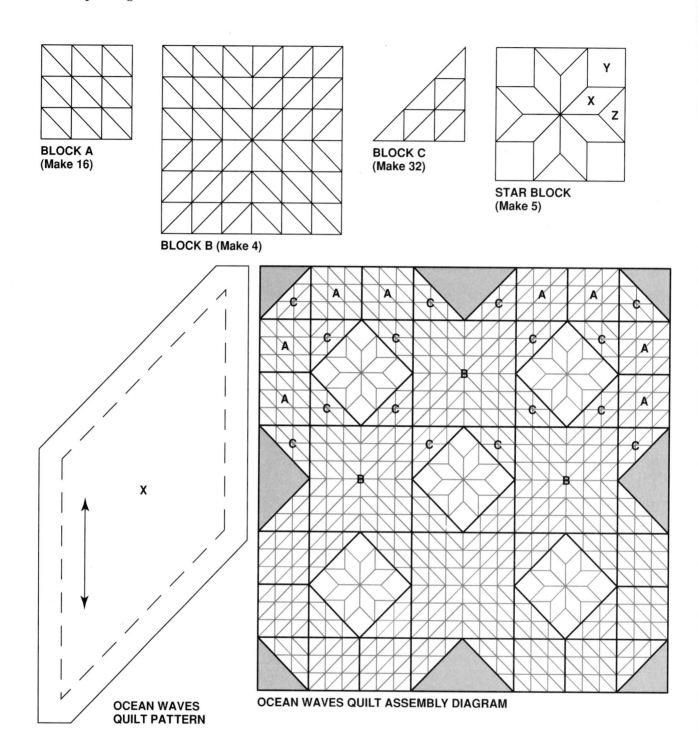

BLOCK A
(Make 16)

BLOCK B (Make 4)

BLOCK C
(Make 32)

STAR BLOCK
(Make 5)

OCEAN WAVES
QUILT PATTERN

OCEAN WAVES QUILT ASSEMBLY DIAGRAM

Be sure the seam lines in all the squares are angled in the same direction as shown in the block diagram, *top, left*. Make 16 of Block A.

2. Make four more of Block A and join them to make one of Block B. Refer to the block diagram, *top, center*, to see how the seam lines are angled in each quadrant of the assembled block. Make four of Block B.

3. Referring to the block diagram, *top, center*, combine three triangle-squares with three individual triangles of scrap fabric to make Block C. Make 32 of Block C.

Making the star blocks

1. Join eight X diamonds to make each star, alternating yellow and lavender diamonds.

2. Referring to the star block diagram, *top, right*, set a Z triangle into alternate openings around the star. (See page 163 for tips on setting in.) Set a Y square into the remaining openings. Make five star blocks.

3. Stitch a completed C block onto opposite sides of each star block; press the seam allowances toward the star. Add a C unit onto the remaining block sides in the same manner.

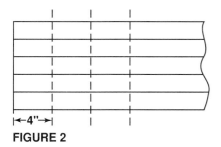

FIGURE 2

Assembling the quilt top

Referring to the quilt assembly diagram, *opposite,* join the units in five horizontal rows. For rows 1, 3, and 5, join C units onto the black setting triangles as shown. Join the rows to complete the quilt top.

Adding the borders

1. Join five 2x38-inch strips of scrap fabric as shown in Figure 2, *above.* Press the seam allowances to one side. Make three strip sets.
2. Cut nine 4-inch-wide units from each strip set as shown in Figure 2.
3. Cut eight 2x4-inch pieces from the one remaining 2x38-inch strip.
4. Sew one 2x4-inch piece onto both ends of one pieced unit. Add five more pieced units end to end to make one border strip. Compare the border strip to one side of the quilt top. Add or subtract 2x4-inch segments to the border strip to match the length of the side, then stitch the border onto the quilt top. Repeat to add a border strip to the opposite side of the quilt top.
5. Join seven pieced units and two 2x4-inch units to make a border for each of the remaining sides. Adjust the length of the border strip as before, if necessary. Stitch these borders onto the quilt top.
6. Stitch the 8½x58-inch black borders onto opposite edges of the quilt. Press the seams toward the black fabric; trim excess border fabric even with the sides. Add the 73-inch-long strips onto the remaining edges.

Quilting and finishing

BACKING: Divide the backing fabric into two 2¼-yard lengths. Sew the two panels together; press the seam allowance open. Layer backing, batting, and quilt top; baste the three layers together.

QUILTING: The quilt pictured on page 149 has outline quilting ¼ inch from each seam line. Quilt as desired.

BINDING: Cut seven 3½x42-inch strips of binding fabric. Stitch the strips together end to end to make approximately 290 inches of straight-grain binding. See page 307 for tips on applying binding. To fill out the wide binding typical of Amish quilts, take a ½-inch seam when stitching this binding onto the quilt top.

Making a larger quilt

The size of this quilt is ideal for a large wall hanging or a short twin-size coverlet (without a pillow tuck). To make a 94x94-inch quilt, make the center area of the quilt with five rows of five blocks each. Draw an assembly diagram like the one *opposite* before starting.

———————————— *CHALLENGING* ————————————

Princess Feathers Quilt

Shown on page 150.
The finished quilt measures approximately 82x82 inches. Each Princess Feathers block is 33 inches square.

MATERIALS

6½ yards of gold solid fabric for the blocks, borders, and binding
3½ yards of green solid fabric
2¼ yards of red solid fabric
2½ yards of 90-inch-wide sheeting for backing fabric
90x108-inch precut quilt batting
Template material

INSTRUCTIONS

Elaborate appliquéd quilts, such as this one, are rare in Amish country. Red, green, and gold were popular colors among the Amish and Mennonites at the turn of the century, but the predominance of gold and the appliqué used in this quilt are somewhat unusual. Since the quilt originated in Pennsylvania, it most likely was made by a Mennonite woman or another quilter influenced by Pennsylvania Dutch colors and motifs.

PRINCESS FEATHERS QUILT BLOCK

The same fabrics were used to piece the quilt's backing in the traditional Amish Bars pattern (see photo on page 151), making it a reversible quilt. Although the same fabrics are used on front and back, no special economy is gained when using 44-inch-wide cotton goods—the same amount of fabric is needed as listed for both quilts, so the only saving is in using a single batt.

Cutting the fabrics

Refer to page 288 for tips on making templates for appliqué. Make a template for each of patterns A through I on pages 170 and 171. For the feather (C), make a complete template by joining the two parts of the pattern on page 171.

For the center daisy (A) and the tulip petals (D, E, and F), you can either make a template of the complete shape or place a template of the half pattern on the fold of the fabric.

When cutting appliqués from fabric, add a ³⁄₁₆-inch seam allowance around each piece.

From the gold fabric, cut:
◆ Four 34-inch squares.
◆ Two 5½x74-inch strips and two 5½x84-inch strips for the outer border.
◆ Four 1½x72-inch strips for the inner border.
◆ Five 2½x72-inch strips for straight-grain binding.
◆ 32 of Pattern B.
◆ 16 of Pattern F.

continued on page 172

169

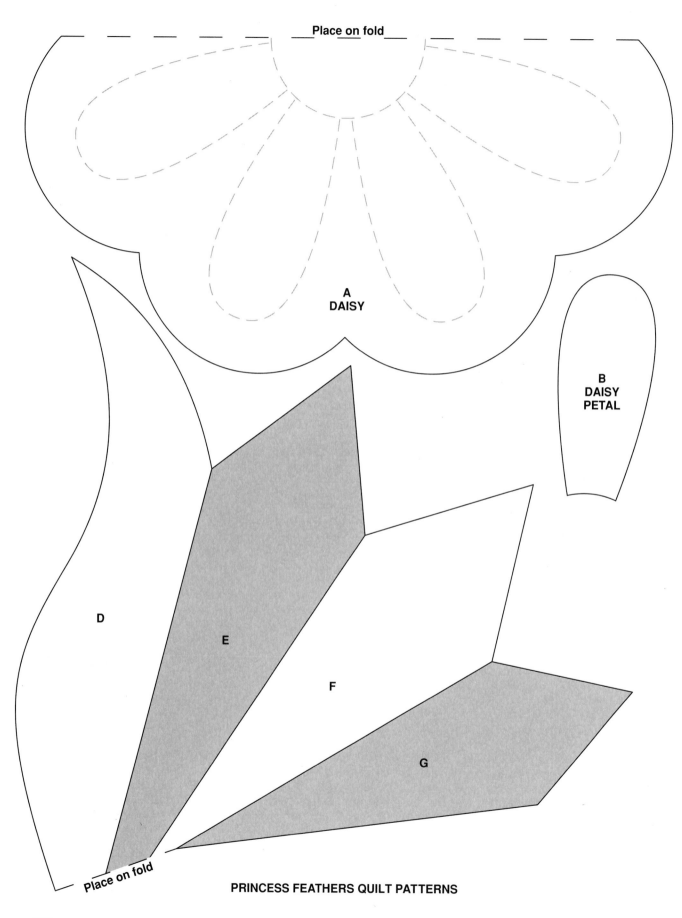

Place on fold

A
DAISY

B
DAISY
PETAL

D

E

F

G

Place on fold

PRINCESS FEATHERS QUILT PATTERNS

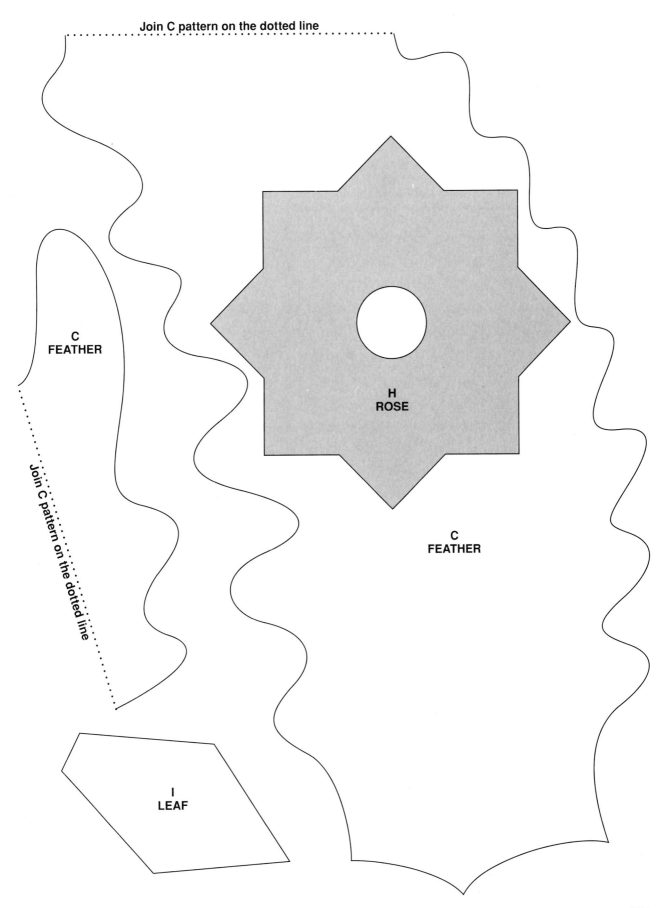

Join C pattern on the dotted line

C
FEATHER

Join C pattern on the dotted line

H
ROSE

C
FEATHER

I
LEAF

171

From the green fabric, cut:
- ◆ Four 1½x74-inch strips for the third inside border.
- ◆ One 17½x42-inch piece. From this piece, cut sixteen 1¾x10-inch strips for the long stems and thirty-two 1¾x7½-inch strips for the short stems.
- ◆ 16 *each* of patterns C, D, and G.
- ◆ 64 of Pattern I.

From the red fabric, cut:
- ◆ Four 1½x70-inch strips for the first inside border.
- ◆ Four of Pattern A.
- ◆ 16 of Pattern E.
- ◆ 32 of Pattern H.

Preparing stems for appliqué

With right sides together, fold one stem piece in half lengthwise. Machine-stitch ¼ inch from the raw edge. Press the seam allowance open, centering the seam line in the middle of the strip. Turn the strip right side out and press again.

Seam all the stem strips in this manner. The ends will be covered by other pieces, so it is not necessary to finish those edges.

Positioning the appliqué

1. Fold each 34-inch background square in half vertically, horizontally, and diagonally; lightly press the folds to establish placement guidelines for the appliqué. If desired, trace the complete design on the background fabric with an erasable fabric marker.

2. Prepare the appliqué pieces for each block by basting back the seam allowances. It is not necessary to turn under edges that will be covered by other pieces, such as the bottom edge of the feathers. Clip seam allowances as necessary to achieve nice points and curves. Cut out the center of each H rose, trimming the seam allowance to ⅛ inch. Do not turn this edge under yet.

3. Appliqué the eight petals (B) onto the center daisy (A), positioning the petals as indicated on the A pattern given on page 170.

4. Referring to the block diagram on page 169, pin or baste all pieces in place on the background square before appliquéing them. Start by positioning the daisy in the center of the block. Slip one end of a long stem under the daisy at each diagonal placement line. Center a feather (C) over each vertical and horizontal placement line, slipping the bottom of each feather under the daisy.

5. Position petals for each tulip (D, E, F, and G) at the end of each long stem. The tip of the G diamond should be aligned with the diagonal placement line. Working out from the center of the flower, pin the F petals in place and then the E petals. The straight edges of the D piece will cover the raw edges of the E petals and the top of the stem.

6. Referring to the block diagram, position a short stem on both sides of each long stem approximately halfway between the daisy and the tulip. Tuck the ends of the short stems under the long stems. Pin a rose (H) in place at the end of each short stem.

7. Position pairs of small leaves (I) in place as shown in the block diagram, slipping the blunt end of each leaf under the long stem piece.

Appliquéing the blocks

1. Stitch all leaf and stem pieces in place first to anchor the other pieces.

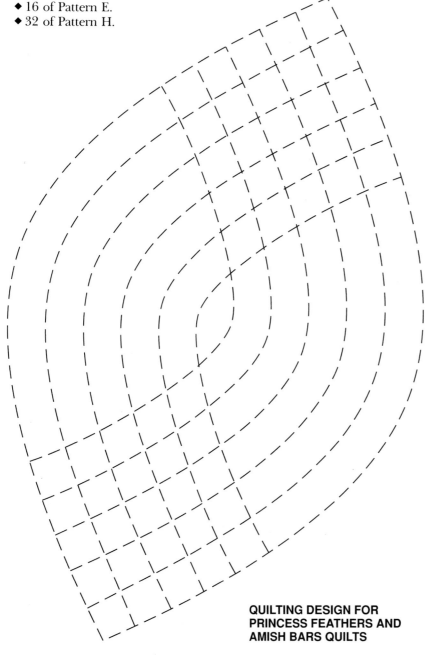

QUILTING DESIGN FOR PRINCESS FEATHERS AND AMISH BARS QUILTS

2. Appliqué the feathers (C) in place next, then stitch the center daisy (A) over the ends of all the long stems and feathers.

3. Stitch the roses in place. In the center of each rose, use your needle to turn back and appliqué the edge of the red rose fabric, revealing the gold base fabric underneath. Appliqué the four tulips.

4. Complete four Princess Feathers blocks. Press each appliquéd block. Trim the blocks to 33½ inches each.

Assembling the quilt top

1. Join the four blocks in two rows of two blocks each; join the rows into a 66½-inch square. Press the seam allowances to one side.

2. Sew a 1½x70-inch red border strip onto the side of the quilt top that you've designated as the top; add a second red strip to the opposite side. Press the seam allowances toward the borders, then trim the border fabric even with the sides of the quilt top.

3. Stitch the remaining red border strips onto the sides of the quilt top. Press the seam allowances toward the border; trim excess border fabric.

4. Add the gold and green narrow borders in the same manner, sewing the border strips to the top and bottom edges of the quilt first and then stitching the side borders.

5. Stitch the 5½x74-inch strips of gold fabric onto the green borders at the top and bottom edges of the quilt. Press the seam allowances toward the gold fabric. Complete the quilt top by adding the 5½x84-inch gold borders to the sides.

Quilting and finishing

Layer backing, batting, and quilt top; baste the three layers together.

Quilt as desired. The quilt pictured on page 150 has outline quilting around each appliquéd shape and in the narrow borders. A diagonal grid of ½-inch squares is quilted in the background of the appliqué. A pattern for the cable design quilted in the outer border appears *opposite*.

Use the five 2½x72-inch strips of gold fabric to make approximately 340 inches of straight-grain binding. Refer to page 307 for tips on applying binding.

———————— *BASIC* ————————
Amish Bars Quilt

Shown on page 151.
The finished quilt measures approximately 82x82 inches.

MATERIALS

2¾ yards of red solid fabric
2⅛ yards *each* of gold and green solid fabrics (includes binding)
2½ yards of 90-inch-wide sheeting for backing fabric
90x108-inch precut quilt batting
Rotary cutter, mat, and acrylic ruler

INSTRUCTIONS

Bars quilts were popular with the Amish because they were so practical—they require little sewing time to assemble and they use up scraps, so they cost almost nothing to make. The Bars quilt pictured on page 151 is the back of the Princess Feathers quilt shown on page 150.

Cutting the fabrics

From the red fabric, cut:
◆ Four 5½x71-inch strips for bars.
◆ Three 6½x71-inch strips for the outer bars and bottom border.
◆ Two 6½x36-inch cross-grained strips for the top border.

From the gold fabric, cut:
◆ Five 5½x71-inch strips for bars.
◆ Five 2½x71-inch strips for the binding.

From the green fabric, cut:
◆ Five 5½x71-inch strips for bars.
◆ Four 6½-inch squares for the border corners.

Assembling the quilt top

This quilt is assembled in two halves, then the top border is added to each half so that the center seam is continuous from the top of the quilt to the bottom border.

continued

Grn	Red										Red								Grn
Red	Gold	Grn	Red	Gold	Grn	Red	Gold		Grn	Red	Gold	Grn	Red	Gold	Grn	Red			
Grn	Red																		Grn

AMISH BARS QUILT ASSEMBLY DIAGRAM

173

1. Referring to the quilt assembly diagram on page 173, assemble the left half of the quilt top. Begin with a 6½-inch-wide strip of red fabric, and add a strip of gold fabric to one long side.
2. Add a strip of green fabric onto the gold strip. Continue adding strips in a red-gold-green sequence as shown until eight strips are joined, ending with a gold strip. Press all seam allowances toward the red or green strips.
3. Join the remaining strips in this manner to complete the right half of the quilt top. Start with a green strip, then add strips in a red-gold-green sequence, ending with a 6½-inch-wide red strip.
4. Stitch a green corner square onto one end of each 36-inch-long red border strip. Press the seam allowances toward the red fabric.
5. Matching the seam lines of the corner square and the outer red bar, stitch one border strip onto the top edge of both quilt halves. Press the seam allowances toward the borders; trim excess border fabric even with the sides of the quilt top.
6. Join the two quilt halves, stitching from the top border down to the bottom of the bars. Press the seam allowance to one side.
7. Sew a green square onto each end of the remaining red border strip. Matching the seam lines of the squares with the outer red bars, stitch the border strip to the bottom edge of the quilt. Press the seam allowance toward the border fabric.

Quilting and finishing
Layer backing, batting, and quilt top; baste the three layers together.

QUILTING: The quilt shown on page 151 is quilted to accommodate the Princess Feathers design on the reverse side. The cable design quilted in the border fits nicely centered in each bar (the pattern is given on page 172). Quilt as desired.

BINDING: Use the five 2½x71-inch strips of gold fabric to make approximately 340 inches of straight-grain binding. Refer to page 307 for tips on applying binding.

—BASIC—
Amish Shadows Quilt
Shown on page 152.
The finished quilt measures approximately 39½x46 inches. The finished block is 6⅜ inches square.

MATERIALS
1⅜ yards of black solid fabric
¾ yard of burgundy solid fabric for the patchwork, inner border, and binding
⅛ yard *each* of five more solid fabrics for the patchwork
1⅜ yards of backing fabric
45x60-inch precut quilt batting
Acrylic right triangle
Rotary cutter, mat, and acrylic ruler

INSTRUCTIONS
A traditional Amish Shadows Quilt is always made with solid colors and a black background. The quilt shown on page 152 has somber fabrics, but it also can be made with bright, bold colors for a more contemporary look. When made with print fabrics, this block is called Roman Stripes.

This is an ideal project for the quiltmaker who is unsure about picking fabrics, because any color combination works in this versatile design, especially if black is used for the background. Black makes the other patchwork colors sparkle. Try a polished cotton for some of the patchwork stripes to give the quilt extra interest.

If black doesn't suit your style, consider navy, brown, gray, or muslin for the background. However, these colors may require more careful fabric selection of the patchwork colors.

Our quilt is made of 20 blocks in a 4x5-block straight set. It is the perfect size for a wall hanging or a crib quilt.

Instructions are given for making the blocks with quick-piecing techniques. A template is not necessary.

Cutting the fabrics
A rotary cutter is recommended for cutting these strips and triangles.

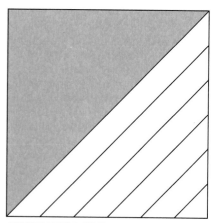

AMISH SHADOWS BLOCK

From the black fabric, cut:
◆ Two 5¾x48-inch strips for the outer border, cutting on the lengthwise grain.
◆ Two 5¾x30-inch strips for the outer border, cutting on the crosswise grain.
◆ Ten 7½-inch squares.
   Cut each square in half diagonally to obtain 20 triangles.

From the burgundy fabric, cut:
◆ One 9x42-inch piece for the binding.
◆ Two 2¼x37-inch strips and two 2¼x27-inch strips for the inner border.
◆ Three 1¼x42-inch strips for the patchwork.

From each of the remaining five solid fabrics, cut:
◆ Three 1¼x42-inch strips for the patchwork.

Strip piecing the striped triangles
If you were to cut individual pieces for each stripe in the triangles, you would have many difficult angles to match and bias edges to handle. So, the striped triangle is ideal for strip piecing. See page 18 for additional tips on strip piecing.
1. Join six 1¼x42-inch strips, one of each color, into a strip set, arranging the colors as desired. Keep in mind that the strips on the outside edges of the set will be the most dominant in the finished triangles. Press all seam allowances in the same direction.

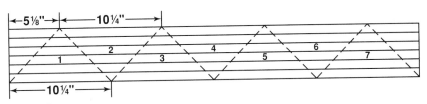

|←5⅛"→|←——10¼"——→|

|←——10¼"——→|

FIGURE 1

2. On one short side of the strip set, use your rotary cutter and acrylic ruler to cut a straight side, perpendicular to the long edge of the strip set.

3. Referring to Figure 1, *above,* measure 5⅛ inches from the top left-hand corner along the top edge of the strip set. Place the right-angle corner of the acrylic triangle at this point. With the rotary cutter, cut out the triangle. Cut out six more striped triangles from the strip set as illustrated in Figure 1.

Note: Handle these triangles carefully during and after cutting; all the new edges are on the true bias and can be stretched and distorted easily.

4. Make two more strip sets. These can be the same as the first one or you can rearrange the fabric colors in each strip set for greater variety in the finished triangles. Cut seven triangles from each strip set (this includes one extra triangle, since only 20 are needed for this quilt).

Piecing the Amish Shadows block
To allow for minor distortion in cutting and sewing the striped triangles, the plain black triangles were cut slightly larger than necessary. If your plain triangles appear to be too big, do not trim the excess fabric yet.

1. Center a striped triangle atop a plain triangle with right sides together. Stitch the two triangles together along the long edge (hypotenuse).

2. Before you press, check the accuracy of the square. Match the right-angle corner of the acrylic triangle with the corresponding corner of the fabric triangle. Trim excess fabric from the sides of the triangle as necessary.

3. Make 20 Amish Shadows blocks. Press the center seam allowance toward the plain triangle.

Assembling the quilt top
Before assembling the blocks, see page 91 for suggestions on making Log Cabin sets. These sets also are appropriate for the Amish Shadows block. Or, experiment with the blocks to make your own arrangement.

Join the blocks in five horizontal rows of four blocks each. Assemble the rows to complete the quilt top.

Adding the borders
1. Stitch a 2¼x27-inch strip of burgundy fabric to each short edge of the quilt top. Press the seam allowances toward the border fabric; trim excess border fabric even with the sides of the quilt.

2. Add the 2¼x37-inch burgundy strips to the long sides of the quilt. Press the seam allowances toward the border fabric; trim excess border fabric even with the ends of the quilt.

3. Join the black borders to the quilt top in the same manner, adding the short strips to the ends first and then the longer strips to the sides.

Quilting and finishing
Layer backing, batting, and quilt top; baste the three layers together.

QUILTING: The quilt shown on page 152 has outline quilting in the striped triangles and a diagonal grid of 1-inch squares in the black triangles. A cable design is quilted in the inner border; the outer border is quilted with a design of interlocking squares. Quilt as desired.

BINDING: From the 9x42-inch piece of burgundy fabric, cut five 1½x42-inch strips for straight-grain binding. These strips are cut wider than usual to imitate the wide bindings customary on traditional Amish quilts. For the long sides of the quilt, piece binding strips as necessary. See page 307 for tips on applying binding.

Pennsylvania Dutch Tulip Quilt

Shown on pages 152 and 153.
The finished quilt measures approximately 74½x90 inches. The finished block is 11 inches square.

MATERIALS
5½ yards of red solid fabric
2¼ yards of yellow solid fabric
2 yards of pink solid fabric
1 yard of green solid fabric
1 yard of binding fabric
5½ yards of backing fabric
81x96-inch precut quilt batting
Template material

INSTRUCTIONS
The primitive style of this quilt's tulip appliqués and the bright colors of the solid fabrics are typical of Pennsylvania Dutch folk art. The quilt has 14 appliquéd blocks in a diagonal set with plain blocks and setting triangles. By turning the blocks in different directions, the appliquéd tulips meet in the center to form an interesting design.

Cutting the fabrics
Refer to page 288 for tips on making and using templates for hand appliqué. Prepare templates for patterns A through F on page 176. Add a ³⁄₁₆-inch seam allowance around each piece when cutting the fabrics.

From the red solid fabric, cut:
- Two 10½x92-inch strips and two 10½x57-inch strips for the outer border.
- Three 17-inch squares.
  Cut each square in quarters diagonally to obtain 10 setting triangles and two extras.
- Eighteen 11½-inch squares.
  Fourteen of these squares are for the appliqué blocks and four are for setting squares.
- Two 8⅝-inch squares.
  Cut each square in half diagonally to obtain four corner setting triangles.

continued

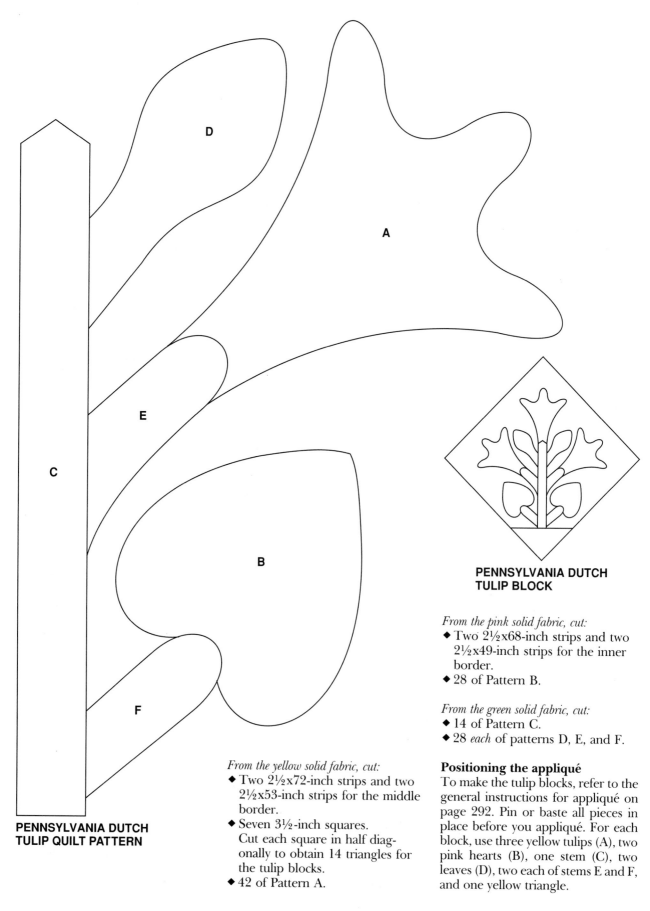

PENNSYLVANIA DUTCH TULIP BLOCK

From the pink solid fabric, cut:
◆ Two 2½x68-inch strips and two 2½x49-inch strips for the inner border.
◆ 28 of Pattern B.

From the green solid fabric, cut:
◆ 14 of Pattern C.
◆ 28 *each* of patterns D, E, and F.

Positioning the appliqué
To make the tulip blocks, refer to the general instructions for appliqué on page 292. Pin or baste all pieces in place before you appliqué. For each block, use three yellow tulips (A), two pink hearts (B), one stem (C), two leaves (D), two each of stems E and F, and one yellow triangle.

PENNSYLVANIA DUTCH TULIP QUILT PATTERN

From the yellow solid fabric, cut:
◆ Two 2½x72-inch strips and two 2½x53-inch strips for the middle border.
◆ Seven 3½-inch squares. Cut each square in half diagonally to obtain 14 triangles for the tulip blocks.
◆ 42 of Pattern A.

1. Fold one 11½-inch red square in half *diagonally;* lightly press the fold to establish a placement line.

2. Prepare the appliqués by basting back the seam allowances. Do not turn under edges that will be covered by another piece, such as the bottom edges of the leaves, tulips, or stems. Clip seam allowances as necessary to achieve nice points and curves. For the yellow triangles, turn under only the edge of the long side.

3. Begin by pinning the stem (C) on the diagonal placement line. Position the unturned bottom edge of the stem 1⅞ inches from the corner of the square, centering the stem on the line. Pin the yellow triangle over the bottom of the stem, aligning the unturned triangle edges with the sides of the red square.

4. Referring to the block diagram, *opposite,* pin or baste the remaining pieces in place on the background fabric before appliquéing. Slip the ends of the stems, leaves, and the top tulip under the prepared stem piece; then position the hearts and the side tulips, slipping the end of each piece under the adjacent stem piece.

Appliquéing the blocks

Appliqué the tulips and hearts in place first, then stitch the leaves and the four short stems. Keep the center stem fabric out of the way until these pieces are sewn in place, then pin it in place again.

Appliqué the center stem, covering the unturned ends of the flowers, leaves, and short stems. Complete the appliqué by stitching the long

edge of the yellow triangle in place over the bottom of the stem.

Appliqué 14 tulip blocks.

Assembling the quilt top

Referring to the quilt assembly diagram, *below,* lay out the appliquéd blocks with the plain red squares and setting triangles. Note the direction of each tulip block; the four blocks in the center of the quilt are positioned so that the yellow triangles meet.

Stitch the blocks and the setting triangles together in diagonal rows as indicated by the red lines on the diagram. Join the assembled rows to complete the quilt top.

Adding the borders

1. Stitch a 2½x49-inch strip of pink fabric onto the bottom edge of the quilt top. Trim the excess border fabric even with the sides of the quilt. Repeat, adding another pink strip at the opposite (top) edge. Press the seam allowances toward the borders.

2. Add the 2½x68-inch strips of pink fabric onto the sides of the quilt top in the same manner.

3. Sew the yellow middle border and red outer border onto the quilt top in the same manner, sewing the borders to the top and bottom first and then to the sides.

Quilting and finishing

BACKING: Divide the backing fabric into two 2¾-yard lengths. Sew the two panels together; press the seam allowance open.

Layer backing, batting, and quilt top; baste the three layers together.

QUILTING: On the quilt pictured on pages 152 and 153, the four center blocks have outline quilting inside and around each appliqué piece. The remaining blocks and the narrow borders are quilted with a grid of 1-inch squares. An interwoven cable is quilted in the wide outer border.

Quilt as desired. For the cable, use a purchased stencil of a design approximately 8 inches wide.

BINDING: Make approximately 340 inches of bias or straight-grain binding. See pages 306 and 307 for tips on making and applying binding.

PENNSYLVANIA DUTCH TULIP QUILT ASSEMBLY DIAGRAM

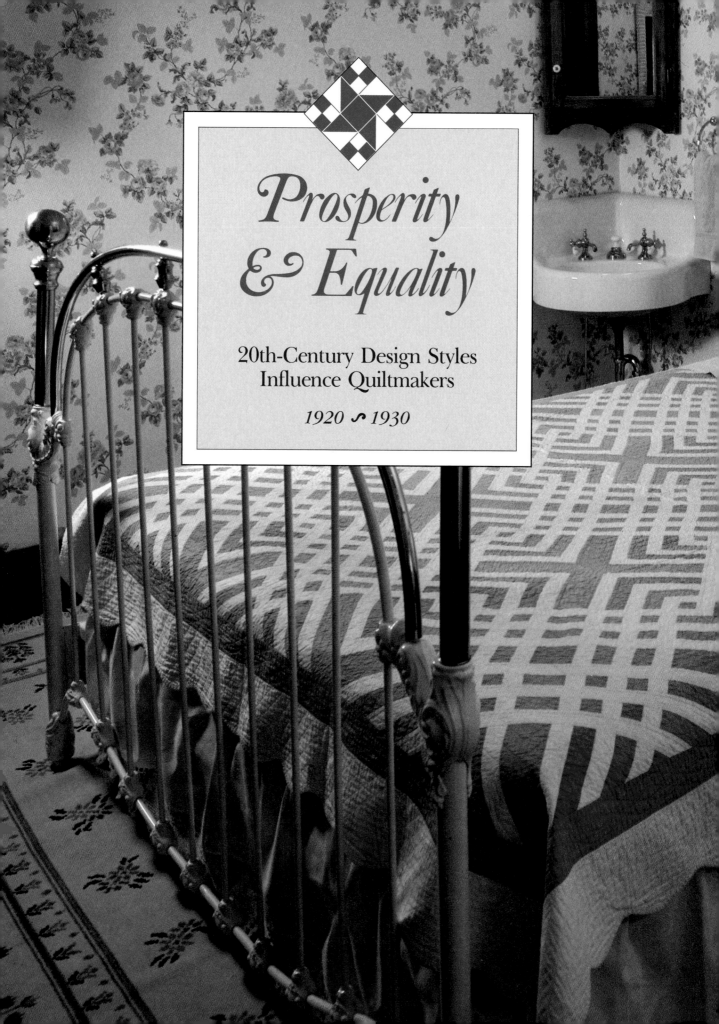

Prosperity & Equality

20th-Century Design Styles
Influence Quiltmakers

1920 ～ 1930

◆ *Carpenter's Square,*
c. 1928; 86x109 inches.
Instructions begin on
page 188.

Prosperity & Equality
1920–1930

*It took me more than 20 years, nearly 25, I reckon,
in the evenings after supper when the children were all
put to bed. My whole life is in that quilt . . . All my
joys and all my sorrows are stitched into those
little pieces . . . I tremble sometimes when I remember
what that quilt knows about me.*

Marguerite Ickis, quoting her
great-grandmother

The 1920s were years of prosperity and change. The modern woman was different from her mother and grandmother. By 1921, she had won the right to vote and was liberated by new technology from the household drudgery of the past.

Electricity, gas, and water lines revolutionized American life. Automobiles, telephones, washing and sewing machines, radio, motion pictures, and other inventions and conveniences quickened the pace of everyday life.

As if to deny the hustle of modern times, designers looked to the past. While young Americans danced the Charleston and speakeasies flourished in defiance of Prohibition, the so-called Colonial Revival was evident in fashionable buildings, furnishings, and decorating.

The hodgepodge of styles popularized by the Colonial Revival were all inaccurately labeled "colonial." These supposed Early American reproductions replaced Victorian decor. Quilts fit the romanticized colonial ideal, so women brought down old quilts from the attic to enhance their new furniture.

If a family heirloom was not available, the 1920s woman had the money to buy one, or at least to buy materials. Encouraged by new products and vast amounts of published material, American women found renewed interest in making quilts.

◆ *Kaleidoscope (left),
c. 1926; 83x99 inches.
Instructions begin on
page 201.*

181

◆ *Lindy* (above), c. 1930, from a pattern published by Capper's Weekly; 74x85 inches. Instructions begin on page 193.

*T*he nationwide publication of quilt patterns during the 1920s and '30s forever altered the quilting tradition. Quiltmakers once limited to regional patterns and local customs were now exposed to ideas from outside sources.

Many newspapers and national magazines introduced regular quilting columns in the 1920s. For the first time, women in all parts of the country

saw the same patterns and fabric suggestions at the same time.

While quilting was a magazine tradition dating back to *Godey's Lady's Book* of the 1800s, it was new for newspapers, and very successful. A 1930 Gallup survey named quilt columns as the most popular feature in six major city newspapers.

The *Kansas City Star*, which printed separate editions for five states, was an important source of quilt patterns in this period. Beginning in September 1928, the *Star* published a quilt pattern every week for 34 years.

During those years, three different women designed or illustrated the *Star* patterns. Ruby McKim was first, followed by Eveline Folard. Both were designers who contributed quilt patterns of distinctive style. However,

when Edna Marie Dunn took over the column in 1933, she often used patterns sent in by readers. Quiltmakers faithfully collected these columns, pasting the newspaper clippings into scrapbooks.

Magazines also carried regular articles and patterns on quilting. Marie Webster's original designs appeared in *Ladies' Home Journal* magazine from 1911 to 1917 and greatly influenced quiltmaking trends of the 1920s. Another important quilt designer was Anne Orr, needlework editor of *Good Housekeeping*, who contributed a page to that magazine every month from 1919 to 1940.

Magazines for farmers and their families also took part in the quilting revival. Farm women were among the most devoted and productive quilt-makers of the 1920s and 1930s, encouraged by regular features in *Farm and Fireside*, *Ohio Farmer*, and *Successful Farming* magazines.

Designers, such as Orr and Webster, created quilt patterns in updated styles and colors. Partial to appliquéd floral motifs, they retained the use of solid-colored appliqués on a light background, but they substituted scalloped edges and soft pastels for the hard lines and strong colors of the 1800s.

◆ *Pomegranate Medallion* (above), c. 1928; 82x82 inches. Instructions begin on page 197.

Prosperity & Equality

1920–1930

*E*ntrepreneurs found numerous money-making opportunities in the new enthusiasm for quilts.

For years, quiltmakers had used time-honored methods of making patterns, marking and cutting fabric, and sewing pieces together. Quilting the top required still more patterns and marking. Enterprising inventors set out to devise all sorts of ingenious timesaving devices.

For example, the Sears catalogs of the mid-1920s advertised perforated quilting stencils with stamping wax as a means to eliminate "tiresome marking of quilts in the old-fashioned way." The stamping kit included stencils of traditional quilting designs and a jar of black or yellow paste.

The quilter placed the stencil on the quilt and rubbed the waxy paste over it with a cotton ball that had been dipped in gasoline. This left a dot-ted line on the cloth to follow when quilting. Of course, it also left a residue of paste and gasoline.

Mail-order companies provided a host of products for quilters. Well-known editors and designers, such as Marie Webster, Anne Orr, and Ruby McKim, ran mail-order pattern companies, as did Carlie Holmes, a contributor to *Better Homes and Gardens* magazine.

Other successful mail-order firms included the Ladies Art Company of St. Louis, and Old Chelsea Station Needlecraft Service of New York.

◆ *Milky Way (above), made by Anne McCartney of Mitchellville, Iowa, c. 1930; 44½x48½ inches. Instructions begin on page 199.*

◆ *Tulip Garden (right), Oklahoma, c. 1925; 79½x97 inches. Instructions begin on page 190.*

184

burned in the Chicago fire of 1871. The reproduction she made was the first of many quilts that combined her appreciation of antiques and unique design talent.

A graduate of the Art Institute of Chicago and a skilled seamstress, Kretsinger mixed art nouveau style with traditional quilt motifs. Floral wreaths, trailing vines, and elaborate borders were her trademarks, highlighted by feather quilting that gracefully echoed the curves of the swirling appliqué.

Kretsinger made quilts that represented the best of the 1920s. Even copies made by her neighbors are now in the collections of prestigious museums. Like most influential designers of the day, she favored floral appliqué in an updated medallion setting, scalloped borders, and clear, light colors.

These design ideas, especially the preference for pastel colors, gained universal acceptance with quiltmakers and remained firmly entrenched for the next 40 years. The widespread publication of patterns through magazines, newspapers, and mail-order companies left valuable documentation of an extraordinarily creative period in American quiltmaking.

◆ *Orchid Wreath* (above), made by Rose Kretsinger of Emporia, Kansas, c. 1929. Courtesy of the Spencer Museum of Art, University of Kansas. Instructions are not available for this quilt.

*T*he fashion for quilts created interest in their history as well as a desire to make them. The first books devoted solely to quilting were published in the 1920s. Among them was *The Romance of the Patchwork Quilt in America*, coauthored by Carrie Hall and Rose Kretsinger.

Carrie Hall was a dressmaker in Leavenworth, Kansas, who used published patterns to make 16 quilts and more than 800 blocks during the 1920s. She used these blocks to illustrate talks about quilting to Kansas women's groups.

The Orchid Wreath quilt, *above*, that was pictured on the cover of their book was one of the many outstanding quilts designed and made by Rose Kretsinger of Emporia, Kansas.

Kretsinger took up quilting at age 40 during the height of the Colonial Revival when she decided to follow the advice given by popular magazines to make a copy of an old quilt for her bed.

From her maid, Kretsinger borrowed fragments of an antique quilt

◆ *Snowball* (opposite), c. 1925; 88½x88½ inches. Instructions begin on page 202.

Carpenter's Square Quilt

Shown on pages 178 and 179.
The finished quilt measures approximately
86x109 inches. Each Carpenter's Square
block is 23 inches square.

MATERIALS
7 yards of white solid fabric for
  patchwork, border, and binding
5 yards of blue solid fabric
3¼ yards of 90-inch-wide sheeting
  for backing
120x120-inch precut quilt batting
Fabric marker
Rotary cutter and mat
24-inch-long acrylic ruler marked in
  ⅛-inch and ¼-inch increments

INSTRUCTIONS
The Carpenter's Square block has
hidden potential. A single block is interesting, but when the 12 blocks are
joined in a straight set, the contrasting fabrics create an illusion of intri-
cately interwoven strips.

This block looks more complex to
make than it is. It is so well suited to
rotary cutting and strip piecing that
we do not recommend traditional
methods.

Referring to the block diagram,
right, identify the diagonal rows that
are the basic units of the Carpenter's
Square block. Rows 1, 2, and 3 are
white strips. Rows A, B, and C are cut
from one strip set. The corners (Unit
D) are made separately.

Cutting the fabrics
Cut all 42½-inch-wide strips cross-
grain to make efficient use of the fabric. The narrower strips can be cut
from the width remaining after the
side borders are cut.

From the white fabric, cut:
◆ One 30x42½-inch piece for the
  binding.
◆ Two 5½x102-inch strips and six
  5½x30-inch strips for the outer
  border.
◆ Twenty-four 1¾x31-inch strips
  for Row 1.
◆ Twenty-four 1¾x26-inch strips
  for Row 2.

◆ One 24x42½-inch piece.
  From this piece, cut twenty-four
  1¾x21-inch strips for Row 3.
◆ One 32x42½-inch piece.
  From this piece, cut eighteen
  1¾x42½-inch strips for the ABC
  strip set.
◆ One 18x42½-inch piece.
  From this piece, cut ten
  1¾x42½-inch strips. Cut each
  strip into five 8½-inch-wide
  segments to obtain forty-eight
  1¾x8½-inch pieces for Unit D.
◆ One 14x42½-inch piece.
  From this piece, cut seven
  1¾x42½-inch strips. Cut each
  strip into seven 6-inch-wide
  segments to obtain forty-eight
  1¾x6-inch pieces for Unit D.
◆ One 7x42½-inch piece.
  From this piece, cut four
  1¾x42½-inch strips. Cut each
  strip into twelve 3½-inch-wide
  segments to obtain forty-eight
  1¾x3½-inch pieces for Unit D.

From the blue fabric, cut:
◆ Four 4x42½-inch strips and two
  4x95-inch strips for the inner
  border.
◆ Twelve 1¾x42½-inch strips for
  the ABC strip set.
◆ Three 3x42½-inch strips for the
  ABC strip set.
◆ Sixteen 3x34-inch strips.
  From these strips, cut forty-eight
  3x9¾-inch pieces for Row A
  and Unit D.
◆ Twenty-four 1¾x34-inch strips.
  From these strips, cut ninety-six
  1¾x7¼-inch pieces for Row B
  and Unit D.
◆ Fifteen 1¾x42½-inch strips.
  From these strips, cut ninety-six
  1¾x4¾-inch pieces for Row C
  and Unit D, plus forty-eight
  1¾x2¼-inch pieces for Unit D.

Making the ABC strip set
See page 18 for additional information on strip piecing. The ABC strip
set is illustrated *opposite, top*.

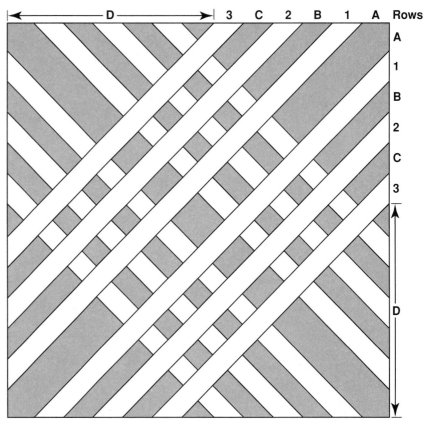

CARPENTER'S SQUARE BLOCK

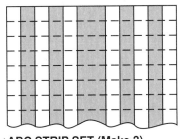

ABC STRIP SET (Make 3)

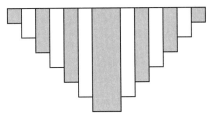

CORNER STRIP SET (Make 24)

Note: Throughout the assembly of rows A, B, and C, press the seam allowances toward the white fabric.

1. Begin with a 3x42½-inch strip of blue fabric for the center of the strip set. Stitch a 1¾x42½-inch strip of white fabric onto both long sides of the center strip.

2. Select four more 1¾x42½-inch strips of *each* fabric. Sew the strips together in blue-white pairs, matching the 42½-inch lengths.

3. Add these units to the center strip to assemble the strip set as illustrated. The completed strip set measures 15½x42½ inches.

4. Referring to the strip-piecing instructions on page 18, cut twelve 3-inch-wide units from this strip set for the center portion of Row A.

5. Make two more ABC strip sets. From these strip sets, cut forty-eight 1¾-inch-wide units for the center portions of rows B and C.

Completing rows A, B, and C

1. To complete Row A, stitch a 3x9¾-inch strip of blue fabric onto both ends of each of the twelve 3-inch-wide units.

2. To complete Row B, add one 1¾x7¼-inch strip of blue fabric onto both ends of each of 24 of the 1¾-inch-wide units.

3. To complete Row C, stitch a 1¾x4¾-inch blue strip onto the 24 remaining 1¾-inch-wide units.

Making the corners (Unit D)

One corner unit is made with 13 fabric strips as illustrated at *left, below.*

Note: Throughout the construction of the corner unit, press all seam allowances toward the blue fabric.

1. Begin with a 3x9¾-inch strip of blue fabric for the center of the strip set. Stitch a 1¾x8½-inch strip of white fabric onto both long sides of the center strip, aligning all three strips at one end. Because the strips are not the same length, the center blue strip extends beyond the two white ones as illustrated. Do not trim the excess fabric.

2. Add a 1¾x7¼-inch strip of blue fabric onto each side of the unit, keeping all the strips aligned at one end as shown.

3. Continue adding strips to both sides of the unit as illustrated, alternating white and blue strips of decreasing length. The last strips on the outside of the unit are 1¾x2¼-inch strips of blue fabric.

Make 24 corner units as shown.

Assembling the block

Note: Throughout the assembly of the block, press each new seam allowance toward the unpieced strip of fabric (rows 1, 2, or 3).

1. Lay out the assembled A, B, and C rows with the white strips cut for rows 1, 2, and 3 as shown in the block diagram, *opposite.*

2. Sew the Row 3 strip onto the pieced Row C, matching the centers of both strips. The strips are not the same length, so there is excess fabric at both ends of the longer row (C). Wait until the blocks are assembled before trimming these irregular ends of fabric, so you minimize the risk of stretching the bias edges.

3. Add Row 2 onto Row C, matching the centers of both rows as before.

4. Stitch Row B onto Row 2 in the same manner, then add Row 1 and Row A, which forms the diagonal center of the block.

5. For the other side of the block, join rows 1, B, 2, C, and 3 in succession as illustrated. If the centers of each row are carefully matched, the piecing in rows A, B, and C will align and create the illusion of interwoven strips.

6. Add a D corner unit to opposite sides of the block. Align the center of each corner unit as you did for the previous rows.

Complete 12 Carpenter's Square blocks. Do not trim the edges of the blocks until after they are joined.

Joining the blocks

Use the acrylic ruler and a fabric marker to draw seam lines around the edges of each block before joining the blocks. Mark the sewing lines on the *wrong* side of each block. Do not cut excess fabric from the block edges until the blocks are joined and you are sure the seam is acceptable.

1. Make a mark in the center of the wide middle strip of one corner unit, ¾ inch from the unstitched end of the strip. This mark pinpoints the corner of the block.

2. On each seam line of that corner unit, measure ¾ inch from the unstitched bottom edge of each of the 12 narrow strips. Make a mark at each of these points.

3. Draw a line on each side of the corner unit connecting the marks and extending across the adjacent block rows to the next corner.

4. Repeat steps 1, 2, and 3 on the opposite corner unit, then measure the square defined by these drawn lines. It should be a precise 23-inch square. However, it is unlikely that anyone's cutting and sewing will result in absolute precision. As you mark each block, you may find your marked squares are slightly larger or smaller—that's fine as long as they are consistent. The borders are cut long enough to accommodate a reasonable variance.

5. Mark sewing lines on all the blocks in this manner.

6. With right sides together and matching seam lines, pin two blocks together. Each row should align with the matching row in the adjacent block. Stitch the blocks together on the marked sewing line.

7. Check the seam on the right side of the joined blocks. The adjacent rows should match nicely. The small blue square formed in the center of the two blocks should be approximately 1¼ inches square.

continued

8. When you are satisfied with the stitched seam, use a rotary cutter and the acrylic ruler to trim the excess fabric from the seam allowance. Press the remaining ¼-inch seam allowance open if there is too much bulkiness to press it to one side.

9. In this manner, join the blocks in four horizontal rows of three blocks each. Join the rows to complete the quilt top, aligning the seam lines of adjacent blocks carefully. Around the outside of the quilt top, leave the jagged edges of the blocks untrimmed until the inner borders are added.

Adding the borders

1. Stitch one 4x95-inch strip of blue fabric to each long side of the quilt top, using the marked lines on the blocks as a sewing line. When you are satisfied with the seam, trim the excess fabric of the blocks from the seam allowance. Press the remaining ¼-inch seam allowances toward the border fabric.

2. Join two 4x42½-inch strips of blue fabric to make one 84½-inch-long border strip. Matching the center seam of the border with the center of the bottom edge of the quilt, stitch the border onto the quilt. In the same manner, add a blue border strip to the top edge. Trim excess fabric from the seam allowances and press.

3. Sew one 5½x102-inch strip of white fabric onto each long side of the quilt. Trim excess border fabric even with the ends of the quilt top.

4. Join three 5½x30-inch white strips to make a border for each of the two remaining sides. Matching the center of the border strip with the center of the quilt edge, stitch the borders onto the top and bottom of the quilt.

Quilting and finishing

MARKING: Mark the desired quilting design on the quilt top. The quilt shown on pages 178 and 179 has simple outline quilting around the block patchwork and a small cable quilted in the narrow border. The outer border is quilted with diagonal lines spaced 1¼ inches apart.

You can leave the borders straight or make a scalloped edge similar to the one pictured. If you want a scalloped edge, use a saucer or small bowl as a template and trace gentle curves along the outer edge of the quilt. Do not cut the scallops until after the quilting is complete.

QUILTING: Sandwich the batting between the backing fabric and the marked quilt top; baste the three layers together. Quilt as desired.

BINDING: Use the remaining white fabric to make approximately 410 inches of binding. See pages 306 and 307 for tips on making and applying binding. If you are making a scalloped edge, follow the instructions on page 306 to prepare continuous bias binding; stitch the binding onto the quilted top before cutting the scallops from the outer border fabric.

Tulip Garden Quilt

Shown on pages 184 and 185.
The finished quilt measures approximately 79½x97 inches. Each block is 12½ inches square.

MATERIALS
7¾ yards of white fabric
3 yards of green solid fabric
1¾ yards of red solid fabric
6 yards of backing fabric
90x108-inch precut quilt batting
Template material

INSTRUCTIONS
An appliquéd border makes a stunning framework for this classic red, white, and green tulip design. The quilt has 12 appliquéd blocks assembled in an alternate diagonal set.

Cutting the fabrics
See page 288 for tips on making templates for patchwork and appliqué. Make appliqué templates for patterns A, B, C, and D, *opposite*, and a patchwork template for Pattern E, *below.*

When cutting the A, B, and C appliqués from fabric, add a ³⁄₁₆-inch seam allowance around each piece. Add a full ¼-inch seam allowance at the straight ends of each D piece as indicated on the pattern, since the D pieces are seamed together.

From the white fabric, cut:
◆ One 29x42-inch piece for the binding.
◆ Two 14x103-inch border strips.
◆ Two 14x84-inch border strips.
◆ Three 19-inch squares.
  Cut each of these squares in quarters diagonally to obtain 10 setting triangles.
◆ Two 10-inch squares.
  Cut both squares in half diagonally to get four corner triangles.
◆ Eighteen 13-inch squares.

From the red solid fabric, cut:
◆ 12 of Pattern A.
◆ 76 of Pattern B.

continued

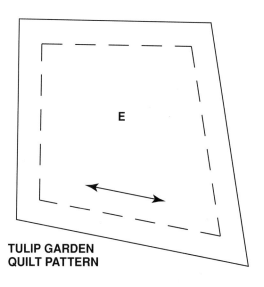

**TULIP GARDEN
QUILT PATTERN**

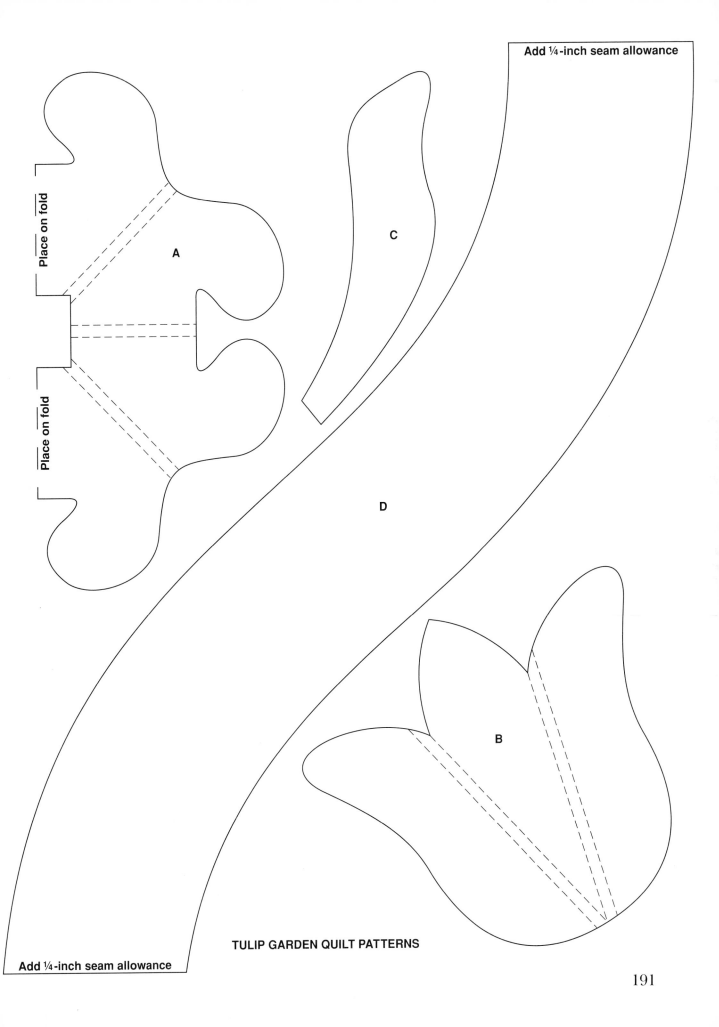

Add ¼-inch seam allowance

Place on fold

Place on fold

A

C

D

B

Add ¼-inch seam allowance

TULIP GARDEN QUILT PATTERNS

191

From the green solid fabric, cut:

◆ Five 1x42-inch strips for the tulip stems.
◆ One 32x42-inch piece.
   From this piece, cut 76 of Pattern C and 76 of Pattern C reversed.
◆ One 63x42-inch piece.
   From this piece, cut 14 of Pattern D and 14 of Pattern D reversed.
◆ Four of Pattern E.

Preparing stems for appliqué

1. With right sides together, fold one 1x42-inch green strip in half lengthwise. Machine-stitch a scant ¼ inch from the raw edge of the strip.
2. Press the seam allowance open, centering the seam line in the middle of the strip. Turn the strip right side out and press again.
3. Stitch the remaining four stem strips in this manner. If you find it easier to turn a shorter strip, cut each 42-inch-long strip into two 21-inch-long pieces and prepare them in the same manner.
4. Cut 2½-inch-long segments from these strips for the tulip stems. Cut 76 stems. It is not necessary to turn under the short ends as these will be covered by other pieces.

Appliquéing the block

1. Turn under the seam allowances on one A center piece, including the little square in the middle of the fabric. Clip the seam allowance as needed to achieve nicely curved edges.
2. Turn under the edges of four tulips and eight leaves (four of Pattern C and four of Pattern C reversed). Do not turn under the straight edges of the leaves since these will be covered by the stems.
3. Fold one white square in half vertically, horizontally, and diagonally; finger-press each fold to mark placement lines.
4. Referring to the block diagram, *above,* pin the appliqués in place. Align the deep indents of the A piece on the horizontal and vertical placement lines and the center of each curved section on the diagonal lines. Tuck a stem under the A piece at each diagonal placement line. Position C and C reversed leaves on opposite sides of each stem. Place a B tulip at the top of each stem.

TULIP GARDEN BLOCK

5. When all the pieces are correctly positioned, appliqué them in place. For the center of the A piece, use your needle to turn back and appliqué the edge of the inner square, revealing the white fabric underneath.
   Make 12 appliquéd blocks.

Assembling the quilt top

Refer to page 295 for a diagram of a diagonal set. Use this diagram as a guide to lay out the appliquéd blocks, the six setting squares, and the setting triangles in diagonal rows.
   Assemble the blocks and setting pieces in diagonal rows, then join the rows. The assembled quilt top without the border should measure approximately 53x71 inches.

Adding the appliquéd swag border

1. Stitch one 14x84-inch border strip to the top and bottom edges of the quilt, matching the center of each strip with the center of the edge of the quilt top. Sew a 14x103-inch border strip onto the side edges of the quilt and miter the corners. See page 299 for instructions on making mitered corners.
2. Machine-stitch each D piece to one D reversed piece with a ¼-inch seam allowance. Press the seam allowances open to avoid bulkiness when turning the edges for appliqué. Each of these pairs is one swag of the border.
3. To make a curved swag border for one short side of the quilt, join three swags end to end. Turn under the curved edges to prepare the border for appliqué.

4. Center and pin the prepared border on one short side of the quilt, matching the center seam of the swag border with the center of the white border strip. In the same manner, prepare a three-swag border for the opposite side of the quilt.
5. Join four swags end to end for each side border. Stitch an E piece onto each end of both four-swag strips. Turn under the edges of each swag strip to prepare it for appliqué.
6. Center a four-swag border on each long side of the quilt, matching centers. If your stitching has been precise, the diamond-shaped E piece will straddle the mitered seam of the white borders and align with the swag border on the adjacent side. Some adjustment may be required to align the swag borders.
7. When all four swag borders are correctly positioned, baste them in place. Tuck a stem under the swags at each seam line and at the tip of each E corner piece. The stems at the E corner piece will point to the outside corner of the quilt and the other stems will alternate directions, half the stems pointing toward the inside of the quilt and half pointing toward the outside edge (see photo on pages 184 and 185). Pin a tulip and two leaves in place on each stem.
8. Appliqué the swags and the border tulips in place on the white fabric.

Quilting and finishing

BACKING: Cut the backing fabric into two 3-yard pieces. Sew them together to make one wide panel.
   Layer backing, batting, and quilt top; baste the three layers together.

QUILTING: Quilt as desired. The quilt shown has a diagonal grid of 1-inch squares quilted in the white areas and outline quilting around the appliqué pieces. Quilting lines for the center pieces and tulips are shown on the A and B patterns. Parallel lines of quilting follow the curves in the appliquéd border swags.

BINDING: Use the remaining white fabric to make approximately 365 inches of bias or straight-grain binding. Refer to pages 306 and 307 for tips on making and applying binding.

Lindy Quilt

Shown on page 182.
Finished quilt is approximately 74x85
inches. Each block is 11 inches square.

MATERIALS
5¼ yards of muslin or white fabric
3 yards of gold solid fabric for
  patchwork, borders, and binding
Gold embroidery floss and
  embroidery needle
5 yards of backing fabric
81x96-inch precut quilt batting
Template material
Tracing paper and pencil
Nonpermanent fabric marker
Rotary cutter, mat, and acrylic ruler

INSTRUCTIONS
This quilt is an alternate straight set
of 42 blocks joined in seven rows of
six blocks each. Twenty-one airplane
blocks alternate with muslin blocks
that are embroidered with an eagle,
another American symbol of flight.

Cutting the fabrics
See page 288 for tips on making templates for patchwork and appliqué.
Make templates for patchwork patterns A through F and appliqué pattern G, *below* and on page 196.

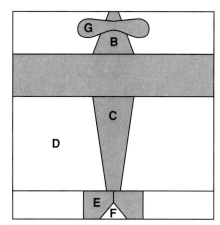

AIRPLANE BLOCK

From the muslin, cut:
◆ Twenty-one 11½-inch squares.
◆ 21 *each* of patterns A, A reversed,
  D, D reversed, and F.
◆ Forty-two 2x4⅜-inch strips for
  the bottom of the block.

From the gold fabric, cut:
◆ One 25x42-inch piece for the
  binding.
◆ Four 4½x80-inch border strips.
◆ 21 *each* of patterns B, C, E, E
  reversed, and G.
  Add a ³⁄₁₆-inch seam allowance
  around the template when cutting
  the G propellers.
◆ Twenty-one 2¾x11½-inch strips
  for the airplane wings.

Making the airplane blocks
The airplane block is made in four
horizontal rows as illustrated in the
block diagram, *left*.
1. To make Row 1, the top row, stitch
one A and one A reversed onto the
long sides of one B piece. Press the
seam allowances toward the gold B
piece.
2. Make Row 3 in the same manner,
stitching one D piece and one D reversed piece onto the long sides of
one C piece.
3. Sew a 2x4⅜-inch muslin strip onto
a long side of one E piece. Stitch another muslin strip onto one E reversed piece. Press the seam
allowances toward the gold fabric.
4. Stitch these E pieces together,
joining the short edges of the two
pieces as shown in the block diagram.
Press the seam allowance open. Set
the muslin F piece into the angle between the two E pieces.
5. Using a 2¾x11½-inch strip of
gold fabric for Row 2, join the rows.
6. Turn under the edges of the propeller (G) piece. Center the propeller
over the gold B piece, positioning it
approximately ¾ inch from the edge
of the block. Appliqué the propeller
in place.

Make 21 airplane blocks.

continued

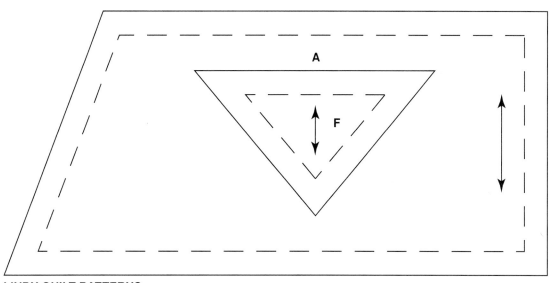

LINDY QUILT PATTERNS

Join eagle pattern on the dotted lines

**EMBROIDERY PATTERN
FOR LINDY QUILT**

Embroidering the eagle blocks

Trace the two parts of the eagle embroidery pattern, *right* and *opposite,* to make a complete pattern.

Center one muslin square over the traced pattern. Use a washout fabric marker or pencil to lightly trace the design onto the fabric. Using two strands of floss, embroider the eagle design in outline stitch (see page 137 for stitch diagram).

Make 21 eagle blocks.

Assembling the quilt top

See page 295 for an illustration of an alternate straight set.

1. Join the blocks into seven horizontal rows of six blocks each, alternating the two kinds of blocks. Four rows will begin at the left-hand side with airplanes and three rows will begin with eagles. Press the seam allowances toward the eagle blocks.

2. Join the rows, matching the block seam lines. The quilt top should be approximately 66½ x 77½ inches.

Adding the borders

Sew one border strip onto each long side of the quilt top. Press the seam allowances toward the borders; trim excess border fabric even with the ends of the quilt top.

Add the two remaining border strips to the top and bottom edges of the quilt top in the same manner.

Quilting and finishing

BACKING: Cut the backing fabric into two 2½-yard lengths. Sew the two panels together side by side; press the seam allowance open.

Sandwich the batting between the backing and the quilt top. Baste the three layers securely together.

QUILTING: The quilt shown has a diagonal grid of 1-inch squares quilted in the background of the eagle and airplane blocks as well as straight line quilting on the airplane wings. Diagonal lines of quilting zigzag along each border. Quilt as desired.

BINDING: Use the remaining gold fabric piece to make approximately 325 inches of bias or straight-grain binding. See pages 306 and 307 for tips on making and applying binding.

Join eagle pattern on the dotted lines

195

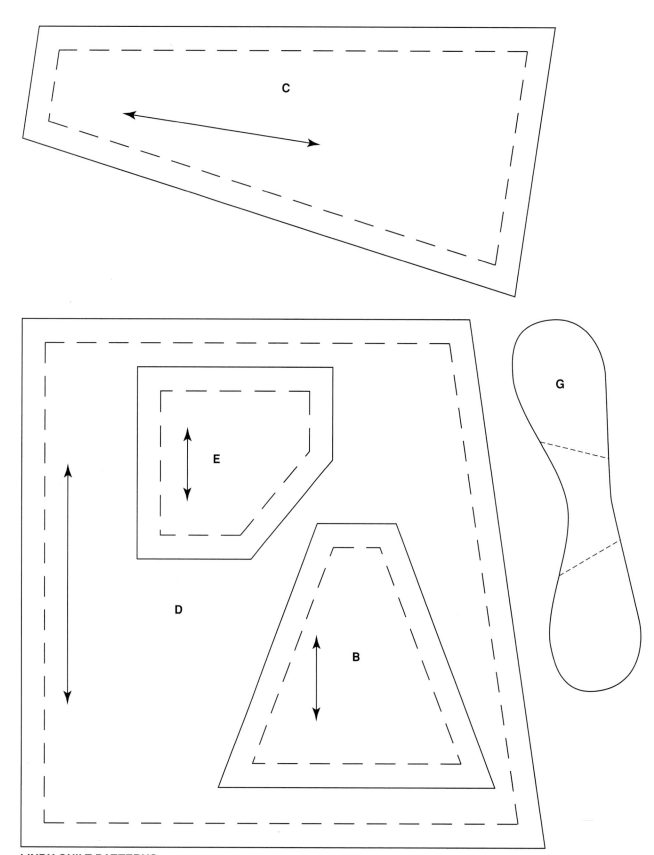

LINDY QUILT PATTERNS

Pomegranate Medallion Quilt

Shown on page 183.
The finished quilt measures approximately 82x82 inches.

MATERIALS

4 yards of muslin
2½ yards *each* of green, pink, and gold solid fabrics
2½ yards of 90-inch-wide sheeting for backing fabric
81x96-inch precut quilt batting
Template material

INSTRUCTIONS

This quilt has triple flower motifs appliquéd on a center square and four side panels. The same flowers are appliquéd on the corner squares in a narrowed arrangement.

Cutting the fabrics

See page 288 for tips on making templates for appliqué. Make templates for patterns A, B, and C, *below.* Pattern A is used for both the leaves and the tulip petals. When cutting the appliqués from fabric, add a ³/₁₆-inch seam allowance around each piece.

From the muslin, cut:
◆ One 38½-inch center square.
◆ Four 16½x38½-inch side panels.
◆ Four 16½-inch corner squares.

From the green fabric, cut:
◆ Four 2½x86-inch border strips.
◆ One 27x32-inch strip for binding.
◆ Four 1½x32-inch strips for the *straight stems.*
  From these strips, cut four 13-inch-long stems and six 9-inch-long stems.
◆ One 22-inch square.
  Cut this square into 1½-inch-wide *bias* strips for the *curved stems.* From these, cut twelve 1½x13½-inch stems and eight 1½x9½-inch stems.
◆ 20 *each* of Pattern A and Pattern A reversed.
◆ 60 of Pattern B.

From the gold fabric, cut:
◆ Four 2½x86-inch border strips.
◆ 30 of Pattern C.

From the pink fabric, cut:
◆ Four 2½x86-inch border strips.
◆ 30 *each* of Pattern A and Pattern A reversed.

Preparing stems for appliqué

1. Fold a straight-grain stem piece in half lengthwise with right sides together. Machine-stitch ¼ inch from the edge of the long side. Press the seam allowance open, centering the seam in the middle of the strip.
2. Stitch ¼ inch from the edge of one end of the stem, sewing across the pressed seam allowance. Turn the strip right side out and press again. Prepare all the straight-grain stem strips in this manner. The other end will be covered by a flower, so it is not necessary to finish those edges.
3. Stitch the bias stems as you did the straight stems, but leave both short ends unstitched as they are both covered by other pieces.

Positioning the appliqué

Referring to the quilt assembly diagram on page 198, pin or baste the appliqués in position on the muslin, as described below, before stitching them in place. The measurements shown on the assembly diagram are for the finished quilt; measurements in these instructions include the seam allowances for individual blocks.

1. Prepare the appliqué pieces for each block by basting back the seam allowances. It is not necessary to turn under edges that will be covered by another piece, such as the bottom edges of the A and C flower pieces. Clip seam allowances as necessary to achieve nice points and curves.
2. Fold the 38½-inch muslin square in half vertically and horizontally; finger-press the folds to establish placement guidelines for appliqué.
3. Center one 9-inch-long straight stem on the horizontal guideline, placing the finished end of the stem 1 inch to the *right* of the vertical guideline. Position another 9-inch-long stem on the horizontal placement line with its finished end 1 inch to the *left* of the vertical guideline.
4. Pin a C piece at the top of each straight stem, lapping the unturned end of the C piece over the unturned edge of the stem. The top of each C piece should be approximately 6¼ inches from the edge of the muslin.
5. Place one pink A piece and one pink A reverse piece over each C piece as indicated on the C pattern, *below.* Cover the unturned edges of

continued

Lap tulip petals (A) over tip

C

B

A

POMEGRANATE MEDALLION QUILT PATTERNS

the stem and the A and C pieces with two green B pieces, overlapping the tips of the two pieces in the center of the flower.

6. Pin a 13½-inch-long bias stem on each side and 1 inch from the bottom of each straight stem, as shown in the quilt assembly diagram, *below.* Tuck the end of each bias stem under a straight stem and then curve the bias stems as shown. Pin the bias stems in place on the background fabric.

7. Pin flower pieces at the end of each side stem. Adjust the positions of the stems and flowers using the measurements in the diagram as a guide. One petal tip (A) of each side flower should be 4½ inches from the center vertical guideline, or 9 inches from the opposite flower.

8. Place green leaves (A) on the stems as shown.

9. Position the stems and pomegranates on each 16½x38½-inch side

panel in the same manner, using the measurements shown on the assembly diagram as guidelines (don't forget to add seam allowances).

10. Fold each muslin corner square in half diagonally; finger-press to make a placement guideline. Center a 13-inch-long straight stem on the guideline, positioning the finished (bottom) edge of the stem approximately 3⅛ inches from the corner of the muslin square.

POMEGRANATE MEDALLION QUILT ASSEMBLY DIAGRAM

11. Pin a C piece at the top of the stem, placing the tip of the C piece approximately 4½ inches from the corner. Pin the A and B tulip pieces in place on top of the C piece.

12. Add the side stems and flowers as shown, then position the leaves.

Appliquéing the blocks
Stitch the stem pieces and leaves in place first. Appliqué each tulip in place next, starting with the center C piece. Stitch the pink petals in place; appliqué the green B pieces last.

Assembling the quilt top
To join the blocks, refer to the quilt assembly diagram to assemble three horizontal rows. To make the top row, stitch a corner square onto both short sides of one 16½x38½-inch side panel. Position the pomegranate flowers as shown in the assembly diagram. Make the bottom row in the same manner.

Sew the two remaining side panels onto the side edges of the 38½-inch center square. Join the three rows to complete the quilt top.

Adding the borders
Sew a green border strip between a pink and a gold border strip to make one 6½x86-inch border unit. Press both seam allowances toward the green strip. Make three more border units in the same manner.

Add one border unit to each side of the quilt and miter the corners. See page 299 for instructions on making mitered corners.

Quilting and finishing
Sandwich the batting between the backing fabric and the quilt top; baste the three layers securely together.

QUILTING: Quilt as desired. The quilt shown on page 183 has a diagonal grid of 1½-inch squares quilted in the muslin areas and outline quilting around the appliqué pieces and in the borders.

BINDING: Use the remaining green fabric to make approximately 340 inches of bias or straight-grain binding. Refer to pages 306 and 307 for tips on making and applying binding.

Milky Way Quilt

Shown on page 184.
The finished quilt measures approximately 44½x48½ inches. Each finished block is 6 inches square.

MATERIALS
2¼ yards of muslin
3¾ yards of pink solid fabric for the patchwork and backing
½ yard of pink print fabric for binding
48x60-inch precut quilt batting
Rotary cutter, mat, and acrylic ruler

INSTRUCTIONS
The magic of this quilt is that the pieced sashing creates the illusion of a contrasting block. Since the quilt is made with two contrasting fabrics, it is difficult to distinguish the blocks from the sashing when the quilt is complete.

The Milky Way block is assembled like a nine-patch by joining one plain square, four pieced triangle-squares, and four four-patch squares. The same basic units are used to make the sashing. Instructions are given for quick piecing, but are adapted easily to traditional methods.

Cutting the fabrics
A rotary cutter, used with an acrylic ruler, is ideal to cut all the pieces for this quilt. Templates are not needed.

From the pink solid fabric, cut:
◆ One 54x42-inch piece and one 5x54-inch piece.
   Set these aside for the backing.
◆ One 7x51-inch piece.
   From this piece, cut two 1¾x51-inch strips and two 1¾x47-inch strips for the borders.
◆ Eight 1½x42-inch strips for the four-patch units.
◆ Three 2½x42½-inch strips.
   From these strips, cut forty-nine 2½-inch squares for the blocks and the sashing.
◆ Five 15x18-inch rectangles for the triangle-squares.
   There is enough fabric to cut an extra rectangle if you need it.

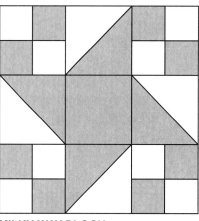

MILKY WAY BLOCK

From the muslin, cut:
◆ One 12x51-inch piece.
   From this piece, cut four 1½x47-inch strips and four 1½x51-inch strips for the borders.
◆ Eight 1½x42-inch strips for the four-patch units.
◆ Three 2½x42½-inch strips.
   From these, cut fifty 2½-inch squares for the sashing units.
◆ Five 15x18-inch rectangles for the triangle-squares.
   Enough fabric is allowed to cut an extra rectangle if you need it.

Making the triangle-squares
Refer to page 114 for more detailed instructions on quick-pieced triangle-squares.

1. On each 15x18-inch muslin piece, mark a 4x5-square grid of 2⅞-inch squares as shown in Figure 1, *below.* Draw the diagonal lines through the squares as shown.

continued

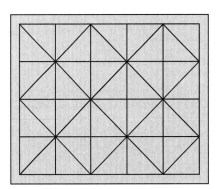

FIGURE 1

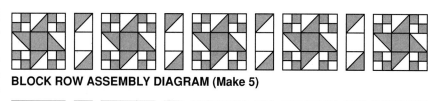

BLOCK ROW ASSEMBLY DIAGRAM (Make 5)

SASHING ROW ASSEMBLY DIAGRAM (Make 6)

2. Layer each muslin square, marked side up, atop a matching 15x18-inch piece of pink fabric.

3. For traditional piecing, cut the triangles apart on the marked lines; use a fabric pencil and a gridded ruler to mark ¼-inch seam allowances on each triangle.

4. For quick piecing, stitch the grid as described in Step 3 on page 114. Each grid makes 40 triangle-squares.

5. Repeat the procedure with the remaining 15x18-inch pieces to make 200 triangle-squares. Press the seam allowances toward the pink fabric.

Making the four-patch units

TRADITIONAL PIECING: Cut the 1½-inch-wide strips of *each* fabric into 1½-inch squares, cutting 200 squares of each color. Assemble the squares into four-patch units as shown in Figure 2, *below.* Make 100 units. Press seam allowances toward the pink fabric.

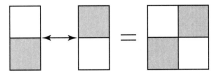

FIGURE 2

STRIP PIECING: See page 18 for tips on strip piecing.

Stitch each 1½x42-inch strip of pink fabric to a matching muslin strip to make a 2½x42-inch strip set; press the seam allowances toward the pink fabric. From each of the eight strip sets, cut twenty-five 1½-inch-wide segments.

Use two segments to make each of 100 four-patch units, turning one segment upside down to position the fabrics as shown in Figure 2, *above.*

Making the Milky Way blocks

Refer to the block diagram on page 199 to assemble each block. Join the prestitched units in three rows of three squares each.

1. To assemble the top row of the block, stitch a four-patch unit onto opposite sides of one triangle-square,

positioning the fabrics as shown in the diagram. Assemble a triangle-square and two four-patch units for the bottom row in a similar manner. Press all the joining seam allowances toward the four-patch units.

2. For the middle row, sew triangle-squares onto opposite sides of a plain pink square, positioning the fabric colors as shown in the diagram. Press the seam allowances toward the center square.

3. Join the three rows to complete the block. Make 25 Milky Way blocks.

Assembling the pieced sashing

Use the remaining triangle-squares for the sashing. All 50 of the sashing units are the same.

Stitch triangle-squares onto opposite sides of one 2½-inch muslin square, always sewing muslin edges together. Position the triangles to make a finished sashing unit as illustrated in the row assembly diagrams, *above.* Make 50 sashing units in this manner; press the seam allowances toward the muslin square.

Assembling the quilt top

See page 295 for an illustration of a straight set with sashing.

1. Select five blocks for each row. Join the blocks as shown in the Block Row Assembly Diagram, *above, top,* with a sashing unit between each pair of blocks. Make five block rows.

2. Each row of horizontal sashing is made by alternating 2½-inch pink squares with pieced sashing units. Starting with a pieced unit, sew five sashing units and four squares together to make a row as illustrated in the Sashing Row Assembly Diagram, *above, bottom.* Make six rows of horizontal sashing.

3. Matching seam lines carefully, sew a row of horizontal sashing to the top of each block row.

4. Join the rows, sewing the top of the sashing row to the bottom of the adjacent block row.

5. Complete the quilt top by sewing the remaining row of sashing to the bottom of the fifth block row.

Adding the borders

Refer to page 299 for instructions for borders with mitered corners.

1. For each side of the quilt, sew a muslin border strip on both long sides of each pink border strip.

2. Sew the 51-inch-long border units onto the sides of the quilt top and the 47-inch-long border units to the top and bottom edges. Miter the corners, then trim the excess border fabric from the seam.

Quilting and finishing

BACKING: Stitch the two pieces of backing fabric together along their 54-inch lengths to make one 46½-inch-wide panel; press the seam allowance open.

Layer backing, batting, and quilt top; baste the three layers together.

QUILTING: The quilt shown has diagonal lines quilted through each pink square of the four-patch units. These lines cross and form an X in the center of each muslin sashing square. The triangle-squares and the borders have outline quilting. Quilt as desired.

BINDING: Use the ½ yard of print fabric to make approximately 190 inches of either bias or straight-grain binding. See pages 306 and 307 for tips on making and applying binding.

Kaleidoscope Quilt

Shown on pages 180 and 181.
The finished quilt measures 83x99
inches. Each block is 8 inches square.

MATERIALS

2¾ yards of muslin
⅞ yard *each* of light peach, red,
    green, blue, yellow, lavender,
    dark pink, and light pink solid
    fabrics for the block patchwork
¾ yard of dark peach solid fabric
    for the inner border
⅓ yard of gold solid fabric for the
    block centers
1 yard of binding fabric
3 yards of 90-inch-wide sheeting for
    backing fabric
90x108-inch precut quilt batting
Template material

INSTRUCTIONS

Each of the eight triangles in this
block is a different color. The same
colors are used, in the same positions, in all the blocks. A gold circle is
appliquéd in the center of the blocks
where the triangle points meet.

This bright and cheery quilt has 99
Kaleidoscope blocks arranged in a
9x11-block straight set.

Cutting the fabrics

Refer to page 288 for tips on making
templates for patchwork and appliqué. Make templates for patterns A,
B, and C, *right*. Add a ⅛6-inch seam
allowance to each C piece when cutting out the traced circles.

From the muslin, cut:
◆ Four 4½x94-inch borders.
◆ 396 of Pattern B.

From the gold fabric, cut:
◆ 99 of Pattern C, adding the seam
    allowance.

From each of the colored fabrics, cut:
◆ 99 of Pattern A.

From the dark peach fabric, cut:
◆ Four 2x42-inch strips for the end
    borders.
◆ Six 2x30-inch strips for the side
    borders.

Making the Kaleidoscope block

Select one A triangle of each color to
make one block. Refer to the block
diagram, *right*, for color placement as
you make each block.
1. Begin by sewing pairs of A triangles together. Stitch the red triangle
to the green one and the peach triangle to the lavender one. Press the
seam allowances toward the red and
the lavender fabrics.
2. Join the two pairs by sewing the
red and peach triangles together;
press the seam allowance toward the
peach triangle.
3. Make the other half of the block in
the same manner, stitching the dark
pink and yellow triangles together,
then joining the blue triangle to the
light pink one. Press the seam allowances toward the yellow and pink triangles. Join the two pairs to make a
half-block.
4. Join the block halves to form an
octagon. Don't worry if the triangle
points don't come together exactly in
the center as this will be covered by
the C circle.

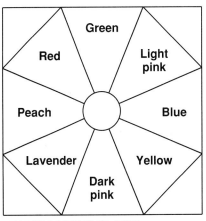

KALEIDOSCOPE BLOCK

5. Stitch the long side (hypotenuse)
of a muslin B triangle to the edges of
the yellow, lavender, light pink, and
red edges; press the seam allowances
toward the B triangles.

continued

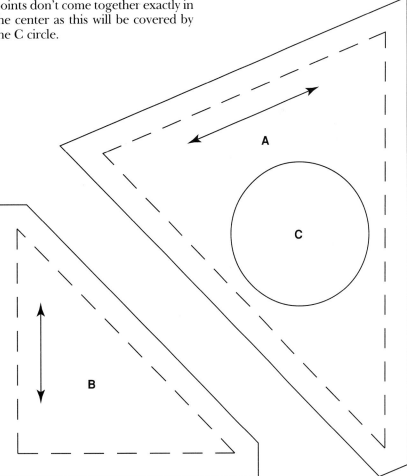

KALEIDOSCOPE QUILT PATTERNS

6. Turn under the edge of a gold C circle. Appliqué the circle in place over the center of the block.

Make 99 Kaleidoscope blocks.

Assembling the quilt top

Join the blocks in 11 horizontal rows of nine blocks each. When piecing a row, join the peach triangle of each block to the blue triangle in the adjacent block. This keeps all the blocks in the same relative position.

Stitch the rows together to complete the quilt top.

Adding the borders

INNER BORDER: Stitch three 2x30-inch strips of dark peach fabric together end to end to make a border strip for each long side of the quilt. Match the center of the border strip with the center of one side of the quilt top; stitch borders in place on both sides. Press the seam allowances toward the borders, then trim the excess border fabric even with the top and bottom edges of the quilt top.

Join two 2x42-inch strips of dark peach fabric to make a border strip for the top and bottom edges. Add these borders in the same manner as the side borders.

OUTER BORDER: Stitch a muslin border strip onto each long side of the quilt top. Press the seam allowances toward the inner border; trim excess border fabric even with the edges of the quilt top.

Repeat to add borders to the top and bottom edges.

Quilting and finishing

Sandwich the batting between the quilt top and the backing. Baste the three layers securely together.

QUILTING: Quilt as desired. The quilt pictured has outline quilting inside each colored triangle. The borders are quilted with diagonal lines, 1 inch apart.

BINDING: Make approximately 370 inches of bias or straight-grain binding. See pages 306 and 307 for tips on making and applying binding.

— BASIC —

Snowball Quilt

Shown on page 187.
The finished quilt measures approximately 88½x88½ inches. Each Snowball block is 8 inches square.

MATERIALS

5 yards of muslin or white fabric
4 yards of pink solid fabric
2¾ yards of backing fabric
90x108-inch precut quilt batting
Template material
Rotary cutter, mat, and acrylic ruler

INSTRUCTIONS

The Snowball Quilt is an example of the Robbing Peter to Pay Paul effect created by alternating images of two contrasting fabrics. When the blocks are set together, the octagons and triangles create the illusion of white stars on a pink background—or is it pink stars on a white background?

Eighty-one Snowball blocks in this quilt are assembled in a 9x9-block straight set framed by a three-strip border with pieced corners.

Cutting the fabrics

Refer to page 288 for tips on making templates for patchwork. Make a window template for Pattern A, *opposite*. You can make a template for the half-pattern as given and mark on folded fabric, or you can make a template for the complete shape so you can mark on a single layer of fabric. Mark both cutting and sewing lines for piece A.

From the pink fabric, cut:
◆ One 13x86-inch piece for the borders.
  From this piece, cut four 3¼x79-inch strips for the middle border and eight 3¼-inch squares for the corners of the other two borders.
◆ Ten 3⅝x29-inch strips.
  From these strips, cut eighty 3⅝-inch squares. Cut each square in half diagonally to obtain 160 triangles.
◆ 41 of Pattern A.

SNOWBALL BLOCK

From the white fabric, cut:
◆ One 25x42-inch piece for the binding.
◆ One 26x84-inch piece for the borders.
  From this piece, cut four 3¼x73-inch strips for the inner (first) border and four 3¼x84-inch strips for the outer (third) border. From the scrap at the end of the shorter borders, cut four 3¼-inch squares for the corners of the middle border.
◆ Twenty-one 3⅝x16-inch strips. From these strips, cut eighty-two 3⅝-inch squares. Cut each square in half diagonally to obtain 164 triangles.
◆ 40 of Pattern A.

Making the Snowball block

Throughout the construction of the blocks, press the seam allowances toward the darker fabric.
1. Stitch a pink triangle onto one diagonal edge of a white octagon (A). Add pink triangles to the three remaining diagonal edges to complete the block. Make 40 Snowball blocks in this manner.
2. Repeat, sewing four white triangles onto each pink octagon. Make 41 of these blocks.

Assembling the quilt top

Join the blocks into nine horizontal rows of nine blocks each, alternating pink and white centers. Make five rows that have pink-centered blocks at each end and four rows that have white-centered blocks at each end.

Join the rows, alternating the block colors and matching seam lines carefully. The assembled quilt top should be approximately $72\frac{1}{2}$x$72\frac{1}{2}$ inches.

Adding the borders

1. Stitch a $3\frac{1}{4}$x73-inch white border strip onto the top edge of the quilt. Add a matching border strip to the bottom edge. Press the seam allowances toward the border strips; trim borders even with the sides of the quilt top.

2. Add a $3\frac{1}{4}$-inch square of pink fabric to both ends of the remaining 73-inch-long border strips. Join these to the sides of the quilt top, matching the seam lines of the corner squares with the seam lines of the top and bottom borders. Adjust the corner square seams to make the side borders shorter or longer as necessary.

3. Stitch the middle border in the same manner, adding pink strips at the top and bottom edges of the quilt top and then adding the side borders with white corner squares.

4. Use the $3\frac{1}{4}$x84-inch white strips for the outer (third) border. Add pink squares to the side borders.

Quilting and finishing

Layer backing, batting, and quilt top; baste the three layers together.

QUILTING: On the quilt pictured on page 187, there are six different designs quilted in the white octagons. We show one of these quilting designs on Pattern A, *right*. The pink octagons are quilted with a grid of 1-inch squares, and the triangles have outline quilting inside the seam lines. A cable of interlocked ovals is quilted over the combined width of the border strips. Quilt as desired.

BINDING: Make approximately 360 inches of bias or straight-grain binding. See pages 306 and 307 for tips on making and applying binding.

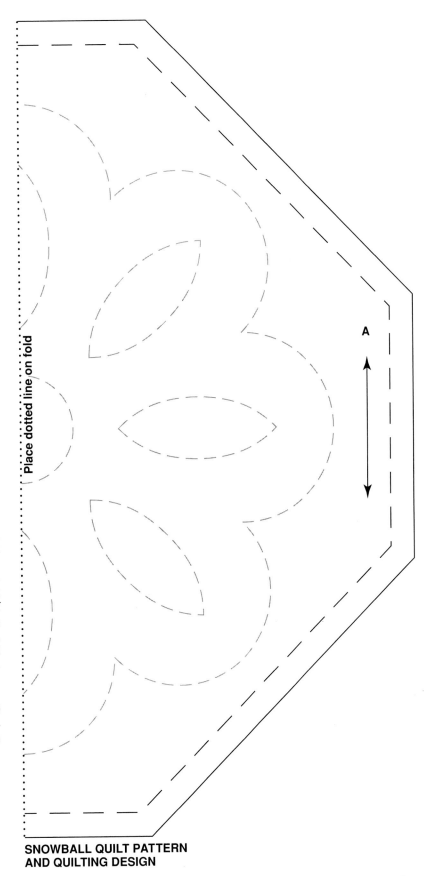

Place dotted line on fold

A

**SNOWBALL QUILT PATTERN
AND QUILTING DESIGN**

◆ *Tulip Circle, c. 1938;*
70x85 inches. Instructions
begin on page 214.

Triumphs IN Hard Times

Quiltmakers Overcome
The Great Depression

1930 ∾ 1945

Triumphs in Hard Times
1930–1945

*'Most all my work has been the kind that perishes with
the usin', as the Bible says . . . if a woman was
to see all the dishes she had to wash before she died, all
piled up before her in one pile, she'd lie down and
die right then and there. When I'm gone, ain't nobody
goin' to think o' the floors I've swept . . . But when one of
my grandchildren or great-grandchildren sees one
o' these quilts, they'll think of Aunt Jane, and, wherever
I am then, I'll know I ain't forgotten.*

Eliza Calvert Hall, *Aunt Jane of Kentucky*

*I*t was a time of making do or doing without, of worrying, scrimping, and outright despair. But many quilts made during the Great Depression of the 1930s belie the hard times in which they were made. Regardless of pattern or place of origin, most 1930s quilts were pretty, pastel, and surprisingly sophisticated.

The story of quiltmaking in the 1930s begins in the previous decade. The 1920s were years of prosperity that saw enormous change in the American way of life. The rural, farm-based society of the late 1800s was transformed into an industrial colossus built around

thriving urban centers. Many of the time-honored traditions of American life had simply faded away.

Having come to rely on ready-made commodities, most Americans no longer could afford them when the hard times came. Getting by in the Depression meant relearning the skills of earlier days. But the times had changed and quilt-making, like most art forms, incorporated both the old and the new.

◆ *Dogwood (right), made from a published Laura Wheeler pattern, c. 1938; 83x83 inches. Instructions begin on page 216.*

206

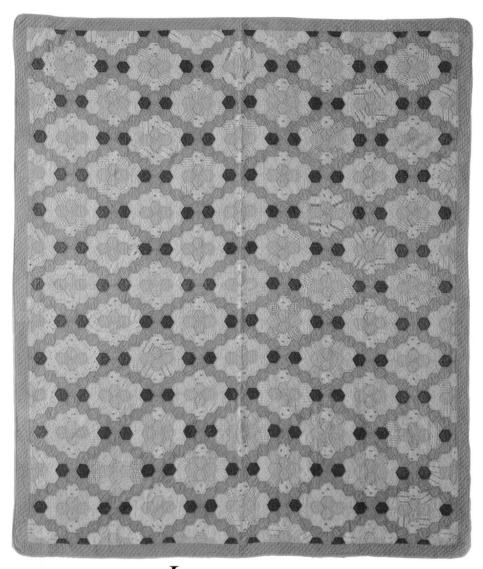

◆ *Rainbow Tile* (above),
c. 1936; 68x89 inches.
Instructions begin on
page 218.

*I*n the catastrophic
economic climate of the
Depression, federal recovery programs used folk
art, such as quiltmaking,
to create cottage indus-
tries, social occasions, and
a demand for domestic
textiles. The idea was to
solve the crisis with good
old American know-how
and fortitude by making

the most of time-honored
traditions. National pride
and confidence were the
keys to recovery.

Depression era quilts
were based on traditional
patterns and techniques.
But the strong colors of
authentic early patchwork
clashed with 1930s styles,
so new pastel colors and
the influence of design
styles, such as art deco
and art nouveau, were
mixed with old designs to
create a new look.

These soft, sometimes
elegant designs contrasted
with the stark reality of

the hard times facing
quiltmakers. By concen-
trating on making
something beautiful, the
quilter could block out
poverty and deprivation.

Quiltmakers clamored
for new ideas and vari-
ations, and many
publishers were glad to
provide them. Most
women's magazines of the
1930s simply ignored the

country's woes. Nobody
wanted to read bad news,
and products associated
with hard times did
not sell. Publishing took
the same optimistic,
escapist approach as
movie moguls, who
served up Shirley Temple,
lavish musicals, and
rags-to-riches plots to
Depression era audiences.

Those hardest hit by
poverty had no delusions
of themselves as artists
maintaining America's
heritage—they were just
making do. But these
quilters, too, were swayed
by publications that
brought new styles to the
most isolated farms.

◆ *Grandmother's Flower*
Garden (opposite),
c. 1935; 85½x91 inches.
Instructions begin on
page 222.

◆ *Laurel Wreath Quilt* (above), c. 1936, 66¼x79 inches. Instructions begin on page 224.

*A*lthough 1933 was the Depression's worst year, it was an important time for quilting. In that year, Prohibition was repealed, banks failed, and President Franklin Roosevelt told Americans, "The only thing we have to fear is fear itself." In 1933, Americans also experienced the biggest quilt contest of all time.

Sears, Roebuck & Co. sponsored the contest to coincide with the 1933 Chicago World's Fair. Keyed to the fair's "Century of Progress" theme, the contest was a high point in the resurgence of quiltmaking.

Two paragraphs in the January 1933 catalog announced the contest, which offered a $1,000 grand prize. By the May 15 entry deadline, nearly 25,000 quilts were registered, the most entered in any contest before or since.

Extra prize money was promised if the winning quilt represented the "Century of Progress" theme. Scores of theme quilts were submitted, many making extensive use of pictorial appliqué. However, the judges were firm traditionalists who

ignored these "modern" quilts, much to the outrage of the makers. Not one theme quilt won a regional contest.

Local and regional contests were held to narrow the field. The winning quilts earned ribbons and a place in the exhibit in the Sears pavilion at the fair, where they were viewed by more than five million people.

The grand prize winner was Margaret Caden of Lexington, Kentucky, but she did not make her quilt. One of Caden's employees pieced the Feathered Star quilt and added elaborate trapunto; another woman did the quilting, making 15 stitches to the inch. After the contest, the quilt was presented to Eleanor Roosevelt, but it has since disappeared.

The contest was a public relations bonanza. Quilt displays inspired many women to stop by the fabric department in each Sears store. Sears and other companies sold booklets and patterns of the winning quilts.

In such hard times, however, materials for a prizewinning quilt were too expensive for many people. Instead, some used printed feed and grain sacks to make quilts, as well as their clothing and underwear.

Considered charming today, the use of sacks labeled the maker as poor or frugal, and from a rural community.

◆ *Bride's Bouquet* (opposite), c. 1940; 83½x98 inches. Instructions begin on page 226.

*O*f the thousands of quilt patterns distributed throughout the country in the 1930s, some were so widely accepted that they became classics. Grandmother's Flower Garden, Double Wedding Ring, Dresden Plate, and Sunbonnet Sue quilts in soft pastel colors were made by the thousands in all parts of the country.

While magazines and mail-order firms provided patterns, retailers found that a quilting demonstration resulted in brisk sales of notions and fabric. Even major department stores, such as Macy's, supported quilting.

In 1932, Scioto Danner was hired to show the quilts, kits, and patterns that she sold from her home in El Dorado, Kansas, at Macy's New York store for two weeks. Many New York women didn't know what a quilt was and asked if it was some sort of table pad, but Danner's visit was a success nonetheless. Customers drawn by her window display lined up to make their purchases.

After her success at Macy's, Danner was wooed by every major department store in the country and was sometimes booked two years in advance. She appeared

frequently in stores in Kansas City and other midwestern cities.

Danner understood that women, charmed by the romanticized colonial ideal, wanted to make pretty, updated reproductions of antique quilts. For example, her Ladies' Dream Quilt, *above*, was copied from one that had been in a Missouri family for six generations; folklore had it that the design came to the maker in a dream. With such a pedigree, quilters snapped up Ladies' Dream patterns.

Danner is a wonderful example of an American entrepreneur who rose above the hard times. Her work force came from the

local high school; a bookcase in her home was the warehouse. She sold patterns for 25 cents to $2 each, as well as kits, marked quilt tops, and finished quilts.

With the U.S. entry into World War II in 1941, the quilting revival declined. During the war, women went to work; later, they transferred their attention to babies, mortgages, fin-tailed cars, and television—anything new and modern, rather than antique and colonial. Quiltmaking never died out, but it would be 35 years before making quilts became fashionable again.

♦ *Star Bouquet* (opposite), *c. 1938, made from a Nancy Cabot pattern; 76x89 inches. Instructions begin on page 229.*

♦ *Ladies' Dream* (above), *c. 1935, made from a kit or pattern sold by Mrs. Danner's Quilts; 89x89 inches. Instructions begin on page 232.*

213

—————BASIC—————
Tulip Circle Quilt

Shown on pages 204 and 205.
The finished quilt measures approximately
70x85 inches. Each finished block is 15
inches square.

MATERIALS
4½ yards of muslin
3 yards of teal solid fabric for
  leaves, stems, borders, and
  binding
¾ yard of pink solid fabric for the
  tulips
½ yard *each* of lavender and purple
  solid fabrics for the posies
¼ yard of gold solid fabric for the
  posy centers
5¼ yards of backing fabric
81x96-inch precut quilt batting
Template material
Gold embroidery floss (optional)

INSTRUCTIONS
The Tulip Circle quilt is made of 20
appliquéd blocks joined in a straight
set of five horizontal rows of four

TULIP CIRCLE BLOCK

blocks each. The relatively simple
shapes of the flowers make this block
an excellent choice for beginners in
appliqué.

Cutting the fabrics
Refer to page 288 for tips on making
templates for appliqué. Prepare templates for patterns A through E, *oppo-*
site. When cutting the appliqués from
fabric, add a ³⁄₁₆-inch seam allowance
around each piece.

Cutting requirements for the block
appliqués are given for one block,
with the number required for the entire quilt shown in parentheses. Appliqué a single block to test the
accuracy of your templates before
cutting the remaining fabric.

From the muslin, cut:
◆ Twenty 15½-inch squares.

From the teal fabric, cut:
◆ Two 5½x90-inch border strips.
◆ Two 5½x65-inch border strips.
◆ One 25x31-inch piece for the
  binding.
◆ Five 1½x42-inch strips for the
  stems.
◆ One 20x65-inch piece.
  From this piece, cut eight (160)
  of Pattern E.

From the lavender fabric, cut:
◆ One (20) of Pattern A.

From the purple fabric, cut:
◆ One (20) of Pattern B.

Place on fold

ONE-HALF OF QUILTING DESIGN FOR TULIP CIRCLE QUILT

From the gold fabric, cut:
◆ One (20) of Pattern C.

From the pink fabric, cut:
◆ Four (80) of Pattern D.

Preparing stems for appliqué
With right sides together, fold one 1½x42-inch teal strip in half lengthwise. Machine-stitch ¼ inch from the raw edge. Press the seam allowance open, centering the seam line in the middle of the strip. Turn the strip right side out and press again.

Stitch the other four stem strips in the same manner. From each prepared strip, cut sixteen 2½-inch-long stem pieces.

The ends of the stems will be covered by other pieces, so it is not necessary to finish those edges.

continued

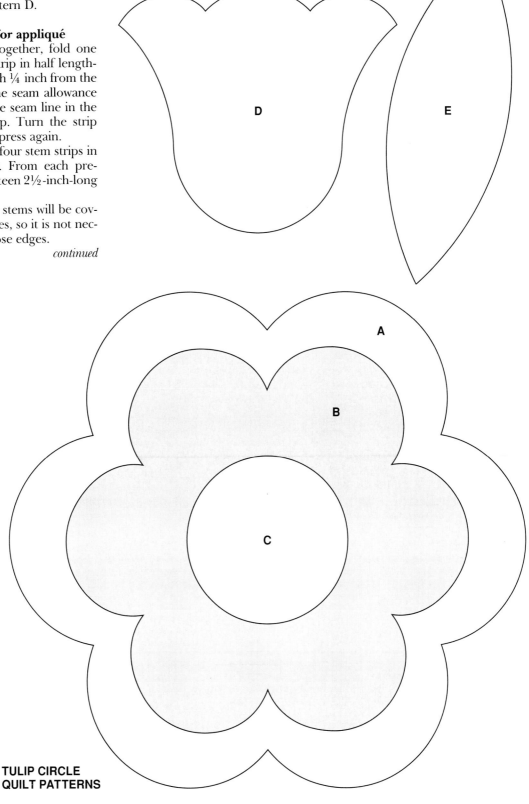

**TULIP CIRCLE
QUILT PATTERNS**

Appliquéing the block

1. Turn under the seam allowances on all the appliqué pieces. Clip the seam allowances as needed to make nicely curved edges.
2. Fold one muslin square vertically, horizontally, and diagonally; press each fold to mark placement lines.
3. Referring to the block diagram on page 214, position and pin the appliqués in place on the muslin. Begin by pinning a lavender A piece in the center of the block, aligning the horizontal and vertical centers of the piece with the placement lines on the muslin block. Pin B and C pieces in place atop the A piece.
4. Tuck four stems under the A piece, centering them on the horizontal and vertical placement lines. Position a pink tulip at the other end of each stem. Adjust the length of each stem so the top of each tulip is approximately 1¼ inches from the raw edge of the muslin block.
5. Position pairs of E leaves between the tulips as shown in the block diagram. The two leaves in each pair meet on the diagonal placement line.
6. When all pieces are correctly positioned, appliqué them in place. Stitch the stems first, then the A posy piece. Appliqué the B posy and the C center in place, then stitch the tulips and the leaves.
7. The quilt shown has buttonhole-stitch embroidery around the edge of the gold posy center. Add this stitching last, if desired.

Make 20 Tulip Circle blocks.

Assembling the quilt top

Join the completed blocks in five horizontal rows of four blocks each. Sew the rows together. Without the borders, the quilt top will measure approximately 60½x75½ inches.

Adding the borders

Stitch the two 5½x65-inch border strips to the top and bottom edges of the quilt top. Press the seam allowances toward the borders, then trim the excess border fabric even with the sides of the quilt top. Add the two 5½x90-inch border strips to the quilt sides in the same manner.

Quilting and finishing

BACKING: Cut the backing fabric into two equal lengths. Sew the two panels together side by side; press the seam allowance open. Layer the backing, batting, and quilt top; baste the three layers securely together.

QUILTING: Quilt as desired. The quilt shown has outline quilting inside each appliqué piece. The background inside each circle is filled with a diagonal grid of ¾-inch squares.

Where four blocks come together, a space is formed between the circles. The quilt shown has a posy design quilted over the seam lines in each space. The pattern for this design is on page 214. The same posy, without leaves, is quilted in the borders.

BINDING: From the remaining teal fabric, make 320 inches of bias or straight-grain binding. See pages 306 and 307 for tips on making and applying binding.

———CHALLENGING———

Dogwood Quilt

Shown on pages 206 and 207.
The finished quilt measures approximately 83 inches square. Each Dogwood block is 11 inches square.

MATERIALS

4¾ yards of pink solid fabric for patchwork, borders, and binding
4¼ yards of muslin for patchwork
3⅛ yards of green print fabric for patchwork
¼ yard of yellow print fabric for patchwork
One 7-inch square *each* of 49 assorted pastel print fabrics
2½ yards of 90-inch-wide sheeting for backing
90x108-inch precut quilt batting
Template material

INSTRUCTIONS

This quilt is a straight set made in seven rows of seven blocks each. The fabrics in each of the 49 Dogwood blocks are the same except for the B pieces that form the large center flower. Different print fabrics in a rainbow of pastel colors give this quilt a feeling of spring flowers.

Curved seams and set-in pieces make this block a challenge. Because of these difficulties, most quilters will prefer to do some or all of the patchwork by hand. Take extra care to ensure accuracy in cutting and piecing.

Cutting the fabrics

Refer to page 288 for tips on making templates for patchwork. Review the instructions for the patchwork, then decide whether to piece the Dogwood block by hand or by machine. Prepare a template for each of patterns A through G, *opposite*.

From the yellow print fabric, cut:
◆ 49 of Pattern A.

From the muslin, cut:
◆ 196 of Pattern C.
◆ 196 of Pattern E.
◆ 196 of Pattern F and 196 of Pattern F reversed (Fr).

From the green print fabric, cut:
◆ 196 of Pattern E.
◆ 196 of Pattern G.

From each print fabric square, cut:
◆ Four of Pattern B.

From the pink fabric, cut:
◆ Four 3½x85-inch borders.
◆ One 27x42-inch piece for the binding.
◆ 196 of Pattern D and 196 of Pattern D reversed (Dr).

continued

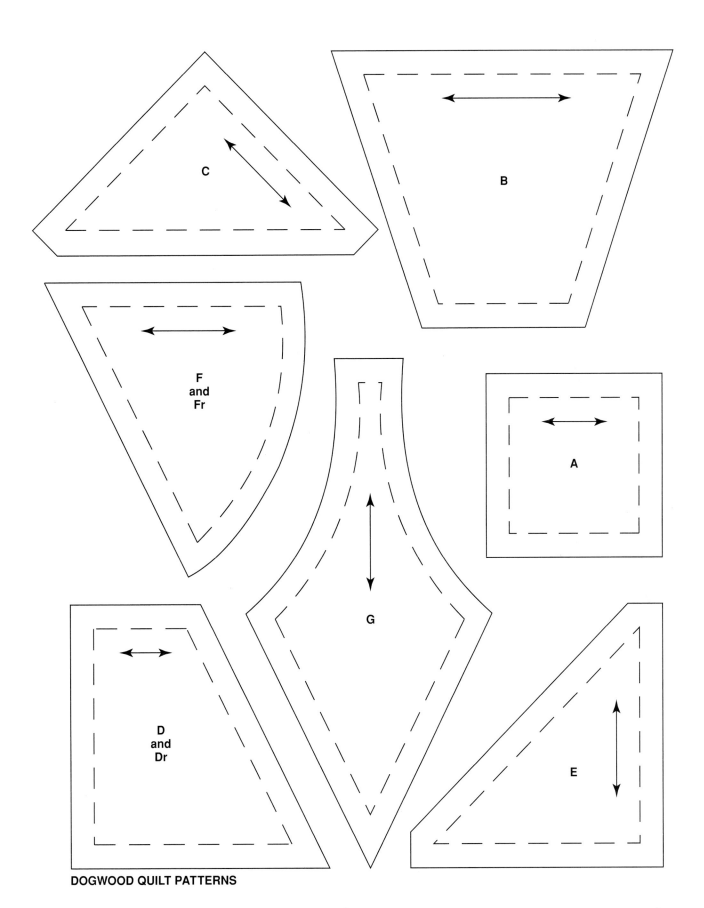

DOGWOOD QUILT PATTERNS

217

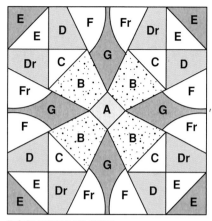

DOGWOOD BLOCK

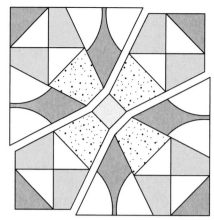

**DOGWOOD BLOCK
ASSEMBLY DIAGRAM**

Making the Dogwood block

Make center and corner units as described below. Each block has four corners and four center units.

CORNER UNITS: Refer to the corner unit assembly diagram, *below,* to join the pieces for each corner.
1. Join muslin and green E triangles to form a square; sew a D piece onto the muslin side of the square as shown. Press the seam allowances away from the muslin triangle.
2. Sew a C triangle onto the bottom edge of a D reversed piece, as shown *below;* press seam allowance toward the D piece. Add a B piece to the long side of the C triangle as shown.
3. Join the EED/BCDr units to complete the corner unit. Make 196 corner units, four for each block.

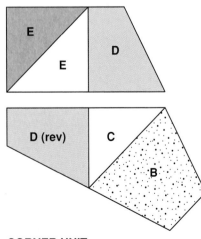

**CORNER UNIT
ASSEMBLY DIAGRAM**

CENTER UNITS: Sew the curved side of one F piece and one F reversed piece to the curved sides of each G piece as shown in the block assembly diagram, *above.* See page 71 for tips on stitching curved seams. Press the seam allowances toward the F pieces.

Make 196 center units, four for each block.

JOINING THE UNITS: Refer to the block assembly diagram, *above,* to make each block. Use four corner units, each with the same B fabric, and four center units for one block.
1. Join two corner blocks in a diagonal row with an A square between them. Leave ¼ inch of the seam allowance unstitched at both ends of each seam. Press seam allowances toward the center square.
2. Stitch a center unit onto both sides of the two remaining corner units. Press seam allowances toward the corner units.
3. Join the three sections to complete the block.

Complete 49 Dogwood blocks.

Assembling the quilt top

Refer to page 294 for a diagram of a straight set. Join the blocks in seven horizontal rows of seven blocks each. Matching seam lines carefully, stitch the rows together to complete the quilt top.

Adding the borders

Sew a pink border strip onto opposite sides of the quilt top. Press the seam allowances toward the borders, then trim the excess border fabric even with the sides of the quilt top. Add borders to the remaining sides in the same manner.

Quilting and finishing

Sandwich the batting between the backing and the quilt top. Baste the three layers securely together.

QUILTING: The quilt pictured on pages 206 and 207 has outline quilting around the patchwork pieces and a simple cable quilted in the borders. Quilt as desired.

BINDING: Use the remaining pink fabric to make approximately 340 inches of bias or straight-grain binding. Refer to pages 306 and 307 for tips on making and applying binding.

———————*CHALLENGING*———————

Rainbow Tile Quilt

Shown on page 208.
The finished quilt measures approximately 68x89 inches.

MATERIALS

4¾ yards of pink solid fabric for patchwork, border, and binding
1 yard *each* of red, yellow, and light blue solid fabrics for patchwork
Eighteen ¼-yard pieces or scraps of assorted pastel print fabrics for patchwork
5¾ yards of backing fabric
90x108-inch precut quilt batting
Template material
Bond paper (optional)

INSTRUCTIONS

This quilt, also known as Diamond Field, is made of 59 "tiles" and additional partial tiles. When the tile units are joined, a latticelike path of pink hexagons separates the tiles.

Hand piecing is recommended for this quilt because of the challenging set-in seams. Before beginning, review the English paper piecing technique described on pages 220 and

221 and the tips on page 163 for stitching set-in seams. To assemble the quilt, use the method that works best for you.

Cutting the fabrics

See page 288 for tips on making and using templates for patchwork. Make a window template for the hexagon pattern on page 222.

Note: If you prefer to buy ready-made templates, they are available for hexagons in a variety of sizes. For this quilt, buy a window template for a 1-inch (finished size) hexagon.

From the pink solid fabric, cut:
◆ One 32-inch square for binding.
◆ Two 2½x74-inch strips and two 2½x90-inch strips for the border.
◆ 574 hexagons.

From each of the red, yellow, and light blue solid fabrics, cut:
◆ 154 hexagons.

From the print scrap fabrics, cut:
◆ 714 hexagons.

Making the basic tile units

For each tile unit, use eight pink hexagons and two hexagons *each* of the red, yellow, and blue fabrics.

Choose 10 print hexagons for each tile, using the same fabric or mixing the scraps. Refer to the basic tile unit illustrated in the quilt assembly diagram, *below,* as you make each unit.

Begin by sewing the two blue hexagons together, using either traditional sewing or the paper piecing method. Join the yellow hexagons to the blue hexagons as shown, then add the encircling row of 10 print hexagons.

Stitch the two red hexagons at both ends of the tile unit as illustrated, then complete the unit with the partial row of eight pink hexagons.

Make 59 tile units.

Making the partial tile units

Partial units fill in the spaces between the joined tile units around the outside edges of the quilt top (see photo on page 208). The quilt assembly diagram, *below,* illustrates the bottom left corner of the quilt and shows the three kinds of partial units needed to finish the quilt top.

For the top and bottom edges of the quilt, make a unit that is a horizontal half of the basic tile unit. Make four partial units for the bottom of the quilt as shown, then make four units for the top of the quilt adding

eight pink hexagons on the outside edge of these units.

Make six side units for the left side of the quilt as shown. For the right side of the quilt, make six more units that have the pink hexagons on the opposite side of the unit.

Make one corner unit as shown. Assemble all the hexagons in the quilt top before making the remaining corner units to avoid confusion in color placement.

Wait until the quilt top is completely assembled before trimming the excess fabric at the edge of each partial unit.

Assembling the quilt top

Referring to the quilt assembly diagram, join the tile units. Because every seam is set in, you can join the units in any order you like. Some quiltmakers prefer to make horizontal rows, others like to join the units in undefined groups.

When all the units are joined, including the four corner units, trim the uneven edges of the partial units.

Adding the border

Stitch the two 2½x74-inch border strips to the top and bottom edges of the quilt top. Press the seam allowances toward the border strips, then trim the excess border fabric even with the sides of the quilt top. Add the two 2½x90-inch border strips to the quilt sides in the same manner.

Quilting and finishing

BACKING: Cut the backing fabric into two equal lengths. Sew the two panels together side by side; press the seam allowance open. Layer the backing, batting, and quilt top; baste the three layers securely together.

QUILTING: Quilt as desired. The quilt shown has outline quilting inside each hexagon and diagonal lines stitched in the borders.

BINDING: From the remaining pink fabric, make 350 inches of bias or straight-grain binding. See pages 306 and 307 for tips on making and applying binding.

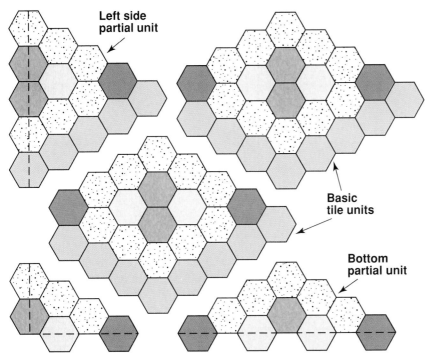

Left side partial unit

Basic tile units

Bottom partial unit

RAINBOW TILE QUILT ASSEMBLY DIAGRAM

PAPER PIECING (ENGLISH PATCHWORK)

When patchwork was in its infancy, a quilt made of pieced hexagons was one of the first pieced designs to win widespread popularity. Often named Mosaic or Honeycomb, so many all-over hexagon quilts were made in England between 1750 and 1850 that the design became known as English patchwork. Today that term also is applied to the particular hand-sewing technique that has been associated with hexagon quilts for centuries.

The Honeycomb was so ingrained in the culture of English Pilgrims that it was often the design used to teach sewing in colonial times. Young girls had to meet their daily quota of pieced hexagons before they were allowed out to play.

Though time-consuming, English patchwork is ideal for those who like hand sewing. It results in accurate piecing and is ideal for joining many-sided shapes and curved patches. Although most commonly associated with hexagons, English paper piecing can be used with other shapes, such as clamshells and diamonds.

Piecing with papers

English patchwork always is sewn by hand. Each hexagon is basted onto a paper shape, which is cut the size of the *finished* patch. The seam allowances are pressed over the edge of the paper and tacked on the wrong side of the patch. The hexagons are joined with tiny overcast stitches sewn through the fabric only. When all sides of the hexagon are sewn, the paper is removed.

Nearly any type of paper will do. Newspaper was used widely in the past. If the paper is to be reused, typing paper and other bond papers that have more weight will hold their shape better than lightweight papers.

During hard times, when batting or some other filler was unavailable, papers were sometimes left in place to give the finished quilt a little extra warmth. Much information about the quilts and their makers can be gathered from these bits of paper.

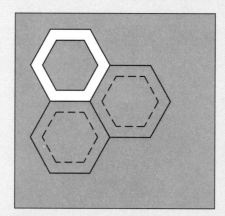

1 **Use a window template** to cut the fabric pieces. Mark sewing and cutting lines on the *right* side of the fabric. When cutting multiple hexagons from one piece of fabric, mark the pieces side by side to create mutual cutting lines as illustrated *above*. Cut the fabric hexagons apart on the drawn lines.

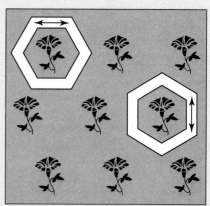

2 **To center a fabric motif** inside the hexagon, use the window template to frame the desired area; mark cutting and sewing lines around the motif on the right side of the fabric. The grain line on the template can be parallel with either the lengthwise or crosswise grain of the fabric.

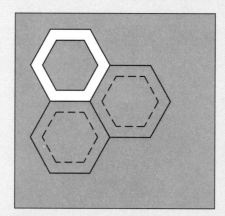

3 **Trace the** *finished* **size** of the patch onto paper. From the paper, cut at least as many hexagons as there are in each unit. The papers can be reused, but it is necessary to leave the papers in the hexagons at the outside edge of each unit until the units are joined.

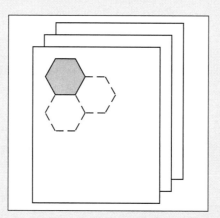

4 **Center a paper patch** on the *wrong side* of a fabric hexagon and pin it in place. Fold one edge of the fabric hexagon over the paper, being careful not to crease the paper. Make a basting stitch through both fabric layers and the paper as illustrated *above*.

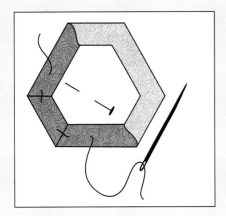

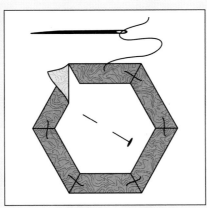

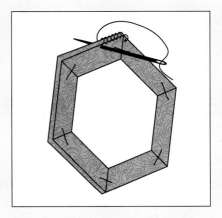

5 Fold the next seam allowance over the paper in the same manner, mitering the fabric at the corner. Baste over the folded corner to secure it, bringing the needle up in the middle of the next seam allowance as shown *above*. Repeat for all the remaining edges of the hexagon.

6 To finish the final corner, slip the excess fabric of the last seam allowance under the first one. Baste over the corner to hold both edges in place. Cut the basting thread, leaving a short free end. Remove the pin and press the basted patch. Prepare all the hexagons in the same manner.

7 To join two adjacent hexagons, place them with right sides of the fabrics together and carefully match the corners of the two patches. Whipstitch the folded edges on one side together, taking care not to catch the papers in the stitching. Sew from corner to corner, backstitching at the ends to secure the stitches.

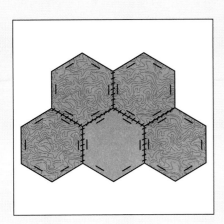

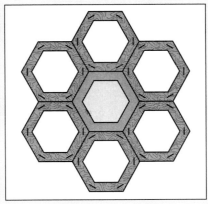

8 Join additional hexagons in the same manner. Stitch the entire length of each seam. The stitches should barely show on the right side of the joined pieces. Do not break the sewing thread when stitching the patches together; sew continuously from one seam to the next.

9 Remove the paper from each hexagon only when it is bordered on all sides by another sewn patch. Remove the basting thread from the hexagon by pulling one end of the loose thread, then lift the paper out. Gently press the finished patchwork unit. If the paper is not torn or creased, it can be used in another unit or saved for another project.

——————*CHALLENGING*——————

Grandmother's Flower Garden Quilt

Shown on page 209.
The finished quilt measures approximately 85½x91 inches.

MATERIALS

5 yards of muslin for patchwork and first border

2 yards of lavender solid fabric for patchwork, outer border, and binding

1¼ yards *each* of light yellow and light green solid fabrics for patchwork and borders

Fifty-two 6x9-inch scraps of assorted solid fabrics for patchwork

Fifty-nine 9x12-inch scraps of assorted print fabrics for patchwork

3 yards of 90-inch-wide sheeting for backing fabric

90x108-inch precut quilt batting

Template material

Bond paper (optional)

INSTRUCTIONS

This classic Depression era quilt has 59 "flowers" set along a pieced "garden path." Each flower has a solid yellow center, enclosed by an inner circle of six solid-colored hexagons, a ring of 12 print hexagons, and an outer circle of 18 muslin hexagons.

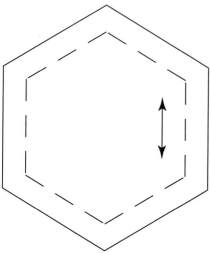

PATTERN FOR RAINBOW TILE AND GRANDMOTHER'S FLOWER GARDEN QUILTS

When the flower units are joined, wide paths of muslin separate them. Four borders of hexagons in muslin, light yellow, light green, and lavender complete the quilt with an edge that follows the hexagonal pieces.

This quilt, with its set-in pieces, can be sewn by hand or by machine, but hand piecing is recommended. Before beginning, review the English paper piecing technique described on pages 220 and 221 and the tips on page 163 for stitching set-in seams. To assemble the quilt, use whichever method works best for you.

Cutting the fabrics

See page 288 for tips on making and using templates for patchwork. Make a window template for the hexagon pattern, *below, right*.

Note: If you prefer to buy ready-made templates, they are available for hexagons in a variety of sizes. For this quilt, buy a window template for a 1-inch (finished size) hexagon.

From the muslin, cut:
◆ 1,062 hexagons for 59 flower units.
◆ 220 hexagons for the first border.

From the light yellow fabric, cut:
◆ 59 hexagons for flower centers.
◆ 226 hexagons for the second border.

From the light green fabric, cut:
◆ Six hexagons for one flower unit.
◆ 232 hexagons for the third border.

From the lavender fabric, cut:
◆ One 38-inch square for binding.
◆ 36 hexagons for six flower units.
◆ 238 hexagons for the outer border.

From each solid scrap fabric, cut:
◆ Six hexagons for one flower unit.

From each print scrap fabric, cut:
◆ 12 hexagons for one flower unit.

Making the flower units

Referring to the flower unit assembly diagram, *above*, join 37 hexagons to make one unit. Using either traditional sewing or the paper piecing

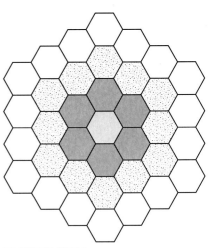

FLOWER UNIT ASSEMBLY DIAGRAM

method, sew six solid-colored hexagons around the yellow center. Add 12 print hexagons in the next ring, then complete the unit with an outer ring of 18 muslin hexagons.

Make 59 flower units.

Assembling the quilt top

Referring to the quilt assembly diagram, *opposite*, join the flower units. Because every seam is set in, you can join the units in any order you like. Some quiltmakers prefer to make horizontal rows, others join the units in undefined groups.

Adding the borders

For the first border, add a row of muslin hexagons around the outside edge of the quilt top. Add the second border of light yellow hexagons, then stitch a border of light green hexagons. Complete the quilt top with a row of lavender hexagons.

Quilting and finishing

Layer the backing, batting, and quilt top; baste the three layers together.

QUILTING: Quilt as desired. The quilt shown has outline quilting inside each hexagon.

BINDING: From the remaining 38-inch square of lavender fabric, make approximately 375 inches of bias binding. See pages 306 and 307 for tips on making and applying continuous bias binding.

GRANDMOTHER'S FLOWER GARDEN QUILT ASSEMBLY DIAGRAM

223

Laurel Wreath Quilt

Shown on page 210.
Finished size is 66¼x79 inches.
Finished block is 10¼ inches square.

MATERIALS

2¼ yards of green solid fabric for sashing
½ yard of red and yellow print fabric for sashing squares
Thirty ⅛-yard pieces of assorted light-colored fabrics for the blocks
Thirty ⅛-yard pieces of assorted red fabrics for the block backgrounds
4¼ yards of backing fabric (includes binding)
72x90-inch precut quilt batting
Template material
Rotary cutter, mat, and acrylic ruler

INSTRUCTIONS

This block was published as Laurel Wreath by both *Capper's Weekly* and *Prairie Farmer* magazines in 1931. In the late '30s, Mrs. Danner (see page 213) sold a pattern for this block, calling it Dove at the Windows.

Our quilt has 30 Laurel Wreath blocks joined in six horizontal rows of five blocks each. Sashing strips of the particular green that was so popular during the 1930s, punctuated with sashing squares of a red and yellow print, organize and complement the scrap fabrics in the blocks.

Cutting the fabrics

See page 288 for tips on making templates for patchwork. Make templates for patterns A, B, C, and D, *opposite.*

From each light-colored fabric, cut:
◆ One of Pattern A.
◆ 16 of Pattern C.

From each red fabric, cut:
◆ 16 of Pattern B.
◆ Four of Pattern D.

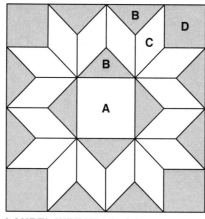

LAUREL WREATH BLOCK

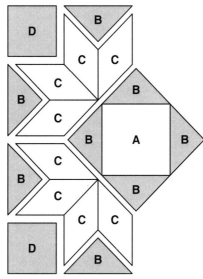

LAUREL WREATH ASSEMBLY DIAGRAM

From the green solid fabric, cut:
◆ Seventy-one 3x10¾-inch strips for sashing.

From the red and yellow print fabric, cut:
◆ Forty-two 3-inch sashing squares.

Piecing the blocks

For each block, select one light fabric and one red background fabric. Refer to the block assembly diagram, *above,* while assembling each block.
1. Sew a B triangle to opposite sides of the A square; press both seam allowances toward the center. Add a B triangle to each remaining side, creating a larger square as illustrated in the assembly diagram.

2. Join four C diamonds into a half-star unit. Press all the seam allowances in the same direction; clip the points of the seam allowances where they meet at the center seam. Make three more units in the same manner, using the same fabrics.
3. Set two B triangles and one D square into each unit as shown.
4. Sew one BCD unit to each side of the center square. It is important to begin and end this stitching precisely so the seam allowance at each side is left free for the seam that will connect adjacent units.
5. To join adjacent units, align the seam lines of the neighboring C diamonds. Begin sewing at the inside corner and stitch toward the outside edge. Press seam allowances open or to one side, whichever way your patchwork lays flat.
   Make 30 Laurel Wreath blocks.

Joining the horizontal rows

When assembling the rows, refer to the illustration of a straight set with sashing on page 295.
1. Sew one vertical sashing strip to the left side of each Laurel Wreath block; press seam allowances toward the sashing strips.
2. On the floor or a table, lay out the blocks in a pleasing arrangement; separate the blocks into six horizontal rows with five blocks in each row.
3. Join the blocks in Row 1, sewing each block to the sashing strip of the adjacent block.
4. Complete the row by adding a sashing strip to the right side of the last block in the row. Press all sashing seam allowances toward the sashing.
5. Join rows 2–6 in the same manner.

Assembling the quilt top

1. Each row of horizontal sashing is made by alternating the green sashing strips with squares of the red and yellow print fabric. Starting with a square, sew five sashing strips and six squares together to make a row. Make seven rows of sashing.
2. Matching seam lines carefully, sew a sashing row to the top edge of each of the six block rows. Press seam allowances toward the sashing rows.

3. Join the rows, sewing the top of the sashing row to the bottom of the adjacent block row. Press seam allowances toward the sashing.

4. Complete the quilt top by sewing the remaining row of sashing to the bottom of the sixth block row.

Quilting and finishing

BACKING: Divide the backing fabric into two equal lengths. Sew the two panels together side by side; press the seam allowance open. Sandwich the batting between the backing fabric and the quilt top; baste the three layers securely together.

QUILTING: Quilt as desired. The quilt shown on page 210 has concentric quarter-circles stitched in the bottom portion of the block and adjacent sashing. The rest of the block and sashing is quilted with straight lines and outline stitching.

The leaf-and-vine quilting design on page 312 is suitable for the sashing in this quilt.

BINDING: The edges of the quilt shown are bound by turning the backing over to the front as described below. If you prefer, make and apply separate binding as described on pages 306 and 307.

Trim the batting even with the quilt top. Trim the backing so it is 1½ inches larger on all sides than the quilt top.

Fold the backing in toward the quilt top so the raw edge lays against the raw edge of the quilt top. Turn the folded edge of the backing over onto the quilt top, enclosing all the raw edges. Make mitered or square corners as desired.

Blindstitch the folded edge of the backing on the quilt top by hand or machine-topstitch through all layers.

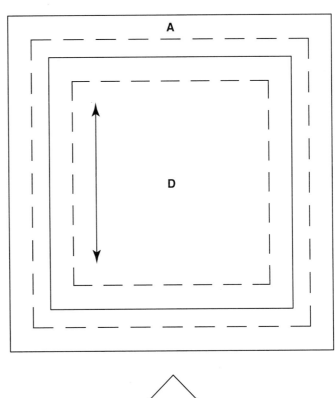

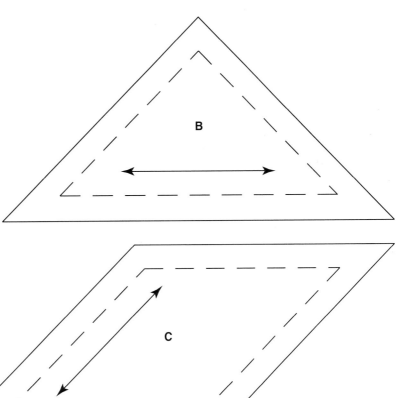

LAUREL WREATH QUILT PATTERNS

——————CHALLENGING——————

Bride's Bouquet Quilt

Shown on page 211.
The finished quilt measures approximately 83½x98 inches. The finished Bride's Bouquet block is 10¼ inches square.

MATERIALS

5½ yards of muslin for the
   patchwork and the inner border
2¾ yards of navy blue pindotted
   fabric for the patchwork, outer
   border, and binding
2 yards of purple solid fabric
1 yard of yellow solid fabric
Scraps of assorted print fabrics
   totaling approximately 2 yards
6 yards of backing fabric
90x108-inch precut quilt batting
Template material

INSTRUCTIONS

This block has several names, including Nosegay and Cornucopia. The Old Chelsea Station mail-order company sold a Laura Wheeler pattern for this quilt in the 1930s, calling it Old-Fashioned Nosegay.

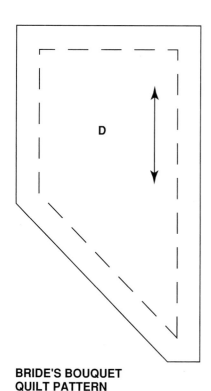

**BRIDE'S BOUQUET
QUILT PATTERN**

BRIDE'S BOUQUET BLOCK

The quilt shown on page 211 has 49 Bride's Bouquet blocks joined in a diagonal set. The triangular spaces at the sides are filled with half-blocks.

Set-in seams make this block a challenge. See page 163 for tips on sewing set-in seams and page 296 for tips on pressing set-in seams.

Cutting the fabrics

See page 288 for tips on making and using templates for patchwork. Prepare window templates for patterns A, C, D, E, and F, *left* and *opposite*.

From the muslin, cut:
◆ Four 4½x89-inch border strips.
◆ 240 of Pattern C.
◆ 180 *each* of Pattern D and Pattern D reversed.
◆ 60 *each* of Pattern F and Pattern F reversed.

From the navy pindot, cut:
◆ Two 2x97-inch border strips.
◆ Two 2x86-inch border strips.
◆ One 34-inch square for binding.
◆ 120 of Pattern A.

From the yellow solid fabric, cut:
◆ Sixteen 2x42-inch strips.
   From these strips, cut 316 B squares, each 2 inches square.

From the purple solid fabric, cut:
◆ 66 of Pattern E.

From the scrap print fabrics, cut:
◆ 240 of Pattern A.

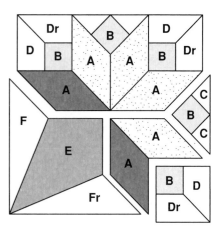

**BRIDE'S BOUQUET BLOCK
ASSEMBLY DIAGRAM**

Making the Bride's Bouquet block
Because this block is relatively difficult, complete one block to gain an understanding of its construction before you proceed. Refer to the block assembly diagram, *above,* as you sew.

To make each block, use two A diamonds of the navy pindot and four A diamonds of scrap fabrics, five B squares, four C triangles, three *each* of D and D reversed pieces, and one *each* of pieces E, F, and F reversed.
1. Referring to the assembly diagram, stitch the six A diamonds together into three pairs. Be careful not to stitch into the seam allowance at the ends of each seam so you can set in the side and corner units.
2. To make each corner unit, join one D and one D reversed piece, as shown. Set a B square into the angle to complete the corner unit. Make three corner units. Set a corner unit into the angle of each diamond pair.
3. To make the CBC side units, stitch a C triangle onto two adjacent sides of a B square.
4. Join two A/corner units as shown at the top of the assembly diagram. Set a CBC side unit into the open angle at the top of the joined unit.
5. Sew the F and F reversed pieces onto the long sides of the E piece. Join the remaining A/corner unit and the FEFr unit.
6. Combine the two halves of the block. Complete the block by setting the remaining CBC side unit into the open angle of the diamonds.

Make 49 Bride's Bouquet blocks.
continued

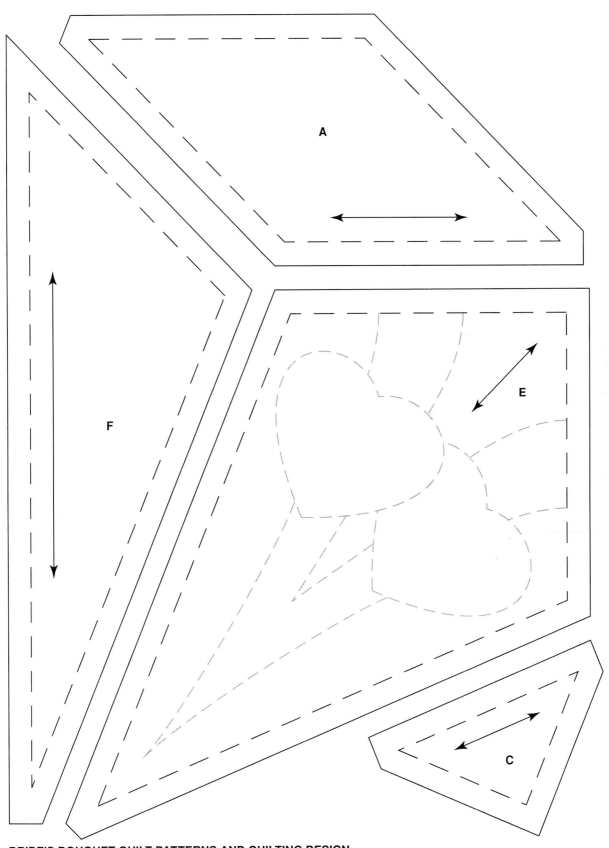

BRIDE'S BOUQUET QUILT PATTERNS AND QUILTING DESIGN

227

TOP HALF-BLOCK (Make 5)   **LEFT HALF-BLOCK (Make 6)**

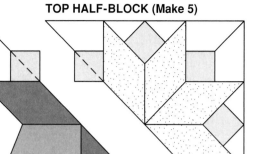
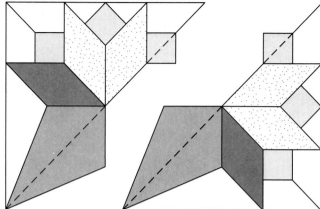

BOTTOM HALF-BLOCK (Make 5)   **RIGHT HALF-BLOCK (Make 6)**

Making the half-blocks

When the blocks are joined in a diagonal set, triangular spaces are left around the sides. Half-blocks fill in these spaces, continuing the repeated pattern of the blocks. (See the quilt assembly diagram, *right*.)

The four types of half-blocks are illustrated *above*. Assemble the half-blocks in the same manner as the full blocks. Make five top half-blocks and five bottom half-blocks as shown. When these are complete, lay a ruler along the diagonal edge of each half-block and trim the excess fabric of the B squares with a rotary cutter.

Make six left half-blocks and six right half-blocks, then trim the excess fabric of the B and E pieces.

Assembling the quilt top

The Bride's Bouquet blocks and half-blocks are stitched together in diagonal rows as indicated by the red lines on the quilt assembly diagram, *right*.

Using the diagram as a guide, lay the blocks on the floor. Picking up one block at a time, join the blocks in each row. Assemble the rows to complete the quilt top, matching the seam lines of adjoining blocks.

Adding the borders

1. Stitch a 4½x89-inch muslin border onto each long side of the quilt top. Press the seam allowances toward the border strip. Trim the excess border fabric even with the top and bottom edges of the quilt top.
2. Stitch the remaining muslin border strips onto top and bottom edges.

BRIDE'S BOUQUET QUILT ASSEMBLY DIAGRAM

3. Sew the navy pindotted borders onto the quilt top, adding the side borders first and then the top and bottom borders.

Quilting and finishing
BACKING: Cut two 3-yard lengths of backing fabric. Sew the panels together side by side; press the seam allowance open. Sandwich the batting between the backing and the quilt top; baste the layers together.

QUILTING: Quilt as desired. The quilt shown has outline quilting inside each patch. The E pieces are quilted with a heart-and-stem motif that complements the bridal bouquet theme; this quilting motif is shown on the E pattern on page 227.

BINDING: Use the remaining navy pindot to make approximately 360 inches of bias or straight-grain binding. See pages 306 and 307 for tips on making and applying binding.

—————CHALLENGING—————

Star Bouquet Quilt

Shown on page 212.
The finished quilt measures approximately 76x89 inches.

MATERIALS
5 yards of muslin for the patchwork and the middle border
3¼ yards of royal blue solid fabric for the patchwork, outer border, and binding
2¼ yards of light green solid fabric for the leaves and inner border
1 yard of yellow solid fabric for star centers and pansy centers
½ yard *each* of five print fabrics for the pansy petals
5¼ yards of backing fabric
81x96-inch precut quilt batting
2 skeins of green embroidery floss
Template material
Nonpermanent fabric marker
Graph paper, pencil, and ruler

INSTRUCTIONS
The quilt shown on page 212 has 32 six-pointed stars joined with blue diamonds. Each star point is embellished with an appliquéd flower and leaf; the flower stem is embroidered.

Because each star shares diamonds with its neighbor, it cannot really be defined as a block. Each star is set into the angles of the adjacent diamonds. Hand piecing is recommended for this quilt because of the many set-ins. See page 163 for tips on stitching set-in seams.

Cutting the fabrics
See page 288 for tips on making templates for patchwork and appliqué. Make templates for appliqué patterns G, H, and I on page 231, and window templates for patchwork patterns A, B, C, D, and F, *below* and on pages 230 and 231.

continued

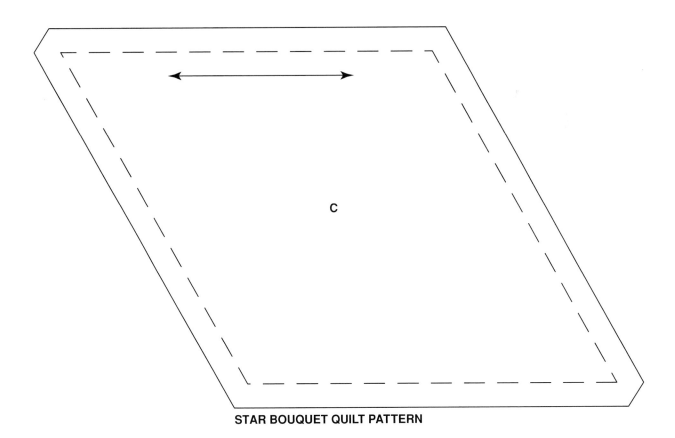

C

STAR BOUQUET QUILT PATTERN

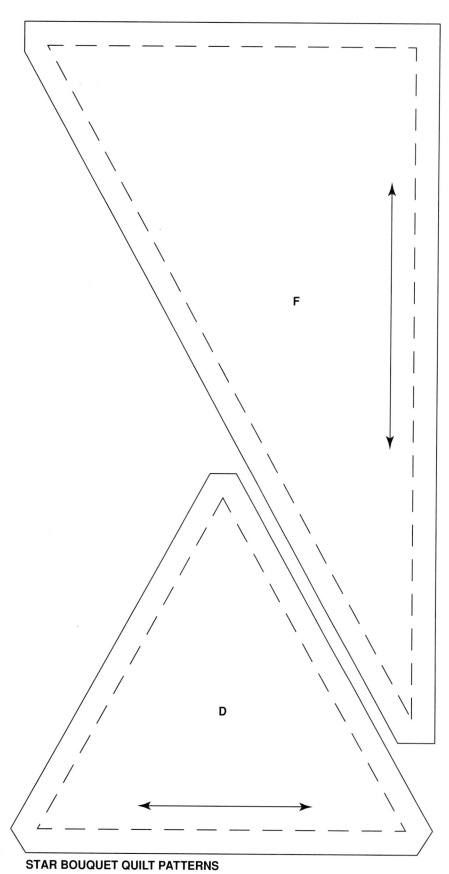

STAR BOUQUET QUILT PATTERNS

FIGURE 1

Figure 1, *above*, is a guide for making a pattern for Triangle E. On graph paper, draw a 6¾x11½-inch rectangle. Define the triangle with a diagonal line from corner to corner. Make a template for this triangle, which includes seam allowances.

From the muslin, cut:
◆ Two 2½x85-inch border strips.
◆ Two 2½x76-inch border strips.
◆ Six 7x24-inch rectangles.
   Fold each rectangle in half, bringing the short ends together. Place the short edge of Template E on the fold of the fabric. Mark and cut six E triangles in this manner. Use the excess fabric from these rectangles to cut the four F pieces.
◆ Two of Pattern F and two of Pattern F reversed.
◆ 192 of Pattern A.
◆ 20 of Pattern D.

From the light green fabric, cut:
◆ Two 2½x81-inch border strips.
◆ Two 2½x72-inch border strips.
◆ 192 of Pattern I.

From the yellow solid fabric, cut:
◆ 32 of Pattern B.
◆ 192 of Pattern H.
   Add a ³⁄₁₆-inch seam allowance around each fabric circle when cutting.

From each of the print fabrics, cut:
◆ 192 of Pattern G.
   Add a ³⁄₁₆-inch seam allowance around each fabric petal when cutting.

From the royal blue fabric, cut:
◆ Two 2½x90-inch border strips.
◆ Two 2½x80-inch border strips.
◆ One 32-inch square for binding.
◆ 119 of Pattern C.

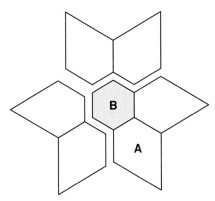

FIGURE 2

Making the stars

As you join the patches, sew on the drawn seam lines only; do not stitch into the seam allowances. It is important to leave the seam allowances available for the next set-in pieces.

1. To make each star, use six A pieces and one yellow B piece. Trace the flower, stem, and leaf onto each A piece as shown on Pattern A, *right*.

2. Join the A pieces in pairs as shown in Figure 2, *above*. Set the B hexagon into the angle of one A pair. Add the two remaining pairs as shown, setting in each seam to complete the six-pointed star.

3. Baste under the seam allowances of one H circle, five G petals, and one I leaf for each star point. Do not baste under the bottom edges of the petals, since these will be covered by the circle. Position the pieces over the tracing on each A piece and appliqué them in place.

4. Use three strands of floss to embroider a stem for each pansy in outline stitch. (See page 137 for stitch diagram.) Embroider veins on each leaf as shown on Pattern I.

Complete 32 stars in this manner.

Assembling the quilt top

Use the quilt assembly diagram on page 232 as a guide to combine the completed stars with blue C diamonds to form the quilt top. Set each diamond into the angled openings of the stars. Add D triangles as shown.

Set E triangles into the angled side openings as shown. Sew an F triangle onto each corner. The assembled quilt top will measure approximately 64½x77½ inches.

continued

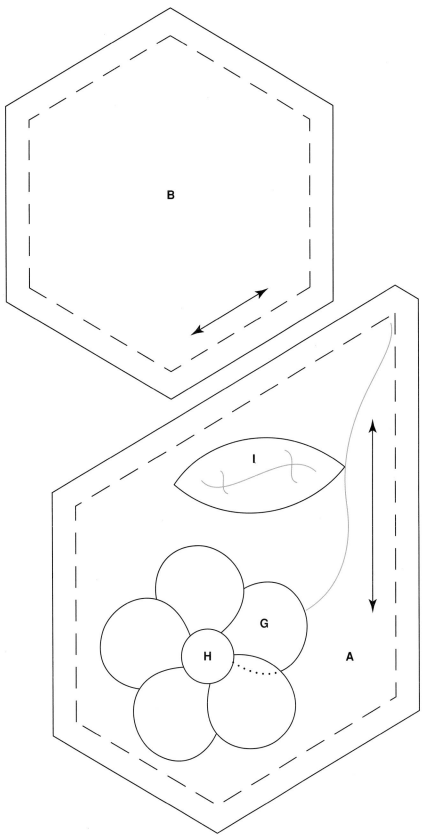

STAR BOUQUET QUILT PATTERNS

231

STAR BOUQUET QUILT ASSEMBLY DIAGRAM

Ladies' Dream Quilt

Shown on page 213.
The finished quilt measures 89x89 inches. Each block is 24 inches square.

MATERIALS
13 yards of muslin for background, binding, and backing fabric
2¾ yards of medium blue solid fabric
1½ yards of dark blue solid fabric
1 yard of blue dotted fabric
120x120-inch precut quilt batting
Template material
Nonpermanent fabric marker

INSTRUCTIONS
This is an authentic Mrs. Danner's quilt. It may have been sold as a kit or a ready-made top. A Ladies' Dream quilt, made with the same fabrics and the same quilting design, is in the quilt collection of the Spencer Museum at the University of Kansas. The museum's quilt, however, has a very different border. The quilt shown on page 213 has the swag-and-bows border that Mrs. Danner advertised.

There are nine appliquéd blocks in this quilt, joined in a straight set.

Cutting the fabrics
See page 288 for tips on making templates for patchwork and appliqué. Make a template for patchwork pattern E, *opposite*, as well as each of the appliqué patterns A, B, C, D, F, G, and H, *opposite* and on page 235. To make a complete template for Pattern F, flip the template plastic to trace the second half of the shape.

For Pattern A, you can either make a quarter-template and cut each piece on the folds as indicated, or make a template for the complete shape so you can cut a single fabric layer. Cut the shaded areas out of the template; use the openings to trace the reverse appliqué shapes onto the fabric.

When cutting appliqués F, G, and H from fabric, add a ³⁄₁₆-inch seam allowance around each traced shape.

From the dark blue fabric, cut:
◆ 72 of Pattern B.
◆ 144 of Pattern E.

Adding the borders
Note: After you sew each border strip onto the quilt top, press the seam allowance toward that strip, then trim excess length from the border strip.
1. Stitch the 2½x81-inch strips of light green fabric onto the long sides of the quilt top. Press the seam allowances and trim excess border fabric even with the edges of the quilt top.
2. Stitch the 2½x72-inch light green strips onto the top and bottom edges of the quilt top. Press and trim.
3. Add the muslin border in the same manner, stitching the 85-inch strips onto the long sides of the quilt top and then sewing the 76-inch strips to the top and bottom edges.
4. Join the blue outer borders to the quilt top in the same manner.

Quilting and finishing
BACKING: Cut the backing fabric into two 2⅝-yard lengths. Sew the two panels together side by side; press the seam allowance open. Sandwich the batting between the backing and the quilt top; baste the three layers securely together.

QUILTING: Quilt as desired. The quilt shown has the pansy-appliqué motif quilted in the yellow centers of the stars and outline quilting on the other patches. A braided cable is quilted in the three-strip border.

BINDING: Use the remaining royal blue fabric to make approximately 340 inches of bias or straight-grain binding. See pages 306 and 307 for tips on making and applying binding.

LADIES' DREAM BLOCK

From the blue dotted fabric, cut:
◆ 72 *each* of patterns D and E.
◆ Nine of Pattern A for the reverse appliqué.

From the muslin, cut:
◆ Two 42x99-inch pieces and one 16x99-inch piece for the backing.
◆ Two 9x91-inch border strips.
◆ Two 9x74-inch border strips.
◆ One 24x46-inch piece for the binding.
◆ Nine 24½-inch squares.

From the medium blue fabric, cut:
◆ Nine of Pattern A.
Trace reverse appliqué sections indicated by the shaded areas on the pattern onto these pieces, but do not cut out these sections yet.
◆ 72 of Pattern C.
◆ 28 of Pattern F.
◆ 56 of Pattern G.
◆ 56 of Pattern H.

Appliquéing the blocks
1. Fold each 24½-inch background square in half vertically, horizontally, and diagonally; lightly press the folds to establish placement guidelines for the appliqué. If desired, trace the complete design on the background fabric with the nonpermanent fabric marker. The A and B patterns, *below,* are spaced properly to facilitate tracing the design onto fabric.

continued

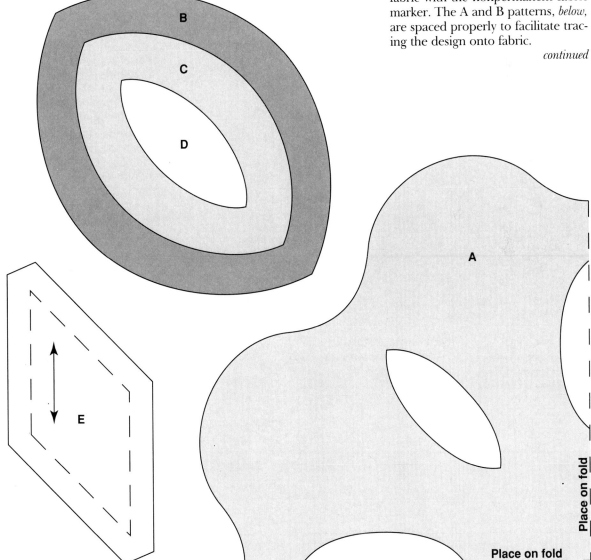

LADIES' DREAM QUILT PATTERNS

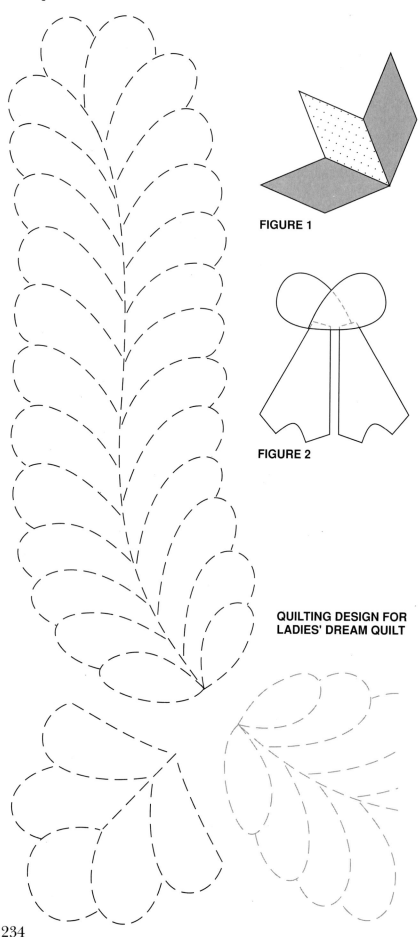

FIGURE 1

FIGURE 2

QUILTING DESIGN FOR LADIES' DREAM QUILT

2. Prepare one A piece of medium blue solid fabric for each block. Baste back the seam allowance around the outside edge, clipping the seam allowance as necessary to make smooth curves. Use a small scissors to carefully slit the center of each of the eight reverse appliqué areas. Do not turn back these edges yet.

3. Trim ¼ inch from the edge of each dotted-fabric A piece. Place a dotted A piece under each blue A piece so the dotted fabric shows through the slits cut in the blue fabric. Baste the two pieces together.

4. Center a prepared A piece on each muslin square, aligning the eight slit openings with the placement lines on the background square. Pin the A piece in place. Appliqué the edge of the A piece onto the muslin.

5. Clip the edges of each reverse appliqué opening. Use your needle to turn under the edges to reveal the underlying piece and stitch the rolled edges in place. Remove the basting.

6. Turn under the seam allowances of each B, C, and D piece. Referring to the block diagram on page 233, pin eight B pieces on each block. Leaving approximately ½ inch between each B piece and the center A piece, align each B piece with one of the placement lines on the muslin square.

7. Pin or baste a C piece atop each B piece, then pin a D piece on top of each C piece.

8. Join three E diamonds into a unit by machine-stitching a dark blue diamond onto two sides of a dotted diamond as shown in Figure 1, *left, top.* Press the seam allowances open to reduce bulk, then turn under the seam allowances on the unstitched edges of each diamond.

9. Pin a three-diamond unit at the top of each B piece so the point of the center (dotted) diamond barely touches the top of the B piece. Align the center diamond with the appropriate placement line on the muslin square. The tops of the center diamonds on the horizontal and vertical placement lines should be approximately 1¼ inches from the raw edge of the square. Adjust the diamond units and BCD units as necessary, spacing them evenly. When all the units are correctly positioned, appliqué them in place.

Complete nine appliquéd blocks in this manner. Press all the blocks.

Assembling the quilt top
See page 294 for an illustration of a straight set.

Join three blocks to make a row; make three rows. Assemble the three rows. The resulting quilt top is approximately 72½ inches square.

Adding the appliquéd borders
Refer to the photo on page 213 for guidance in appliquéing the swags and bows on the border strips.
1. Stitch the 74-inch muslin border strips onto opposite sides of the quilt top. Press the seam allowances toward the border strips, then trim the excess border fabric even with the quilt top. Sew the 91-inch border strips to the remaining edges in the same manner.
2. Prepare the F, G, and H pieces by turning under the seam allowances on each piece. Do not turn under the ends of the F swags or the top edges of the G ribbons, since these will be covered by the bowknot pieces.
3. Find the center of each border. Center one F swag on each border strip, matching the middle of the swag with the middle of the border.
4. At each end of the pinned swag, pin a complete bow comprised of two H bowknot pieces and two G ribbon pieces. Refer to Figure 2, *opposite,* for guidance in positioning each bow piece. The straight edges of the G pieces will be approximately ⅜ inch apart. The left H piece will be covered by the H piece on the right.
5. Continue alternating swags and bows on each border strip, pinning them in place as you work from the center toward the ends of the border strip. Position six bows and seven swags on each strip. Pin a bow at each corner, angling it so the bowknot covers the ends of the adjacent swags.
6. When you are satisfied with the position of all the bows and swags, appliqué them in place.

Quilting and finishing
MARKING: The quilt shown has a feather plume stitched in each corner of the Ladies' Dream blocks. Make a stencil or template for the feather plume from the pattern *opposite.*

Position the outside edges of the stencil ¼ inch from the seam lines of each block. Mark the corner and one feather plume, then turn the stencil or tracing over and mark a mirror image of the plume on the other side of the corner motif.

Use a coin or some other round object to trace randomly placed small circles on the appliquéd blocks. Mark the borders as desired; the border of the quilt shown is quilted with a diagonal grid of ¾-inch squares.

BACKING: Sew the 16x99-inch muslin panel between the two 42x99-inch panels. Press the seam allowances open. Sandwich the batting between the quilt top and the backing; baste the three layers together.

QUILTING: Quilt as desired. In addition to the feather quilting design, the quilt shown has outline quilting on the inside edge of each piece on the blocks and around the outside of each border bow and swag.

BINDING: Use the remaining muslin to make approximately 360 inches of bias or straight-grain binding. See pages 306 and 307 for tips on making and applying binding.

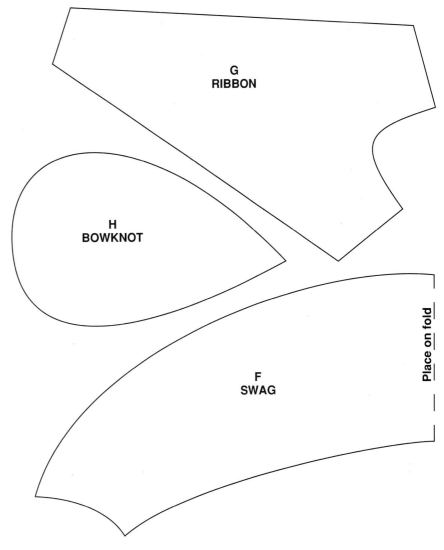

LADIES' DREAM QUILT PATTERNS

Traditions Remembered

A New Generation Discovers The Heritage of Quilting

1965 ∽ 1991

◆ *Iris Germanica, Dallas, Texas, 1990; 91¼x91¼ inches. Instructions begin on page 245.*

*No matter how simple or traditional
a pattern, the effect of a quilt is still absolutely
original because no two people handle fabric
and color the same way.*

Beth Gutcheon

*T*he popularity of quilts declined during the 1950s and '60s. All things old-fashioned and hand-made were out of style; modern chic demanded store-bought bedcovers made of synthetic material. Although some people continued to make quilts during this period, the general public saw little value in them. Quilts were banished to the attic or, worse, thrown away.

In the late 1960s, however, the pendulum of public opinion began to swing again. The back-to-nature ideas of a new generation planted a seed of interest in age-old crafts that would blossom in the next decade.

For charter members of this new quilt renaissance, resources were scarce. In

1965, aspiring quiltmakers used patterns yellowed with age because there was nothing new in print. Fabric was inexpensive, but what was available was polyester, double knit, or printed in garish colors and patterns.

As in the 1920s, magazines played a role in the quilt revival of the 1970s. *Quilter's Newsletter,* founded in 1969, was the first special interest magazine for quiltmakers. It became a mecca for people whose interest in quilts had been stirred by the tidbits that appeared in mainstream publications.

Another landmark in quilt appreciation was the 1971 exhibit of antique quilts curated by Jonathan Holstein and Gail van der Hoof at the Whitney Museum of Art in New York. For the first time, quilts were hung on the walls and presented as art and important artifacts of American history.

◆ *Linked Squares (left), Macomb, Illinois, 1990, an updated variation of a 1930 Nancy Cabot design; 85x109 inches. Instructions begin on page 248.*

*T*he Bicentennial celebration of 1976 was important to the renewal of a widespread interest in quilts. In the best tradition of quiltmaking, this special event in U.S. history spurred countless groups and individuals to record their national pride in quilts. In a flurry of red, white, and blue, the quiltmaking revival surged into full bloom.

Like generations of quiltmakers before them, Americans stitched patriotism and political sentiment into commemorative quilts. Historical societies, church groups, and civic organizations in every town and city re-created local and national history in fabric to mark America's birthday.

Nationwide promotions and contests encouraged individuals to make quilts, too. In the Bicentennial spirit, many people who had never made a quilt purchased kits and patterns of historic antique quilts so they could duplicate a piece of America's heritage.

◆ *Twilight Star and Twisted Square* (opposite), Linn, Kansas, c. 1985; 80½x95 inches. Instructions begin on page 250.

Quilter's Newsletter magazine received more than 500 entries in its Bicentennial quilt contest. The number of entries in other national contests offered ample proof that Americans were making new and exciting quilts in record numbers.

The interest in quilts did not end with the Bicentennial year. Many people were introduced to quiltmaking in 1976 and 1977 by a record-setting promotion in *Woman's Day* magazine that sold more than 150,000 Log Cabin quilt kits and patterns.

In 1977, nearly 10,000 quilters entered a national contest sponsored by *Good Housekeeping* magazine. The first-prize winner, Jinny Beyer of Fairfax, Virginia, catapulted to celebrity status among quiltmakers worldwide.

◆ *Tree of Paradise* (above), Winterset, Iowa, c. 1985; 29¾x29¾ inches. Instructions begin on page 254.

*A*mericans greeted the 1980s with a thirst for new materials and information about quilts.

Publishers and manufacturers met the demand with a cornucopia of new products. Magazines and books about quilts multiplied; 100-percent-cotton fabric designed for quilters was printed in a rainbow of colors and patterns. Tools such as rotary cutters and plastic templates revolutionized patchwork techniques.

Perhaps the most significant development in the 1980s was the unprecedented networking that developed among quilt enthusiasts everywhere. Local and state guilds were organized, as were national groups for quilt research and appreciation. Conventions, exhibits, and workshops attracted people from every state and from around the world who shared their knowledge of and enthusiasm for quilts.

The Kentucky Quilt Project, completed in 1982, was among the first organized efforts to catalog antique quilts within a state. Other state projects were conducted throughout the 1980s.

Research continues to expand people's knowledge of and appreciation for the quilts of America's past and to ensure their preservation. Today's quiltmakers have secured the legacy of their forebears and are moving forward to stitch the heritage of tomorrow.

♦ **Bear's Paw** *(above), Iowa, 1988; 44½x44½ inches. Instructions on page 258.*

♦ **Country Tulip** *(left), Lonmor, Iowa, c. 1984; 85x102 inches. Instructions begin on page 256.*

243

244

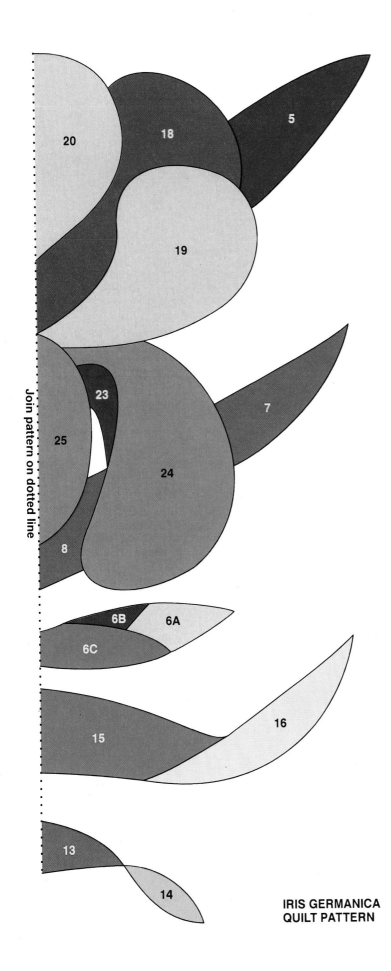

Join pattern on dotted line

**IRIS GERMANICA
QUILT PATTERN**

Iris Germanica Quilt

*Shown on pages 236 and 237.
The finished quilt measures approximately
91¼ inches square. Each block is 11¼
inches square.*

MATERIALS
4¼ yards of seafoam green solid
    fabric for blocks, setting squares,
    and sawtooth triangles
2¾ yards of dark purple solid
    fabric for outer border
2 yards of mauve solid fabric for
    setting and sawtooth triangles
1⅜ yards of olive green solid fabric
    for the inner border and binding
¼ yard *each* of six different green
    solid fabrics, ranging in color
    from lime to forest green, for the
    iris leaves
Scraps of assorted pink, blue,
    mauve, purple, peach, and gold
    solid fabrics in light, medium,
    and dark shades for the flowers
2⅞ yards of 108-inch-wide sheeting
    for backing fabric
120x120-inch precut quilt batting
Template material
Nonpermanent fabric marker
Tracing paper and pencil

INSTRUCTIONS
Fabrics in six different greens and an
assortment of pastels create a lovely
palette in this prizewinning quilt.
Each of the 16 appliquéd iris blocks
has a different combination of colors.

    The appliquéd blocks and setting
squares, joined in an alternate diagonal set, form a light, central garden of
flowers against the darker setting triangles and borders.

Cutting the fabrics
From the seafoam green fabric, cut:
◆ Sixteen 14-inch squares for the
    appliqué blocks.
◆ Nine 11¾-inch squares for the
    setting squares.
◆ Five 2¾x28-inch strips and two
    2¾x42-inch strips.
    From these strips, cut seventy-
    eight 2¾-inch squares. Cut each
    square diagonally in half to yield
    156 sawtooth triangles.

continued

245

From the mauve fabric, cut:
◆ Three 17⅛-inch squares.
   Cut each square diagonally in quarters to obtain 12 setting triangles.
◆ Two 11½-inch squares.
   Cut each square diagonally in half to obtain four corner triangles.
◆ Six 2¾x42-inch strips.
   From these strips, cut seventy-eight 2¾-inch squares; cut each square diagonally in half to yield 156 sawtooth triangles.
◆ Sixteen 2⅜-inch squares for the sawtooth patchwork.

From the olive green fabric, cut:
◆ 1 yard for the binding.
◆ Eight 1½x42-inch strips for the inner border.

From the dark purple fabric, cut:
◆ Four 10½x99-inch border strips.

Preparing the blocks for appliqué

Trace the iris pattern on pages 244 and 245 onto tracing paper. Join the two parts of the pattern as indicated to make a complete tracing. Number each part of the drawing as shown; include the center mark (+) located near the left edge of piece 25.

1. Fold each of the 14-inch seafoam green squares in half vertically and horizontally; finger-press each fold to mark a crease.

2. Tape the paper pattern to a window or a light box. Place one green square atop the pattern, matching the center of the square with the center mark on the pattern. Using the nonpermanent fabric marker, lightly trace the iris design onto the fabric.

Trace the design onto each of the remaining 15 background squares.

Preparing the appliqué fabrics

Note: We recommend that you prepare appliqués for one iris block and assemble that block before cutting the remaining fabrics. The following instructions are given for one block.

See page 288 for tips on making templates for appliqué.

1. Using the traced pattern as a guide, make a template for each of the iris pieces. Label each template with its number.

2. For the bud tips, cut one *each* of patterns 1A, 2A, 6A, 9A, and 17A from one or more of the flower fabrics. Add a ³⁄₁₆-inch seam allowance when cutting each piece.

3. From the same fabrics, or a different combination, cut one *each* of patterns 18 through 25 for the iris. In the quilt shown, most blocks use three or four fabrics for each iris. Patterns 19 and 20 are the same fabric, as are 21 and 23. The lower petals, 22, 24, and 25, also are cut from one fabric. Pattern 18 is sometimes the same as one of the three other fabrics, but it also can be different.

Note: The pattern on pages 244 and 245 is shaded to assist you in identifying the pieces. This is just one of the many ways that this design can be shaded. Experiment with placement of light and dark values as you compose each block.

4. Using a variety of green fabrics, cut one *each* of the remaining patterns for the leaves and buds.

Making the bud units

Assemble the five bud units as described here before you appliqué the block. You can appliqué the parts of these buds directly onto the background square if you prefer, but we found these small pieces easier to manage without the bulk of the background fabric.

Referring to your numbered pattern, group the pieces for buds 1, 2, 6, 9, and 17 for one iris block.

1. Turn under the seam allowances on the top edges of piece 1A, forming a nice sharp point. Press or baste the edges in place. Leave the bottom edges flat where the B and C pieces will overlap.

2. Turn under the top edges of piece 1B in the same manner; appliqué or seam the B piece to the A piece as shown on the pattern. Stitch the 1C piece in place in the same manner so it overlaps the bottom edges of both the 1A and 1B pieces. The prepared bud is now ready to appliqué onto the background fabric as a single unit.

3. Prepare buds 2, 6, 9, and 17 in the same manner.

Appliquéing the iris block

The number on each part of the traced pattern indicates the order in which the pieces are appliquéd onto the background fabric. Use the numbers as a guide to stitch the block.

1. Align Bud 1 on its traced outline on the background square, then appliqué it in place. It is not necessary to turn under the edge that will be covered by Bud 2.

2. Appliqué pieces 2, 3, 4, and 5 in place in the same manner, aligning each piece with its traced outline.

3. Position and appliqué Bud 6 in place, leaving a space unstitched as indicated on the pattern. Bud 17 will be inserted in the space later.

4. Appliqué the remaining pieces, adding each one in numerical order. Most pieces will overlap one or more of the pieces already in place. Insert the bottom of Bud 17 under the stem of Bud 6 with its tip lying atop piece 15. Stitch the bud in place, then close the opening in Bud 6 before continuing with the remaining appliqué.

5. Appliqué 16 iris blocks as described. Trim each completed block to 11¾ inches square, measuring 5⅞ inches from the center mark of the iris along each of the four creased center lines. Steam-press the block to remove all creases and puckers.

Making the sawtooth triangles

1. Stitch the small green and mauve triangles together in pairs to form 156 triangle-squares.

2. Join five triangle-squares in a row, positioning the fabric colors as indicated in Figure 1, *opposite, top;* end the row with a 2⅜-inch mauve square.

3. Sew the assembled row onto one leg of a mauve setting triangle. Make six pieced setting triangles as illustrated in Figure 1. In the same manner, assemble six more pieced setting triangles, positioning the fabric colors as shown in Figure 2, *opposite, top.*

4. Join six of the remaining triangle-squares in a row, positioning the fabric colors as shown at the top of Figure 3, *opposite.* Make 14 sawtooth strips in this manner. Set these strips aside for the quilt assembly.

FIGURE 1 (Make 6)

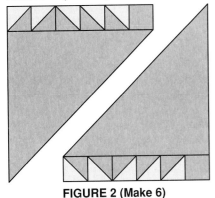

FIGURE 2 (Make 6)

5. Assemble two more strips in the same way, adding a mauve square at both ends of each strip as shown at the bottom of Figure 3. Stitch these strips onto the long diagonal edges of the two mauve corner triangles.

Assembling the quilt top

1. Lay the appliquéd blocks and the 11¾-inch green setting squares on the floor, arranging them in diagonal rows as illustrated in the quilt assembly diagram, *right*.

2. Stitch the blocks together for rows 2, 3, 4, 5, and 6. Add a six-square sawtooth strip to both ends of each row, positioning the fabric colors as shown in the assembly diagram. Do not add the setting triangles yet.

3. To make Row 1, sew a six-square sawtooth strip to opposite sides of the iris block as shown in the diagram. Add a corner triangle with sawtooth edging to the outside edge of the block. Join setting triangles to the sides of the block as shown.

4. Make Row 7 in the same manner as Row 1, positioning the fabric colors as shown in the assembly diagram.

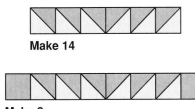

Make 14

Make 2

FIGURE 3

5. Join rows 1 and 2, then sew a setting triangle onto both ends of Row 2 as shown. Add Row 3, then join the setting triangles for that row.

6. Stitch Row 4 onto the edge of Row 3; do not add the corner triangles yet. Set aside rows 1–4 for now.

7. Stitch Row 6 onto Row 7, then add the setting triangles to Row 6. In the same manner, add Row 5 and then the setting triangles for that row.

8. Join the assembled unit of rows 5–7 onto the remaining edge of Row 4. Press all the row seam allowances toward the center. Finally, add corner triangles at the ends of Row 4.

Adding the borders

1. Stitch the 1½x42-inch strips of the olive fabric together in pairs, making four 1½x83-inch border strips.

2. Match the seam line of each green border strip with the center of one purple border strip and stitch them together; the purple strip will be 8 inches longer on each end. Make four border strips in this manner.

3. See page 299 for tips on mitering border corners. Following these instructions, stitch the border strips onto the edges of the quilt top.

Quilting and finishing

Sandwich the batting between the quilt top and the backing fabric. Baste the three layers together.

QUILTING: Quilt as desired. The quilt shown has a feather wreath quilted in each setting square and a grid of small squares quilted over the rest of the quilt top. A feather vine is quilted in the wide purple border.

BINDING: Use the remaining olive fabric to make approximately 380 inches of bias or straight-grain binding. Refer to pages 306 and 307 for tips on making and applying binding.

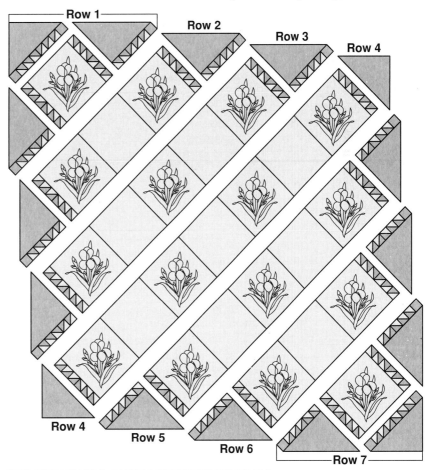

Row 1   Row 2   Row 3   Row 4   Row 4   Row 5   Row 6   Row 7

IRIS GERMANICA QUILT ASSEMBLY DIAGRAM

Linked Squares Quilt

Shown on pages 238 and 239.
The finished quilt measures approximately
85x109 inches. Each finished block is
12 inches square.

MATERIALS

4¾ yards of ecru print fabric for
  the patchwork and middle border
4½ yards of medium blue striped
  or print fabric for the patchwork,
  outer border, and binding
2¾ yards of dark blue print fabric
  for patchwork and inner border
3¼ yards of 90-inch-wide sheeting
  for the backing
120x120-inch precut quilt batting
Template material
Rotary cutter, mat, and acrylic ruler

INSTRUCTIONS

When the 35 blocks of this quilt are
joined in a 5x7-block straight set,
they form a wonderful pattern of interlocked squares. The block is not
difficult to stitch, but its assembly requires a partial seam. If this technique is new to you, read the block
assembly instructions carefully before you begin.

Cutting the fabrics

Refer to page 288 for tips on making
templates for hand or machine patchwork. Prepare templates for patterns
B, C, and D, *opposite.*

From the ecru print fabric, cut:
◆ Two 5x76-inch strips and six
  5x31-inch strips for the middle
  border.
◆ Thirty-five 4¾-inch squares (A).
◆ 140 of Pattern B.

From the medium blue print fabric, cut:
◆ One yard for the binding.
◆ Two 6x90-inch strips and
  two 6x101-inch strips for the
  outer border.
◆ 70 *each* of patterns C and D.

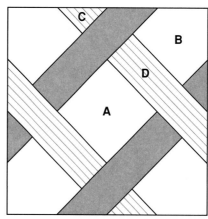

LINKED SQUARES BLOCK

From the dark blue print fabric, cut:
◆ Two 3x68-inch strips and
  two 3x87-inch strips for the inner
  border.
◆ 70 *each* of patterns C and D.

Making the Linked Square blocks

Each block contains one A square
and two each of units 1 and 2. Make
these units as described below before
assembling the blocks.
1. Refer to Figure 1, *below,* to make
Unit 1. Begin by joining a dark blue C
triangle onto one side of a B piece,
positioning these pieces as shown;
press this seam allowance toward the
C triangle. Add a medium blue D
piece to the diagonal edge of the BC
piece; press this seam allowance toward the D piece. Make 70 of Unit 1
(two for each block).
2. Referring to Figure 2, *below, right,*
make Unit 2 in the same manner. Use
medium blue C triangles and dark
blue D pieces. Make 70 of Unit 2.
3. With right sides together, match
the corner of a Unit 1 D piece with
one corner of an A square. Stitch

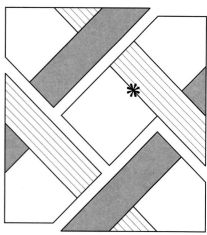

LINKED SQUARES
BLOCK ASSEMBLY DIAGRAM

from the corner of the square to the
halfway point of the side (indicated
by the asterisk in the block assembly
diagram, *above*). This seam is completed after the last quarter-section is
added to the center square. The ADB
edge created by this partial seam
gives you a straight edge on which to
add the next unit.
4. Working *counterclockwise,* stitch a
Unit 2 onto the edge of the ADB unit.
Press the seam allowance toward the
D piece of Unit 2.
5. Add another Unit 1 and then another Unit 2 to the center square as
illustrated. Press each new seam allowance toward the unit just added.
Keep the first unit out of the way as
you stitch the last Unit 2 onto the
A square.
6. Match the unstitched edge of the
first Unit 1 to the edge created by the
A square and the last Unit 2; stitch
the remaining portion of the seam.
  Make 35 Linked Square blocks.
continued

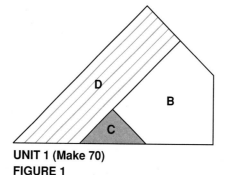

UNIT 1 (Make 70)
FIGURE 1

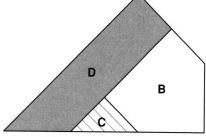

UNIT 2 (Make 70)
FIGURE 2

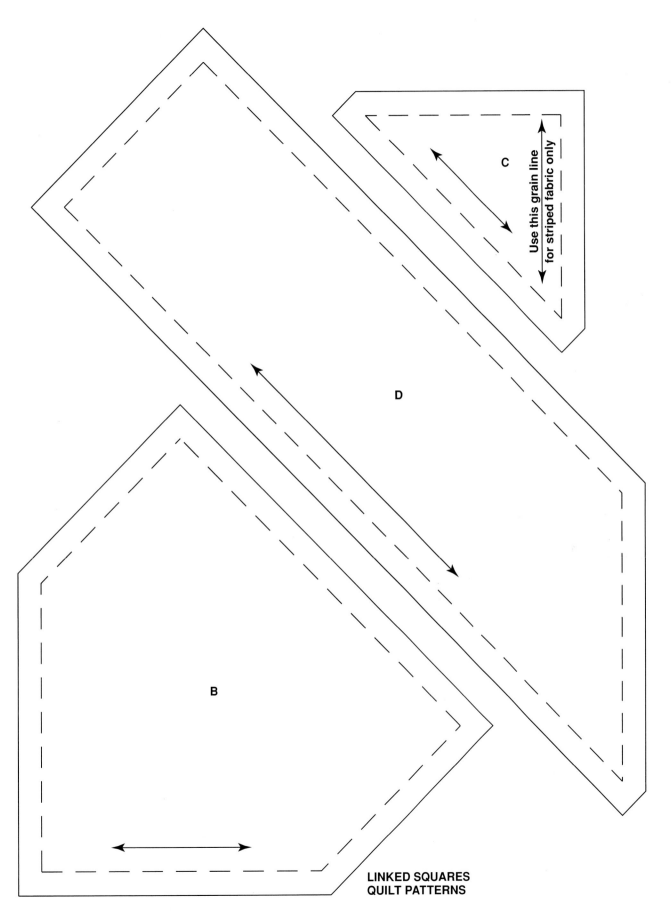

C

Use this grain line
for striped fabric only

D

B

**LINKED SQUARES
QUILT PATTERNS**

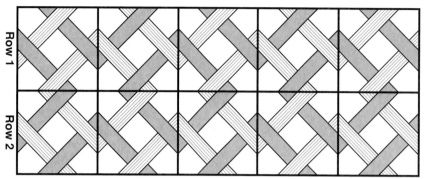

FIGURE 3

Assembling the quilt top

1. Lay out five blocks in a row, turning the blocks to position the colors as shown in Row 1 of Figure 3, *above*. Join the blocks, keeping each one in its correct position. Make four of Row 1.

2. Referring to Figure 3, make three of Row 2 in the same manner.

3. Stitch the assembled rows together in three pairs, stitching one of Row 1 to one of Row 2. Match the block seam lines carefully. Join the three pairs to complete the quilt top, adding the extra Row 1 at the bottom of the last Row 2.

Adding the borders

1. Stitch an 87-inch-long dark blue border strip onto each long side of the quilt. Press the seam allowances toward the borders; trim excess border fabric even with the ends of the quilt top.

2. Stitch the 68-inch-long dark blue border strips onto the top and bottom edges of the quilt. Press the seam allowances toward the dark blue fabric; trim excess border fabric.

3. Join three 5x31-inch strips of ecru print fabric to make a border strip for each long side of the quilt. Add these border strips to the quilt top, then add the 5x76-inch top and bottom borders. Add the medium blue borders in the same manner to complete the quilt top.

Quilting and finishing

Layer backing, batting, and quilt top; baste the layers together.

QUILTING: The quilt shown on pages 238 and 239 has concentric circles quilted over the blocks and a co-

ordinating braided cable stitched in the borders. Quilt as desired.

BINDING: Use the remaining medium blue print fabric to make approximately 400 inches of binding, either bias or straight-grain. Refer to pages 306 and 307 for tips on making and applying binding.

───────CHALLENGING───────

Twilight Star and Twisted Square Quilt

Shown on page 240.
The finished quilt measures approximately 80½x95 inches. Each block is 10¼ inches square.

MATERIALS

6¼ yards of beige/black print fabric for the blocks, borders, and binding

2¾ yards of black print fabric for blocks and borders

2 yards of gray-on-white pindot for the blocks and pieced border

1⅛ yards of a dark border stripe fabric that has at least five repeats of a 2⅝-inch-wide stripe for the pieced border

⅓ yard *each* of pink solid fabric and muslin for Twilight Star blocks

3 yards of 90-inch-wide sheeting for backing fabric

90x108-inch precut quilt batting

Template material

Rotary cutter, mat, and acrylic ruler

INSTRUCTIONS

This quilt has two patchwork blocks that alternate in a diagonal set. Six

Twilight Star and 12 Twisted Square blocks combine to form an interweaving design that is strengthened by the placement of light, medium, and dark fabrics.

Half-blocks of the Twilight Star block form the 10 setting triangles around the edges of the diagonal set, and quarter-blocks are used for the four corners. The assembled blocks are framed by a series of borders, including a challenging pieced border that combines the block fabrics with a coordinating border stripe.

Cutting the fabrics

See page 288 for tips on making templates for patchwork. Prepare window templates for patterns A, E, F, and I, *opposite*. All the other pieces can be measured with a ruler and cut using a rotary cutter. Refer to the block diagrams on page 252 and Figure 1 on page 253 to identify the patches for which patterns are not given.

From the pindot, cut:
◆ Ten 2⅝x42-inch strips.
  From these strips, cut 96 of Pattern A for the Twilight Star blocks and partial-blocks.
◆ One 25x42-inch piece.
  From this piece, cut 12 of Pattern E for the Twisted Square blocks.
◆ Thirty-six 3⅛-inch squares for the J square in the pieced border.

From the black print fabric, cut:
◆ Two 2x84-inch strips and two 2x96-inch strips for the fourth border.
◆ 48 of Pattern F.
  To cut these pieces, position the F template with the longest side parallel to the crosswise grain of the fabric.
◆ Twenty-four 3⅞-inch squares.
  Cut each square diagonally in half to obtain 48 G triangles for the Twisted Square blocks.
◆ Seventy-two 3⅛-inch squares for the J square in the pieced border.

From the muslin, cut:
◆ Ninety-six 2-inch squares for the B square in the Twilight Star blocks and partial-blocks.

continued

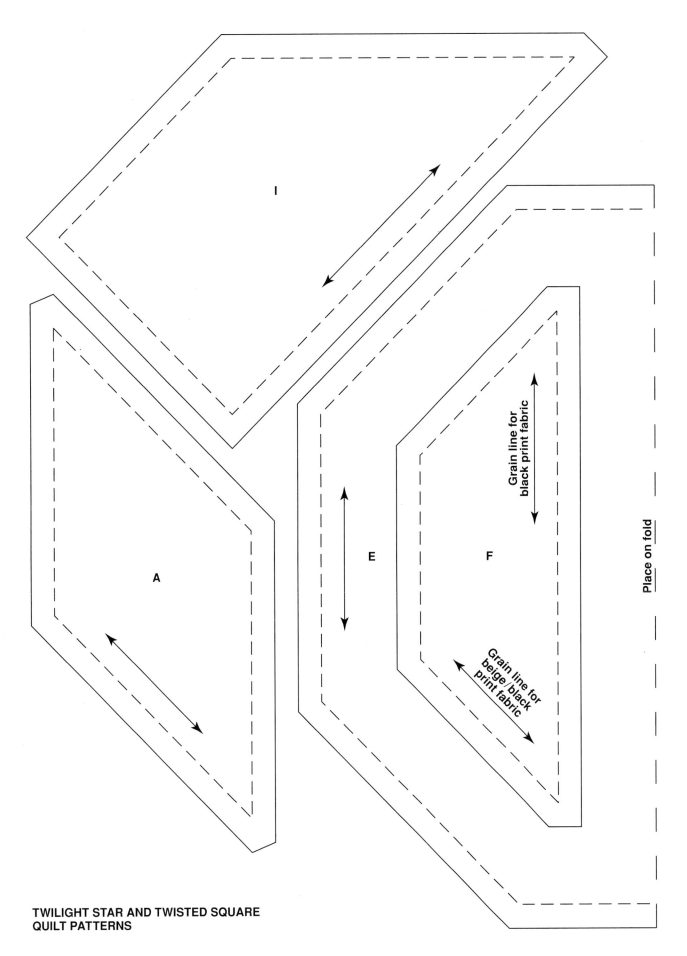

I

A

E

F

Grain line for
black print fabric

Grain line for
beige/black
print fabric

Place on fold

**TWILIGHT STAR AND TWISTED SQUARE
QUILT PATTERNS**

251

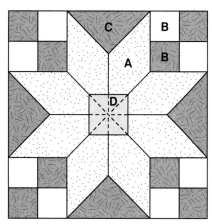

TWILIGHT STAR BLOCK (Make 6)

From the pink solid fabric, cut:
- Twenty 2½-inch squares for the D square in the Twilight Star blocks and partial-blocks.

From the beige/black print fabric, cut:
- One yard for the binding.
- 3¼ yards for the borders. Cut two 5x58-inch strips for the first border, cutting both strips from the same edge of this fabric. Cutting across the remaining fabric width, cut two 5x73-inch strips for the first border, two 4½x81-inch strips and two 4½x96-inch strips for the third border, and two 1½x101-inch strips and two 1½x86-inch strips for the last border.
- 124 B squares, each 2 inches square, for the Twilight Star blocks and partial-blocks.
- One 12x42-inch piece. From this piece, cut twelve 5⅝-inch squares. Cut each square diagonally in quarters to get 48 C triangles for the Twilight Star blocks and partial-blocks.
- One 27x42-inch piece. From this piece, cut 48 of Pattern F. To cut these pieces, place the grain line parallel to the diagonal edge of the template.
- Thirty-six 5⅛-inch squares. Cut each square diagonally in quarters to obtain 144 H triangles for the pieced border.

From the border stripe fabric, cut:
- 36 of Pattern I and 36 of Pattern I reversed.

Making the Twilight Star blocks
Make six Twilight Star blocks, referring to the block diagram, *left*, for guidance. See page 163 for tips on sewing set-in seams.

1. Stitch two A diamonds together, being careful to end the stitching ¼ inch from the end of the seam. Press the seam allowance to one side, then set a C triangle into the angled opening of the diamonds. Make four ACA units for each block.

2. Sew these units together in pairs, then join two pairs to complete the star. Leave ¼ inch unstitched at the ends of the seams to receive the set-in corner squares. Don't worry if the center of the star, where all eight seams meet, is not perfectly flat, since the D square will cover the center.

3. Join eight pairs of muslin and print fabric B squares; press each seam allowance toward the print fabric. Join two pairs to make a square. Make four of these squares for each block. Set a four-patch square into each opening of the star diamonds.

4. Turn under the ¼-inch seam allowance on all sides of the D square. Fold the D square in half vertically

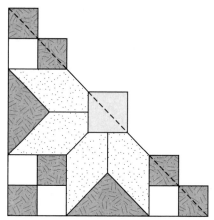

TWILIGHT STAR HALF-BLOCK (Make 10)

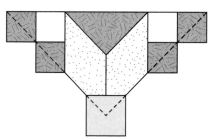

TWILIGHT STAR QUARTER-BLOCK (Make 4)

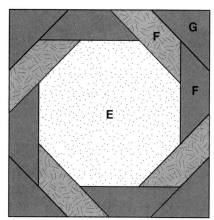

TWISTED SQUARE BLOCK (Make 12)

and horizontally and insert a pin through the center point. Push the pin through the center point of the star to position the D square. Appliqué the square in place.

Making the partial-blocks
For the setting triangles, make 10 Twilight Star half-blocks and four quarter-blocks as illustrated, *left*.

As each unit is completed, align the acrylic ruler with the unstitched edge of the A diamonds and use your rotary cutter to trim the excess fabric from the B and D squares at the edges of each unit.

Making the Twisted Square blocks
Make 12 Twisted Square blocks, referring to the block diagram, *above*. Each block requires one E piece, four black print F pieces, four beige/black print F pieces, and four G triangles.

1. Designate one edge of the E piece as the top. With the right sides of the fabric together, align the *longest* side of one black print F piece with the top edge of the E piece, matching the diagonal edges on the *right-hand* edge. If you marked sewing lines on the fabric, push a pin through both layers to align the right corners of the seam lines on the two pieces.

2. Starting at the matched corner, stitch approximately 1½ inches of this seam. Leave the rest of the seam unstitched for now; it will be completed after the last F piece is joined to E. When the F piece is smoothed to the right side, the diagonal edges of both pieces should align.

3. Working *clockwise* around the center piece, add F pieces, alternating the two fabric colors. Press each seam allowance away from the center piece as you work. When the last F piece is sewn in place, complete the seam of the first F piece.

4. Complete the block by adding a G triangle to each corner; press the seam allowance toward the triangle.

Assembling the quilt top

The blocks and partial-blocks are stitched together in diagonal rows as indicated by the red lines on the quilt assembly diagram, *right*.

Using the diagram as a guide, lay the blocks on the floor. Picking up one block at a time, join the blocks in each row. Assemble the rows to complete the quilt top, matching the seam lines of adjoining blocks.

Center a 5-inch-wide border strip of beige/black print fabric on each edge of the quilt top. Refer to page 299 for instructions on sewing borders with mitered corners. The quilt top should measure approximately 53x67½ inches for the pieced border to fit.

Making the pieced border

1. Stitch each I piece to an I reversed piece, matching diagonal edges.

2. Set a black print J square into the open angle of four pieced I units; set a pindotted J square into each remaining unit.

3. Sew H triangles onto two adjacent sides of each remaining J square, making 72 triangular units.

4. Combine these units to make each border strip as illustrated in the quilt assembly diagram. Join the units in diagonal rows as shown in Figure 1, *below,* turning each unit to position the colors as necessary. Join these rows to complete each border.

5. Sew the pieced border strips onto the quilt top, then carefully stitch the four mitered seams.

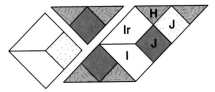

FIGURE 1

TWILIGHT STAR AND TWISTED SQUARE QUILT ASSEMBLY DIAGRAM

Adding the borders

Separate the shorter border strips of each width from the longer ones. Use the shorter strips to make borders for the top and bottom edges of the quilt top and the longer ones for the sides.

Sew together the strips for the three remaining borders and add them to the quilt top as one piece. Sew the two beige/black print strips onto opposite sides of the black print strip, matching the centers of all three strips.

Add the borders onto the quilt top, following the directions on page 299 for making mitered corners. Trim excess fabric from the seam allowances.

Quilting and finishing

Sandwich the batting between the quilt top and the backing fabric; baste the three layers together.

QUILTING: Quilt as desired. The quilt shown has outline quilting inside the seam lines of each patch. See page 203 for a suitable quilting design to fill the centers of the Twisted Square blocks.

BINDING: Use the remaining print fabric to make approximately 365 inches of bias or straight-grain binding. See pages 306 and 307 for tips on making and applying binding.

Tree of Paradise Wall Hanging

Shown on page 241.
The finished wall hanging is approxi-mately 29¾ inches square. The Tree of Paradise block is 12½ inches square.

MATERIALS
1 yard of a border stripe fabric with two or more designs for the inner and outer borders and for the block (Each stripe must repeat at least four times across the width of the fabric.)
½ yard of blue print fabric for the middle border
¼ yard or 14-inch square *each* of gray solid, and ecru and black print fabrics for the block patchwork and the setting triangles
⅛ yard *each* or scraps of rust, dark brown, and light brown print fabrics for the block patchwork
One 17-inch square of tan fabric for the binding
36-inch square *each* of backing fabric and quilt batting
Template material
Rotary cutter, mat, and acrylic ruler

INSTRUCTIONS
The stripes of the two narrow bor-ders in this wall hanging were cut from one fabric. Border stripe fabric usually has several lengthwise de-signs that can be cut apart and used to add linear interest in patchwork. The design for the inner border was 1½ inches wide; the one used for the outer border was 2½ inches wide. Since widths of border stripes vary, adjust the instructions as necessary for designs of different widths.

Cutting the fabrics
See page 288 for tips on making and using templates for patchwork. Make a template for Pattern F, *opposite.* The other pieces can be measured with a ruler and cut using a rotary cutter. Refer to the block assembly diagram, *below, right,* to identify the patches for which patterns are not given.

From the blue print fabric, cut:
◆ Four 4x28-inch strips for the middle border.

From the gray solid fabric, cut:
◆ Two of Pattern F.
◆ One 5⅞-inch square.
Cut this square diagonally in half to get two D triangles.
◆ Five 2⅛-inch squares.
Cut each of these squares diago-nally in half to get 10 B triangles.
◆ One 1¾-inch A square.

From the ecru print fabric, cut:
◆ Two 7-inch squares.
Cut each of these squares diago-nally in half to get four setting triangles.
◆ Two 2⅛-inch squares.
Cut each of these squares diago-nally in half to get three B triangles and one extra.

From the border stripe fabric, cut:
◆ Nine 2⅛-inch squares.
Cut each of these squares diago-nally in half to get 18 B triangles.
◆ Eight 2x11-inch strips for the first border.
The design for this border should be 1½ inches wide and have sufficient fabric on each side for seam allowances.
◆ Four 3x33-inch strips for the outer border.
If the border stripe design (not including seam allowance) is more than 2½ inches wide, increase the length of the strips to accommodate the extra width for mitering.

From the rust print fabric, cut:
◆ Three 1¾-inch A squares.
◆ Nine 2⅛-inch squares.
Cut each of these squares diago-nally in half to get 18 B triangles.

From the black print fabric, cut:
◆ Six 3⅜-inch squares.
Cut each of these squares diago-nally in half to get 12 C triangles.

From the light brown print fabric, cut:
◆ Two 2⅝-inch squares.
Cut each of these squares diagonally in half to obtain three E triangles and one extra.
◆ One 4⅝-inch square.
Cut this square diagonally in half to get one G triangle and one extra.

From the dark brown print fabric, cut:
◆ Two 2⅝-inch squares.
Cut each of these squares diagonally in half to obtain three E triangles and one extra.

Making the Tree of Paradise block
1. Join six B triangles of border print fabric to six B triangles of gray solid fabric, making six triangle-squares. Press the seam allowances toward the gray fabric.
2. Join six more border print B trian-gles to six rust print B triangles in the same manner. Press the seam allow-ances toward the rust fabric.
3. Referring to the block assembly diagram, *below,* for fabric placement, combine these triangle-squares with the remaining B triangles of gray and rust fabrics to make larger triangular units. Combine these triangle units with C triangles to make squares.
4. Referring to the assembly diagram for piece placement, make three quadrants of the block by joining the assembled units with the remaining A squares and C and D triangles.
5. Make three triangle-squares with the E triangles, joining one light brown and one dark brown triangle

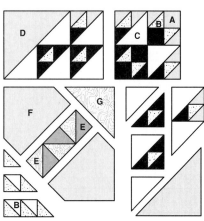

**TREE OF PARADISE
BLOCK ASSEMBLY DIAGRAM**

in each square. Press the seam allowances toward the dark fabric. Join these three triangle-squares in a row to make the tree trunk, turning the squares to alternate the fabrics as shown in the diagram.

6. Stitch an F piece onto each long side of the tree trunk. Press the seam allowances toward the F pieces. Sew the light brown G triangle onto the top edge of the trunk unit.

7. Make three triangle-squares with B triangles of ecru and border print fabrics. Press the seam allowances toward the ecru fabric. To make the tree base, join these triangle-squares with the remaining B triangles of border print fabric, as illustrated. Add the resulting triangle to the bottom of the trunk unit.

8. Combine the four quadrants to complete the block.

Adding the setting triangles
1. Stitch a 2x11-inch border stripe piece to both short legs of each ecru setting triangle, making a mitered corner. (See page 299 for tips on making mitered corners.) Press the seam allowances toward the borders.
2. Use the long edge of the ecru triangle as a guide to trim the excess border fabric. Align the edge of the acrylic ruler with the edge of the triangle so that the ruler extends over both borders. Use the rotary cutter to trim the border strips along the edge of the ruler.
3. Stitch a pieced setting triangle onto one side of the block, then stitch another setting triangle onto the opposite side. Press the seam allowances toward the triangle units. Add setting triangles to the remaining sides of the block.

Adding the borders
Center the blue print border strips on each edge of the quilt top. Refer to page 299 for tips on sewing borders with mitered corners.

Add the outer border strips in the same manner.

Quilting and finishing
Sandwich the batting between the quilt top and the backing fabric; baste the three layers securely together. Quilt as desired. The quilt shown has a feather motif in the setting triangles and an undulating feather plume in the middle border.

See page 308 for tips on adding a hanging sleeve to the back of the quilt.

BINDING: Use the tan fabric to make approximately 125 inches of binding, either bias or straight-grain. Refer to pages 306 and 307 for tips on making and applying binding.

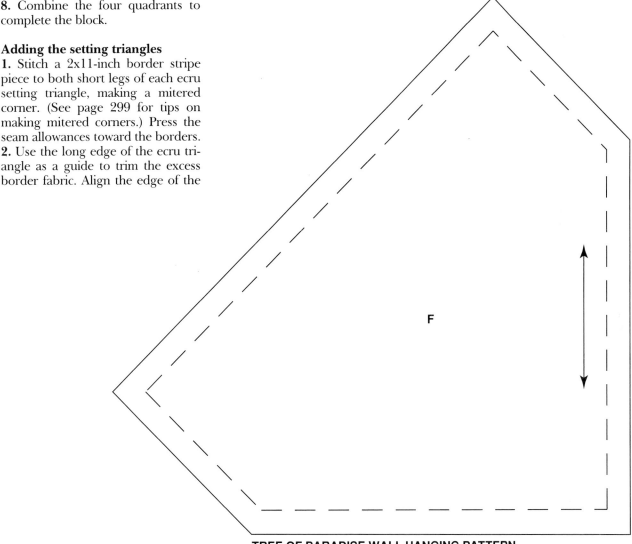

F

TREE OF PARADISE WALL HANGING PATTERN

Country Tulip Quilt

Shown on pages 242 and 243.
The finished quilt measures 85x102
inches. Each Country Tulip block is
6 inches square.

MATERIALS

5¾ yards of mauve print fabric for
   the tulip blocks, setting squares
   and triangles, the border
   triangles, and binding
4 yards of cream print fabric
1 yard *each* of green solid and blue
   print fabrics for the tulip blocks
¼ yard *each* of blue solid and
   mauve solid fabrics for tulip tips
3 yards of 90-inch-wide sheeting for
   backing fabric
90x108-inch precut quilt batting
Template material
Rotary cutter, mat, and acrylic ruler

INSTRUCTIONS

There are 120 tulip blocks in this
quilt, 60 with mauve tulips and 60
with blue tulips. Two blocks of each
color are joined to make each of the
twenty 12-inch blocks that are assembled in an alternate diagonal set. The
border is comprised of forty 6-inch
tulip blocks of alternating colors.

Cutting the fabrics

Before cutting the fabrics, read the
following assembly instructions; decide whether you will use traditional
or quick-piecing techniques to piece
the tulip blocks.

   See page 288 for tips on making
and using templates for patchwork.
For traditional hand or machine sewing, prepare window templates for
each of patterns A, B, C, and E, *opposite*. If you decide to make the tulip
blocks using the quick-piecing method, make a window template only for
Pattern E.

From the blue print fabric, cut:
◆ Ten 2½x42-inch strips for the
   tulips.
   For traditional piecing, cut 60 of
   Pattern A and 60 of Pattern A re-
   versed from these strips.

From the mauve print fabric, cut:
◆ Ten 2½x42-inch strips for tulips.
   For traditional piecing, cut 60 of
   Pattern A and 60 of Pattern A re-
   versed from these strips.
◆ One 30-inch square for binding.
◆ Twelve 12½-inch setting squares.
◆ Four 18¼-inch squares.
   Cut each of these squares diago-
   nally in quarters to yield 14
   setting triangles and two extras.
◆ Four 9⅜-inch squares.
   Cut each of these squares diago-
   nally in half to yield eight corner
   triangles.
◆ Eighteen 9¾-inch squares.
   Cut each of these squares
   diagonally in quarters to yield 72
   border triangles.

From the cream print fabric, cut:
◆ Forty 1x42-inch strips.
   For traditional piecing, cut 240 of
   Pattern B and 240 of Pattern B
   reversed from these strips.
◆ Thirteen 1½x42-inch strips.
   From these strips, cut 120 of
   Pattern E and 120 of Pattern E
   reversed.
◆ Fifteen 4⅞x42-inch strips.
   From these strips, cut 120
   squares, each 4⅞ inches square.
   Cut each square diagonally in
   half to yield 240 F triangles.

From the green solid fabric, cut:
◆ Twenty 1½x42-inch strips for the
   tulip leaves.
   For traditional piecing, cut 120 of
   Pattern C and 120 of Pattern C
   reversed from these strips.

From each of the mauve and blue solid
fabrics, cut:
◆ Three 1½x42-inch strips.
   From these strips, cut sixty
   1½-inch squares of each color for
   the tulip tips.

Making the tulip blocks

TRADITIONAL PIECING: Referring to the block assembly diagram,
right, make the Country Tulip block
in three sections according to the following instructions.

1. Stitch a B piece onto both long
sides of one C piece. If you have
marked the sewing lines on each
piece, push a pin through both layers

of fabric to align the seam lines before you sew.

2. Add a mauve print A piece onto
one end of the BCB unit as shown;
press all seam allowances toward the
A piece.

3. Assemble a matching unit for the
opposite side of the block, using the
reversed pieces of A, B, and C. Press
the seam allowances of this unit away
from the A piece.

4. Stitch these two units together,
matching seam lines of opposing
pieces where they meet. Stop stitching ¼ inch from the top edge of the
tulip fabric to leave the seam allowance available for the set-in corner
unit. Press open the seam allowance
of this center seam.

5. Add an F triangle to both sides of
the tulip as shown; press these seam
allowances toward the triangles.

6. Join one E piece and one E reversed piece as shown. Do not stitch
beyond the seam line of the E pieces
so the seam allowance will be available to receive the set-in D square
(see page 163 for tips on stitching
set-in seams). Set a D square of blue
solid fabric into the angled opening
of the E pieces.

7. Set the corner unit into the angled
opening of the A tulip pieces to complete the block.

   In this manner, make 60 tulip
blocks using mauve print A pieces
and blue solid D squares. Make 60
more tulip blocks using blue print A
pieces and mauve solid D squares.

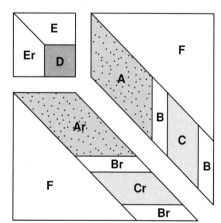

COUNTRY TULIP BLOCK
ASSEMBLY DIAGRAM

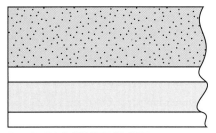

TULIP BLOCK STRIP SET

STRIP PIECING: See page 18 for basic tips on strip piecing.

1. Stitch 1-inch strips of cream fabric onto both long sides of one green strip. Add a strip of mauve print fabric to one edge to complete the strip set as illustrated *above*.

2. Make 10 of these strip sets. Separate these into two groups of five. For one group, press the seam allowances *toward* the mauve print tulip fabric; for the second group, press the seam allowances *away* from the mauve print fabric. Sort the strip sets into five pairs, with one strip set from each group in each pair.

3. Lay one strip set pair on the cutting mat with right sides together, matching the outer edges of both units. The opposing seam allowances will help you match the seam lines.

4. With the acrylic ruler and rotary cutter, square off the *left* edge of the stacked strip sets so you have a straight edge from which to start.

5. Measure 4½ inches from the left edge across the top of the strip set. Draw a diagonal line from this point down to the bottom left corner of the strip set as shown in Figure 1, *below*.

6. Starting from this first line, mark diagonal lines 2 inches apart along the length of the strip set until you have marked 12 segments. Using a rotary cutter, cut on the drawn lines

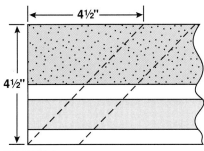

FIGURE 1

through both layers of the stacked strip sets to obtain 12 pairs of mirror-image tulip units.

7. Stitch each pair together, matching seam lines of opposing pieces where they meet. Stop stitching ¼ inch from the top edge of the tulip fabric to leave the seam allowance available for the set-in corner. Press open the seam allowance of this center seam.

8. Add an F triangle to both sides of the tulip as shown; press these seam allowances toward the triangles.

9. Join one E piece and one E reversed piece as shown in the assembly diagram. Set a D square of blue solid fabric into the angled opening of the E pieces (see page 163 for tips on set-in seams). Set the resulting corner unit into the angled opening of the tulip to complete the block.

Make 60 blocks using mauve print tulip fabric and blue solid D squares. Repeat steps 1 through 9 with blue print tulip fabric and mauve solid D squares to make 60 more blocks.

continued

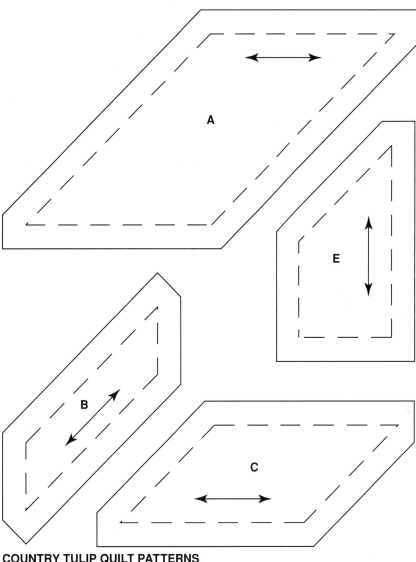

COUNTRY TULIP QUILT PATTERNS

COUNTRY TULIP QUILT ASSEMBLY DIAGRAM

Assembling the quilt top

1. To make each 12½-inch block, join four tulip blocks (two of each color) as shown in the quilt assembly diagram, *above*, placing like-colored tulips opposite each other in each block. Make twenty 12½-inch blocks.
2. The blocks and setting pieces are joined in the diagonal rows indicated by red lines on the assembly diagram. Lay the blocks on the floor, turning them as shown so that mauve tulips always face blue ones (see the photo on pages 242 and 243). Alternate the tulip colors around the border.
3. Join border blocks and triangles to make units for each diagonal row as shown in the assembly diagram.
4. Picking up one unit at a time, join the blocks, setting pieces, and border units in each diagonal row. Join the rows to complete the quilt top.

Quilting and finishing

Sandwich the batting between the backing and the quilt top; baste the layers together.

QUILTING: The quilt shown has outline quilting in the tulip blocks and a feathered wreath stitched in each setting square. A suitable wreath design is given on page 25. Quilt as desired.

BINDING: Use the remaining square of mauve print fabric to make approximately 380 inches of bias or straight-grain binding. See pages 306 and 307 for tips on making and applying binding.

Bear's Paw Wall Hanging

Shown on page 243.
The finished quilt measures approximately 44½x44½ inches. Each Bear's Paw block is 10½ inches square.

MATERIALS

2¾ yards of dark blue print fabric for border, binding, and backing
1⅜ yards of ecru/rose print fabric for the block background
½ yard of dark rose print fabric for sashing
⅛ yard of light blue print fabric for sashing squares
Nine 9x20-inch pieces of one or more print fabrics for the Bear's Paw blocks
48-inch square of quilt batting
Template material
Rotary cutter, mat, and acrylic ruler

INSTRUCTIONS

This wall hanging has nine Bear's Paw blocks in a straight set with sashing strips and squares between them. Five different fabrics were used for the blocks in our quilt; you can use the same fabric for all the blocks or as many different fabrics as you like.

Cutting the fabrics

For efficient use of fabric, cut large pieces in the order stated below, then cut these into the strips and squares listed below the large pieces.

From the dark blue print fabric, cut:
◆ Four 4x46-inch strips for the border.
◆ One 29x49-inch piece and two 9x49-inch pieces for the backing.
◆ Four 2x49-inch strips for straight-grain binding.
Use the remainder of this fabric for Bear's Paw blocks, if desired.

From each 9x20-inch print fabric piece, cut:
◆ One 9x13-inch piece for the triangle-squares.
◆ Four 3½-inch squares.
◆ One 2-inch square for the block center.

From the ecru/rose print fabric, cut:
◆ Nine 9x13-inch pieces for the triangle-squares.
◆ Thirty-six 2x5-inch pieces for the block crossbars.
◆ Thirty-six 2-inch squares.

From the dark rose print fabric, cut:
◆ Eight 2x42-inch strips.
From these strips, cut twenty-four 2x11-inch strips for the sashing.

From the light blue print fabric, cut:
◆ Sixteen 2-inch squares for the sashing squares.

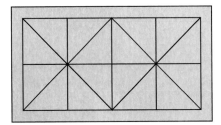

FIGURE 1

Making the triangle-squares
See page 114 for more instructions on quick-pieced triangle-squares.
1. On the wrong side of each 9x13-inch piece of ecru print fabric, mark a 2x4-square grid of 2⅜-inch squares as shown in Figure 1, *above*. Draw diagonal lines through the squares as shown. With right sides together, layer each ecru print square atop one 9x13-inch piece of print fabric.
2. For traditional piecing, cut the triangles apart on the marked lines, cutting through both layers of fabric. For hand piecing, mark ¼-inch seam allowances on each triangle.
3. For quick piecing, stitch the grid as described in Step 3 on page 114. Each grid makes 16 triangle-squares.
4. Using either piecing method, make 16 triangle-squares of each fabric combination. Press the seam allowances toward the darker print fabric.

Making the Bear's Paw blocks
Refer to the block assembly diagram, *right,* to make each Bear's Paw block.
1. Join the triangle-squares in pairs, sewing the ecru side of one square onto the colored side of the adjacent square. Make eight pairs of triangle-squares for each block.

2. Sew a pair of triangle-squares onto one side of each 3½-inch square of colored fabric. Press the seam allowance toward the large square.
3. Stitch a 2-inch square of ecru print fabric onto the colored end of each remaining pair of triangle-squares. Press the seam allowance toward the ecru square. Then join this three-square unit to the rectangular unit as shown in the diagram. Make four of these quarter-block sections with the same fabrics for each block.
4. Stitch a quarter-block section onto both long sides of two 2x5-inch strips of ecru print fabric. Press the seam allowances toward the center strips.
5. For the crossbars, sew a 2x5-inch ecru strip onto opposite sides of each 2-inch colored square. Press the seam allowances toward the ecru strips.
6. Join the three rows of each block by stitching the quarter-block rows onto opposite sides of the center crossbar row as shown in the diagram. Press each seam allowance toward the center row.
Make nine Bear's Paw blocks.

Joining the horizontal rows
While assembling the rows, refer to the illustration of a straight set with sashing on page 295.
1. Sew one dark rose sashing strip to the left side of each block; press the seam allowances toward the sashing.
2. On the floor or a table, lay out the blocks in a pleasing arrangement; separate the blocks into three rows with three blocks in each row.
3. Join the blocks for Row 1, sewing

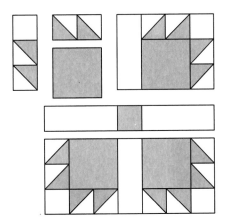

BEAR'S PAW BLOCK ASSEMBLY DIAGRAM

each block to the sashing strip of the adjacent block. Complete the row by sewing a vertical sashing strip to the right side of the last block in the row. Press all sashing seam allowances toward the sashing. Repeat for rows 2 and 3.

Assembling the quilt top
While assembling the quilt top, refer to the photo on page 243.
1. Each row of horizontal sashing is made by alternating light blue sashing squares with dark rose sashing strips. Starting with a square, sew three sashing strips and four squares together to make a row; make four rows of horizontal sashing.
2. Matching seam lines carefully, sew a row of horizontal sashing to the top of each of the three block rows. Press seams toward the horizontal sashing.
3. Join the rows, sewing the top of the sashing row to the bottom of the adjacent block row. Stitch the remaining row of sashing to the bottom of the third block row. Press seam allowances toward the sashing.

Adding the border
Stitch a dark blue border strip onto opposite sides of the quilt top. Press the seam allowances toward the border strips; trim excess border fabric even with the quilt top. Add the remaining border strips to the other edges in the same manner.

Quilting and finishing
BACKING: Stitch a 9x49-inch strip of backing fabric onto each side of the 29x49-inch panel. Press the seam allowances open.

Layer backing, batting, and quilt top; baste the three layers together.

QUILTING: The quilt shown has diagonal lines of quilting in the Bear's Paw blocks and outline quilting in the sashing strips and squares. A twisted braid is quilted in the borders. Quilt as desired.

BINDING: Use the 2x49-inch strips of the border fabric for the binding. See page 307 for tips on applying straight-grain binding.

259

Today's Quilters

Profiles of Ten Quiltmakers in the 1990s

Glendora Hutson

*My quilts are traditional.
I make quilts for many of the
same reasons my ancestors
did. Even when I use my own
original designs, the
traditional roots are evident.*

A teacher of quilt-making since 1976, Glendora Hutson makes classic quilts using 20th-century tools.

"It never seems necessary to me to title my quilts. The names are well known to quilters today as well as to quilters of our great-grandmothers' generation," Glendora says. "The quilts speak for themselves."

Glendora is a legal administrator from Berkeley, California, whose interest in quilts began with antiques. She speculated about each quilt, when and where it was made, how it was used, and, most of all, who made it.

"Early quiltmakers used their craft as a means of cementing friendships around the quilting frame and passing on tradition," Glendora says. "I feel at home in this heritage and I make quilts for many of the same reasons."

Glendora usually makes crib-size quilts like the Lone Star, *right,* and Peony, *opposite.* She likes machine piecing, hand appliqué, and hand quilting. She uses a rotary cutter and other popular tools in her work and teaching.

Jennifer Patriarche

*Quiltmaking
puts you between the past and
the future, where your
grandmother's and your quilts
will hopefully be joined by
your granddaughter's.*

Jennifer Patriarche's prizewinning quilts almost always begin with a piece of fabric that she just can't resist.

With *Iris Germanica,* shown on pages 236 and 237, the beginning was the soft green background fabric that seemed to demand a flower. The iris on this quilt is reminiscent of Jennifer's garden. The borders of the quilt are purple because "I have a passion for green and purple together," Jennifer says.

Iris Germanica took top honors in the appliqué category at the 1990 American Quilter's Society show in Paducah, Kentucky, as well as awards in several other national competitions.

Handcrafts were part of Jennifer's life before she learned to quilt in 1981. Knitting, smocking, and sewing were good training for quiltmaking, she says, because they each incorporate color, texture, design, and precision workmanship.

Jennifer credits the local quilt guild and other groups in her home city of Dallas, Texas, with helping her become a prizewinning quiltmaker. "We critique one another's work and help with the development of new ideas," she explains about her guild. It is a support system rooted in the traditions of American quilters.

Jennifer has a constant urge to handle fabric, and has too many ideas to work on only one quilt at a time. While she has an appliqué quilt in progress, Jennifer likes to work on three or four pieced quilts so she can vary machine sewing with handwork. She developed *Seventy Swans A-Swimming,* shown *opposite,* from a pattern in *Quilter's Newsletter* magazine during the same period she was working on the iris quilt.

Quilts—both finished and in progress—are everywhere in Jennifer's Dallas home. Even the dog has been carefully trained not to walk on a quilt being basted on the floor. Jennifer's husband and sons feel free to make suggestions on each current project, especially if the quilt she's making is for one of the boys.

Between quilt projects, Jennifer's spare time is devoted to learning to fly an airplane.

Suzanne Marshall

If I'm ever uptight about anything, quilting calms me down and eases the snags that come up in life.

Quilting captivated Suzanne Marshall almost by accident. A library book and fabric scraps from a lifetime of sewing launched the career of this prizewinning quilter who finds inspiration wherever she goes.

And she seems to go everywhere. Home is Clayton, Missouri, but her pharmacology professor husband, Garland, lectures all over the world. Now that their four children are grown, Suzanne often travels with him, taking appliqué along.

"It's amazing what an icebreaker it can be," Suzanne says. "Strangers will tell me about their quilts and, before you know it, I'm hearing their family history."

Suzanne worked on *Scherenschnitte*, shown on page 268, in New Guinea,

surrounded by native children interested in learning about quilts. This quilt later won the appliqué grand prize in the 1990 Better Homes and Gardens Books Blue Ribbon Quilt Awards (the second of Suzanne's quilts to win) and Best Workmanship Award at the 1991 Quilter's Heritage Celebration in Lancaster, Pennsylvania.

Full Bloom, shown *opposite*, was chosen by the Dairy Barn Arts Center of Athens, Ohio, to be part of an international exhibit touring Europe and Japan.

"The quilts I make are always a surprise to me when they are finished," Suzanne says, because she doesn't start with a plan. Instead, she begins with an idea and experiments with the quilt as it grows.

Self-taught with much trial and error, Suzanne has perfected her "slow, old-fashioned" appliqué technique—basting pieces onto the background, then needle-turning the edges. She prepares basted appliqué or a small
continued

267

finished quilt to work on while she travels.

"Because I don't use a hoop or a frame for quilting, I can quilt just about anywhere," Suzanne says. "Quilting is very soothing for me; it actually can be a form of meditation."

The travels of the Marshall family sometimes appear in Suzanne's quilts. Exotic animals and insects are appliquéd on *Full Bloom*, as well as on a Baltimore Album-style quilt that Suzanne titled *Marshall Menagerie*.

Suzanne's family takes great pride in her success and cherishes the quilts she makes. Since she has become an acclaimed quiltmaker, the Marshalls have added quilt shows to their travels. Garland enjoys helping Suzanne critique each quilt.

268

Jackie Leckband

It's okay to use primitive stitches. It gives the piece a simple, old-fashioned look.

Recycling is just a side benefit of Jackie Leckband's craft. She finds new uses for old clothing and blankets by cutting them into primitive, folk-art appliqués.

Buttonhole-stitch appliqué is an age-old craft. At home in rural Earlham, Iowa, Jackie studies 19th-century examples of this appliqué technique to get ideas for 20th-century creations. Ever frugal in their use of scraps, early American women made penny rugs using circles of wool sewn side by side, sometimes in layers, onto a backing of felt or burlap. Tossed over a table or on the floor, rugs with designs of flowers and fruit brightened dark cabins and warmed cold, bare floors.

Using old clothing and other wool scraps, Jackie makes pincushions, pillows, ornaments, and sachets for sale as well as embellished clothing.

Because wool doesn't ravel, it can be stitched in place without turning the edges. Felt, leather, and other nonwoven materials—any material you can get a needle through—can be used for this style of appliqué.

Intrigued by the vivid colors of wool, Jackie emphasizes the hues by using bright, contrasting colors of embroidery floss or crochet thread for the buttonhole stitches. She also uses running stitches, cross-stitches, and French knots to embellish the appliqué.

There are no rules governing how wool appliqué should be done, Jackie says, which makes it an ideal craft for beginners. The informal style of the appliqué is ideal for simple shapes such as a child's drawing or coloring book illustrations.

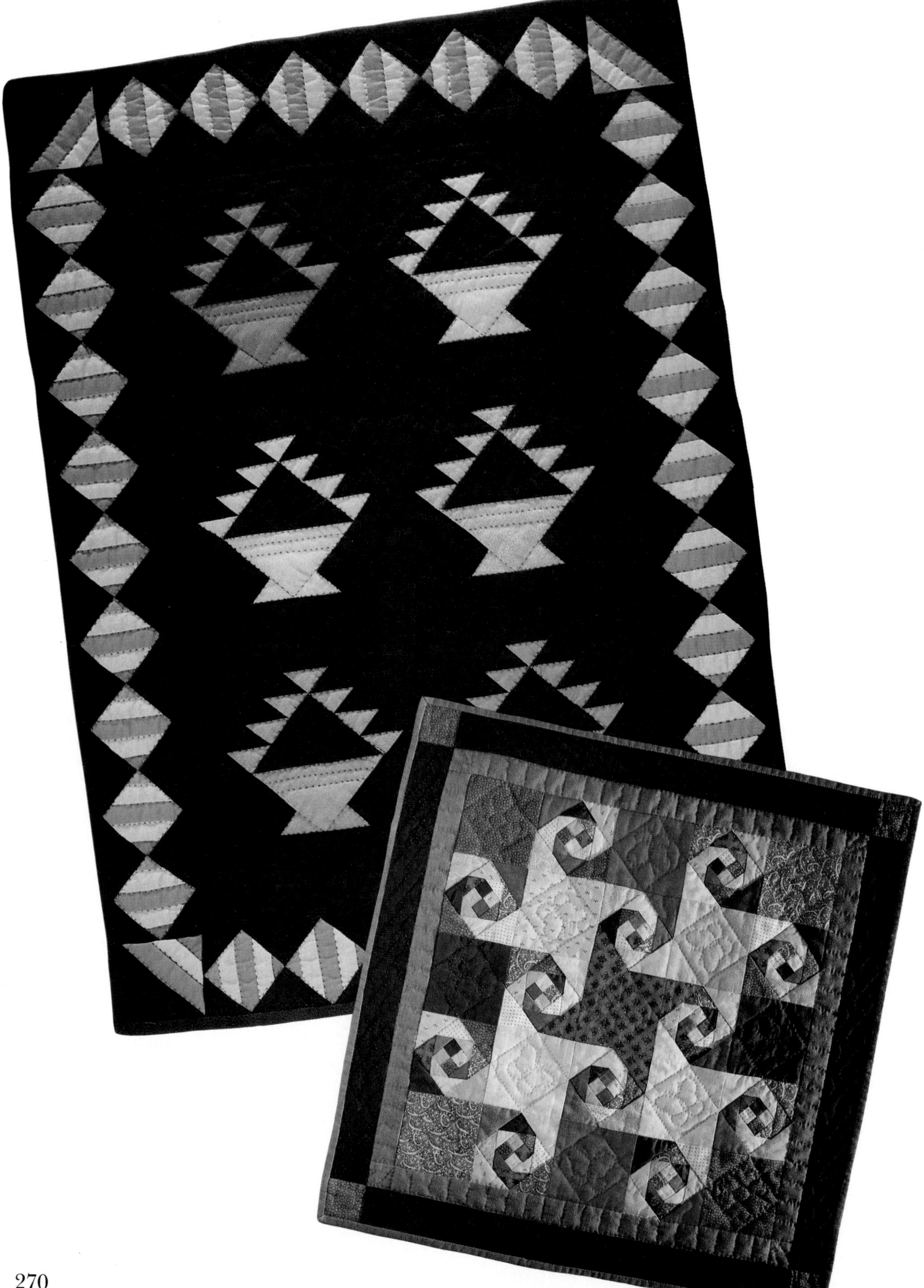

Vicky Haider

I put parts of different things together so my quilts don't look like everyone else's.

Since teaching herself to quilt in 1983, Vicky Haider has made more than 100 quilts. The thousands of hours she has spent perfecting her craft is evident in her nicely pointed stars and small, even quilting stitches.

Vicky is a deliberate traditionalist—she selects or dyes fabrics to achieve the look of the antique quilts that she loves.

A two-time winner of the Better Homes and Gardens Books Blue Ribbon Quilt Award for patchwork at the North Dakota State Fair, Vicky

previously did cross-stitch and needlepoint, but has given them up for the satisfaction she finds in quiltmaking.

"I like to incorporate a number of traditional designs in my quilts," Vicky says. The wall hanging at *top, right,* combines

Flying Geese, Log Cabin, and Pine Tree patterns with a star of hearts in a work entitled *Placid Pines.* "My favorite quilting time is winter, so my designs often have a Christmas look," Vicky says. "I so enjoy the serenity and peace of that season."

The Haiders' home in Minot, North Dakota, is filled with antiques and old-fashioned ambience, as well as a quilt in progress. Vicky's husband, Tom, participates by cutting patches for her.

"I draw on paper until I can come up with something that works in fabric," Vicky says. The majority of her quilts are small pieces, but she makes full-size quilts, too. One quilt that took 3,000 hours to complete was exhibited at Disneyland.

Like many quiltmakers, Vicky shares her enthusiasm for quilts with others in her community. A member of the Prairie Quilters of Minot, Vicky teaches quiltmaking in local workshops and adult education classes.

Edmund Anthony

*Quilting grabs hold
of you and
doesn't turn you loose!*

Edmund Anthony considers himself a quiltmaker, not a quilt artist. Although he occasionally does hang quilts on the wall, his quilts are designed and made to be used on beds.

Edmund enjoys all the attention he gets from his quilting friends (mostly women) as much as he enjoys quiltmaking, or so his wife says. Joy Anthony is also skilled with a needle, but it's Edmund who takes part in local quilting groups and wins ribbons at quilt shows.

One prizewinning quilt is *Baltimore Revisited,* shown *opposite,* which won the Better Homes and Gardens Books Blue Ribbon Quilt Award for appliqué at the 1990 Tennessee State Fair.

Edmund began this quilt in a class on advanced appliqué, using patterns from *Spoken Without a Word* by Elly Sienkiewicz and border ribbons designed by Joan Kost. "This mixture of the past and present expresses the timeless appeal of the Baltimore Album quilts and their influence on today's quilters," he says.

Joy designed Edmund's quilt, *Eye of the Hurricane,* shown *left,* which also has won several prizes.

Edmund started making quilts after a 1980 visit to Pennsylvania, where he saw quilts made by his daughter's mother-in-law. "Maybe I can do something like that," he thought. He and Joy discussed the idea on the trip home to Murfreesboro, Tennessee.

Referring to a book, Edmund machine-pieced a star quilt that he paid someone to quilt. The cost of quilting three more tops led him to take up quilting himself.

Now Edmund does a little quilting every day; he finds it a relaxing way to wind down from the stress of his job as a psychology technician at a veterans hospital.

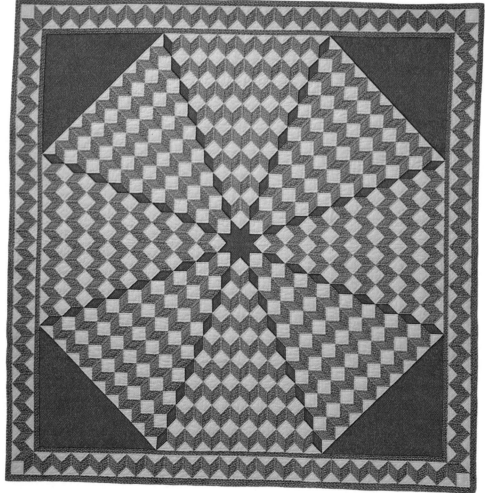

272

Caroline Alderman

Patchwork and quilted garments don't go out of fashion. I have things that are just as wearable today as when I made them years ago.

*C*aroline Alderman tried other crafts, but they didn't mix well with small children. For example, ceramics was too messy and demanded more than 10 minutes between interruptions. Sewing seemed the best choice—it didn't require water and she could stop and start at will.

So Caroline sewed up a storm. As her girls got older, she made cute appliquéd sunsuits, then complete outfits, and, finally, unique garments for herself.

"I liked that our clothes were different than everyone else's," Caroline says. One thing led to another until she began making custom-designed clothes as a business. Caroline also taught classes throughout the Midwest before the Alderman family moved to Hilton Head, South Carolina. In addition to designing clothing, Caroline participates in style shows and does gallery exhibits of her wearable art.

Although she combines patchwork, appliqué, and quilting techniques in her designs, the only quilts Caroline has made are a few small wall hangings.

She explains, "With a quilt, you have to pick up your house so people can come over and see it. With clothing, you can put it on and take it with you wherever you go!"

Caroline's clothes are a wonderful icebreaker. Strangers are so interested in what she is wearing that they often approach her to ask about her one-of-a-kind outfits.

Khang Yang

I sewed to feed the children.

Khang Yang never learned to read or write, and her English is still limited. She lets her needlework tell her story.

In intricate appliqué and embroidery, Khang's work depicts life in a Laotian village—women feeding chickens, men planting corn, and livestock gathered around the watering hole.

Khang's family fled their war-torn homeland in the 1970s. During the year they spent in a Thai refugee camp, Khang's mother taught her to sew. The handwork was their only livelihood—even Khang's husband, Doua, helped embroider. Like many women who immi-grated to the United States before her, Khang sewed to feed her family.

With her mother and sister-in-law, Khang continues to make and sell Hmong-style handwork from her home in Brooklyn Center, Minnesota. Each piece is based on traditional Laotian motifs or is a pictorial appliqué of village life.

Judith Reilly

The most exciting aspects of quilting are the learning process and sharing inspiration. I urge myself and my students to expand our comfort zones, not leave them. And always, always to have fun!

The quilt, *Warning: Some Colors May Run,* shown *opposite,* is an example of what Judy calls "wonderful fun." She encourages her students in Brookfield, Connecticut, to create surprises in a design, to be unpredictable. "If my work brings viewers a feeling of delight or inspiration, then maybe they will take that feeling home."

A sense of humor and a thirst for originality influence Judy Reilly's approach to quiltmaking.

"Although my work is based on traditional techniques and design elements, I consider myself a contemporary quilter," Judy explains.

For Judy, "contemporary" is defined as fresh and inspired, receptive and ever-growing, but not necessarily abstract. She loves traditional patterns, but feels quiltmaking should be a personal challenge, not just a hobby.

"I design, quilt, exhibit, and teach because I can encourage others to grow and to cherish their individual creativity," Judy says. "If someone values the importance of an idea and translates it to cloth, some of the qualities learned—patience, determination, curiosity—may be reflected in other aspects of their life."

Judy's work reveals her sense of fun. Details in *The Yarn Spinner and Other Cat Tails,* shown *right,* will tickle any cat lover, and *My Fair Lady,* shown *above,* is "udderly" charming.

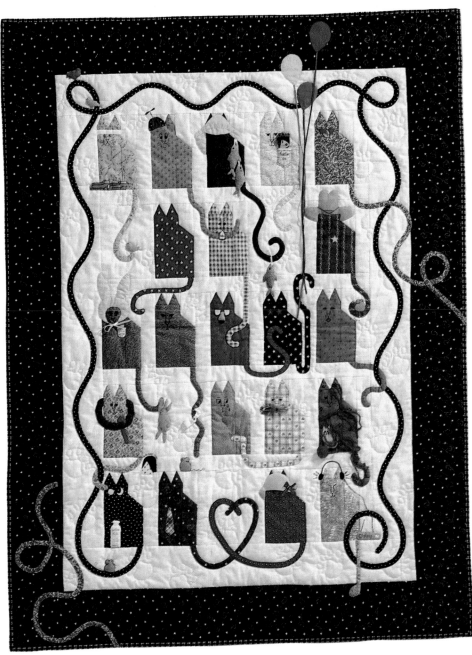

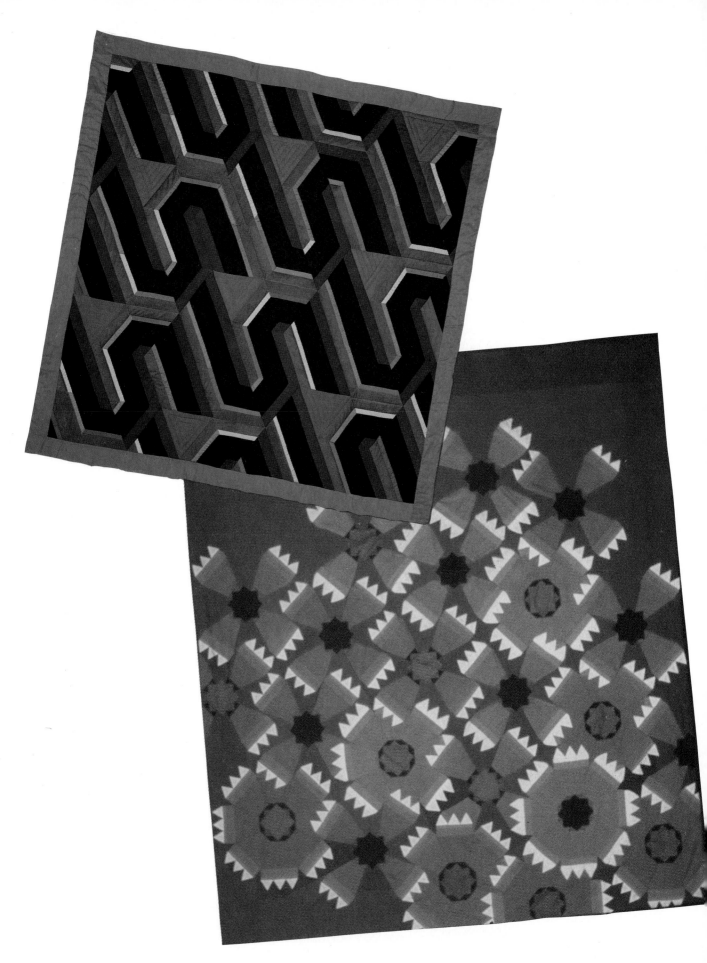

Nancy Whittington

In my quilts, I try to re-create different sensations of light through the use of color and pattern.

*B*lending painters' theories of color and light with the traditional skills of quiltmaking is a process that absorbs Nancy Whittington. Working in her Carrboro, North Carolina, studio, she experiments with color and contrast in fabric.

"I use color in a painterly fashion, exploring color gradations and light-dark contrast to suggest different sensations of light," Nancy says.

She begins work on each quilt with the desire to create a vibrant surface of pattern that appears filled with light. With specific color relationships in mind, she draws pattern variations until "I can't stand not handling the fabric."

Working with fabric is a personal and unique art for Nancy. A graduate of the Rhode Island School of Design, she paints and dyes fabrics to achieve the gradations she wants.

Silk—one of Nancy's favorite fabrics because of its glow and ability to absorb dye—is used in *Leaf Symmetry II*, shown *right*. She combined silk with fabrics of other textures, such as wool and Ultrasuede, in *Coming to Meet*, shown *opposite, top*, and *Gaillardia*, shown *opposite, bottom*.

"My favorite part of quiltmaking is the actual joining of colored shapes, because I finally get to see if the original idea succeeds in being as vibrant and balanced as I wanted," Nancy says.

She machine-stitches the straight seams and hand-sews more intricate seams using English paper techniques. "I like the relaxation of the hand piecing . . . and the portability," Nancy says.

Even for art quilts, the quilting and finishing "can seem endless." Nancy listens to music while she quilts and dreams of "a big, church quilting bee showing up at my door."

Quilter's Schoolhouse

General Instructions
for Quiltmaking

◆ **Schoolhouse Quilt,**
 c. 1935; 68x94 inches.
 Instructions begin on
 page 310.

SELECTING A PROJECT AND FABRICS

Making a quilt can be as simple or as demanding as you wish to make it. A quilter can find satisfaction in completing a traditional quilt or designing and making an original work. There are so many variations and combinations of patchwork, appliqué, and quilting that there is always something new and exciting to make.

START SIMPLE
Patchwork became part of the American tradition as a sensible way to teach basic sewing skills to young girls. According to folklore, a girl made a dozen quilts before she married, each more complex and skillfully made than the last. When she became engaged, a girl made the thirteenth quilt—her masterpiece.

This old tradition holds a lesson for today's beginning quilters: Learn the basics and work your way up to more complex projects; don't feel you have to create a masterpiece with your first quilt. Begin as girls did in colonial times by making a basic design that will cultivate your ability to select fabrics, combine colors, cut, sew, and quilt.

"BASIC"
Some of the projects in this book are marked as "Basic." A beginner should probably select one of these for a first project. Be advised that "basic" is a relative term—the project is, in our opinion, more quickly and easily completed than the average quilt. The time required to actually complete a project depends greatly on the skills of the individual.

"CHALLENGING"
This book also contains projects designated as "challenging." These are quilts that we believe require advanced skills and patience. They are not recommended for beginners.

FIGURING YARDAGES
In this book, all yardages are given for 44/45-inch-wide fabrics. We have allowed for short widths and shrink-age by figuring each needed yardage based on a 42-inch fabric width. If your fabric is less than 42 inches wide, you probably will need more fabric than is given in the materials list, even though we allow at least ¼ yard for error in most cases.

USE 100 PERCENT COTTON
It is not just an old wives' tale that 100 percent cotton is the best fabric for quiltmaking. Most of the beautiful antique quilts of the 19th century are made of cotton. Cotton fabric is lightweight, easy to handle and to sew through, durable, and easily washed.

Cotton has the following inherent qualities that make it superior to other fabrics in most cases.

Easy to press and crease. Polyester blends, by their very nature, resist creasing. This makes them ideal for some garments, but inappropriate for quilting. Cotton, on the other hand, retains its pressed shape. This quality gives sharp crispness to a seam or to the edge of an appliqué.

Cotton is flexible enough that a good steam pressing can work out little puckers or tension pulls, making the piece lie flat. Blends usually must be ironed with a cooler iron, so your seams must be more exact.

Easy to quilt. Most quilters agree that 100 percent cotton is easier to quilt than blends. The same hardness of fibers that makes polyester resistant to creasing also makes it difficult to push a needle through.

Minimizes distortion. Using fabrics of 100 percent cotton throughout your quilt lessens the chance for distortion in the patchwork. Mixing cottons and blends sometimes (but not always) results in puffy, mismatched seams despite careful sewing.

CHOOSING FABRICS
There is one fundamental principle to remember when selecting fabrics: It doesn't matter what anyone else thinks, as long as *you* like it.

It's fine to seek advice from friends or helpful store clerks—another perspective is sometimes illuminating—but don't feel obligated to heed it. All that matters is that you are happy with the fabrics you select.

Not every fabric in the project has to be a stunner—some have to recede so that others stand out. This is particularly true of background fabrics or materials used in scrap quilts.

You may determine a quilt's color scheme by the room where it will be used or, if the quilt is a gift, by the preference of the recipient. You might find one fabric you love and build around it. But color is not the only factor in selecting fabric—value (light and dark) and scale (size of the print) are important, too.

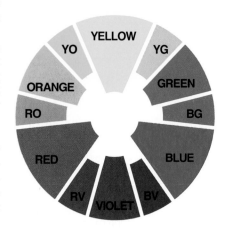

The color wheel. The color wheel, *above,* is a helpful tool in selecting fabrics. Even if you decide on a dominant color, what do you put with it? Let the color wheel help you decide.

The primary colors are red, yellow, and blue. Green, orange, and purple are secondary colors, each made by combining two primaries. Between the primary and secondary colors are tertiary colors. All colors are made by mixing different values of these hues.

Monochromatic. A monochromatic color scheme uses tints and shades of one color. Be sure to use contrasting values of that one color and different scales of print, such as those shown in the collection *above;* fabrics will blend together if they are too much alike, losing the definition of the design.

An example of use of a monochromatic color scheme is the Jacob's Ladder Quilt in Chapter 7.

Analogous. Three adjacent colors on the wheel, in any tint or shade, make an analogous color scheme. If blue is the main color, give the scheme sparkle by adding adjacent colors—green and purple, red and purple, or green and yellow—as well as neutrals (gray, white, or black).

The three Amish pillows pictured in Chapter 7 are examples of use of analogous color schemes.

Rob Peter to Pay Paul. A two-color scheme of high-contrast fabrics used in equal proportions causes an optical illusion in some designs. The eye cannot determine which is the background and which is the foreground because there is balanced interplay between the two fabrics.

In quilting, this is referred to as a "Rob Peter to Pay Paul" scheme (see the quilt on pages 16 and 17), even when a different block is used. Examples include the Hearts and Gizzards Quilt in Chapter 2 and the Snowball Quilt in Chapter 8.

A two-color scheme with highly contrasting light and dark fabrics has a crisp, clean look. A tried-and-true combination is to mix any color with either white or black.

White makes an adjacent color appear to recede, while black makes the same color seem to advance. White brightens almost any color; black clarifies a color and makes it seem like a jewel tone in a dark setting.

Complementary. A complementary color scheme uses colors opposite one another on the color wheel, such as blue and orange or violet (purple) and yellow. The most popular complementary color scheme is red and green, often used with white. The Swirling Peony Quilt in Chapter 2 is a classic example.

Value placement. Changing the position of light and dark fabrics within a block can produce dramatically different results. For example, the Burgoyne Surrounded block, *above,* looks very different when light and dark fabrics are reversed.

In most two-color designs, light and dark fabric placement is crucial to the character of the quilt, as seen in the Fruit Basket and the Checkers and Rails quilts in Chapter 3.

Scrap bag. The scrap quilt is nearly foolproof as far as selecting fabrics goes—virtually any combination of fabrics will work. Depending on the nature of the available scraps, you can still choose to use a monochromatic, analogous, or complementary color scheme; however, fabrics for many of the best scrap quilts are chosen completely at random.

For many quiltmakers, the greatest challenge of a scrap quilt is to resist the urge to coordinate or to develop organized placement of colors or prints. Attempting to instill order among the scraps can be deadly—it is precisely the randomness and spontaneity of a scrap quilt that makes it successful.

Scrap quilts are great for using up fabrics that seem dull or unattractive, nice fabrics that don't "go with" anything, and leftover odds and ends.

continued

FABRIC SELECTION AND PREPARATION

MIXING PRINTS AND SOLIDS

The most successful quilting projects achieve a balance of small and large prints and solids, as well as color. The rule of thumb to remember is: *Avoid too much of the same thing.*

Resist the urge to be conservative, to avoid a fabric collection that has no pizzazz. The coordinated fabric lines in today's shops make it easy to fall into this trap. In each quilt, try to use one fabric you think is daring, even if you use it only as an accent.

There is a multitude of beautiful print fabrics available today—make the most of them. If you can find one print that contains all the colors in your scheme, even in tiny amounts, it becomes a unifying element.

Solid fabrics. Using all solid fabrics is usually safe, but safe is not always what you want. A solid fabric scheme can be very contemporary, especially with highly contrasting fabrics.

Solids are also effective for defining or offsetting one or more prints.

Small-scale prints. A small, subtle print looks solid from a distance, but adds texture that a solid lacks. Therefore, small-scale prints are often ideal background fabrics.

Avoid small prints that are widely spaced on the background color—when you cut this fabric into small pieces, many of the pieces will be plain unless each patch is cut with the printed motif carefully centered on it.

Large-scale prints. Many people are intimidated by big, splashy prints, but such fabrics are full of possibilities.

The variety of the patches cut from a fabric with a big print can contribute movement and excitement to the overall look of a quilt. Also, many of the paisley and floral prints available today have the flavor of 18th- and 19th-century fabrics; if you want an antique look, a richly colored elaborate print may be ideal.

Big prints also make wonderfully dramatic borders.

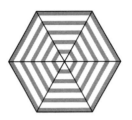
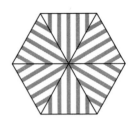

Stripes and checks. Stripes require special attention when cutting, but the results can be spectacular. Diamonds and triangles cut from stripes create fascinating effects when sewn together, as in the examples *above.*

Extra yardage may be required to make the most of a striped fabric.

Avoid checks larger than ¼ inch square, as they exaggerate even the slightest irregularity in the grain, the cutting, or the stitching.

PURCHASING FABRIC

The first rule of buying fabric is to buy the very best you can afford. Fabric is a critical element of the quilt and it just doesn't make sense to skimp on something so important.

Be sure you buy enough fabric to finish the project. If you run short, you might not be able to get more of the same fabric, and the alternatives may leave much to be desired. In this book, most yardages listed include up to ¼ yard of extra fabric "for good measure."

Buying fabric for a quilt requires a financial commitment that you may not be willing to make if you are unsure about your choices. If you're uncertain, start with enough fabric to make one or two trial blocks. Just don't let too much time go by before deciding to purchase the rest of your fabric; otherwise it may be sold out.

In specialty shops, skilled shop personnel can be helpful in making fabric selections, but don't let them make decisions for you. Also, spread out your choices and then step back so you can see the fabric from a distance—this is an excellent way to see if something is really out of place or more dominant than you want.

PREWASHING

There are conflicting opinions about the need for prewashing fabric. The debate is a modern one because most antique quilts were made with unwashed fabric. However, the dyes and sizing used today are very different from those used a century ago.

We recommend that you prewash a scrap of each fabric to test it for shrinkage and bleeding.

Advantages: The biggest advantage to prewashing is certainty. Today's fabrics resist bleeding and shrinking, but some of both can occur in some fabrics—an unpleasant prospect if the quilt is already assembled. Another advantage is that some quilters feel prewashed fabric is easier to quilt.

Disadvantages: Many quilters contend that today's fabrics are so reliable that prewashing is not necessary. There's no doubt that the wrinkled mass that comes out of the washer is a chore to press and straighten.

The crispness of unwashed fabric is ideal for machine piecing. And, if fabric with the same fiber content is used throughout the quilt, then any shrinkage that occurs in its first washing should be uniform. This small amount of shrinkage is what gives antique quilts the slightly puckered look we find so charming today.

Prewashing: Unfold the fabric to a single layer for even saturation. Wash it in warm water to allow the fabric to shrink and/or bleed. If the fabric bleeds, rinse it until the water runs clear. Hang the fabric up to dry, or put it in the dryer until it is just slightly damp. It will need a good pressing before it can be marked and cut.

FINISHED QUILT SIZES

Finished size is an important factor in selecting a project and in buying fabric. A quilt made for a particular bed should fit it, just as a garment fits a person. If the quilt is too long, too short, too wide, or too narrow, then it won't be a success, no matter how well it's made.

The ideal finished size varies with each quilt. Consider the quilt's design, the size and style of the bed, and your personal preferences before determining a finished size.

PERSONAL CHOICES

The size and style of the bed will influence some decisions about the quilt's finished size. For example, for a sleigh-style bed with a solid, high footboard, there is no need for the quilt to have significant length. A quilt for a modern, platform-style bed needs much less length and width than one for a four-poster.

Size is also affected by your decision to use a dust ruffle or let the quilt hang to the floor. Even with a dust ruffle, the necessary length and width should be calculated carefully.

Also, decide whether to add length for a pillow tuck or if the quilt will lie flat with the top covered by pillows.

STANDARD MATTRESS SIZES

Spring mattresses are made in six standard sizes; the size of waterbed mattresses may vary slightly. Following are the width and length of the mattress *surface* for each size:

    Crib—27x52 inches
    Youth—33x66 inches
    Twin—39x74 inches
    Full—54x74 inches
    Queen—60x80 inches
    King—78x80 inches

COMMERCIAL BEDCOVERS

Ready-made bedspreads and comforters can help you choose the best size for your quilt. The following dimensions are *average* sizes; individual bed coverings can vary in size by as much as 6 inches.

Comforters. A comforter is generally designed to be used as a blanket. Most comforters cover a mattress with little extra size to spare; they do not necessarily cover the box springs, nor do they allow for a pillow tuck.

Use the following sizes as guidelines for a quilt that will be used with a dust ruffle and that does not cover pillows. These sizes represent minimum dimensions for a bed covering.

    Twin—66x86 inches
    Full—76x86 inches
    Queen—86x88 inches
    King—102x88 inches

Bedspreads. A bedspread covers the bed, falls almost to the floor (assuming the top of the mattress is the standard 20 to 21 inches from the floor), and allows for a pillow tuck.

The following represent the maximum dimensions for a bedspread.

    Twin—80x108 inches
    Full—96x108 inches
    Queen—102x118 inches
    King—120x118 inches

OUR AVERAGE FINISHED SIZE

With the information given above, we determined *average* dimensions for the four most popular quilt sizes. We allow a 14-inch drop on three sides and 9 inches for a pillow tuck.

In this book, instructions are given for a size that approximates one of the sizes listed below. The finished size given for each quilt is a mathematical calculation; the effects of sewing and quilting will probably vary the finished size.

    Twin—67x97 inches
    Full—82x97 inches
    Queen—88x103 inches
    King—106x103 inches

CALCULATING FINISHED SIZE

To determine the best finished size for your quilt, start with the dimensions of the mattress. If you want the quilt to cover pillows, add 8 to 12 inches to the length for a pillow tuck.

Decide how much drop you want on each side. To determine the drop, measure from the top of the mattress to just below the top of the dust ruffle, all the way to the floor, or some point in between. For most quilts, you will want to add one drop to the length and two drops to the width.

Finally, add 2 to 3 inches to both the width and the length to allow for take-up by the quilting.

Example: Let's figure the size of a quilt for a queen-size bed with a dust ruffle and matching pillow shams.

We know the mattress measures 60x80 inches. Since shams will cover the top of the quilt, no addition is needed for a tuck.

The dust ruffle is only 8 inches from the top of the mattress, but a longer drop of 16 inches is desired.

To figure the quilt width, add 16 inches twice to the width of the mattress: 60 + 16 + 16 = 92 inches.

To figure length, add 16 inches to the length of the mattress: 80 + 16 = 96 inches. It is not necessary to add a second drop to the length because the quilt stops at the headboard or the edge of the mattress.

If we add 2 inches for take-up in quilting, the desired finished size of this quilt is 94x98 inches.

ADAPTING A DESIGN TO SIZE

If the quilt you want to make is not the desired finished size, there are several ways to adapt the design.

To make a quilt smaller, eliminate a row of blocks, set the blocks without sashing, and/or narrow the border widths.

For a larger quilt, make extra rows of blocks, add sashing, and/or add multiple borders. Each addition will require extra yardage, which you should estimate before you buy.

Quilts that are not made for a bed have few limitations. A doll quilt or wall quilt can measure 10 inches, 10 feet, or anything in between.

Lap quilts or quilts "just for show" also can be almost any size you like.

EQUIPMENT, TOOLS, AND GADGETS

Little special equipment is needed for quiltmaking if you already sew. Most basic quilting tools are common household sewing items. Specialized products that are marvelous time- and labor-saving devices are available for quick cutting and marking of fabrics, but they are not mandatory for a successful project.

GENERAL SEWING SUPPLIES

Iron and ironing board. Pressing is important in achieving a smooth and accurate quilt top, so a good iron is a must. If a steam iron is not available, use a water sprayer or mister. Keep the ironing board conveniently close to your work area.

Needles. Use sharps or regular sewing needles for hand sewing and betweens for quilting.

Pins. Have a good supply of round-headed pins. Buy the longest ones you can; they are helpful when pinning multiple layers. Do not use pins that are thick or rusted that might leave holes or marks in the fabric.

Scissors. Use small, sharp embroidery scissors to clip threads and seam allowances. If you are marking and cutting fabric with scissors, a good, large pair of dressmaker's shears is necessary; be sure the blades are clean and very sharp. You will need separate scissors for cutting paper; never cut paper with sewing shears as this will quickly dull the blades.

Sewing machine. Almost any machine will work for piecing. Patchwork does not require fancy stitches, only a simple straight stitch. The bobbin tension must be properly adjusted to produce seams that are free of puckers and distortion.

Sewing thread. Use 100 percent cotton or a cotton-covered polyester thread. If the machine tension is properly adjusted, it is not necessary to use matching colors for machine piecing. Using a large cone of ecru or gray thread is more economical than buying individual spools. For any type of hand sewing, use thread colors that match your fabric.

MATERIALS FOR MAKING PATTERNS AND TEMPLATES

Compass. Use a drafting compass to draw accurate circular patterns.

Graph paper. To draft geometric patterns, use graph paper with four or eight squares per inch. Marking pattern lines on graph paper using a pencil and ruler ensures accurate lines and angles.

Protractor. Use a protractor to draft patterns with angles that are not easily verified on graph paper.

Template plastic. Available at craft and quilting shops, this semitransparent plastic is preferable to other materials, particularly opaque ones. It is easier to position a transparent template accurately over stripes or other fabric motifs. The plastic is thin and easy to cut, improving the accuracy of the template. The edges of a plastic template will not fray even with repeated use, making the template reusable. This type of plastic is also recommended for making quilting-design stencils.

TOOLS FOR MEASURING, MARKING, AND CUTTING

Acrylic ruler. A ruler of thick, clear plastic acts as a straightedge with a rotary cutter. Appropriate rulers are available in a variety of sizes and shapes. The most versatile is 22 to 24 inches long and marked with straight lines in ¼-inch increments as well as 45-degree and 60-degree angles.

Pencils. Use a regular lead pencil, well sharpened, for tracing templates onto fabric. Some specialty shops now stock marking pencils in removable white, yellow, blue, and silver for marking on dark fabrics.

Rotary cutter and mat. This round-bladed cutter quickly cuts strips and straight edges through four to six layers of fabric. It is indispensable for strip piecing. Always use the cutter with a mat designed for rotary cutting. In addition to protecting the table, the mat grips the fabric to help keep it from shifting while you cut.

Triangle. A large 45-degree draftsman's triangle is useful for marking miter lines as well as cutting right triangles with a rotary cutter. Metal or plastic triangles are available at art supply stores.

SEWING GADGETS

Bias bar. This narrow metal bar is used to press under the edges of bias strips. Bias bars vary in size from ¼ inch wide to ½ inch wide.

Bias folder. This device prepares strips for bias appliqué. The fabric is inserted into the tube which folds both edges into the center, ready for pressing. Bias folders are available for several widths of bias strips.

Open-toed appliqué foot. A sewing machine foot with a wider-than-usual space between the toes, an open-toed foot allows the needle to swing back and forth to make a wide stitch. It affords good visibility for the maneuvering needed for machine appliqué. The bottom of the foot is channeled so it travels smoothly over the heavy line of stitches.

Seam guide. A transparent plastic rod that is ¼ inch square, a seam guide is used to mark ¼-inch seam allowances on patchwork pieces.

Seam ripper. It's nice to think you'll never need one, but we all make mistakes. This is an essential tool for removing machine stitches.

Tube turner. This long, hooked tool is handy for turning seamed bias for bias appliqué.

QUILTING AIDS

Artist's (drafting) tape. Available at art supply stores, ¼-inch-wide tape can be used instead of marking to guide outline quilting ¼ inch from seam lines. This kind of tape does not leave a sticky residue on fabric.

Chalk pencil or wheel. Chalk makes a removable white line on a dark fabric. It also is widely available in yellow, pink, and other colors.

Design stencil. An outline of the quilting design, stencils made of plastic, cardboard, or metal can be traced onto the quilt top.

Even-feed walking foot. For machine quilting, a special walking foot regulates the movement of the fabric without the action of the feed dogs.

Invisible thread. A clear monofilament, invisible thread is often used for machine quilting. Its lack of color makes it "invisible" on the fabric even though the stitched design has the dimension of other quilting.

Quilting frame. A large assembly of wooden poles and slats, a frame holds the three layers of a quilt in place during the quilting process.

Quilting hoop. A quilting hoop has deeper sides than an embroidery hoop to accommodate the thickness of the backing, batting, and quilt top. A hoop 14 to 22 inches in diameter is commonly used when a frame is not available or practical.

Quilting needles. Use betweens for hand quilting. They are available in sizes 8 to 10.

Quilting thread. Stronger than regular sewing thread, quilting thread is now available in dozens of colors. It is often coated to prevent tangling, eliminating the need to use beeswax as pioneer women did.

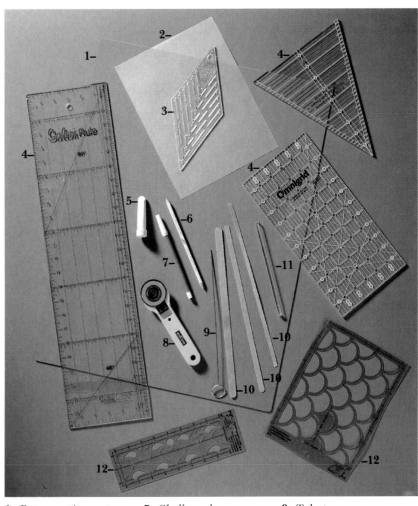

1. *Rotary cutting mat*
2. *Template plastic*
3. *Ready-made template*
4. *Acrylic rulers*
5. *Chalk marker*
6. *Marking pencil*
7. *Water-erasable marker*
8. *Rotary cutter*
9. *Tube turner*
10. *Bias bars*
11. *Seam guide*
12. *Quilting design stencils*

Safety pins. Some quilters like to use 1-inch-long rustproof safety pins for basting. Since they are reusable, they are more economical than thread in the long run.

Thimble. Even if you've never used a thimble for sewing, you should learn to use one for quilting. The difficulty of pushing a needle through several layers makes a thimble a necessity. In addition to metal thimbles, some shops carry flexible leather thimbles.

Washout markers. Felt-tip pens and other markers with water-dissolving ink should be tested before use. Read and follow the manufacturer's directions carefully—most warn against applying heat or using any type of soap before removing the marks. A mist or spray of clear water usually works better than soaking. In some cases, repeated application of water is necessary for satisfactory results.

MAKING AND USING TEMPLATES

A template is an exact duplication of a printed pattern that is traced onto fabric for cutting.

Many straight-sided shapes can be marked directly on the fabric with a ruler, but templates are necessary to mark other shapes. Some quilters use templates for all shapes.

MAKING TEMPLATES

A template can be made by gluing a paper pattern onto sandpaper or cardboard, but these materials can be difficult to cut and will fray with repeated use.

We recommend template plastic, available at craft supply stores. This material can be used indefinitely and its transparency allows you to trace a pattern directly onto its surface. The plastic is lightweight and easy to cut. Even on plastic, use a ruler to accurately trace lines and corners.

All the patterns in this book are full-size. Patchwork patterns show both the seam line (dashed) and the cutting line (solid), and always include a ¼-inch seam allowance.

No seam allowance is given on appliqué patterns. Add a ³⁄₁₆-inch allowance when cutting these pieces for hand appliqué. When a large pattern is split and given in two pieces, such as the large leaf in the Rose Wreath Quilt in Chapter 2, make a single template for the piece.

Mark each template with its letter designation, grain line, and block name. Verify the template's size by placing it over the printed pattern. Templates must be accurate or the error, however small, will be compounded many times over as the quilt is assembled.

To check the accuracy of your templates and marking, make a test block before cutting out more pieces.

TRACING THE TEMPLATE

To mark on the fabric, use pencil, a white dressmaker's pencil, chalk, or some other marker that makes a *thin,* accurate line. Do not use a ballpoint or ink pen that may bleed if washed.

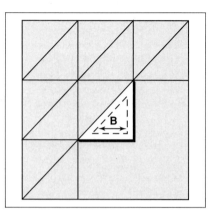

1 For hand piecing, templates are usually cut to the exact *finished* size of the patch, without seam allowances added. Place the template *facedown* on the *wrong side* of the fabric; position the tracings at least ½ inch apart. These marked lines are *sewing lines.* Some quilters also mark cutting lines, but experienced quilters cut the pieces apart by eye, adding a ¼-inch seam allowance around each piece.

2 For machine piecing, templates are made with the seam allowances included. This enables you to mark pieces using common lines for efficient cutting. Place the templates *facedown* on the *wrong side* of the fabric and mark around them. Using sharp scissors or a rotary cutter, cut exactly on the drawn lines.

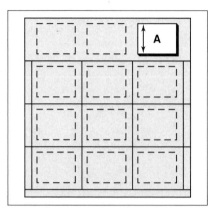

3 Window templates can be used for hand or machine patchwork. By drawing both the cutting and sewing lines, precision is enhanced for both methods. The guidance of a drawn seam line is especially useful for setting in pieces by machine, when pivoting at a precise point is critical. Used on the right side of the fabric, window templates also enable you to cut out specific motifs with accuracy.

4 Templates for hand appliqué are always made the *finished* size. Place templates *faceup* on the *right side* of the fabric. Position tracings ½ inch apart. Cut out each shape, adding a ³⁄₁₆-inch seam allowance around each piece. The drawn line provides a guideline for turning under the seam allowance for sewing.

CUTTING FABRIC

Careful, precise cutting is essential for a successful quilt. When patches are accurately cut, even a beginning quiltmaker can assemble the pieces without much difficulty.

CUTTING LIST GUIDELINES

For each project in this book, cut the pieces of each fabric in the order in which they are listed. This makes the most efficient use of the yardage.

Each ◆ designates a major step in the cutting. In many cases, this step will list a large piece followed by instructions to cut that piece into smaller patches or strips.

The dimensions of large, regularly shaped pieces such as setting triangles, squares, and borders are listed *with seam allowances included,* but no pattern is given. Measure and mark these pieces directly onto the fabric using a ruler, T-square, triangle, or similar tool to mark accurate angles.

The lengths given for borders are slightly longer than needed; trim the excess border fabric when sewing is complete.

SCISSORS VS. THE ROTARY CUTTER

Scissors and rotary cutters each have their advantages—in different situations. Sharp scissors that are used only for cutting fabrics are necessary to cut irregular shapes and curves.

A rotary cutter, used with a self-healing protective mat and a thick acrylic ruler, is quick and efficient for straight cuts. Handling a cutter takes some getting used to, but it is ideal for cutting strips, squares, and most triangles. For this type of cutting, a rotary cutter is faster and more accurate than scissors.

Rulers in many different shapes and sizes are now marketed for use with rotary cutters. Cutting mats also are available in a wide range of sizes; some are printed with grids to help in the measurement and alignment of straight edges.

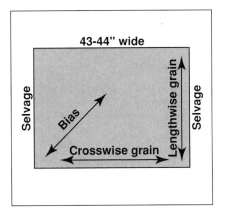

1 **Consider fabric grain** before cutting patches. One or more straight sides of the patch should follow the lengthwise or crosswise grain of the fabric. This is especially true of sides that will be placed on the outside edge of a block or the quilt top. Align the grain line on the template with the fabric grain.

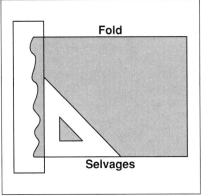

2 **Square up the fabric edges** to ensure straight cuts. Align the base of a right-angle triangle with the selvage, then place your acrylic ruler against the upright straight edge of the right triangle as shown. Cut along that line. By trimming off the ragged edge of the fabric (usually not more than an inch or two), you'll have a clean, straight edge on which to begin cutting the pieces for the quilt.

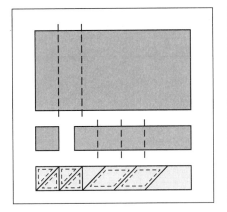

3 **Cut strips or rectangles** on the crosswise grain. Trim selvages from both ends, then follow the directions to cut each strip into smaller units as shown. Even when you are using templates, it can be advantageous to cut strips that match the width of the patch; then the template can be aligned with the edge as shown. Position templates to take advantage of common cutting lines.

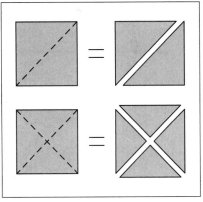

4 **Cut triangles from squares**. The cutting instructions often direct you to cut a square in half or in quarters diagonally as shown to obtain right-angle triangles. The sides of the triangle along an outside edge of the square are on the straight of the grain; the triangle sides on the diagonal lines are on the bias.

HAND PIECING

Whether to sew by hand or machine is a personal choice. The earliest patchwork was, of necessity, sewn by hand. Even after the invention of the sewing machine in 1846, hand sewing remained popular with quiltmakers. Even today, some people believe hand piecing is the only "real way" to make a quilt.

Working by hand may be slow, but many people find it a soothing and pleasant pastime. You can join family discussions or watch television while you work. Also, handwork is easy to take along when traveling.

In hand piecing, seams are sewn only on the marked sewing lines rather than from one raw edge of the piece to the other. The advantage of hand piecing is that the seam allowances can be pressed in any direction because they are not sewn down.

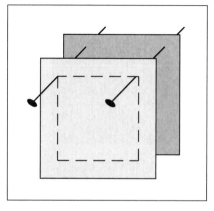

1 Match the edges of the two pieces to be joined with the right sides of the fabrics together. Sewing lines should be marked on the wrong side of both pieces. Push a pin through both fabric layers as shown *above* to align the corners. Secure the pins perpendicular to the sewing line. Insert one or more pins between the corners.

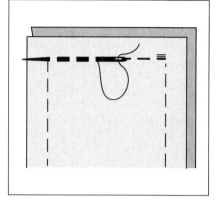

2 Insert the needle through both fabrics at the seam-line corner. Make one or two backstitches atop the first stitch to secure the thread. Weave the needle in and out of the fabric along the seam line, taking four to six tiny stitches at a time before you pull the thread taut. Remove the pins as you sew. Turn the work over occasionally to see that the stitching follows the marked sewing line on the other side.

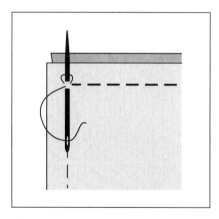

3 Sew eight to 10 stitches per inch along the seam line. At the end of the seam, remove the last pin and make the ending stitch through the hole left by the corner pin. Backstitch over the last stitch and end the seam with a loop knot as shown *above*.

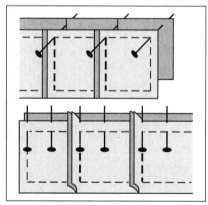

4a To join rows of patchwork by hand, hold the sewn pieces with the right sides together and match the seams. Insert a pin through the seams and corners of the matching pieces. Add additional pins as necessary, securing each pin perpendicular to the sewing line.

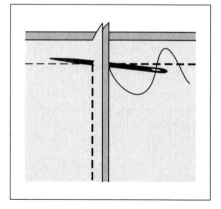

4b Stitch the joining seam as before, but do not sew across the seam allowances that join the patches. At each seam allowance, make a backstitch or a loop knot as described in Step 3, then slide the needle through the seam allowance as illustrated *above*. Knot or backstitch again to give the intersection strength, and continue to sew the remainder of the seam. Press each seam as it is completed.

MACHINE PIECING

Quilt historians have documented machine-stitched quilts almost as old as the sewing machine—proof that many quiltmakers of the 19th century were quick to embrace the new time-saving device. Proponents of machine piecing contend that it is faster, more efficient, and often more durable than hand piecing.

SEWING MACHINE BASICS

You don't need fancy stitches or accessories to do machine patchwork; any machine that makes a satisfactory straight stitch can be used. However, it is important to adjust the tension in both the top and bobbin threads to have smooth, even stitching on both layers of fabric. When the tension is properly set, no stitches are visible on the right side of the fabric.

The width of the presser foot is very important. The right edge of the foot is used as a guide for ¼-inch seam allowances. If the toe of your foot is not ¼ inch wide, purchase another foot. Quilt shops and sewing machine dealers sell an inexpensive generic "quilter's foot" that fits most machines.

An alternative is to put masking tape on the throat plate with the left edge of the tape exactly ¼ inch from the needle hole. When you stitch, you will run the edge of the fabric against the edge of the tape.

Set the stitch length at 12 to 15 stitches per inch. This will be small enough to hold the patches securely together but not too small for you to rip out in case of error.

THREAD COLORS

Having two threads—one on the top of the machine and one in the bobbin—allows you to use thread colors that match your fabrics. If your quilt has many fabrics, it is most practical to use a neutral color, such as gray or beige, throughout the quilt. When the machine tension is properly set, the thread color won't matter.

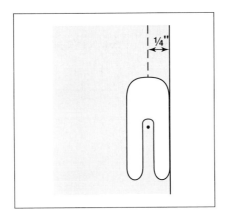

1 **A consistent seam allowance** is important for successful machine piecing. As you sew the patches together, keep the matched raw edges together and aligned with the edge of the presser foot to maintain a ¼-inch seam allowance.

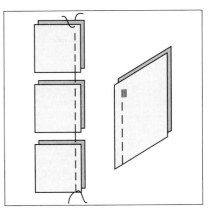

2 **Stitch seams** from edge to edge. Chain-piece, whenever possible, by feeding patches under the needle without lifting the foot or clipping the threads. The stitched patches will be linked by short lengths of thread. In most cases, it is not necessary to backstitch, but when you are joining patches that will receive a set-in piece, such as the diamonds *above right*, stop ¼ inch from the edge and backstitch.

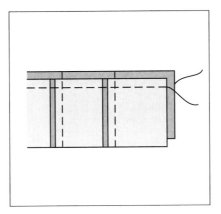

3 **Pin rows together** as shown in Step 4a of the hand-piecing tips, *opposite*. Matching seam allowances must be pressed in opposite directions before you sew to reduce bulk. Stitch across the seam allowances as shown *above*. If one row is slightly longer than the other, pin matching seams and stitch with the short piece on top—the feed dogs will help to ease the fullness of the bottom row.

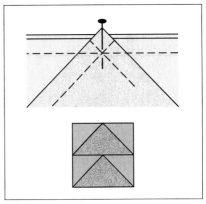

4 **To match points accurately,** push a pin through the two patches to align the seam allowances properly. Pin the rest of the seam normally and stitch. In the Flying Geese example *above*, the new line of stitching should cross the tip of the large triangle at the exact intersection of the adjoining seams. Remove each pin just before the needle reaches it. Sewing over pins can be dangerous and often results in broken needles.

APPLIQUÉ

"Words can scarcely describe this triumph of the needle," Ruth Finley wrote about appliqué in 1929. Appliqué is a method of stitching fabric pieces atop a base to create a picture. The edges of each piece are turned under and sewn to the base fabric by hand with hidden slip stitches or, in some cases, embroidery stitches.

Appliqué is one of the oldest of needle arts; examples have been found in ancient Egyptian tombs and medieval tapestries. In the United States, appliqué had its heyday in the album quilts of the mid-1800s and in 1920s and '30s masterpieces inspired by art nouveau.

Beginners should select an appliqué design with straight lines and gentle curves. Learning to make good points and tiny stitches takes practice.

Machine appliqué requires different skills and procedures. Few, if any, designs in this book are suitable for machine appliqué.

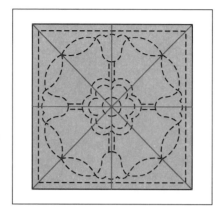

1 **Finger-press the base** square vertically, horizontally, and diagonally to make placement guidelines. Use a nonpermanent marker to *lightly* trace the block seam lines and the appliqué design on the right side of the fabric. Do not trace the exact outline of each piece as the marks may be difficult to erase from the edges of the finished work; mark just inside the lines to indicate placement of each piece.

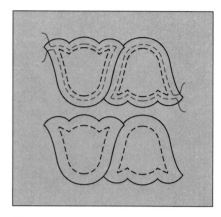

2 **Trace each appliqué shape** on the appropriate fabric, using templates as described on page 288. Before cutting, an optional step is to stay-stitch the appliqués. By hand or machine, work small stitches just outside the marked sewing line of each piece. Stay-stitching strengthens the edge and allows it to roll under more easily. Cut out each appliqué, adding a ³/₁₆-inch seam allowance.

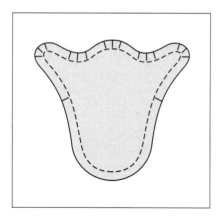

3 **Carefully clip the curves** of each appliqué piece to the marked sewing line or stay-stitching line. Clip just to the line, not beyond it. This enables the turned-under allowance to spread as needed, creating a smooth curve along the edge of the appliqué. Make extra clips along deep curves for ease in turning. Straight edges do not require clipping.

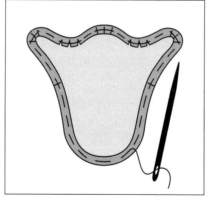

4 **Fold under the allowance** along the drawn sewing line and baste it in place on the wrong side of the piece. The turned seam allowance, in some areas, may form little pleats that should be basted in place; these should not be visible on the right side of the appliqué. Quiltmakers with advanced appliqué skills often skip this step and use their needle to turn under the edges as they sew. Press the prepared appliqué pieces.

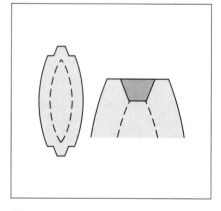

5 **To achieve sharp points** on leaves and similar pieces, trim the seam allowances as shown, *above, left.* Fold the blunted points down as shown, *above, right,* then turn the seam allowances under on both sides of the leaf. The side seam allowances will overlap slightly at the tips, forming nice, sharp points. Press the prepared leaf with spray starch to hold the edges in place.

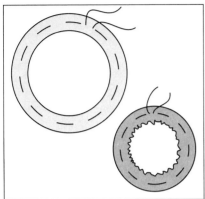

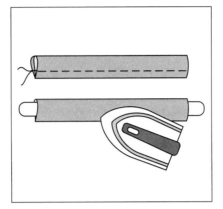

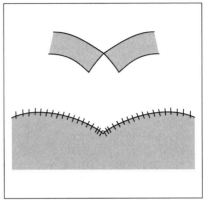

6 **To prepare a circle** for appliqué, run a gathering thread around the edge of the circle as shown, *above left.* Center the template on the wrong side of the circle and gently pull the thread tails, gathering the circle around the template. Press the circle, using spray starch to set the edges. Let the fabric cool completely before you remove the template.

7 **Stems and vines** usually are made from bias strips. Fold each strip in half lengthwise with *wrong* sides together. Machine-stitch ¼ inch from the fold to make a ¼-inch-wide stem. For stems of different widths, adjust the space between the stitching and the fold. Slip a bias bar into the stitched tube, centering the seam on the back; press, then remove the bar. Trim the seam allowance to ⅛ inch.

8 **A deep indentation** in an appliqué piece is sometimes called a "valley." Valleys are typical in hearts, as well as many flower shapes. When the seam allowance is clipped to the sewing or stay-stitching line, it separates when turned under, leaving no fabric at the point. To secure the raw edges and prevent raveling, work the appliqué stitches closely together at the point of the indentation.

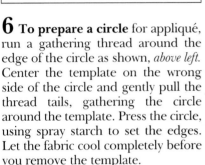

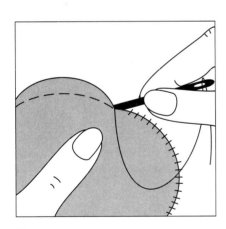

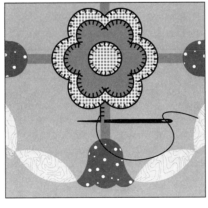

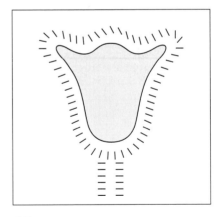

9 **Pin or baste** the appliqués in place, covering the traced outlines. Overlap pieces as necessary. Using thread that matches the appliqué, sew each piece onto the base (or atop a previously stitched appliqué) with small slip stitches. Catch just a few threads of the fold of the appliqué with each stitch. Pull stitches taut but not so tight that they pucker the fabric. Use the needle tip to manipulate the appliqué edges as desired.

10 **Buttonhole-stitch** embroidery is an alternative to regular appliqué. (See the stitch diagram on page 137.) It is ideal for use with felt, wool, and nonwoven materials because they do not require a turned-under seam allowance. For cotton fabric, work tiny, close stitches if you have not turned under a seam allowance. Stitched with two or three strands of floss, embroidery adds additional texture and design to the piece.

11 **Cut away the fabric** under the appliqué if it shows through the top fabric. Trimming also reduces the bulk of multiple layers, which is desirable if you intend to quilt the appliqué. To trim under the appliqué, use small embroidery scissors and work from the back side of the base fabric. Trim the underlying fabric to within ¼ inch of the appliqué stitches. Be careful not to cut the appliqué fabric.

293

SET VARIATIONS

The arrangement of blocks in a set is an important part of quilt design. The same block will look different in different sets. A Sawtooth Star block is used in all the illustrations on these two pages. In each drawing, dark lines indicate rows for assembly.

STRAIGHT SET

When blocks are set together square, edge to edge, the blocks interact to form new designs where they meet, creating effects not present in a single block. Examples are the Optical Illusion Quilt in Chapter 3 and the Arrowhead Star Quilt in Chapter 6.

To assemble a straight set, sew the blocks together in rows, either horizontally or vertically, then join the rows. Matching seam lines at each juncture is crucial to achieve the desired effect.

ALTERNATE STRAIGHT SET

An alternate set is assembled in the same manner as a regular straight set, but plain squares are placed between the blocks, checkerboard style. The plain setting squares can be of a matching or contrasting fabric in a print or solid. A solid setting square is ideal to showcase fancy quilting.

Separating the design blocks emphasizes the individual blocks rather than the interaction between them. The Nine-Patch Variation and Sawtooth Star quilts in Chapter 1 are examples of alternate straight sets.

STRAIGHT SET WITH SASHING

Sashing between blocks defines each block, giving the quilt a feeling of order and uniformity. The sashing fabric should be a unifying element, tying the blocks together.

Sashing can be plain or pieced. Use of contrasting squares at the sashing intersections is typical of pieced sashing, as in the Schoolhouse Quilt on pages 280 and 281.

Pieced sashing can contribute to the overall design, such as in the Burgoyne Surrounded Quilt on page 21.

STRAIGHT SET

DIAGONAL SETS

Turned on point, a block takes on a whole new character. Some blocks, particularly pieced basket designs, are almost always set diagonally.

A diagonal set is assembled in diagonal rows, with setting triangles added to both ends to fill in all sides and corners of the quilt top.

An example of a diagonal set is the Bride's Bouquet Quilt in Chapter 9; an alternate diagonal set is the Country Tulips Quilt in Chapter 10. The Fruit Basket Quilt in Chapter 3 is an example of a diagonal set with pieced sashing.

OTHER SETS

Strip sets, such as the Flying Geese and Little Baskets quilts in Chapter 5, have vertical rows of design blocks with one or more strips of vertical sashing between the rows.

In an allover design, such as the Clamshell in Chapter 5, the same element is repeated over the entire quilt, not separated into blocks.

The Diamond-in-the-Square Quilt in Chapter 7 is a classic example of a medallion quilt, which has a central design surrounded by multiple borders. The Tree of Paradise Wall Hanging in Chapter 10 is another example of a medallion set.

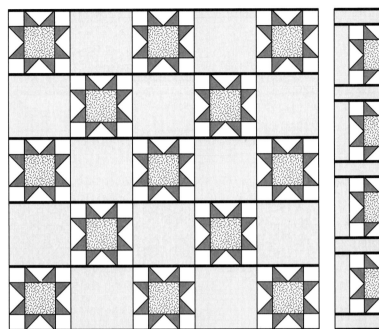

ALTERNATE STRAIGHT SET

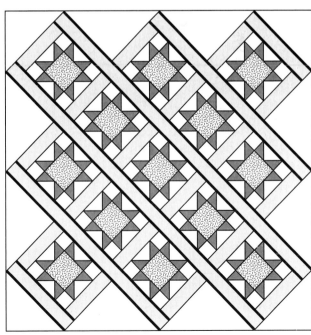

STRAIGHT SET WITH SASHING

DIAGONAL SET

DIAGONAL SET WITH SASHING

IRONING AND PRESSING

A good pressing iron is a must for every quiltmaker. The heat, pressure, and steam moisture set the seams and remove wrinkles.

Set the ironing board at a comfortable height; constantly bending over the board puts stress on your back.

There is a big difference between ironing and pressing. You want to iron your fabric before you cut it, then press the patchwork seams.

IRONING
Ironing is the sliding motion of the iron back and forth over a large piece of fabric to remove wrinkles. Each fabric should be well ironed to ensure accurate cutting.

PRESSING
To press patchwork, set the iron firmly on the fabric, then lift it, setting the iron down again in the desired position rather than sliding it over the fabric.

Don't push and pull at the fabric. This may stretch the fabric off grain and distort the patchwork.

Press appliqué pieces before turning edges under. When appliqués are sewn in place, press again very lightly; over-pressing appliqué can make an impression of the seam allowance on the right side and cause glazing.

RIGHT SIDE, WRONG SIDE
Some quilters like to press the right side of the fabric, others prefer to press the back, and some cover all the bases by pressing the back first and then the front to be sure the seams are smooth on both sides.

If you press the right side, be careful that the iron is not too hot or it may glaze the fabric. Use a pressing cloth to guard against glazing.

PRESS SEAMS TO ONE SIDE
Always press patchwork seam allowances to one side, not open as in dressmaking. The general rule of thumb is to press the seam allowances toward the darker fabric, but this is not always possible.

1 In patchwork, press all new seam allowances before continuing to the next step in the assembly. Whenever possible, press the seam allowance toward the darker fabric as shown *above*. It is important, however, to avoid pressing seam allowances over each other, which creates bulk.

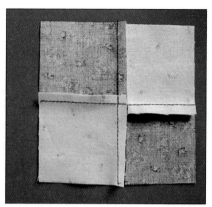

2 To reduce bulk where the seams meet, press the seam allowances in opposite directions; this will sometimes require pressing toward the lighter fabric. Press the joining seam toward the darker fabric, if possible.

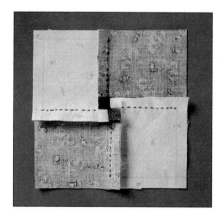

3 To press a hand-sewn junction of four seams, swirl the seam allowances clockwise as shown *above* to reduce bulk where they meet in the center. Press gently on both sides.

4 To press a machine-sewn set-in seam, press both seam allowances of the set-in piece flat toward the two pieces that create the angle, while pressing their joining seam to one side as shown *above, top*. To press a hand-sewn set-in seam, spread the seam allowances open in the center as shown *above, bottom* to reduce bulk where the seams meet.

JOINING BLOCKS

Pressing and pinning are crucial when joining blocks so that seam lines match as exactly as possible. Seam allowances in adjacent blocks must be pressed in opposite directions to reduce bulk and to facilitate the matching of seams. Before sewing blocks together, it is best to pin adjoining points and seams together to achieve an accurate match.

Once a quiltmaker's skills are more developed, these steps become less critical. A practiced hand can smooth and match the seam allowances without the aid of ironing and pinning.

The simplest way to join blocks is in rows, since you will sew them together in a straight line. Arrange the blocks and any setting pieces on the floor to clearly identify the pieces in each row and how they are positioned. As you join each row, pick up one block at a time from the floor to avoid confusion.

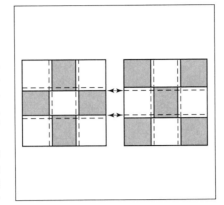

1a **When blocks** are sewn together, adjoining seam allowances should be pressed in opposite directions. Plan ahead as you make each block. The blocks *above* show correct pressing. At *left,* horizontal seam allowances are pressed toward the center row; at *right,* they are pressed away from the center. Some blocks can be pressed all the same and rotated to achieve opposing seam allowances.

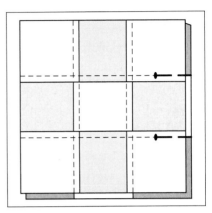

1b Pin blocks together at each seam line, right sides facing, to keep them in place during sewing. Each pin should go through the stitching of both seam lines to hold the seams together. Use additional pins as needed. You may find some blocks are larger than others; pinning helps determine where easing is required. A blast of steam from the iron may help fit the blocks together.

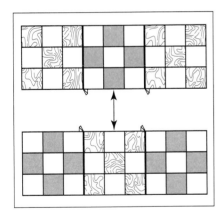

2 **When a row is assembled,** press all seam allowances between blocks in the same direction. For the adjacent row, press seam allowances in the opposite direction as illustrated *above.* In an alternate set, always press the seam allowances between blocks toward the setting squares and triangles; this creates the least bulk and always results in opposing seam allowances in adjacent rows when they are joined.

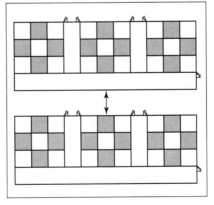

3 **Sashing eliminates** the need to worry about opposing seam allowances. Assemble horizontal rows with vertical sashing strips between the blocks; press the new seam allowances toward the sashing. If necessary, ease or stretch the sides of a block to match the length of the sashing strip. Assemble the quilt top with horizontal sashing between the rows; press these seam allowances toward the horizontal sashing strips.

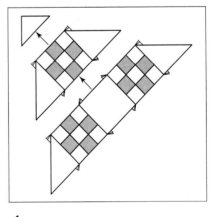

4 **Diagonal sets** are composed of diagonal rows of blocks and setting pieces. Because they are on the diagonal, adjacent rows will be different lengths. Lay all the blocks and setting pieces on the floor to identify the pieces in each row. Start by assembling one corner, as shown *above,* then join the blocks in each row. Each row has a setting triangle at each end.

ADDING BORDERS

Most quilts have one or more borders that frame and enhance the central design of the quilt top.

There are many types of borders and different ways to stitch the corners. A quilt can have one wide border or several narrow ones. Corners are either square (butted) or mitered.

Precise work is required to make a pieced border such as the one on the Twilight Star and Twisted Square Quilt shown on page 240. It is a challenge to make this type of border fit the quilt top. Because fabric stretches and seams differ, the piecing rarely measures exactly what it should after it is assembled.

MEASURING FOR BORDERS

It may be necessary to ease or stretch opposite sides of a quilt top to fit border strips of the same length. If the finished sides are unequal, the quilt will ripple and refuse to lie flat.

Measure the quilt from top to bottom through the middle of the quilt. (This measurement usually is different from the length of the sides.) This middle measurement is the correct length for the side borders, including top and bottom seam allowances.

Find the center of the side border strips. Mark the center and the desired ends of the each strip with pins. Sew these strips onto the quilt top following the instructions given on this page or *opposite*, depending on the type of corners you choose to make.

To determine the required length for the top and bottom borders, measure from side to side through the middle of the quilt top. Pin and sew these borders in the same manner as the side border strips.

When making square corners, you do not need to measure for subsequent borders, since the first one should square the quilt.

In this book, cutting instructions include extra length for borders, which allows for size variations in the assembled quilt top.

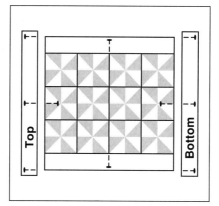

1a **Square-cornered borders** are easiest to stitch. To begin, find the center of each edge of the quilt top and place a pin at those points. Border strips usually are sewn onto the long sides first, as illustrated *above*. When border strips are added to the top and bottom edges, they cross the seam line of the side borders and extend to the side edges. Subsequent borders are added in the same order.

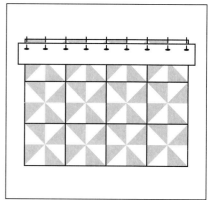

1b Pin a border strip onto one side edge, matching the pinned centers of the strips and the quilt top. Then match the pins at the ends of the border strip with the ends of the quilt top. Ease or stretch the quilt to fit between the pins, pinning as necessary. Sew borders on both sides before adding the top and bottom borders. Press seams away from the center of the quilt top.

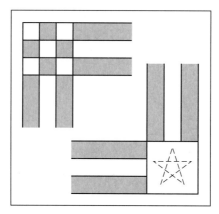

2 **A contrasting corner** is stitched like a square corner. Add side borders as described in Step 1b. If the borders are composed of multiple strips, as in the examples *above*, join the strips and add each border as one piece. Stitch a contrasting square to each end of the top and bottom border strips, then add the borders onto the quilt. Adjust the seams of the squares as necessary to align them with the side border seams.

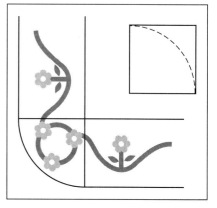

3 **Rounded corners** work well with appliquéd borders, particularly if the design curves at the corners. Stitch rounded-corner borders in the same manner as a contrasting corner. To make the corner pattern, draw a square the *finished* size of a contrasting corner; use a compass to draw a quarter-circle, as shown *above*. Add seam allowances when cutting corner pieces from the border fabric.

MAKING MITERED BORDER CORNERS

Mitered corners enhance a pieced border or plain border made with striped fabric by creating the illusion of a continuous line around the quilt.

When making mitered corners in a pieced border, sew multiple strips together so the border for each side can be handled as one piece.

Measure the quilt top to determine the desired length of each border strip, as described *opposite*. Mark the center and ends of each strip with pins. Do not trim the border strips until each corner is stitched.

Pin borders onto the quilt top, aligning the pinned match points. If one edge is longer than the other, distribute the fullness evenly when pinning. Pressing may help fit the two edges together, since steam both shrinks fabric and enables it to stretch. Machine-stitch with the longer piece on the bottom so the feed dogs can take up the extra fullness.

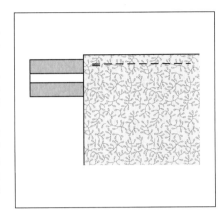

1 **Sew the borders** onto the quilt top, as described in Step 1b, *opposite.* Begin and end each seam line ¼ inch from the edge of the quilt top. Excess border fabric will extend beyond each edge. Stitch all four border strips onto the quilt top in this manner. Press borders and seam allowances before sewing the corners.

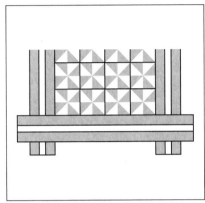

2a **For hand sewing** the mitered corners, an appliqué technique is preferred, especially if you are matching stripes. Lay the quilt top on the ironing board or a table, right side up. Lap the horizontal (top or bottom) border facing you over the side borders, as shown *above*.

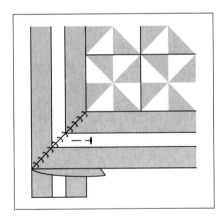

2b At one corner, turn the horizontal border under to make a diagonal fold. Press the fold and pin it in place on the side border, which is still lying flat. Hand-stitch the fold with an appliqué stitch. Press the stitched corner, then trim excess fabric to a ¼-inch seam allowance on the back.

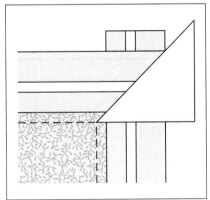

3a **Machine-stitched mitered corners** can be made in several different ways. The easiest method is to mark seam lines on the *wrong side* of each border, match the lines, and sew the seam. To mark a seam line, align one point of a right triangle where the border seams meet, as shown *above;* draw a line on the border fabric along the long edge (hypotenuse) of the triangle. Lap the adjacent border on top and repeat.

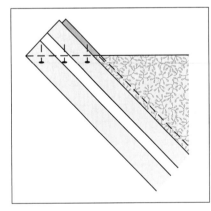

3b With right sides of adjacent borders together, match the marked seam lines and pin. Beginning with a backstitch at the inside corner, stitch exactly on the marked lines to the outside edge. Check the right side of the corner to see that it lies flat and that stripes match as desired, then trim the seam allowance. Some quiltmakers press these seam allowances to one side; others prefer to press them open.

CHOOSING A QUILTING DESIGN

A top is not a finished quilt until it is joined to batting and backing with quilting stitches.

Quilting serves a practical purpose—it holds the three layers of a quilt together in a manner that keeps them from shifting. However, quilting also enhances the look of the finished quilt, so the choice of quilting designs deserves careful thought.

Several factors should be weighed when choosing a quilting design.
◆ What kinds of fabrics are in the quilt? Quilting is visible on light fabrics more than dark ones and on solid fabrics more than prints. A fancy quilting design will be hidden in an area of dark print fabric.
◆ Which parts of the quilt will show off the quilting designs? Wide, plain borders or alternate unpieced blocks are perfect places for lots of quilting.
◆ Is a traditional or contemporary look best for your quilt? Traditional designs are more formal and symmetrical than free-form designs.
◆ How will the quilt be used? It probably isn't practical to do a lot of quilting on a quilt that will be used on a teenager's bed.
◆ What is your skill level? Simple designs with straight lines are best for beginners. Also, quilting across seam lines—and the extra thickness of the seam allowances—may be difficult for an inexperienced quilter.
◆ Can you use a quilting design that adds personal meaning to the quilt? If the quilt is to be a wedding gift or an anniversary tribute, motifs such as hearts and true lover's knots are appropriate. School mascots, favorite pets, objects associated with a hobby, and other images also can personalize a quilt.

OUTLINE AND ECHO QUILTING
The simplest quilting is stitched without planning or marking simply by following the lines of the patchwork or appliqué.

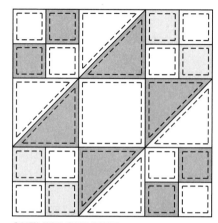

OUTLINE QUILTING

Outline quilting on patchwork is stitched ¼ inch from the seam lines, just past the extra thickness of the pressed seam allowances. Many quilters like to use ¼-inch-wide masking tape as a stitching guide. Used in small segments and removed as you stitch, masking tape leaves no residue on the fabric.

Quilting can be closer to the seam line on the side of the seam that does not have seam allowances. This is called quilting "in the ditch," and is more subtle than outline quilting because it tends to disappear into the seam lines. On appliquéd quilts, in-the-ditch quilting is stitched closely around the edge of each design to raise it from the surface of the quilt.

ECHO QUILTING

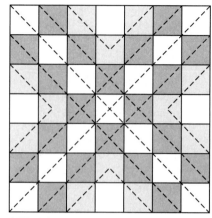

STRAIGHT LINE QUILTING

Echo quilting is multiple lines of quilting that follow the outline of an appliqué, so the quilting repeatedly "echoes" the shape. Also known as wave quilting, this style often is associated with Hawaiian appliqué.

CROSSING THE LINE
Lines of quilting can be used to complement the patchwork, directing the viewer's eye by emphasizing selected aspects of the block or the overall quilt design.

In quilts such as the Irish Chain pictured on page 15, for example, diagonal lines of quilting through each square of the block reinforce the illusion of continuous diagonal chains formed by the joined blocks.

Some quilters contrast geometric patchwork with rounded or curved quilting. The Linked Squares Quilt pictured on pages 238 and 239 is an example—quilted concentric circles soften the linear look of the patchwork without detracting from the visual effect of interlocked squares.

FILLING IN THE SPACES
Large areas of unpieced fabric generally look best with more quilting. Plain squares and/or triangles in alternate sets, sashing strips, and plain medallion squares are greatly enhanced by a pretty quilting design.

The Diamond-in-the-Square Quilt shown on pages 144 and 145 is a good example of how quilting complements simple patchwork by filling in open spaces. The large medallion square would have little visual interest without the texture and pattern of the quilted star and wreath.

Two more examples are in Chapter 1—the Pinwheel Quilt setting squares are quilted with a feathered wreath, and the Nine-Patch Variation Quilt has a large leaf quilted in the setting squares.

Designs such as the wreath are formal and symmetrical, as are lover's knots, pinwheels, and fancy hearts. The leaf, on the other hand, is informal. It can be positioned at a different angle in each block or several leaves may be overlapped, creating additional interest to the overall design of the quilt.

Select a quilting design that fits the area to be filled, allowing for ⅜ inch on all sides between the quilting and the seam lines. If the motif you like is not the right size, reduce or enlarge the drawing in a photocopy machine.

BACKGROUND FILLERS
Some quilts have simple background designs quilted in open spaces. Also, designs such as hearts and wreaths can have filler grids quilted in the spaces inside and around them.

FEATHERED WREATH

BACKGROUND FILLER DESIGNS

Most background fillers are patterns of straight lines—single or closely spaced double lines stitched vertically, horizontally, or diagonally. Crossing lines make grids of squares or diamonds. These fillers are easy to mark using only a marker and a ruler.

The Checkers and Rails Quilt shown on page 59 shows an effective use of background quilting. The grid of squares stitched in each setting square echoes the checkerboard pattern of the pieced sashing.

Allover patterns ignore the natural boundaries of patchwork. Quilting designs for this type of filler are basket weave, clamshells, and concentric circles.

FABULOUS FEATHERS
The feather is a centuries-old decorative motif. Medieval monks illustrated parchments with swirling lines of feathers much like the curving border designs quilters have always loved.

Colonial Americans inherited the feather tradition from English quilters. Since then, many feather quilting designs—circles, hearts, and undulating borders—have evolved.

Feather motifs can be customized to the specifications of your quilt, but the details are too complex to include here. Ready-made stencils of feather designs are available in a wide variety of shapes and sizes.

BORDERS AND CORNERS
An old superstition says a continuous design should be quilted in the border of a bridal quilt because a broken border foretells sorrow and strife. Continuous quilting designs magnify the framing effect of a border, but separate corner motifs are fine, too.

In fact, how to mark the corner is an important decision when selecting a border design. Feathers, cables, and chains are wonderful border designs, but they require planning to turn around the corners.

Whether you use a contrasting corner design or a connecting one, you must measure the repeat of the quilting design to see that it will fit the length of each border evenly. For a continuous border design, work out a motif that connects the vertical and horizontal borders appropriately.

PRECUT STENCILS AND HOUSEHOLD OBJECTS
Today's quilters have access to many ready-made stencils and books of quilting designs. It is easy to make a stencil by cutting out a traced design from stencil or template plastic, using a double-bladed art knife.

Any simple drawing can be used as a quilting design. A child's coloring book is a good design source. Common household objects, such as teacups and cookie cutters, can be used as templates.

CABLE BORDER

MARKING QUILTING DESIGNS

Marking the quilt top can be done by drawing in stencil slots, outlining a template, or tracing a drawing. Free-style, outline, and in-the-ditch quilting do not require marking.

Press the quilt top before marking. If you use a water-erasable marker, do not press the top again until all marks are completely removed. Complete all marking before layering the top with batting and backing.

PREPARATION

A ready-made stencil needs no preparation. You can make your own stencil by cutting template plastic with a double-bladed art knife.

To mark directly from a drawing, go over the drawn lines on paper with a black *permanent* marker; other inks may leave traces on the fabric. Let the inked pattern dry. To see the design through dark fabric, you may have to tape the drawing and the quilt top over a light box or window.

1 **Test any marker** on *each* fabric to make sure it shows up and is easy to remove when the quilting is done. Suggested markers (shown left to right, *above*) for light-colored fabrics include a Number 3 lead pencil, a water-erasable marking pen, chalk pencil, and a chalk dispenser; for dark fabrics, try a soapstone marker, yellow and silver pencils, a sliver of soap, and a chalk dispenser.

2 **Mark fine lines;** heavy lines are difficult to remove and may lead you slightly astray as you quilt. The lines should be durable enough to last until the quilting is completed. When using a stencil or a ruler, lay the quilt top on a flat surface and draw the lines on the fabric. Especially on borders, you may want to draw guidelines to be sure the stencil is straight and properly positioned as you mark.

3 **To mark a drawn design,** secure the drawing on a flat surface with masking tape. Matching the quilt top seams with the edge guides on the pattern, tape the quilt top in place over the pattern. Position a pin at the middle of each border strip to aid in aligning the quilt top with the border design. Firmly secure the quilt top so it will not shift as you mark it.

4 **Begin marking at the center** of the quilt top and work out toward the borders. Mark larger and/or more complex designs first, then fill in the small details in each area.

5 **Mark the background filler** pattern last, if you choose to quilt one, by using a ruler as a guide to draw straight lines. Position the ruler carefully, keeping the lines equidistant and parallel. A grid is usually easier to mark if you draw all the parallel lines in one direction before marking the lines in the opposite direction.

BASTING THE QUILT LAYERS

Properly assembling the layers of a quilt ensures a smooth, wrinkle-free surface for quilting. Follow the tips below to prepare the backing and batting before basting them together with the quilt top.

PREPARING THE BACKING

Backing fabric should be the same type as the quilt top; 100 percent cotton usually is recommended.

Quilts more than 42 inches wide require either a pieced backing or extra-wide sheeting. Some fabric and quilting shops sell sheeting by the yard in 90-inch and 108-inch widths.

A pieced backing can have one center seam or two seams that connect a narrow panel to each side of a wide center panel. Position the seams parallel to the side edges of the quilt. Press the seam allowances open.

Cut or piece a backing that is at least 3 inches larger on all sides than the quilt top.

SELECTING THE BATTING

Batting is now available in a variety of choices in fiber content, loft, warmth, ease of needling, softness, and washability. The qualities of the batting you use should complement the nature and future use of your quilt.

No batting manufacturer has yet eliminated bearding, the migration of batting fibers through a quilt's outer layers of fabric. Black or gray batting is recommended for quilts made with predominantly dark fabrics.

Bonded polyester batting is by far the most popular in use today. It is lightweight, easy to stitch, washable, and does not shift as readily as cotton or wool batting. This batting has a slightly higher loft than cotton or wool, which puts the quilting stitches in high relief. Available in a variety of sizes and weights, bonded batting does not require a lot of quilting—lines every 2 to 4 inches are sufficient.

Cotton and wool batts give a quilt the flat, thin appearance of antiques. They are not recommended for beginners because both require very close quilting, at least every inch, and are not as easy to needle as polyester. Cotton batting usually shrinks when washed; wool batting is not washable.

Needlepunch batting also has a low loft, but it is more dense and provides extra warmth.

PREPARING THE BATTING

Precut batting is widely available in five standard sizes, although some shops sell batting by the yard. The batt listed for each project in this book is the most advantageous of the standard precut sizes.

Fluff precut batting in a clothes dryer for a few minutes on an air-dry setting to remove wrinkles. Trim the batt, as necessary, cutting it 2 inches larger all around than the quilt top.

1 **Tape the backing** to a smooth work surface, *wrong* side up. (Don't use a fine table because you may scratch its surface.) If the backing is larger than the table, let the extra length hang over one end; the pull of the hanging fabric keeps the backing taut while you baste the section on the tabletop. Center the batting atop the backing, smoothing it flat; tape or pin them together at the edges. Center the quilt top on the batting.

2 **Baste the three layers** together, working from the center toward each edge. Baste a horizontal and a vertical line through the center, then baste diagonal lines from corner to corner, as shown *above*. If the quilt has sashing strips, baste along the strips first. Fill in additional basting, making stitches about 2 inches long and 4 inches apart; lap quilting requires closer basting since the quilt is handled more.

3 **For hoop or lap quilting,** fold the backing over the front and baste a temporary hem in place for the duration of the quilting. This prevents the edges of the batting and fabric from fraying as the quilt is handled. The hemming is not necessary when using a quilting frame.

QUILTING

Quilting is a series of small, even stitches made by hand or by machine to secure the three layers of a quilt. Quilting adds texture and additional design to a quilt's appearance.

MACHINE QUILTING

Quilting by machine is more than 100 years old, but until recent years it required superior machines and sewing skills. Today's improved sewing machines and presser feet now make machine quilting practical.

The steps to successful machine quilting are too numerous to include here. Several excellent books on machine quilting are sold at fabric and quilting shops.

HAND QUILTING

Quilting by hand is viewed by many as the traditional and preferred method of quilting. Hand-quilting a bed-size quilt can take more time than sewing the quilt top, but quilters consider it a personal commitment to fine craftsmanship and a labor of love to stitch the layers by hand.

Hoops and frames

Some quilters like to hold the quilt loosely in their laps, but most feel they get straighter, smaller stitches if the work is held taut in a hoop or frame.

Many frames are now available at reasonable prices. Large ones accommodate several quilters at a time, others are designed for one person. A frame supports the quilt's weight, ensures even tension throughout the quilting, and frees both the quilter's hands for quilting. Once set up, however, a frame cannot be disassembled until the quilting is complete.

A hoop is both portable and inexpensive. Made in several sizes and shapes, quilting hoops are deeper than embroidery hoops because of the thickness of the quilt layers.

When using a hoop, keep all the layers evenly taut. Check for wrinkles in the backing before you begin to

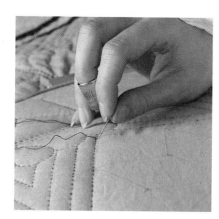

1 Hold the needle between your thumb and first finger as shown *above*. Place your other hand *under* the quilt, with the tip of the index finger in the spot where the needle will come through the quilt back. With the needle angled slightly away from you, push the needle through the layers until you feel the tip of the needle with the finger beneath the quilt.

2 When you feel the needle tip, slide the finger underneath the quilt toward you, pushing up against the side of the needle to help return it to the top. At the same time, with your top hand, roll the needle away from you. Gently push the needle forward and up through the quilt layers, until the amount of needle showing is the length you want the next stitch to be.

stitch. Rest one side of the hoop against a table edge to support your work as you quilt.

Needles and thread

A quilting needle is a "between"—a short needle with a small eye. Common sizes are 8, 9, and 10; a higher number indicates a smaller needle. Expert quilters may use a size 12 between, but 8 is best for beginners.

Quilting thread is stronger than regular sewing thread. Some quilters select one or more colors that match the fabrics in the quilt top. Others use contrasting colors to make the quilting stitches more noticeable.

The mandatory thimble

Beginners may find it hard to get used to wearing a thimble on the middle finger of the quilting hand. Without it, however, hand quilting can be *painful*—pushing the needle through three layers drives the needle deep into an unprotected finger.

Popping the knot

No knots should show on the front or back of a hand-quilted quilt. Instead, hide the beginnings and ends of each thread as described below.

To begin, thread a between with 18 inches of quilting thread, knotting one end. Insert the needle through the top and the batting (but not the backing) a few inches away from the quilting area; bring the needle back to the surface in position to make the first stitch. Gently tug the thread, just enough to pop the knot through the fabric and embed it in the batting.

To end stitching, wind the thread twice around the needle close to the quilt top, making a French knot. Then run the needle through the top and batting, bringing it out again a few inches away from the stitching. Tug the knot under the surface.

Hold the thread *taut* and clip it close to the top before releasing it; relaxing the tension on the thread snaps the thread end out of sight.

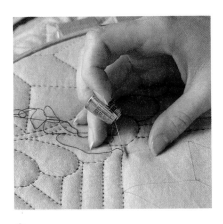

3 **Lift the eye of the needle** with the thimble finger, positioning your thumb just ahead of the stitching. Rock the needle upward until it is almost perpendicular to the quilt top. Push down on the thimble until you feel the tip of the needle on your finger underneath the quilt. It takes practice to learn not to prick this finger. A variety of tools is available for use under the quilt to turn the needle and save the finger.

4 **Push the needle** tip up to the quilt top with your finger underneath the quilt. At the same time, with your thimble finger, roll the eye of the needle down and forward to help return the tip to the surface.

5 **Repeat the rock-and-roll** motion of steps 3 and 4, filling the needle with evenly spaced stitches. Uniformity of stitching is more important than size, but eight or more stitches per inch is considered fine quilting. When the needle is full, pull it away from the quilt until the stitches are snug. If you find it difficult to pull the needle out, use small pliers to grip the needle tip and pull it through.

TYING YOUR QUILT

Tying, or tufting, is a quick-and-easy alternative to quilting. It is an appropriate, useful finish for a quilt that will get a lot of wear and tear. Save your fine hand stitching for a quilt that will be cared for and treasured.

The best materials for tying are perle cotton, sport-weight yarn, or narrow ribbon. A tie is sewn through all three layers of the quilt—backing, batting, and quilt top—and knotted on the surface of the quilt top. In some cases, the knot is on the back.

Quilts that are tied have a puffier look than those that are quilted. For extra puffiness, use a thick batting, or even multiple layers of batting.

For an added touch, sew buttons or other colorful ornaments onto the quilt layers as you tie.

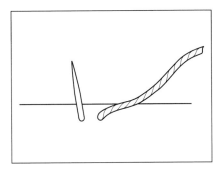

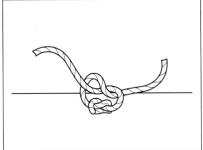

1 **From the right side,** push the threaded needle down through all layers of the quilt. Pull the needle through, leaving a 3-inch-long tail of thread on the surface. Push the needle back to the quilt top about ⅛ inch from the first tail. Push the needle back down to the back of the quilt through the *first* hole of the stitch.

2 **Bring the needle up** to the surface again through the *second* hole. Cut the thread, leaving a second 3-inch-long tail of thread. Tie the clipped threads in a square knot close to the surface of the quilt top. Don't pull the thread too tightly, or it will create a pucker in the fabric.

305

MAKING BINDING

There are several ways to bind the edges of a finished quilt. Most methods require extra fabric to make a separate binding strip.

The binding is the part of the quilt that receives the most wear. For added durability, we recommend making French-fold (double-layer) binding, which is more resistant to wear than a single layer. Instructions given in this book are for French-fold binding.

For each project in this book, yardage is included to make French-fold binding cut 2 inches wide on either the bias or straight grain. This width makes a finished binding approximately ⅜ inch wide.

BIAS OR STRAIGHT-GRAIN?

Whether you choose to cut binding strips on the bias or straight of the grain is a personal choice.

Bias binding has a stretch that helps it lie smooth, turn curves, and miter nicely at corners. When applied to the quilt edge, the bias threads of the weave crisscross each other over the edge, creating a strong finish. Straight-grain binding has single threads running parallel to the quilt edge that weaken with wear.

Cutting straight-grain binding

One way to make straight-grain binding is to cut *lengthwise* strips, each slightly longer than the quilt edge.

To make continuous straight-grain binding, piece cut strips end to end. You can also cut straight-grain binding with the continuous-cut method described at *right*, eliminating Step 1 and marking the fabric as described in Step 2. Press the seam allowances open to distribute the bulk.

Making continuous bias

Refer to steps 1–4 at *right* to make continuous bias. This method can be used to make continuous bias of any width, whether it is to be used for appliqué or for binding.

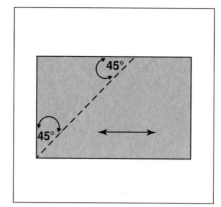

1 **Start with a square** or rectangle of fabric. Draw a diagonal line from the bottom corner of the fabric to the top edge as shown. Use a large acrylic triangle to square up the left edge of the fabric and to draw an accurate 45-degree angle. Cut the fabric on the drawn line. Handle the edges carefully to avoid distorting the bias.

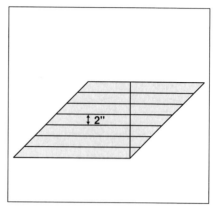

2 **Sew the two pieces together** with a ¼-inch seam allowance, matching the straight edges as shown. Press the seam open. Use a pencil or marker with a ruler to draw parallel lines across the length of the seamed fabric. The space between the lines is the desired width of the binding strip, including seam allowance. For example, cut a 2-inch-wide strip to make a ⅜-inch-wide finished binding.

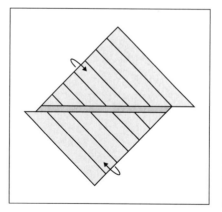

3 **Bring the bias edges together,** matching raw edges and right sides, to create a tube of fabric. Shift one edge down so that the top of one edge aligns with the first marked line of the opposite edge as shown. The other end also becomes offset. Holding the fabric in this position, seam the two edges together. Press the seam open.

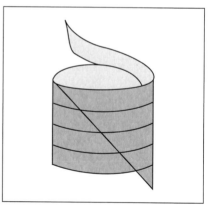

4 **Begin cutting** at one uneven end along the marked line. Each time you cut across the seam, you'll be moving down one marked line, cutting a continuous spiral.

APPLYING BINDING

The quilt top should be quilted and securely basted around the edges before any binding is applied.

BACKING-FABRIC BINDING

Turning the backing over to the front of the quilt is a quick and easy way to cover the edges. All it requires is an extra inch of backing fabric around the quilt top. This inch of fabric is turned over on itself, then the fold comes over the edge of the quilt and is hand-stitched onto the front.

This same method can be used to turn quilt top fabric over to the back.

This technique eliminates the need to make and apply a separate binding, but does not have the durability that the French-fold method offers.

MITERED, SQUARE CORNERS

This decision is a personal choice, but one rule of thumb can be applied—if the borders are made with square corners, then square corners should be used for binding as well.

Straight-grain binding is used for square corners. For mitered corners, it is necessary to make continuous binding, either bias or straight-grain.

SEWING BINDING ONTO THE QUILT

Refer to the opposite page for tips on making French-fold binding.

Bring the raw edges of the binding strip(s) together, folding the fabric in half lengthwise with the wrong sides together; press the fold.

Trim batting and backing to within 1 inch of the quilt top. Match the raw edges of the binding strip with the edges of the quilt top, right sides together. Using a standard ¼-inch seam allowance, stitch the binding to the quilt; sew through the binding, quilt top, batting, and backing.

Before applying the binding, read steps 1–3 at *right* for tips on making mitered corners or Step 4 for information on making square corners.

After the binding is sewn to the quilt, trim the batting and backing even with the seam allowance.

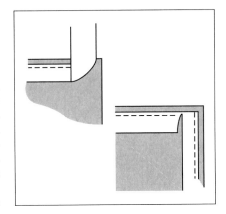

1 **For mitered corners,** use continuous binding. *Turn over a ½-inch hem* at one end of the binding; start sewing that end to any side of the quilt top. Stop ¼ inch from each corner. Fold the binding up as shown at *upper left.* Holding the fold in place, bring the binding down in line with the next side as shown at *lower right.* Start stitching again at the top fold of the binding, sewing through all layers.

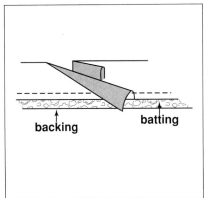

2 **Stitch around the quilt** in this manner. When you return to the starting point, overlap the end of the binding beyond the fold in the first end as shown *above.* Turn the binding over the edge of the quilt to the back, covering the raw edge of the second end. Hand-stitch the binding in place on the backing fabric.

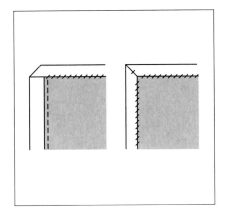

3 **To finish miters on the back,** hand-stitch right up to the corner as shown, *left,* and then fold the binding over the next side as shown *right.* Tack a stitch or two in the miter fold to secure it, then proceed along the next edge.

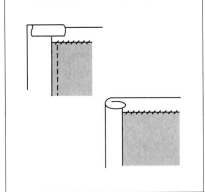

4 **For square corners,** sew binding onto opposite sides of the quilt. Fold binding over the edge; hand-sew it to the quilt back. Trim excess binding at each end. Sew binding to remaining sides, overlapping the bound edges. Trim, leaving ½ inch of extra fabric at both ends. Fold fabric over bound edge as shown at *upper left.* Turn binding to the quilt back, enclosing edges, *lower right.* Hand-sew binding onto the backing fabric.

HANGING QUILTS

Hanging quilts on the wall has become increasingly popular in recent years. A quilt adds color and drama to nearly any decorating scheme, whether modern, country, or traditional. However, it is important to protect a quilt while showing it off.

Only a sturdy quilt that is not too heavy should be hung. If a quilt is in delicate condition, hanging will only accelerate its deterioration. Alternate quilts between storage and display every few months to minimize the effects of fading.

HANGING METHODS

The method used most frequently to hang a quilt is to stitch a sleeve or casing onto the backing so a rod or dowel can be slipped through it. This method distributes the weight of the quilt across the widest possible area without putting undue strain on any part of it.

Tips for making a hanging sleeve are illustrated at right. If possible, stitch a sleeve onto more than one edge so you can periodically turn the quilt to redistribute the weight.

An alternative method, suitable for small quilts, is to sew tabs or loops to the top edge of the quilt backing. This method is not appropriate for larger quilts because the weight of the quilt will cause distortion at the hanging points.

For the same reason, only a small, very lightweight quilt should be hung with pushpins or small tacks. However, the metal part of the pins might leave rustlike stains where they pierce the fabric.

There are some ready-made hangers available that require no extra piece to be sewn onto the quilt. These are easy to use, but they usually require that one edge of the quilt be encased between the two layers of the hanger. Particularly if the hanger is made of wood, it is imperative that the quilt be turned frequently to avoid damage.

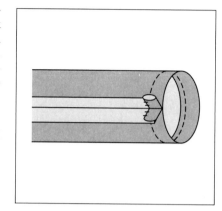

1 **For a sleeve,** cut a 7½-inch-wide piece of prewashed fabric that is 2 inches longer than the quilt edge. Turn in 1½ inches of fabric at both short sides; topstitch a hem. Then fold the fabric in half lengthwise with the *wrong* sides together; stitch the long edges together with a ¼-inch seam allowance. Press the seam open and to the middle of the sleeve as illustrated *above.*

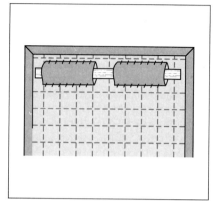

2 **Center the sleeve on the quilt** about 1 inch below the binding with the seam facing the backing. Sew the sleeve to the quilt through backing and batting along both long edges and the ends that lie against the quilt. For large quilts, make two or three sleeve sections as illustrated—this lets you use more nails or brackets to support the rod, and evenly distributes the quilt's weight.

SIGNING YOUR QUILT

It is important to sign and date the quilts you make, for these are the legacies of tomorrow. Most old quilts are now silent about their origin, presenting tantalizing mysteries to quilt historians. So much information has been lost that might have enriched us; we owe future generations a better prospect. In years to come, you may be glad to have the information for your private memories and it will be helpful to your descendants.

There are several ways to permanently mark a quilt, on either the front or back of the quilt. Incorporating your name and a date in the quilting is a time-honored method, as is embroidering these details on the quilt top.

In addition to signing your quilt, write additional information on a label that can be sewn to the quilt back. You might include your name and address, the full date the quilt was completed, who it was made for and why, and any special group or occasion connected with the quilt. You might also list the fabrics used and instructions for care.

Some people embroider or cross-stitch labels, but it is most practical to use a waterproof, permanent marker to write on a plain piece of fabric.

Hem the four sides of the finished label. If you have used embroidery thread, wash the label to guarantee colorfastness before sewing it to the quilt. Slip-stitch the label onto the quilt back, using thread that matches the backing fabric.

CARING FOR QUILTS

Many quilts of bygone days were worn out with hard use. The antique quilts that survive are those that were cherished and carefully stored, to be used only for special occasions.

We are all proud of the quilts we make and want to show them off, but they must be protected from harmful elements. Even a quilt that is stored should be treated in a manner that will preserve it in good condition.

The following suggestions are suitable for the care of most newly made and antique quilts. A museum-quality heirloom deserves special treatment; if you own such a quilt, seek expert advice on its care.

A BREATH OF FRESH AIR
All quilts should be shaken and aired outdoors at least twice a year. A breezy, overcast day is best if it is not too humid. Lay towels on the grass or over a railing, then spread the quilt over the towels. Keep the quilt out of direct sunlight.

STORING QUILTS
A quilt should be stored in a clean container in a cool, dry place in your home. Winter cold and summer heat make attics and garages inappropriate storage areas. Keeping quilts in a basement is unwise if there is the slightest threat of dampness.

Store each quilt either in a cotton pillowcase or wrapped in acid-free paper. Boxes made of acid-free material are also available. Crumple the paper inside each fold to prevent stains and hard creases from developing along the fold lines. These materials allow air to circulate through the quilt and protect it from dust and dampness. Do not store quilts in plastic, as this encourages the growth of mildew.

If you keep your quilt on a wooden shelf or rack, or in a chest (including a cedar chest), put several layers of acid-free paper or muslin atop the wood. A quilt should not be in contact with any wood for a long time, as the natural acids in wood will eventually stain the fabric.

Each time you put the quilt away, fold it in a different way. If possible, it is best to roll the quilt around a tube or cotton towel to avoid folds altogether. Since permanent damage can occur to fabric fibers along a fold line, avoid putting weight on top of the quilt that might increase the chances of fold damage.

DISPLAYING QUILTS
Quilts should be protected from direct light and heat, dust, dampness, cigarette smoke, and aerosol sprays.

If your quilt is hung on the wall, be sure the weight of the quilt is evenly distributed to avoid putting stress on the seams and fabric. Remove any quilt that is in danger of water damage from roof leaks.

When you use quilts on beds, their preservation is the perfect excuse to make more. By changing the quilt in use regularly, no one quilt is exposed to damaging elements for a long period. Ideally, you could have enough quilts so you can rotate them with the change of seasons.

All displayed quilts collect dust. Shake and air your quilts often, whether you use them on beds or as wall hangings. Once per month, gently vacuum the surface of your quilts with a hose attachment to eliminate accumulated dust and dirt.

FACTS ABOUT FADING
No matter how careful you are, a quilt exposed to any kind of light will fade to some degree. Washing also lessens a fabric's original luster.

Unfortunately, some fabrics fade more quickly and more drastically than others and there is no sure way to identify such fabrics before you use them in a quilt. However, there is a simple test that might be worthwhile if you have the luxury of time.

Cut a 4-inch square from each prewashed fabric. Put the squares in front of a bright, sunny window; after two or three weeks, you should see signs of fading.

Compare the squares to the color of the remaining yardage. If all the fabrics have faded to the same degree, then it is safe to assume that the finished quilt will maintain a uniform appearance as it ages. If one of the fabrics has faded more than the others, however, you should think twice before using it in your quilt.

WASHING QUILTS
Any quilt that is used by real people in a real living situation eventually needs to be cleaned. You should be able to wash a new quilt if the fabrics were prewashed and tested for colorfastness before the quilt was made. If in doubt, test a corner of the quilt to be sure the dyes do not bleed.

Some people have enough faith in today's strong, durable fabrics to toss quilts in the washing machine and dryer. Others wash them gently by hand in a large tub or wading pool.

The following tips help ensure that the quilt you make will survive an occasional washing.

● Prewash all fabrics, including the backing. Wash the fabric in the same way you intend to clean the finished quilt, whether that means washing it in the machine or by hand.

● Use washable batting. A bonded polyester quilt batt should wash well. Some batts may require prewashing; others need not be washed at all.

● Use a mild soap in lukewarm water; never use bleach. A heavily soiled quilt may require extra soaking.

● Dry a wet quilt by laying it flat on the floor or outside on the grass on clean mattress pads or towels. A wet quilt is very heavy, so avoid hanging it or lifting it in a way that puts stress on the fabric or stitching.

● Dry cleaning is not advisable because the chemicals in commercial cleaning fluids can be harmful.

Schoolhouse Quilt

Shown on pages 280 and 281.
The finished quilt measures approximately 68x94 inches. Each finished Schoolhouse block is 10 inches square.

MATERIALS
3 yards of yellow fabric for sashing and binding
2⅝ yards of muslin for background of Schoolhouse blocks
35 assorted print fabrics, *each* approximately 10 inches square, for schoolhouses; or 2¾ yards of a single fabric
½ yard of green fabric for sashing squares
5½ yards of backing fabric or 3 yards of 90-inch-wide sheeting
81x96-inch precut quilt batting
Template material
Rotary cutter, mat, and acrylic ruler

INSTRUCTIONS
Blue, navy, and black schoolhouses alternate with more brightly colored Schoolhouse blocks in this twin-size quilt. The thirty-five 10-inch blocks are separated by 3-inch-wide sashing strips in a 5x7-block straight set.

Cutting the fabrics
All measurements given for cutting include seam allowances. Make templates for patterns D, E, F, and G, *opposite* and on page 312; all other pieces are rectangular and can be measured and marked using a ruler. Refer to the block diagram, *above,* to identify patches for which patterns are not given.

Cutting requirements for blocks are given for one block, with the number required for the entire quilt shown in parentheses. Make a single block to test the accuracy of your templates before cutting the remaining fabric.

Note: The horizontal and vertical sashing strips are the same size, but are cut on the crosswise and lengthwise grains, respectively. To avoid confusion, it may be best to cut and sew the vertical sashing strips first, and then cut the horizontal sashing to assemble the quilt.

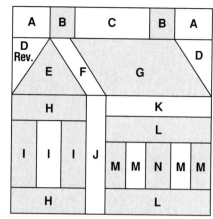

SCHOOLHOUSE BLOCK

From the green fabric, cut:
◆ Forty-eight 3½-inch sashing squares.

From each print fabric, cut:
◆ Two (70) 1¾x2-inch pieces for patch B.
◆ One (35) *each* of patterns E and G.
◆ Two (70) 1¾x4¼-inch pieces for patch H.
◆ Two (70) 1¾x3¾-inch pieces for patch I.
◆ Two (70) 1¾x5¾-inch pieces for patch L.
◆ Two (70) 1½x2¾-inch pieces for patch M.
◆ One (35) 1¾x2¾-inch piece for patch N.

From the muslin, cut:
◆ Eight 2x42-inch strips.
   From these strips, cut two (70) 2x2⅜-inch pieces for patch A and one (35) 2x4¼-inch piece for patch C.
◆ Seven 3¼x42-inch strips.
   From these strips, cut one (35) *each* of patterns D, D reversed, and F.
◆ Four 1¾x42-inch strips.
   From these strips, cut one (35) 1¾x3¾-inch piece for patch I.
◆ Sixteen 1½x42-inch strips.
   From these strips, cut one (35) 1½x6¼-inch piece for patch J; one (35) 1½x5¾-inch piece for patch K; and two (70) 1½x2¾-inch pieces for patch M.

From the yellow fabric, cut:
◆ ¾ yard for binding.
◆ Four 10½x42-inch strips.
   Cut each strip into twelve 3½x10½-inch pieces to obtain 42 vertical sashing strips.
◆ Ten 3½x42-inch strips.
   Cut forty 10½-inch pieces for horizontal sashing strips.

Piecing the Schoolhouse block
Because all the seams are straight and setting-in is not required, this block lends itself to machine piecing, but may be pieced by hand.

The block is pieced in four units that are then joined to complete the block. Refer to the block assembly diagram, *below,* to identify the pieces in each unit.

1. To make Unit 1, sew together two pairs of A and B pieces; complete the unit by stitching both B pieces to opposite ends of a C piece.

2. When making Unit 2, handle the bias edges carefully to avoid distorting the pieces. Sew a D triangle onto the right edge of piece G as illustrated; press seam allowance toward G. Sew the D reversed triangle onto the left side of triangle E and piece F onto the right side; press both seams away from piece E. Complete the unit by sewing the F-G seam; press seam allowance toward F.

3. For Unit 3, sew the muslin I piece between two I pieces of print fabric; press seams toward the center. Complete the unit with H pieces at the top and bottom of the unit; press seams away from center.

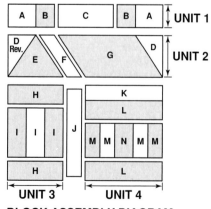

BLOCK ASSEMBLY DIAGRAM

4. To begin Unit 4, join two pairs of muslin and print M pieces, then complete the strip with the N piece in the center. Add L pieces to the top and bottom, then complete the unit with a muslin K piece at the top. Press all seams toward the print fabric.

5. Join units 1 and 2, matching seam lines carefully.

6. Sew Unit 3 to one side of the J piece, then sew Unit 4 to the opposite side. Press seams toward the J piece.

7. Matching seam lines carefully, sew the two pieces together.

8. Make 35 Schoolhouse blocks.

Joining horizontal rows

While assembling the rows, refer to the illustration of a straight set with sashing on page 295.

1. Sew one vertical sashing strip to the left side of each Schoolhouse block; press seam allowances toward the sashing.

2. On the floor or a table, lay out the blocks in a pleasing arrangement; separate the blocks into seven rows with five blocks in each row.

3. Join the blocks for Row 1, sewing each block to the sashing strip of the adjacent block.

4. End the row by sewing a vertical sashing strip to the right side of the last block in the row. Press all sashing seam allowances toward the sashing.

5. Repeat for rows 2–7.

Assembling the quilt top

While assembling the quilt top, refer to the photo on pages 280 and 281.

1. Each row of horizontal sashing is made by alternating green sashing squares with yellow sashing strips. Starting with a square, sew five sashing strips and six squares together to make a row; make eight rows of horizontal sashing.

2. Matching seam lines carefully, sew a row of horizontal sashing to the top of each of the seven block rows. Press seams toward horizontal sashing.

3. Join the rows, sewing the top of the sashing row to the bottom of the adjacent block row. Press seam allowances toward sashing.

4. Complete the quilt top by sewing the remaining row of sashing to the bottom of the seventh block row.

Quilting and finishing

BACKING: Divide the backing fabric into two 2¾-yard lengths; split one piece lengthwise. Sew a narrow panel onto each side of the wide panel.

Layer backing, batting, and quilt top; baste the three layers together.

QUILTING: The quilt shown on page 280 has a pretty vine and leaf quilting design in all the sashing strips. A full-size pattern for this quilting design is given on page 312. An individual leaf motif is repeated in the sashing squares. The blocks are outline-quilted, with diagonal lines quilted on the roof pieces (E and G). Quilt as desired.

BINDING: See pages 306 and 307 for tips on making and applying binding. Use the remaining ¾ yard of yellow binding fabric to make approximately 324 inches of either bias or straight-grain binding.

Making a larger quilt

Adding more rows, vertically and/or horizontally, easily makes this quilt larger. When making a larger quilt, carefully adjust the required yardage for the muslin, the yellow and green sashing fabrics, and the backing fabric. A larger batt also is necessary.

For a full-size quilt, make seven more blocks for another vertical row. The finished size is 81x94 inches.

For a queen-size quilt, make 12 extra blocks for one more vertical row and one more horizontal row. The finished size is 94x107 inches.

To make a king-size quilt, you need 19 more blocks for two additional vertical rows and one more horizontal row. The finished size is 107x107 inches.

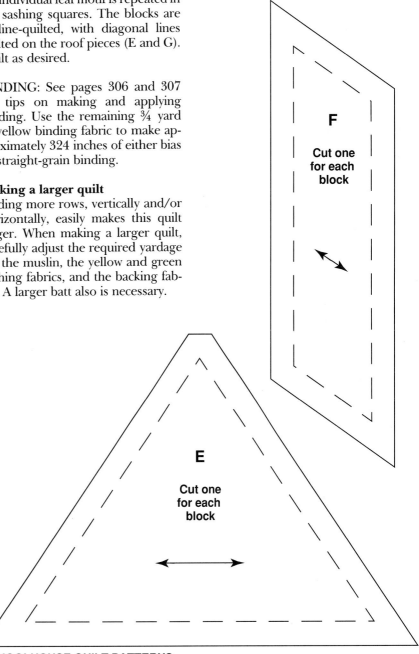

F

Cut one for each block

E

Cut one for each block

SCHOOLHOUSE QUILT PATTERNS

311

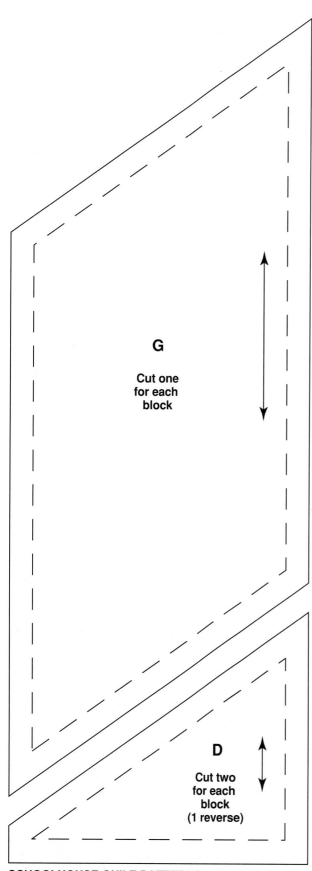

G

Cut one
for each
block

D

Cut two
for each
block
(1 reverse)

SCHOOLHOUSE QUILT PATTERNS

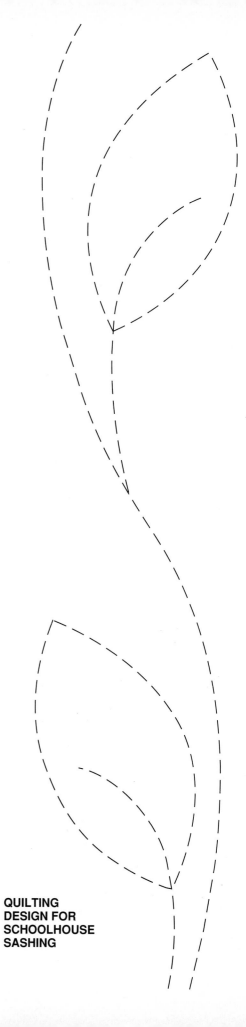

**QUILTING
DESIGN FOR
SCHOOLHOUSE
SASHING**

GLOSSARY

Acid-free paper. Used for storing quilts; available at art supply stores.

Album quilt. *See* Sampler quilt.

Alternate set. An arrangement of blocks in which the design block is combined, or alternated, with plain blocks. Blocks can be straight or turned on point, set together or separated with sashing.

Appliqué. From the French word *appliquer,* which means "to put on" or "lay on." Used as a noun to refer to a piece of fabric that is sewn onto the background fabric either by hand or by machine. Used as a verb to refer to the process of sewing one fabric atop a background fabric.

Backing. The bottom layer of a finished quilt. The backing fabric is cut or pieced to the same size as the quilt top plus 2 to 4 inches on all sides to allow for take-up during quilting.

Basting. Loose hand or machine stitches that temporarily hold layers of fabric together.

Batting. A filling between the quilt top and the backing that contributes to the thickness and warmth of the finished quilt. Bonded polyester batting, which is most widely used, is available at craft and sewing stores in a variety of weights and precut sizes. Batting is also available in cotton, silk, and wool.

Bearding. Pilling on the surface of a quilt caused by loose batting fibers.

Beeswax. Sometimes used to keep quilting thread from tangling.

Between. A needle used for quilting. The higher the number, the shorter the needle. For example, a No. 10 between is a smaller needle than a No. 8 between. Experiment with different sizes to find the one you like.

Bias. The diagonal grain of a woven fabric. The bias runs at a 45-degree angle to the selvage. This is the direction that has the most give or stretch, making it ideal for meandering vines and other curved appliqué, as well as binding for curved edges.

Bias appliqué. An appliqué design that is made with curved strips of bias-cut fabric.

Binding. A narrow fabric strip used to cover the edges of a quilt; the fabric can be cut on the straight grain or on the bias. Also refers to the process of finishing the quilt edges by attaching a separate binding or by folding the backing over the top and stitching it into place.

Block. A single design unit of a quilt, usually repeated to form the design of the quilt. A block can be square, hexagonal, triangular, or rectangular. Some quilts are composed of more than one block design.

Block-style quilt. A quilt composed of separate blocks that are sewn together in rows.

Border. The fabric frame that surrounds the central design area of the quilt top. Often used to showcase fancy quilting, borders can be plain, pieced, or appliquéd. Not all quilts have borders.

Broderie perse. From the French for "Persian embroidery," the term usually describes a technique in which a printed motif, usually a flower or animal, is cut from fabric and appliquéd onto a plain background.

Chain piecing. Machine sewing in which units are sewn one after the other without lifting the presser foot or clipping threads between units. The connecting thread is clipped later when the units are pressed.

Charm quilt. A patchwork quilt composed of one shape in many different fabrics; traditionally, no two pieces are cut from the same fabric.

Comforter. A thick, puffy bed covering designed to be used as a blanket. Most do not allow for a pillow tuck. Comforters often have thicker batting than quilts, which makes them unsuitable for hand quilting. Some are machine-quilted; others are tied.

Corded quilting. A technique that requires parallel lines of quilting stitches through two layers of fabric; cording is inserted between the layers and threaded into the channel formed by the quilting to give dimension to the design. Also known as Italian quilting.

Corner triangles. The triangles that fill the four corner spaces in a diagonal set. *See also* Diagonal set, Setting squares, and Setting triangles.

Crazy quilt. A random arrangement of irregularly shaped pieces, sewn onto a foundation; often made with a variety of fabric types, including silk, velvet, wool, satin, and brocade, as well as cotton. The edges of the patches are usually embellished with embroidery, lace, and/or buttons.

Cutting line. The line on which a patch or appliqué is cut out of the fabric. Patches for machine piecing are cut on the marked lines because those templates include seam allowances. Cutting lines for hand-pieced patchwork and appliqué are generally determined by eye; the quiltmaker adds seam allowances beyond the marked sewing lines because these templates generally do not include seam allowances.

Diagonal set. The arrangement of blocks in diagonal rows, with or without sashing. A diagonal set requires blocks turned on point.

continued

GLOSSARY, *continued*

Echo quilting. One or more lines of quilting that follow the outline of a patchwork or appliqué piece, so the quilting lines "echo" the shape. Multiple echo lines also are known as wave quilting, especially in Hawaiian appliqué. A single line of echo quilting also is called outline quilting.

English piecing. *See* Paper piecing.

Feed dogs. The part of a sewing machine, usually in the center of the throat plate, that moves up and down to propel the fabric under the needle.

Finger-pressing. Using your fingers or a fingernail to flatten or make a crease in fabric.

Foundation. A base fabric for patchwork. Used most with Log Cabin quilts, crazy quilts, and string patchwork, especially when piecing is done by machine.

Fusible webbing. A material composed of fibers that melt when heat is applied to them; used for fusing two layers of fabric together.

Grain. The lengthwise and crosswise threads of a woven fabric. The lengthwise grain, parallel to the selvage, has the least amount of stretch. Crosswise grain, perpendicular to the selvage, has a little more give. For best results, the grain should run in the same direction on all pieces of a quilt block and on the sashing and borders. The edge of any piece that will be on the outside edge of the block or the quilt should always be cut on the straight grain.

Grain line. Indicated on a pattern or a template by an arrow that, when positioned on the fabric, aligns with the lengthwise or crosswise grain.

Grid. A drawing of vertical and horizontal perpendicular lines that form an arrangement of uniform boxes.

Lattice. *See* Sashing.

Layering. The process of sandwiching the backing, batting, and quilt top together for quilting or tying.

Marking. Transferring a quilting design to fabric.

Medallion quilt. Particularly popular in early patchwork quilts, this style uses a large central motif surrounded by several different borders.

Miter. Where vertical and horizontal strips of fabric join at a 45-degree angle to form a corner. Mitered corners are frequently used in borders.

Nine-Patch. A block comprising nine squares, joined in three rows of three squares each. Examples include the Nine-Patch Variation and Pinwheel quilts in Chapter 1.

Notches. Lines marked on the seam line or clips in the seam allowance that indicate points along the seam where the facing patches should be matched. Notches are typically used when sewing curved seams.

Paper piecing. Used in hand piecing when seam allowances are folded over paper templates; the prepared patchwork pieces are then stitched together. The paper is usually removed when piecing is complete, but some old-time quilters, unable to afford batting, left papers in the quilt to add extra warmth. This technique is still widely used for hand-piecing hexagons and diamonds.

Patch. Each individual fabric piece sewn into a quilt. Patches are joined into units, units are joined to make blocks, and blocks are joined, with other components, such as setting triangles, to complete the quilt top.

Patchwork (Piecing). Pieces of cut cloth sewn together to produce a design, usually a block.

Pattern. The printed representation of a patchwork or appliqué shape, which can be traced onto plastic to make a template for cutting.

Prairie points. Squares of fabric that are folded into triangles. Often used as an edging, prairie points also can be sewn into other seams.

Quick piecing. A sewing technique that eliminates some marking and cutting steps. The quiltmaker stitches a large fabric piece that is then cut into individual presewn units. *See also* Strip piecing *and* Triangle-square.

Quilt. A bedcover composed of a top, padding, and a back held together with quilting stitches or ties.

Quilting. Small running stitches that hold the quilt layers together. Quilting can create another design on the quilt top or it can follow the outline of the sewn shapes. Traditional quilting is done by hand, but machine quilting is gaining in popularity.

Quilting hoop. A portable frame used to hold small portions of a quilt taut, facilitating even stitching.

Quilt top. The top layer of a quilt, which can be pieced, appliquéd, embroidered, or a wholecloth.

Reverse appliqué. Areas of an appliqué piece that are cut away to reveal fabric underneath. The appliqué fabric is carefully slit and the edges finished as in regular appliqué. An example is the large leaf of the Rose Wreath Quilt shown in Chapter 2.

Reversed patch. A patch that is a mirror image of another one. In this book, a pattern that is used both right side up and reversed will be labeled accordingly. When cutting a reversed patch, turn the template over (reverse it) to mark the fabric.

Rotary cutter. A device that uses a sharp round blade to cut through layers of fabric. Usually used with a special cutting mat and a thick plastic ruler that serves as a guide for cutting a straight line.

Ruching. A process whereby a fabric piece is tucked and gathered before it is appliquéd onto a background fabric; often seen in classic Baltimore Album quilts. An example is the Rose Wreath Quilt shown in Chapter 2.

Sampler quilt. A block-style quilt in which each block is the same size but a different design; a style popular for friendship quilts and for beginners to learn different techniques.

Sashing. Strips of fabric sewn between blocks of a quilt top. Also known as lattice stripping.

Sashing square. A square of contrasting fabric at the intersection of horizontal and vertical sashing.

Sawtooth. A border or row of pieced triangle-squares.

Seam (Seam line). The junction of two pieces of fabric.

Seam allowance. Fabric between the cut edge and the stitching line. In patchwork, the seam allowance is always ¼ inch unless stated otherwise.

Selvage. The finished edge of a woven fabric, parallel to the lengthwise grain. Because it is more tightly woven than the rest of the fabric, selvage should not be used in a quilt—when washed, it may shrink more than other fabric.

Seminole patchwork. A technique devised by the Seminole Indians of Florida in which strips of fabric are sewn together, then cut into segments and resewn to create intricate geometric designs.

Set (Setting). The arrangement in which blocks are joined in straight or diagonal rows, with or without sashing between the blocks.

Setting-in. Sewing a patchwork piece into the angle or corner made by two other joined pieces.

Setting squares. Plain squares that alternate with design squares to complete the quilt top.

Setting triangles. In a diagonal set, triangles that fill the spaces around blocks at the edges of the quilt top.

Sew order. The sequence in which individual pieces are sewn together to form a unit.

Sleeve. A fabric casing sewn to the back of a quilt through which a hanging rod can be inserted.

Square corner. A corner made by sewing one border to an adjacent border at a 90-degree angle.

Stipple quilting. Quilting stitched in very close, meandering curves that completely cover an area with quilting. Such heavy quilting makes unquilted areas seem puffy by contrast.

String patchwork. Strips of different widths sewn together or onto a foundation to create a design or yardage.

Strip piecing. Sewing strips of fabric together from which pieced units are cut. This is a shortcut technique to avoid marking and cutting separate pieces for machine-sewn patchwork.

Strip set. A combination of pieced strips of a specified width and color. The strips are first sewn, then cut apart into units that are combined with other units to form a design. Some block designs require multiple strip sets. Working with strip sets can eliminate much tedious marking and piecing of individual patches.

Template. A duplication of a pattern that is made of paper, cardboard, plastic, or sandpaper. Templates are used to mark the pattern shape on fabric for cutting. Templates for machine piecing usually include seam allowances; those for hand piecing and appliqué do not. Mark the patch letter and grain-line arrow on each template for identification.

Trapunto. Similar to corded quilting; two layers of fabric are joined with quilting stitches to form a design, then areas of the design are stuffed from the wrong side so that the design stands out in high relief.

Triangle-square. A square that is composed of two right triangles; the seam makes a diagonal line through the center of the square.

Tying. A quick method of securing the layers of a quilt together without traditional quilting. Perle cotton, embroidery floss, or lightweight yarn is stitched through the layers and tied into a square knot on the top of the quilt. Tying is best for quilts and comforters made with thick batting.

Unit. A subdivision of a patchwork block; pieces are joined to form small units, which are then joined to form larger ones until the block is completely assembled.

Wholecloth quilt. A quilt top that is a single piece of fabric, most often a solid color, that is usually elaborately quilted, often with corded quilting or trapunto work.

Yo-yos. Fabric circles that are gathered, flattened, and joined to make a lightweight, unbacked coverlet. Single yo-yos can be used for appliqué.

ACKNOWLEDGMENTS

We express our gratitude and appreciation to the many people who helped produce this book. Our heartfelt thanks go to the following quilt designers and collectors who graciously loaned quilts; to the photographers, for their creative talents; and to all those who in some other way contributed to the production of this book.

QUILT SOURCES

Buckboard Antiques, Oklahoma City, OK—61; 183; 184–185; 210

Margaret Cavigga—11; 14; 36–37; 56–57; 74–75; 82; 130

Marianne Fons—241

Marilyn Ginsburg—110

Donna and Bryce Hamilton—32; 144–145; 280–281

Jeramy Landauer—126–127

Ruth Meyer—240

Marti and Dick Michell—30–31; 34; 60; 108–109; 128–129; 146–147; 150–153; 180–182; 184; 213

Sandra Mitchell—8–9; 21; 59

Jennifer Patriarche—236–237

Judy Pletcher—16–17

Liz Porter—148; 242–243

Shirley S. Sawyer—206–207

Millie Sorrells—238–239

Shelley Zegart—149

TECHNICAL ASSISTANCE

Marianne Fons

Julie Hart

Patty Konecny

Mary B. Larson

Judy Pletcher

Liz Porter

Martha Street

Sara Jane Treinen

PHOTO LOCATIONS

Aldrich Guest House, Galena, IL—183; 236–237

Ulysses S. Grant Home, Galena, IL—74–79; 83; 131

Hellman Guest House, Galena, IL—178–179; 184; 204–205; 212; 240

Living History Farms, Des Moines, IA—54–61; 80–81; 106–112; 180–181; 206–207; 210

Paca House, Historic Annapolis Foundation, Annapolis, MD—8–9; 11; 12; 16–17; 30–37

Pella Historical Village, Pella, IA—184–185; 187; 209; 242–243

Terrace Hill, Des Moines, IA—126–129; 132–133

PHOTOGRAPHERS

Craig Anderson—269

Lydia Cutter—264

DeGennaro Associates—14; 130

Dean Dixon—272, quiltmaker

Susan Gilmore—275

Richard Haggerty—279, quiltmaker

Hopkins Associates—18; 21; 34; 36; 54–61; 82; 96–97; 113; 116; 126–127; 136; 142; 149–150; 152; 182; 184–185; 187; 208–209; 213; 242–243; 283; 287; 296; 302–305

Michael Jensen—cover; 8–9; 11–12; 16–17; 30–34; 36–37; 144–148; 151–153; 280–281

Scott Little—106–109; 111–112; 128–129; 132–133; 180–181; 206–207; 210; 265

Julie Maris/Semel—277, quiltmaker

Garland Marshall—266

Barbara Elliott Martin—267

Sharon Risedorph—260–263

Tom Smesrud—271, quiltmaker

Perry Struse—15; 26; 42; 74–81; 83; 110; 131; 178–179; 183–184; 204–205; 211; 212; 236–241; 268; 270–277, quilts; 274

SOURCE LIST

Quiltmaking supplies are available at many craft and fabric stores, especially those that specialize in quilting. A wide selection of quiltmaking materials and notions is available from the following mail-order catalogs.

Cabin Fever Calicoes
P.O. Box 550106
Atlanta, GA 30355
404-873-5094
Send $1.00 for catalog

Keepsake Quilting
Dover Street, P.O. Box 1459
Meredith, NH 03253
603-279-3351

Quilts and Other Comforts
Box 394
Wheatridge, CO 80034-0394
303-420-4272
Send $1.00 for catalog

Several quotes in this book are excerpted from *Aunt Jane of Kentucky* by Eliza Calvert Hall. This collection of short stories is available from:

R&E Miles
P.O. Box 1916
San Pedro, CA 90733
213-833-8856

Special thanks to Jane Hall and Dixie Haywood for text from *Perfect Pineapples* (C&T Publishing, 1989).

INDEX

*Page numbers in **bold** type refer to photographs with accompanying text; other page numbers refer to how-to instructions or other references. An asterisk (*) following an entry indicates that the word or phrase appears in the glossary on pages 313-315.*